GEORGETTE HEYER

BIOGRAPHY OF A BESTSELLER

Also by Jennifer Kloester

Georgette Heyer's Regency World

GEORGETTE HEYER

BIOGRAPHY OF A BESTSELLER

Jennifer Kloester

WILLIAM HEINEMANN: LONDON

Published by William Heinemann 2011

1 3 5 7 9 10 8 6 4 2

*This project has been assisted by the Australian Government
through the Australia Council, its arts funding and advisory body.*

First published in Great Britain in 2011 by
William Heinemann
Random House, 20 Vauxhall Bridge Road,
London SW1V 2SA

www.randomhouse.co.uk

Addresses for companies within The Random House Group Limited can be found at:
www.randomhouse.co.uk/offices.htm

The Random House Group Limited Reg. No. 954009

A CIP catalogue record for this book
is available from the British Library

ISBN 9780434020713

The Random House Group Limited supports The Forest Stewardship Council (FSC®), the
leading international forest certification organisation. Our books carrying the FSC label are
printed on FSC® certified paper. FSC is the only forest certification scheme endorsed by
the leading environmental organisations, including Greenpeace. Our paper procurement
policy can be found at www.randomhouse.co.uk/environment

Typeset by Palimpsest Book Production Limited, Falkirk, Stirlingshire
Printed and bound by
CPI Group (UK) Ltd, Croydon, CR0 4YY

For

Richard George Rougier
(1932–2007)
friend, raconteur and gentleman

and for

Jane Aiken Hodge
(1917–2009)
who led the way

CONTENTS

ILLUSTRATIONS

22. *Instead of the Thorn* 1924, the first contemporary novel
23. Ronald's father Charles Joseph Rougier, n.d.
24. Ronald's mother Jane (Jean) Henderson Gray Crookston, n.d.
25. Ronald Rougier aged 4, 1904
26. Ronald Rougier, Royal Naval College cadet, circa 1913
27. Ronald Rougier aged 22, 1922
28. Carola and Dulce Oman, 1914
29. Joanna Cannan, circa 1914
30. Georgette Heyer, circa 1922
31. Georgette and Ronald's wedding, 1925
32. George Heyer a few hours before his death, 1925
33. Georgette in Tanganyika 'at the end of a seven mile walk', 1927
34. Georgette outside 'the Manor House', Kyerwa, Tanganyika, 1927
35. Georgette and Ronald in Kyerwa, circa 1927
36. *Helen* 1928, Georgette's most autobiographical novel
37. *The Masqueraders* 1928
38. Georgette and Ronald in Paris, circa 1930
39. Blackthorns, Toat Hill near Horsham, circa 1974
40. Georgette and Misty Dawn, circa 1939
41. Georgette and Richard at Church Cove, the Lizard, Cornwall, 1937
42. Richard and Jonathan Velhurst Viking aka 'Johnny', circa 1940
43. *Pastel* 1929, dedicated to her mother
44. *Barren Corn* 1930, Georgette's last contemporary novel
45. Lieutenant-Colonel Charles Leslie Rougier, circa 1935
46. Sylvia Heyer, n.d.
47. Jean Rougier, n.d.
48. 'Pater' Charles Joseph Rougier, n.d.
49. Georgette by Howard Coster, 1939
50. Dmitri and Dorothy Tornow's wedding, August 1944
51. Ronald, Georgette, Boris and Richard dressed for a wedding, circa 1949
52. Richard, the gillie and Georgette in Scotland, circa 1952
53. A.S. Frere, 1953
54. Patricia Wallace, circa 1938

AUTHOR'S NOTE

I first read Georgette Heyer's novels while living in the jungle in Papua New Guinea and re-read them while living in the desert in Bahrain. A fascination with her historical fiction led me on a ten-year research journey which culminated in this biography. Much of this story of Georgette Heyer's life and writing is drawn from new and untapped archives of her letters. In recent years my discovery of over a thousand pages of her personal writing, dating from when Georgette was eighteen, has made a new biography possible. Access to these letters, so generously given by their owners, has made it a reality. Georgette Heyer's son, Sir Richard Rougier, gave me the necessary copyright permission to quote from his mother's private and public writing. He also gave me unlimited access to her notebooks and private papers and repeatedly told me 'you have *carte blanche*' with the material. Sir Richard's faith and belief in me opened many doors. Georgette Heyer's first biographer, Jane Aiken Hodge, gave me her entire research archive as well as the gift of her friendship, wisdom and advice. Jean and Harry Frere generously gave me sole and exclusive access to all of Georgette Heyer's letters in the Frere Family Archive. Joan Reinhardt kindly allowed me to copy the entire Max Reinhardt Archive and bring it home. The staff of the McFarlin Library at the University of Tulsa in Oklahoma gave me unstinting support and made available a complete copy of their remarkable collection of 'Georgette (Heyer) Rougier letters'. Jean Rose at the Random House Archive helped me to find invaluable letters, photographs and documents and provided access to Georgette Heyer's letters in the Heinemann Archive. Ro Marriott, Roy Pfautch and

Lady Townsend shared their Georgette Heyer letters. Other letters came from Duke University; King's College Library, Cambridge; Reading University and The Society of Authors Archive at the British Library. Georgette's daughter-in-law, Susanna, Lady Rougier, was especially generous in sharing memories and photographs (and a pair of Georgette's York tan gloves). Jeremy and Judith Rougier, Hale Crosse, Sally Tornow and Diane and Antony Price all shared documents, photographs and memories. Judy, Lady Rougier, has been unfailingly kind and her generous support has made possible my continued access to the Heyer family archive. With so many new letters to tell her story, wherever feasible in the biography I have let Georgette Heyer speak for herself as she wrote with a passion and a force that re-writing or paraphrasing would only dilute. For convenience, throughout the book I have referred to her by her Christian name – a familiarity for which I hope she will forgive me.

Jennifer Kloester, 2009

When my biographer collects my letters for publication,
he'll have a job expurgating them, won't he?

Georgette Heyer

PART I

THE YOUNG EDWARDIAN

1902–1919

I

I am to be found in my work.

Georgette Heyer

Georgette Heyer was born an Edwardian. The Victorian Age had ended with the death of Queen Victoria and on 9 August 1902 the new king, Edward VII, was crowned at Westminster Abbey. Georgette was among those born in the first year of his reign. She was also one of the last generation to witness an era which had begun more than one hundred years earlier. Her childhood was alive with traditions that stretched back to the days of the English Regency, many of which remained recognisable, if not unchanged, into the first decade of the twentieth century.

Georgette grew up in a sheltered world in which people were assumed to know their place and many believed that the worth of a man could be told from the cut of his coat. As the eldest child of a mildly affluent middle-class family with aspirations to move up the social ladder, she understood and accepted as natural such things as servants, horses and carriages, good manners, correct speech, the right clothing and a certain level of education and cultural literacy. All of these things had been as much an integral part of life for the moneyed classes in the Regency and Victorian eras as they were in the Edwardian, and they were to have a lasting influence on Georgette.

She was born in the bedroom of the family home at 103 Woodside in Wimbledon. Her parents, George and Sylvia Heyer, had been married only a year and, according to the baby book which Sylvia kept, they were delighted with the safe arrival of their baby daughter, who came into the world at 9.30 a.m. on 16 August 1902 weighing a healthy 8lb 5oz. It was a Saturday and George was enjoying the long summer vacation from his job as French master at King's College School. Georgette was delivered by John Hayward, Wimbledon's most eminent doctor and a family friend, whose presence at the birth reassured Sylvia. At twenty-six she was conscious of being a little older than many first-time mothers. As the youngest of eight siblings and with three unmarried sisters, she knew little about babies and George did not know much more. He was thirty-three but delighted to be a father for the first time.

They named the baby Georgette after her father and grandfather, with the name to be 'pronounced *à la française*'. It was an unusual name and as well as being a feminised version of George was also the name of a new kind of French silk which would (appropriately, given the enduring nature of her future novels) become known for its 'crispness, body and outstanding durability'. The name would also prove prophetic in other ways, for Georgette developed a love of clothes and fabrics which would eventually find an outlet in her writing.

She was a happy baby, with a good appetite who took an active interest in the world around her. Her first weeks were spent largely in the care of the month-nurse, for it was customary for a new mother to remain in bed for at least two weeks while the nurse fed, bathed and cared for the newborn. Georgette was eight weeks old when the month-nurse finally handed her entirely into her mother's care. Sylvia revelled in her daughter's rosy cheeks and silky brown hair that clustered in such pretty curls at the back of her head.

Sylvia recorded many details of Georgette's early months in her baby book, noting that 'Georgette did not take to the perambulator at once when nurse left. She missed the motion of being carried I suppose.' Her baby liked to be with people and woke without fail at the arrival of any meal, crying lustily until she was taken from her cot and brought to join her parents at the table. By four months she had begun to make 'sweet little sounds by way of talking' and loved to visit the clock on the dining-room mantelpiece, where she would make excited noises at its stentorian ticking and musical chimes.

Music was part of daily life in the Heyer household, for George came from a musical family and Sylvia was a graduate of the Royal Academy of Music. She was an accomplished pianist with a lovely singing voice. In the first year of their marriage she and George often spent pleasant evenings at home with piano and book. Sylvia would play and sing, and George would read aloud or recite from his favourite novel or anthology of poems or entertain his appreciative wife with a humorous composition of his own. Georgette loved to hear her mother sing and would turn her head at the sound of her voice when she was only a dozen weeks old. She was delighted by the piano and by the family musical box, which she thought 'a grand source of entertainment'. Pleased to find her baby so captivated by music, Sylvia would often set the music box playing while she gave Georgette her bottle.

Unlike many fathers of his time George took a great interest in his daughter and Sylvia would often put her into their bed with him in the mornings while she was getting up. She loved to watch Georgette and her father 'hold a regular flirtation together' and to listen to her husband talking nonsense to their baby. George was a fine linguist, with a great love of language and poetry in particular, and it afforded him enormous pleasure to watch and listen to this tiny child who made such fascinating noises and looked up at him with her beautiful blue eyes. He thought her entrancing.

He and Sylvia gave Georgette funny little pet names like 'Lillie Solomon', 'Tooley', 'Solly Tolly' and 'Iddy Todgemim dim Bimby'. In February 1903 George wrote a poem for his daughter which he made into a little book tied up with a red ribbon. Entitled *To Georgette Aged Six Months* it began:

> I'll sing a song of you,
>> Georgette,
> I'll sing a song of you;
> You've silky brownish sorts of locks,
> And cheeks of fairest hue;
> You wear such pretty light blue frocks,
> And joy to kick off both your socks,–
> I'll sing a song of you.

And ended:

> And when you are asleep,
>   Georgette,
> Oh, when you are asleep,
> Above the 'broidered coverlet
> The little fingers peep;
> I'd like to venture near, and set
> A kiss upon their tips, Georgette,
> <u>Because</u> you are asleep.

Her father read aloud to Georgette from babyhood, telling her tales from Shakespeare and the Bible, reciting poetry and nursery rhymes and delighting her with made-up stories of long ago. Almost from birth, rhyme, rhythm and metre were an integral part of her life: whether it was her mother's piano-playing and singing, or her father's recitations and storytelling, Georgette's ears were attuned to excellence in music and literature from her infancy.

She was an intelligent baby, fascinated by people and sounds and quick to learn. By fourteen months Sylvia noted that she was crawling everywhere and had begun to walk holding on to the furniture. Her favourite pastime was to stand at the window watching people and things passing by and to look out for her father on whom, Sylvia recorded, 'she was very keen'. Their relationship was to prove pivotal in her life. Her father was a handsome, charismatic man who possessed the knack of bringing the past to life – something which, in time, he would impart to his daughter. Georgette adored him.

George had come to Wimbledon in 1897, at the urgent request of the new headmaster of King's College School. After relocating to Wimbledon from its traditional home in London's Strand, King's had lost several teachers and been desperately in need of a new French master. George was an old boy and a Classics graduate of Cambridge who spoke fluent, idiomatic French and had spent the previous five years teaching at Weymouth College in Dorset. He was a natural and gifted teacher, with a tremendous sense of humour and an energy and enthusiasm that enlivened the classroom and made him a great favourite with his students.

When Georgette was eighteen months old, her mother wrote that 'She dances & plays the piano & sings & pretends to be an old woman,' and observed that, in some ways, she was 'more like a child of 3 or 4'. Georgette and her mother were close in those early years, though this would change in time. Sylvia loved to spend hours with her baby, observing each tiny development and noting with pride every new word or skill accomplished. She described her daughter as 'a darling and so intelligent' and proudly recorded that Dr Hayward considered her 'by far the prettiest baby in Wimbledon'. When Georgette was given her first vaccination, Sylvia felt the pain as much as she did and found herself 'almost hating Dr Hayward' for inflicting it.

By now, Georgette's eyes had turned to a grey-blue (later grey), though her nose was still a 'dear wee snub'. She often sucked her thumb and loved her 'eidy', which she would cuddle when she was tired. Sylvia let her have her first walk out of doors when she was eighteen months old and enjoyed watching her little daughter toddle about the garden. Georgette was fascinated by the world outside the house, with its myriad of things to see and touch and endless new words to learn, as she gradually expanded her horizons and explored the world of Wimbledon and beyond.

Wimbledon was a pleasant place in which to raise a family. A prosperous suburb, it was popular with affluent middle-class professionals who liked its country charm and close proximity to London, just seven miles to the north-east and easily reached by train. Georgette grew up in a world where wooded lanes, hedgerows and fields of wild flowers were part of every daily walk and where the great expanse of Wimbledon Common offered an imaginative child unlimited opportunity for adventure. Her home was not grand, but comfortable and well run, with at least two servants to manage the day-to-day cleaning, cooking and serving of meals. Her father's salary was modest, but in those days a man did not need a vast sum to afford a decent house and domestic help.

The Heyers' house was a pleasant red-brick, three-storey, end-terrace, with steps leading up to a panelled front door beneath an arched portico. A typical middle-class Victorian house, it had its living rooms on the ground floor, bedrooms and the nursery on the first floor and an attic room with a gable window at the top for the servants. Woodside was a quiet street, leading east off Wimbledon Hill Road, conveniently close to the shops in the High Street for Sylvia and within pleasant walking distance of King's College School for George.

Georgette did not spend all of her babyhood in Wimbledon, for Sylvia's mother lived in south-east London and George's parents lived in Worthing, on the Sussex coast. When she was two months old her parents took Georgette on her first outing to her maternal grandmother Annette Watkins' home, at Lee in Lewisham, near Blackheath, to be christened. The service, attended by both sides of the family, was held on 2 October at the Lewisham parish church of St Peter's. This was the first of many visits to 'Grannie' Watkins. Georgette came to adore her grandmother and Sylvia noted that even as a baby she would 'go on anyhow' whenever Grannie came to visit.

The Watkins family was in commerce and well-to-do, and Georgette's Grannie lived at Fairfield, a grand Victorian house set in a large garden at 52 Eltham Road (demolished in 1961 to make way for flats). Sylvia had been born at Fairfield in 1876, and her three unmarried sisters, Cicely, Ellice and Josephine, still lived there with their mother. Sylvia was very fond of her sisters, two of whom, Ellice and Cicely, were nine and ten years older than she was and had helped to raise her. She was also close to Josephine, the youngest of her three sisters and just three years older than Sylvia. Jo, a red-headed beauty, had a strong independent streak. Like her sisters, Ellice and Cicely, she never married. There were also three older brothers, and another sister who had married and moved away when Sylvia was still a child, though she still kept in touch. When Georgette's mother was a girl, Fairfield had accommodated her parents, their eight children, her mother's sister, a live-in cook, parlourmaid, housemaid, and a nurse. Grannie Watkins remained at Fairfield until her death in 1914.

Sylvia's father, William Watkins, had died in 1900, just two years before Georgette was born. He was a tugboat owner, the son of John Rogers Watkins who, in 1833, had founded the first company in the world to run a fleet of tugboats. William and his brother John joined the firm in their teens and over the next three decades helped to build it into a successful business. By the time Sylvia was born, the company was named for her father. William Watkins Limited was one of the leading tugboat operators in the world, with an international reputation for long-distance towing and salvage. Watkins' tugs held records for the world's longest tows, having tugged ships from places as far apart as London and Cadiz, St Helena and Southampton, and Cardiff and St Petersburg. In 1878 it was the Watkins' tugboat, *Anglia*, that brought Cleopatra's Needle up the Thames to its new home on London's Embankment and it is a Watkins' tug, *Monarch*, that is depicted towing the grand old ship in Joseph Turner's painting *The Fighting Téméraire Tugged to her Last Berth to be Broken*. Years later a Watkins' tug would be the first to evacuate troops from the beaches of Dunkirk.

The Watkins bought Fairfield in 1875. It was a happy home. Years of family photographs show that the girls' parents had indulged their daughters' passion for dogs and that the house had been home to a steady stream of small dogs of different breeds. Sylvia's own pet had been a dachshund which had shared her adolescence. After Georgette was born, Sylvia made sure that dogs were a part of her daughter's life, too, and there is a delightful photograph of Georgette and her brothers with a handsome Pekinese taken when Georgette was in her teens.

Like the Watkins, Georgette's paternal grandparents, George and Alice Heyer, had also lived in the Lewisham area. They had moved to Eltham from Highgate in London when George was ten and preparing to start at King's College School. The Heyers lived in a house called 'The Chestnuts' in Court Road which was named for the magnificent chestnut tree in the garden into which (legend had it) the Black Prince had once nailed a horseshoe. In those days, the Heyer and Watkins families lived only two miles apart and both families attended the parish church of St Peter's in Courtlands Road. It was probably here that George and Sylvia first met, although as a twelve-year-old schoolboy George may not have taken much notice of five-year-old Sylvia Watkins. Several years later, in 1895, the Heyers moved into Tudor House, a large property next door to Fairfield, the Watkins' family home, where George would have been a frequent visitor. When they did eventually marry, twenty years after they met, on 10 August 1901, the wedding was at St Peter's.

By the time Georgette was born her Heyer grandparents had left Lewisham and retired to the seaside town of Worthing in Sussex. Although visits there were less frequent because of the distance, when the family did go to Sussex it was usually for several weeks. Georgette's first big trip away from home was to Worthing when she was just four months old. On Christmas Eve 1902, George and Sylvia took her to the seaside town by train. They spent nearly a month with 'Grandpip' and 'Grandmim' at their house in Broadwater Road.

Georgette's grandfather, George Heyer, was a Russian émigré with a white beard and a thick foreign accent that he never lost. He spoke several European languages fluently and on regular family trips abroad enthralled his children with his ability to switch effortlessly from one language to another each time they crossed into a new country. He ensured that his daughters Inez, Ilma and Alice, as well as his son George, learned French and German and insisted on clear enunciation whenever they spoke English. Father and daughters were all musical and young George grew up in a home where an evening's entertainment might include duets from *Il Travatore*, a classical recital on the piano or the family singing Russian folk-songs together.

George Heyer was a passionate man and an affectionate father who was described by his daughter Alice as being 'full of little pithy stories told in a purposely exaggerated broken English and very witty'. He also had what his granddaughter described as a 'Russian Fatalism' tempered by a sense of humour which frequently found expression in all sorts of pranks and practical jokes. He loved to play tricks on unsuspecting friends and family members, and create havoc by introducing people to each other using made-up names. A passion for words often led him to invent outlandish names for everyday things and, in later years, he would tell his grandchildren that he had been picking 'ganzoolias' (marigolds) in the garden. He also loved to tell Georgette tall tales about how, as a nine-year-old, he had escaped from one of the Tsar's pogroms riding on the buffers of a train – at a time when the Russian railways were still in their infancy and the only established line was between St Petersburg and Tsarkoe Selo.

Born in 1832, Georgette's grandfather actually emigrated when he was twenty-seven, leaving Kharkov in southern Russia in 1859. He was a fur merchant born in the village of Kremenchuk, the son of Augustus Heyer, also a merchant, and the family does appear to have been Jewish. This would have made life hard at times, especially for those from towns and villages such as Kremenchuk which were inside the Pale of Settlement – the area within which Jews were allowed to reside permanently and into which they were frequently forced to move after being expelled from cities or provinces within the Russian empire. In 1859, however, Tsar Alexander II had eased many of the restrictions on Jews, making it easier for them to travel. There was a brutal pogrom in Odessa that year and George Heyer seized the opportunity to leave Russia and begin a new life in England. After making the long and difficult journey from Kharkov to London he found work as a warehouseman and, in 1863, successfully applied for British citizenship. By then, George Heyer had pulled himself up the ranks, improving his status and his income, by rising from the position of warehouseman to that of foreign agent for a large woollen wholesaler. Three weeks after his citizenship had been granted, he married Alice Waters at St Luke's Church in Holloway and moved to a new address at 10 Penn Road Villas in Islington, North London.

If George Heyer *was* Jewish, he chose to divest himself of both his ethnic and his religious heritage and to integrate into British society as quickly as possible. His wife was an English girl from an old Norfolk family and their marriage in the Anglican Church and their new house in a fashionable middle-class neighbourhood were all part of his transformation from Russian immigrant to prosperous English businessman. The family surname 'Heyer' was also anglicised from its original Russian pronunciation which would probably have been either 'Geyer' or 'Khyeyir' (the latter being a phonetic spelling as there is no letter 'H' in the Russian alphabet). In its original form the surname was pronounced 'higher' but during the First World War Georgette's branch of the family changed their pronunciation of it to 'hare'.

When his longed-for son was born in 1869, George Heyer appears to have dispensed with the Russian patronymic tradition (in which a son is given his father's first name as his second name) and given him just the one name, 'George', having long since dropped his own second name of Augustus. (A second son, Hubert Claude Heyer, was born in 1875, but died in infancy.) In actively distancing himself from his heritage in this way, Georgette's grandfather may also have unconsciously succumbed to the xenophobia common among the British middle- and upper-classes in the nineteenth and twentieth centuries and set a precedent for a similar stance among his descendants.

Thus, Georgette's family background was mainly middle class and she came from a long line of forebears who, with every new generation, had worked to better themselves and their family's social and economic status. Her father was raised with the expectation that he would become an English gentleman. With this in mind his parents sent him first to a boys' preparatory school on Highgate Hill and then to King's College School in the hope that from there he would gain entrance either to Oxford or Cambridge. He was a bright child with an excellent memory and a gift for recitation that enabled him to perform entire chapters of Dickens by heart. George did well at King's, excelling in mathematics, Greek, French and literature. In 1888 he fulfilled his parents' wish by winning a place at Sidney Sussex College, Cambridge as a Sizar student. Sizar students were those with limited means who were admitted to their College at a lower fee, did not have to pay for food and tuition and were given lodgings at a reduced rate. Originally required to undertake certain domestic duties in return for these allowances, this practice was largely obsolete by the time George went up to Cambridge.

George spent the next four years at Cambridge studying for his

Classics degree, writing poetry and making a name for himself among the literary set. He made many friends and, according to a classmate, achieved the distinction of becoming 'one of the most popular men at Sidney Sussex College'. He had originally wanted to be an archaeologist but in the early 1890s his aspirations were frustrated by a downturn in his family's finances and on leaving Cambridge he was compelled to earn his living as a teacher.

Georgette's mother was from a wealthier background but the Watkins, like the Heyers, were in trade. Without a fortune they were limited in how far up the social ladder they could climb. Sylvia was given an education suited to a well-bred young lady of some means, and her love of music was fully indulged by her parents with lessons on both the cello and the pianoforte. When she was nineteen, they allowed her to audition at one of Europe's most prestigious music schools: the Royal Academy of Music in London. In September 1895 she entered the Royal Academy to begin three years of intense study and musical practice. Supported by her family, who paid the eleven guineas per term tuition, she studied the cello under William Whitehouse, singing under R.E. Miles and took weekly classes in harmony and counterpoint, sight singing and musical dictation. Her parents arranged for her to move into rooms in Osnaburgh Terrace near the Academy and Sylvia gained a new sense of independence living in central London.

She was a fine musician and the only female cellist in her class to receive a Silver Medal in her second year at the Academy, and the only female cellist to obtain a Certificate of Merit in her final year. Sylvia played regularly with the Students' Orchestra and the Students' Chamber Orchestra, performing pieces by Mendelssohn, Tchaikovsky, Saint-Saëns, Dvořák, Rossini, Schumann and Grieg. She loved being at the Royal Academy and for a time dreamed of a career in music. In the late-Victorian era this was not impossible, but it would have been unusual, especially for a female cellist. Sylvia would never be a concert pianist for her hands were too small to stretch further than an octave and her voice, though lovely, was not strong enough for an opera singer. Like most women of her class and time she was also constrained by society's expectations that her career would be that of wife and mother. Three years after leaving the Royal Academy Sylvia married and abandoned her ambition to be a professional musician. A year later she had Georgette.

Georgette was born into a home in which class and breeding were taken for granted as indicators of a person's worth and social acceptability. In the Victorian and Edwardian eras every section of British society was profoundly hierarchical and throughout her childhood Georgette was constantly exposed to the idea of a distinct social order. She knew from personal experience what it was like to be waited on, to have the house cleaned and the food cooked by servants. As a child she quickly absorbed the differences between how people responded to family and friends and the way in which they spoke to the cook or housemaid. As she grew older she also began to understand the various rules and protocols attached to one's own position in the social order and how these affected one's behaviour in different situations.

She was an observant child with an ear for language and a growing ability to discern the subtleties of behaviour that enabled her to recognise the differences between individuals within the various classes. There were innumerable rules for knowing and establishing one's place within the social pecking order and Georgette's perception was that this was particularly true among the servant class, which she quickly discovered could be the most rigidly hierarchical of all. One domestic servant who was known to every well-bred Wimbledon resident, and whom Georgette likely encountered in her childhood, was Roberts, a roving butler whose services were employed across Wimbledon by hosts and hostesses to assist with their dinner parties, dances, garden parties, suppers and soirées. His presence ensured the smooth running of any occasion and, as one Wimbledon resident recorded, he was 'most amusing, sympathetic and competent'. Many of his characteristics match those of the iconic butler who would eventually appear in Georgette's novels.

It was not only Georgette's daily interaction with servants that emphasised ideas about class and breeding, but also the books and popular magazines she read, many of which took for granted concepts of racial and class superiority, the importance of heritage, breeding, and bloodlines, dislike of the foreigner and the Jew, the right of men to rule and the importance of romantic love for women – all of whom apparently wanted to find a husband and live 'happily ever after'. Georgette would have been unusual if she had not absorbed many of the ideas promulgated by the stories she read and heard from her infancy. As well as books by Rudyard Kipling, Robert Louis Stevenson, Charles Dickens, Jane Austen, William Thackeray and Shakespeare, Georgette also grew up reading the novels of Mrs Gaskell, Charlotte Yonge, Harrison Ainsworth, Ouida, Stanley Weyman, May Sinclair, Jeffery Farnol, Ethel M. Dell, D.K. Broster and Baroness Orczy among others. Two of her favourite childhood stories were *The Shepherd's Fairy* by Darley Dale and *The Red Deer* by J.W. Fortescue.

Georgette was given *The Shepherd's Fairy* as a ninth birthday present and never forgot it. It tells the story of a French Comte who is so consumed with jealousy at the birth of his baby daughter that he persuades his brother, Leon, to take the child to England until his wife can be less 'obsessed' with her newborn. Leon sails to England and orders a crewman to give the baby to a shepherd's family. Returning to France, Leon's ship sinks and he is drowned. When the Comte hears of the wreck he assumes that the baby has also perished.

The child, named 'Fairy' by the shepherd's family on account of her dainty appearance, grows up with the shepherd's three sons and although they know nothing about her origins it is 'obvious' that she is of good, even noble birth. Consequently, they see that she is educated in the parson's home and do their best to meet what they perceive to be the needs of a better-born child. Fairy, too, gradually becomes aware of the apparently inevitable differences between herself and the shepherd's family:

As she grew older, Fairy began to realise that there was another difference between her and her foster-parents, besides the difference of education, for she was a lady in thought and feeling as well as by birth and, thanks to Mr Leslie, by education. Not that there was anything to jar upon her feelings in John Shelley or his wife; for, simple, honest folk as they were, there was nothing vulgar about them; and it is vulgarity that jars against a refined mind.

In Georgette's world and in the world of her future novels, vulgarity was the unforgivable sin, for it reflected poor breeding or an ill-formed mind.

The Red Deer was an overtly simple tale about a family of Exmoor deer that emphasised Victorian ideas about a natural social hierarchy. In the novel the red deer are the nobility and all of the other animals take their place beneath them within a rigid class structure. The story takes for granted the importance of manners and birth, *noblesse oblige*, the 'natural' treatment of one class by another and what makes a 'gentleman'. The red deer's mother tells her son:

> "We are never unkind to the Trout," she said, "for they belong to the peat-stream, but you must never become familiar with them. Fallow deer, I believe, treat them as equals," and here she looked very proud, "but we do not. You must never be rude to them, for that would be unworthy of a Red Deer, but you must never make great friends with them."

Georgette's childhood was replete with stories in which the consistent moral and message was that class will cling to class and breeding will always tell. These were themes that she would use repeatedly throughout her writing life. The ideas and attitudes in the novels she read reflected those of a highly structured, class-oriented society, proud of its Empire and sure of its place at the centre of the civilised world. For Georgette, growing up in a family with its own social aspirations, they were not attitudes that needed to be questioned – at least not before the end of the First World War.

2

I inherited my literary bent from my father.

Georgette Heyer

By the time Georgette turned three in 1905, George had grown dissatisfied with his job as a teacher at King's College School and was casting about for something different. Two years earlier he had enjoyed considerable success raising funds for the school's new playing fields. His enthusiasm and organisational abilities eventually brought him to the notice of the Board of King's College Hospital. The hospital was raising funds to relocate from its cramped quarters at Lincoln's Inn Fields in central London to a new 'green-field' site at Denmark Hill, several miles south of the Thames. The Board needed at least £200,000 for the new buildings and in November 1905 they appointed George as Appeals Secretary on a much-improved salary of £300 per year.

A better salary meant a bigger house and in March 1906, two months after George began his new job, the family left 103 Woodside and moved into a spacious new home in another quiet street east of Wimbledon High Street (1 Courthope Road, Wimbledon). It was a good-sized house, double-fronted, and fully detached. This was to be Georgette's home for the next five years and the longest she would live anywhere during her childhood. She stayed with her Grannie Watkins at Fairfield during the move but was excited to come home and explore the new house. She was talking all the time now, having mastered a considerable vocabulary by eighteen months and a fluency by two-and-a-half which prompted her mother to write that 'Babs'

> has quite grown out of a Baby. She is such a dear mite. Her hair curls so prettily & she chatters away to any extent. She knows heaps of nursery rhymes, has known them some time now – she is going to be clever I think, she so soon picks up anything that one reads to her. Also her imagination is very much alive & plays a great part in all her games.

At three-and-a-half Georgette could count up to 100 and knew 'all her letters & can make a few'. Sylvia deliberately refrained from teaching her, however, believing that 'she is so very quick and alert. I think her brain is best left alone for the present.'

While Georgette's birth may have suggested new possibilities for her parents in terms of their respective passions for music and literature, in those early years they chose to foster rather than force her natural interests. Although Sylvia hoped that her daughter would be musical, her feeling that Georgette's brain was 'best left alone' suggests that she wanted her to have an unencumbered childhood, free from pressure and expectation. This did not preclude Sylvia from watching for any signs that might indicate a gift for music.

By the time Georgette was four her mother felt compelled to acknowledge that her daughter had not inherited this particular talent: 'Tooley is quite a big girl now. She is 4½ & tall for her age … Such a sweet nature & so affectionate. She is not musical – she likes to sing "Pop goes the weasel", but the tune is somewhat lacking.' Ten years later she would tell a young schoolfriend of Georgette's that her daughter 'had the most perfect throat and vocal chords for a singer and would have had a lovely contralto voice but she could hardly distinguish one note from another'. It must have been disappointing for such a musical mother to realise that her little girl had no inclination for music other than the enjoyment of listening.

If Sylvia was disappointed by her daughter's lack of musicality, George was delighted to discover that she loved to read. He was a great reader himself and as Georgette grew older he encouraged her to emulate him, giving her books to look at and showing her novels and history books which she might read in time. She read Dickens at a young age and by ten was familiar enough with *David Copperfield* to have absorbed the book's characters and expressions into the family vernacular. As well as recommending books for her to read, her father gave her the run of his library and the freedom to follow her fancy and develop her own literary tastes. It was unusual for a Victorian father to allow his daughter to read at will, for society held strong views about the dangers of exposing young women to what was deemed 'unsuitable' reading matter. George had no such qualms about Georgette, however, and he went on encouraging her to read and to stimulate her imagination. He never forbade her reading a particular book, although he occasionally 'advised her against it', and if he sometimes steered her in certain literary directions, that was natural for a man who had benefited from a Classical education and was passionate about poetry.

George had continued to write poems after leaving Cambridge and was enjoying some success with a number of his verses printed in *The Pall Mall Gazette* and *The Saturday Westminster Review*. His poems were sometimes romantic but more often witty. He had become well known at Cambridge for his poetic humour after he was published in the new university magazine, *Granta*. The editor Rudolph Lehmann (who later joined the editorial board of *Punch*) appreciated George's wit and charm of manner and at one poetry reading expressed his 'frank enjoyment when B.I.N.K., a new man, began with a Pantoum'. B.I.N.K. was George's (inexplicable) nickname at Cambridge and he often used it as his *nom de plume*.

The pantoum (a challenging form of poetry) which Lehmann enjoyed was 'In the Lent Term' – a light-hearted account of George trying to study Greek while a friend tempts him from his books to a tennis match at nearby Leys. It exemplified George's love of writing about the everyday in an effort to capture real moments in his life or mark his enjoyment of ordinary things. He was fascinated by character, personality and the comic eccentricities of his fellow human and had an ear for the vernacular which he was adept at converting into witty dialogue. As a regular contributor to *Granta*, George was among those to be honoured in a tradition that saw regular writers immortalised in biographical verse based on a song from Gilbert & Sullivan's operetta *Patience*:

> A waggish and gay young man,
> A plenty-to-say young man,
> Tell you tales by the score,
> Give you nicknames galore,
> *I*'ll show you the way young man.

But it was not only poetry which excited George's imagination and inspired him to write. His student life had been enriched by the works of many of the great writers, and he was alert to the ways in which the best of them revealed the complexities and subtleties of human nature through satire, drama, romance and brilliant comedy. Although he recognised that he would never reach such heights himself, as a teacher he sought to convey something of the richness and enduring nature of great literature to his students. While at Weymouth College he had instigated an annual tradition of producing the plays of Aristophanes (all of them performed entirely in Greek) and had joined the boys on stage in a leading role. In 1894, George's production of *The Frogs* was positively reviewed in *The Times* and the headmaster acknowledged his 'histrionic talent' and 'genius' for bringing out the best in the boys. At King's College School George produced a number of Molière's plays and became famous for his performance as old Géronte in *Les Fourberies de Scapin*. Years later one of his students, G.S. Szlumper, recalled:

> The most popular master was Heyer. He was young and good humoured and joined in the games and many of the pranks of the boys, but nevertheless worked a good deal of French into the heads of some of us younger boys.

From boyhood, Georgette's father honed his skills writing poetry and short stories, skills which he then sought to impart to his students. He was a compelling teacher, but it required a truly gifted student to fully absorb and then make use of the kinds of literary lessons he had to offer. Ironically, it was not in the classroom but in his own home that George would eventually find that pupil.

From an early age Georgette was the eager recipient of her father's literary heritage and she benefited enormously from his enthusiasm for good literature, his passion for the past, his creative spirit and his love of writing. As well as encouraging her to read widely, George also insisted that she master the intricacies of written English and gain a clear understanding of grammar, syntax and punctuation. He instilled in her a love of the English language and an understanding of its construction, form and usage that would eventually enable her to develop her own stylish prose. They were kindred spirits, these two, and in time George would come to recognise in his daughter the gift of the natural storyteller and a talent for writing which would far exceed his own.

He was a delightful father, with an irrepressible, Peter Pan side to his character which Georgette found immensely attractive. She had grown especially close to him by the time her baby brother was born on 20 August 1907. Coming into the world just four days after her fifth birthday, George Boris Heyer was a source of great interest to his sister, for she was very fond of dolls and quickly discovered that a baby could be just as entertaining. Like Georgette before him Boris was a lively baby, although he did not have her swiftness of mind or her passion for learning. She was not especially perturbed by Boris's arrival or resentful of his demands on her mother. Sylvia's confinement meant more time with Daddy. Father and daughter spent many blissful hours together in the weeks after Boris was born and Sylvia proudly recorded that George 'worships the ground she treads on'.

It is not known when Georgette wrote her first story or poem but she often saw her father writing and may have followed his example early. In 1909, when she was rising seven and Boris was almost two, their father wrote a poem about his son and achieved a long-held ambition when it became the first of several of his poems to be published in *Punch*. 'To Secundus' reveals George's ability to bring a scene to life and infuse it with humour – another talent which he would encourage in his daughter. She also springs briefly into view in the ballad.

To Secundus
(*Aged 20 months*)

You have capable fingers, Secundus my son,
      And a firm yet a delicate touch.
Though you turn out the visiting-cards one by one
And strew them around you, – isn't it fun! –
      They are none of them, bent very much.
And you know it's untidy this game that you play,
For you look up and smile, – and then what can I say?

You've adventurous tastes and a will of your own,
      And I count it the worst of your sins
That you instantly make for the dangerous zone
Of the fender and coal-box, if suffered alone
      To toddle about on your pins;
And your rink-like performance I cannot admire
When you fetch up and balance in front of the fire.

There's a music that lurks in each word that you say
      Be it "tick-tick", or "gee-gee", or "done!"
And the sound of your laughter no words can convey,–
It is really the sparkle alive in the spray
      Of a waterfall lit by the sun.
In your breath there is magic that "Sesame!" cries,
For you blow on my watch – press – and open it flies.

'Tis your quick sense of fun that I like in you best
      And the fact that you never disdain
To evince your delight at my sorriest jest
Which, though often repeated, is welcomed with zest
      And demanded again and again.
You've a joke of your own with the bell-push, but this
Is a joke that the housemaid has taken amiss.

You're so fond of a game that there's trouble unless
    We allow you to join the <u>partie</u>
In whatever's afoot; and it's little you guess
That your vigorous notions of how to play chess
    Have at times inconvenienced me.
And your sister has also been known to refer
To your manner with dolls as distressing to her.

You're a mischievous chap, and I freely admit
    That I like you for being a Turk;
But there's one thing about you disturbs me, – to wit,
Your absurd fascination, – for here do I sit
    When I ought to be up and at work.
You are surely a wizard, Secundus, my lad,
And have bound with a spell your susceptible Dad.

The years following Boris's birth were busy ones for George. As well as his role as Appeals Secretary at King's College Hospital, in 1908 he had also been appointed Secretary to the Dean of the Medical School. He continued directing the hospital's fundraising activities and when, in July 1909, King Edward VII laid the foundation stone for the new hospital George was among those seated on the official platform with the Royal family. He was a key organiser of the grand fundraising carnival held at the Crystal Palace in Sydenham that year and, in 1909 and 1910, George also organised gala charity matinees at the Lyceum Theatre and the Theatre Royal, Drury Lane, in central London. These were very successful and, for a time, put George squarely in one of his favourite milieus – the theatre. He came to know a number of London's leading actors, playwrights and impresarios, as well as several members of the aristocracy, and it was as a result of these connections that, in 1910, he resigned from King's College Hospital to take up the position of Organising Secretary of the Shakespeare Memorial National Theatre Committee.

George was a Shakespeare aficionado and Georgette was raised on the works of the Bard. Her father was enthusiastic about the Committee's plan for a theatre dedicated to producing the works of

Shakespeare and keen to play his part in raising the necessary £500,000 in time for the Shakespeare tercentenary in 1916. The Earl of Lyttleton was committee chairman and his supporters included many of the theatrical, literary, political and aristocratic luminaries of the day. George probably attended the Shakespeare masque held in July 1910 in the park at Knole, the Sackville-Wests' great house in Kent. Ellen Terry, Mrs Winston Churchill, Elizabeth Asquith and Vita Sackville-West all performed at the fund-raiser. George's sister Alice later wrote of him in her memoirs that 'he had charming manners and made many friends among these people and was received at Buckingham Palace'.

By December 1913 George was reported in *The Times* as saying that the Committee had finally settled on a site in central London with frontages on Gower, Keppel and Malet Streets at a cost of £150,000. The balance of the money needed was to be raised by way of an appeal to 'the lovers of Shakespeare', but the First World War threw the Committee's activities into disarray. It was to be nearly one hundred years before Shakespeare's Globe Theatre was eventually built on the south bank of the Thames.

Before his resignation, George had gained a solid reputation in a number of social circles through his work for King's College Hospital and in 1909 he was invited to join the Wimbledon Literary and Scientific Society (WLSS). Founded in 1891 the WLSS was a private society for residents of Wimbledon with an interest in or knowledge of things scientific and literary. Admittance to the Society was considered a great honour, for membership was by invitation only and prior to the First World War members were drawn mainly from Wimbledon's élite – its 'top-of-the-hill' ranks. Members met on a regular basis to hear formal lectures, present papers, and engage in organised debates or informal discussions, many of which were held in Wimbledon's grandest homes.

Georgette sometimes accompanied her father to the WLSS to watch him take part in recitations, readings and literary re-enactments, or in the Society's famous *Conversaziones*. In 1911 George presented a paper to the Society on the poems of François Villon and two years later he and Georgette won great acclaim for their dramatic portrayal of the moment in Shakespeare's tragedy, *King John*, when Hubert is about to put out the eyes of little Prince Arthur. Georgette was convincing as the young prince and the scene, inspired by Yeames' famous painting, was considered very moving. Several Wimbledon families took part in the 'Tableaux from the Poets' and George was not the only literary father to act alongside his daughter that evening. Mr Alfred Percival Graves also led his wife and daughters in the tableau of *Ruth and Naomi* (there is no record indicating whether his fifteen-year-old son, the budding author Robert Graves, had a hand in the production).

Despite its staid exterior, Wimbledon had much to offer a creative, imaginative child like Georgette and her formative years there were to be a major influence on her later writing. Like others of her generation she was a witness to the final years of the equestrian age. There was very little motorised traffic in the suburb before the war and horses were still an essential part of daily life, so as a child Georgette encountered horses and became familiar with carriages in their many forms. Her family does not appear to have owned their own carriage, but there were several livery stables in Wimbledon with horses and carriages for hire. George was a rider and he ensured that Georgette learned the rudiments of the art in childhood.

Georgette also knew many of the local tradesmen's horses. The butcher boy's two-wheeled cart, the baker's van, the fishmonger's gig and the milkman's chariot were all horse-drawn and several times a week the huge, flat, coal carts and open dust-carts made their regular rounds of Wimbledon's streets. She liked to watch the enormous draught-horses with their jangling horse-brasses going down the road. One of the most exciting carriages was the local fire engine, which was drawn by two white horses. Sometimes she would see the horses go galloping down the road pulling the bright red fire engine with its boiler puffing and the firemen furiously clinging on at the back. But the real equestrian highlight came in the summer months when the Box-Hill stagecoach made its run with regular stops at the Dog and Fox Inn in Wimbledon High Street.

Little had changed since the high coaching days of the Regency and Georgette loved to see the stagecoach coming down the street, its four horses glistening with sweat and its scarlet-coated guard holding on at the rear as the coach turned in at the inn yard. The Dog and Fox was where the stagecoach made its first change after leaving London. It was always exciting to watch the ostlers run out as soon as the coach pulled up in the yard and to see how quickly they could unharness the horses and replace them with four fresh ones. Georgette's childhood was filled with the sights, smells and sounds of horses and carriages: she had heard the blare of the guard's coaching horn resonate across the inn-yard as the stage swept out into the street with the horses' hooves clattering on the cobblestones; she understood the urgency of the change and could picture the sudden flurry of activity as the passengers hurried to take their seats in the coach. Years later, when she came to write of such things in her novels, Georgette did not merely imagine these scenes from information culled from history books, she remembered them; one of the reasons she could make such scenes live in her books was because she was writing from life.

Although horses were an important part of the daily routine in Wimbledon, walking was the way most people moved about the town and, like most middle-class Edwardian children, Georgette and Boris had one, or even two, regular daily walks. Accompanied by their mother, Georgette often helped to push Boris in his pram to the shops along the High Street or the Ridgway, or north to Rushmere Pond and the Common. Walks on the Common were sometimes rewarded with a sight of the balloon races that were held regularly in the summer on Saturdays. Looking up, Georgette and Boris might see half-a-dozen huge balloons floating by and would wave to the balloonists travelling overhead in their great basket gondolas. The memory of those balloons and their occupants would appear years later as a scene in her novel, *Frederica*.

Away from the Common, a walk through Wimbledon sometimes meant an encounter with Algernon Swinburne, the famous poet who lived at Putney with his friend, Theodore Watts-Dunton. Swinburne was a familiar sight in Wimbledon where he took his daily walk to the shops and Georgette remembered him once stopping to pat Boris on the head.

A trip to the shops could be a treat, especially if it included a visit to Frost's, the toyshop at 5 High Street. Frost's had a special counter on which was laid out a tantalising array of little tin toys, none of which cost more than a farthing. Georgette chose her dolls at Frost's or, if they were of the more expensive porcelain variety, she might be taken to Mannings, the grand toyshop further down the hill in the Broadway. Two regular sights on the High Street were the Punch and Judy man, who would set up his portable theatre across the road from Frost's, and the organ-grinder, who had several spots along the High Street and the Ridgway where he would stop and churn out popular tunes to entertain the passersby. In the winter months the muffin-man would also make his rounds and sometimes they would buy muffins from the large wooden tray balanced on top of his head.

Georgette spent a happy, untroubled childhood in Wimbledon. She was a healthy, active child, slim of build but strong and very pretty, with long curling brown hair tinted with gold, clear grey eyes and her father's 'strongly marked very individual eyebrows'. She was given ample time to play and read and to absorb the world around her in her own way and at her own pace. School does not appear to have played much of a role in her life before the age of thirteen and it may be that Sylvia's belief that Georgette's brain was 'best left alone' continued to guide her parents' approach to her education. George and Sylvia made sure that she had a sound knowledge of reading, writing and arithmetic, as well as a broad general knowledge and an understanding of languages, French in particular.

Years later, when Georgette wrote her most autobiographical novel *Helen*, she gave the fictional father, Jim Marchant, strong views about education for women which may well have echoed her own father's approach: 'I don't want Helen educated for a profession and made to pass Matriculation. I want her mind to expand. I want her to be accomplished in the sense that she has a wide knowledge of art and history, and literature, and the things that matter.' In the novel

Helen's mother has died giving birth and she is raised by her devoted father. Although the child does not have any formal education before she is ten, she is untroubled by this for 'Himself had taught Helen to read and write, while in long talks with her he had instilled into her a not inconsiderable knowledge of history and literature.' Like Georgette, Helen is happiest in her father's company and has little need for a busy social life or lots of friends.

Georgette was not without friends as a girl but she was a shy child who was happy in her own company and quite content to be left alone with her books and to spend time reading, thinking, and making up stories. Although she sometimes played with other Wimbledon children, she seems to have retained very few of these relationships into adulthood. John Davy Hayward, the son of the family doctor, was an exception. He was two years younger than Georgette, with a sharp intellect and a similar interest in books and writing. John had a quick temper but his conversation was stimulating and Georgette did not seem to mind his tendency to be difficult and acerbic. As she grew older, her own style with those she knew well was to be frank, sometimes to the point of tactlessness, and in John she found someone with whom she could be herself. The two developed a close friendship and the habit of easy intimacy without the complications of romance.

Although he developed a rare form of muscular dystrophy in early adolescence, John eventually went to Cambridge where he became a lifelong friend and confidant of T.S. Eliot's. He and Eliot later ran a minor *salon* from John's flat in Bina Gardens in London and shared rooms for several years before Eliot's marriage. After university John went on to become a successful anthologist and bibliophile and he and Georgette wrote to each other intermittently for many years.

In 1911, when Georgette was nearly nine, her family moved again. Their new home was at 27 Chartfield Road in Putney. It was here that Georgette's brother, Frank Dmitri Heyer, was born on 18 January 1912. By the following August, when she turned ten, Georgette was very much the big sister to both Boris and Frank. She told them stories, pushed Frank in his pram and helped Boris learn his letters.

She loved both boys but was closest to Boris in both age and temperament. The two shared a similar sense of humour and the same direct way of talking. The Heyers did not stay in Putney for much more than two years, for in 1913 the family returned to Wimbledon to live briefly at 119 Ridgway, before leaving England for a new life in France.

3

The modern child isn't brought up on the proper literature.

Georgette Heyer

Early in 1914, George accepted a job as the manager of the Paris branch of Cox's Bank and that spring Georgette and her family moved into a maisonette on the Avenue Marceau. It was an ideal location in the heart of the city, just off the Champs-Elysées, with a view of the Arc de Triomphe and the Étoile. Georgette delighted in her new surroundings with their wide, open boulevards, busy cafés and endless variety of things to see and do. It was a marvellous time to be in Paris, for it was then at its zenith as the cultural centre of the world and an irresistible lure to many of the world's greatest artists, thinkers, writers and musicians. They brought the city to life with conversation and performance, art, music and books and the Heyers revelled in the opportunity to go about the city and absorb some of its cultural riches.

For a literary Francophile like George, the chance to immerse himself in French society, culture and language was especially satisfying. While for Sylvia Paris represented an opportunity to rediscover her music, with its rich offering of concerts, ballets, private *salons* and the great Paris Opéra. Only the year before the Heyers' arrival, Stravinsky's ballet *The Rite of Spring* had caused one of the greatest sensations in the history of music, and the city was alive with the sounds of Ravel, Debussy and Saint-Saëns – whose compositions

Sylvia remembered playing at the Royal Academy. George's position with the bank, his charm of manner and his fluent French brought a number of invitations and Georgette sometimes went with her parents to a *salon* or the theatre. There were also galleries, museums, parks and monuments to see and, already an astute observer, she took note of many things which she would later use in her novel, *Helen*.

In the book Georgette would recall something of those heady Paris months. Part of the story recounts sixteen-year-old Helen's first visit to Paris with her father, Jim Marchant, and her governess, Jane Pilbury. Helen revels in her new home and is fascinated by the city.

> Never were more inveterate sight-seers than Jane and Helen. For over a fortnight they explored Paris . . . They walked round and round the streets which formed an outer circle about the Étoile, trying to decide which view of the Arc was most pleasing. Helen thought she liked the one from the Avenue Marceau, where you saw the Arc three-quarter full, and least the view from the Avenue Wagram . . . They spent hours in the Rue de la Paix gazing at almost incredible frocks and jewels, and marvelled at the size of Napoleon in the Place Vendôme. They crossed the river to the Invalides and the Faubourg Saint Germain, and they went north to the Montmartre . . . and gasped to see the white wonder which, when finished, was to be the Sacré Coeur . . . They talked in exclamation marks, Helen said, and could not find enough words to express what they felt.

Helen attends morning school where she studies history, literature and languages, but 'the afternoons were free for amusement when they would journey down the Seine on little steamboats, or drive out to Fontainebleau. There were concerts too, and theatres, exhibitions and picture galleries, or most enthralling of all, the opera.' Many of Helen's fictional experiences in Paris echo her creator's – although Georgette was to give her heroine a more peaceful departure from the city than she herself would experience.

Conflict came unexpectedly when, on Saturday 1 August 1914, Germany declared war and began its advance towards the French frontier. Three days later, Germany invaded Belgium and on 4 August Britain declared war. Georgette and her family remained in the French capital throughout August and into September and she celebrated her twelfth birthday in Paris. Her parents read the papers and sought information from friends and colleagues while they decided what to do. Like many people in those early weeks of the War, they were not convinced the conflict would last, but as the Germans moved south and west through Belgium reports of the brutality of their advance made those living in Paris increasingly nervous. The Battle of the Marne began on 6 September, with the enemy just thirty miles from the capital, and Georgette always remembered hearing the rumble of the German guns as the Allies fought off the attack. The battle ended six days later with an Allied victory but it was all too close for comfort. Soon afterwards George decided it was time to take his family home.

The Heyers returned to London and tried to settle into normal life. There was an air of uncertainty in England as the War intensified on the Continent. George found that he was unwilling to commit himself to a permanent job until the situation in France was clear. Harold Pullein-Thompson, a young friend of his who had also taught at King's College School, returned from the Front in October after receiving bullet and shrapnel wounds in his arm and shoulder. He was not optimistic about the chances of the conflict being short-lived.

Surrounded by friends and family with loved ones at the Front, Georgette's father (though over-age) began to think about enlisting. It was not a straightforward decision, as he was his family's sole provider and the effect on them was a serious consideration. Georgette was approaching adolescence and, despite an acute intellect, was intensely shy. If her father went to war she would not only lose her dearest companion, she would have to go to school.

Georgette's shyness may have been one reason why her parents were content to educate her at home. George was a gifted teacher more than capable of educating his own children, but the War changed everything. Given his propensity to talk to Georgette on all manner of subjects, her father probably discussed with her the possibility of his enlisting. It cannot have been an easy conversation but, even at twelve, she understood what was expected of someone of her class and upbringing and the need for a 'stiff upper-lip' response. Years later in *Helen* she wrote about a father going off to the War and his explanation to his teenage daughter:

> We thought the War would soon be over. It won't. It's growing. Personal feeling, inclination, everything, must go to the wall before this enormous upheaval. You see that? . . . I've got to go, Helen. It boils down to that. Not because the Country calls, or any other poster cry like that, not because I'm indispensable to the Army, not even because of a patriotic desire to hold England inviolate, as the newspapers would say. It's because of the spirit of adventure that is in every man, and the feeling that one can't be out of it.

Georgette may not have fully understood the War or her father's need to play his part in it, but she loved him and knew that going to France was important to him and that she should cope in his absence. Although she was a sensitive child, she had courage and a strong streak of stoicism that enabled her to internalise her feelings and keep many of the stronger emotions at bay. To those who did not know her well she could sometimes appear unfeeling, and it did not always help that her quick wit and sharp tongue were often used to hide her most private hurts. The heroine in *Helen* similarly suffers after her father and many of her friends leave for the Front: 'She was not cold or hard. Something within her was aching for all these men who were going to Flanders, but she could not show it. "I've got to keep my end up, same as you."'

Georgette kept her end up and when, on 13 September 1915, George applied for 'appointment to a temporary commission in the regular army for the period of the war' she remained stoical. The following day her father was assigned to the British Expeditionary Forces, Central Requisition Office in Rouen. A week later George was commissioned as a lieutenant and on 21 September he embarked for France.

Her father's departure meant Georgette would have to go to school for the first time at the age of thirteen. The institution chosen for her entrance into formal education was the Oakhill Academy at 9 Ridgway Place in Wimbledon. A handsome Victorian terrace house, it was known locally as 'Miss Head's School' and was a popular choice for the daughters of Wimbledon's professional class. In almost every way school was a new experience for Georgette and not altogether a happy one, although her teachers were kind and the principal, Miss Head, took a personal interest in each of the girls. For Georgette, used to the freedom of her father's library, to reading where interest or fancy took her, and to impromptu discussions about poetry, plays, history and language, the formality of school was an adjustment. At Miss Head's she was expected to study set subjects for a specific time, her days regulated by bells and a curriculum. She found the change difficult and, according to an unnamed school friend, [1] for some time her only friends at Oakhill were the teachers, all of whom admired her intelligence and ability and in whose company she was most at ease.

The fact that she got along with adults did not help to endear her to her classmates, but there were also other, more difficult differences to overcome. Georgette's knowledge of history and literature, her experiences in France and her upbringing in general gave her fellow pupils (as the friend later recalled) the sense that 'she had already seen a great deal of the world and a very much wider world than we in our secure little lives in Wimbledon had ever seen.' Georgette was precocious and unusual. This student remembered her 'as an enigma even then; full of intelligence, a very dry caustic wit, and a tremendous sense of humour'.

---

1 Georgette's unnamed school friend wrote to Jane Aiken Hodge after the publication of *The Private World of Georgette Heyer* in 1984. In her letter she gave a detailed description of her friendship with Georgette. Unfortunately, the letter was lost and all that remains from it are the quotations which were included in the paperback edition of the Hodge biography. I have tried various avenues of research and enquiry to try and discover the identity of the unnamed correspondent but to no avail. In her letter she said she was the daughter of a High Court judge who was a widower, that she had attended the Oakhill Academy with Georgette and visited her home regularly over a period of a few years. Although there were several High Court judges who lived in Wimbledon for some or all of the relevant period my research has failed to find a candidate who was a widower with a daughter of the right age.

While she may have inherited her father's love of a joke, George's genius for making friends eluded her. Lacking his gregarious temperament and irrepressible personality, Georgette frequently found the path to friendship tortuous. Her forthright manner and what her classmate described as 'her sharp, all too accurate, caustic tongue', masked her shyness and made her difficult to know. Georgette's deep reserve meant friendship came slowly – although when it did come it was of the enduring kind with a strong element of loyalty. Eventually, she did find a friend at Oakhill and, appropriately, the two girls 'came together over a book'. Their discovery that they had both read and liked *The Red Deer* marked the beginning of a friendship that lasted throughout the War.

Like so many families caught up in the Great War, the Heyers found the changes difficult. Boris was only eight and Frank three when their father left for France. They all felt his absence and for Sylvia and Georgette it was especially hard. Sylvia joined the Red Cross as a volunteer nurse but Georgette was too young to join a formal organisation – although she probably knitted socks and balaclavas for the troops. Her father was never far from her thoughts. Although his job kept him mainly at Army Headquarters and therefore some distance from the battlefront, both mother and daughter were keenly aware of the possibility that he might never return to them.

They did not discuss their feelings much. Sylvia must have been aware of Georgette's emotional struggles and did her best to provide support, but this was not always simple. The distance between mother and daughter had grown over time and Georgette's close relationship with her father had sometimes meant excluding Sylvia, who was now expected to be both mother and father to her children. George's place was not easy to fill and without him to provide for them Sylvia also had to make do financially. She was forced to rely on the income from her share of William Watkins Limited (a few hundred shares bequeathed to her after her father's death), whatever other investments they may have had and on George's Separation Pay (the amount paid to the families of the soldiers on active service), which was less than thirty shillings a week. Her unmarried sisters may have also helped, having come into some money the previous year after their mother bequeathed Fairfield, 'its contents and any money in the bank', to Ellice, Josephine and Cicely. Annette Watkins had died on 9 June 1914 while the Heyers were in Paris, but Georgette's beloved Grannie had remembered her favourite grandchild. The only other bequest in her very brief will read: 'To my granddaughter Georgette Heyer, my watch and chain.'

By the end of 1915, Georgette had lost both her grandmothers to old age. Alice Heyer suffered a stroke two weeks before Christmas and the family travelled to Worthing to be with her and Georgette's grandfather. George Heyer was now eighty-three and facing the prospect of losing his beloved companion. He and Alice had been married for over fifty years and George had always treated his wife 'as if she were a queen'. In her memoir his daughter later recalled that although their mother was a plain woman their father had brought his children up to believe she was beautiful. Now Alice was seriously ill with little hope that she would recover.

It was hard to think of her grandmother dying, but the impending tragedy also brought some days of happiness for Georgette and her family, for her father came home from France to be with his mother in the last week of her life. It was a bittersweet time for everyone. Alice Heyer died on 21 December and George stayed in Sussex just long enough to organise his mother's affairs before leaving to resume his military duties in France. His family returned to Wimbledon and a new address at 19 Homefield Road.

These were gruelling years for everyone as the War raged across Europe and the Middle East. On 1 July 1916 the Battle of the Somme began on the Western Front with an appalling loss of life. Georgette was almost fourteen and aware of many of the horrors being experienced by soldiers and civilians on and around the battlefields. She wrote to her father regularly, regaling him with stories from home and telling him about her activities and those of her brothers. It was part of the unspoken protocol of the time that she should write cheerfully, without reference to her fears for his safety or concerns for those they knew.

By the end of November, fighting on the Somme had killed or injured more than one million Allied and German troops. 146,000 British soldiers were dead or missing and more than 400,000 were wounded. The nation was devastated by a tragedy unlike any it had ever known. The sense of waste and the effects of the horrifying casualty lists would linger on long after the War ended. Christmas 1916 was a sombre time, with many families in mourning. In Britain the general feeling of loss and hardship was only exacerbated by severe food shortages.

The War years were a period about which Georgette chose to write very little. Only in *Helen* does she mention them and even then her heroine merely records her reactions to the early months of the conflict, before an abrupt leap of time moves the story forward four years to find her contemplating the peace. Helen is deeply affected by the War but finds talking of its horrific realities impossible. The deaths of several of her friends at the Front are touched on briefly but, by the end of the conflict, her father returns home safely and life – albeit an irrevocably altered life – goes on. Although Georgette's own father was not at the Front he was not completely shielded from its horrors, for the War took its toll even on those who enjoyed the relative safety of a job behind the lines.

George was a Requisitioning Officer for the Directorate of Hirings and Requisitions attached to Second Army Headquarters. The Directorate was responsible for 'business relations with the French' and for 'the obtaining of sites and buildings' used to accommodate officers and men. George's fluent French and personal charm made him highly effective in gaining entrance to buildings needed by the Army and in overcoming the protests and resistance of their owners, many of whom never forgot 'the persuasive English officer with his perfect French'. Popular with his fellow officers, George was well known for his 'irrepressible optimism and unfailing good temper' and for regularly devoting 'his few spare hours to serving friends less happily quartered'. In October 1916, he was promoted to the rank of Captain with an increase in pay and responsibility.

At home Georgette and Sylvia did their best to maintain a

positive demeanour in the face of increasingly bad war news. In 1917 Sylvia took the children to Bognor Regis to live, for a respite. The move may have been prompted by Boris's continuing poor health (he suffered from a mild form of haemophilia). Bognor was by the sea, only ten miles from George's father at Worthing, and Sylvia must have hoped that the change would do them all good. Although Boris was of an age when most boys went to school, Sylvia continued to teach him at home, despite having received a generous offer for a reduction in fees from Sir Thomas Hughes, the Chairman of Governors at King's College School. It was not the school's usual practice to offer discounts to former masters but Sir Thomas felt that some concession should be made in the case of George Heyer's son, since George was 'not only an Old Boy and ex-master, but one who deserved well of the School'. Mindful of Boris's health, however, Sylvia declined the offer and neither Boris nor Frank went to King's.

In the middle of 1918 the Heyers moved back to Wimbledon, to a new house at 11 Homefield Road – just a few doors from their old address. This was to be the final year of the protracted conflict that was called 'the war to end all wars' and it was to be a long and difficult one. Food rationing was introduced in January and in April conscription was extended to include all able men between the ages of 17 and 51. There were work stoppages and strikes throughout the year in Britain, while on the Continent the fighting continued and the numbers of casualties grew greater by the day. It was a time of considerable strain and hardship, which took its toll on all but the most resilient. The only good news to reach the family from France came in May with news of George's promotion to Staff Captain and his transfer to the General List – a small recognition of his abilities as an administrator.

Georgette turned sixteen in August 1918 and was rapidly growing out of school. She had completed her studies at the Oakhill Academy that year and moved to Wimbledon's most prestigious girls' school, The Study. This school had a reputation for excellence in female education but the narrow curriculum and emphasis on sports held little interest for Georgette. Her time there was brief; too short for her to make her mark scholastically or develop any enduring friendships. Years later all that a fellow student remembered about her was that the family name was pronounced 'higher' and changed after the War.

On 11 November 1918 the declaration of peace saw wild celebrations across Britain. For those families whose loved ones had survived the terrible conflict the relief was overwhelming. Georgette and Sylvia waited impatiently for news of George's return. He finally left France for England on 5 January 1919 and arrived in Wimbledon to a rapturous welcome and a new job at the War Office. It was wonderful for Georgette to have her father home again with time to talk and make plans for the future. He brought the house to life, renewing old acquaintances, playing tennis and bridge, reading, writing, and making them all laugh. If he was affected by the horrors of the War, as most men of his generation were, he kept that part of his life separate, choosing only to remember and talk about his experiences and memories when in the company of his brother officers. George was awarded an MBE for his war service, one of the early recipients of the medal established in 1918 by King George V to honour those who had served in non-combatant roles during the conflict.

George's father did not live long enough to know of the honour. He was eighty-eight when he died on 25 April, soon after his son's return from France. After his wife's death he had remained in the family home cared for by George's sister, Ilma. George Heyer was Georgette's last surviving grandparent; his passing marked the end of an era. He left his estate to be divided among his four children and George invested some of his inheritance in the stock market during the short-lived postwar boom. The extra money also made it easier for Georgette to participate in the glamorous London social scene which came abruptly to life again at the end of the War. As she grew into young womanhood Georgette gradually became less shy; by seventeen she had begun to enjoy going out to dances and parties and meeting new people.

In 1919 she met two young women who shared her literary interests and with whom she would become lifelong friends. Joanna Cannan and Carola Oman had known each other since childhood.

Each was the daughter of an Oxford don and had grown up in Oxford where Joanna's father, Charles Cannan, was Dean of Trinity College and later Secretary to the Delegates (Chief Executive) of Oxford University Press. Carola's father was Sir Charles Oman, the Chichele Professor of Modern History, Fellow of All Souls College and the British Academy, President of the Royal Historical Society and author of A *History of the Peninsular War* in several volumes. Georgette was just seventeen when she first met Carola and Joanna who, at twenty-two and twenty-three respectively, might have been expected to disdain a close friendship with a girl not yet out of her teens. It says much about Georgette's intellect and literary education that she was accepted as an equal by the two older girls.

The three young women met in Wimbledon, where Joanna had come to live after marrying Harold Pullein-Thompson (later known as 'Cappy') in June 1918. Georgette already knew Harold through his friendship with her father. According to Harold's family, she had even fallen in love with him in her early teens, despite the sixteen-year age difference. He was a dashing figure, tall and handsome with dark blue eyes, black hair and a neat military moustache, the sort of man who made an instant impression on women. Joanna Cannan had been love-struck on first meeting the handsome Captain of the Queen's Royal West Surrey Regiment at a dinner at her home in Oxford. Years later her eldest daughter, the novelist Josephine Pullein-Thompson, wrote that:

> Mamma always admitted that she was bowled over by Cappy's good looks, by his assured manner, and his ability to hail taxis and summon head waiters. At thirty-four he was so different from the undergraduates who had previously courted her; and though she refused his first proposal of marriage, when later, on leave from France, he asked her again, she accepted him.

Harold was Georgette's first real-life romantic hero. While his marriage may have brought an end to her adolescent crush, it marked the beginning of her friendship with his wife, Joanna, and her friend, Carola Oman.

They were all ardent readers and keen to make their mark as authors. Carola already had some success as a minor poet with an anthology of war poetry, *The Menin Road and Other Poems*, published by Hodder & Stoughton in October 1919. Like her friends, however, she wanted to write novels. Carola was five when she wrote her first story, a short cautionary tale entitled *Coral and the Bear*. She was six when she visited a wishing-stone patronised by Queen Victoria at which Carola's wish was to write a book. Like Georgette, she grew up reading Shakespeare and had even tried writing sonnets as a girl, submitting them to magazines in the hope of publication and refusing to be deterred by the rejection slips that followed. Later, Carola and Joanna both went to Miss Batty's School for the daughters of Oxford dons (later called the Wychwood School) where they created a forum for their literary ambitions by producing a secret school magazine called the *I.M.* Both girls wrote avidly during their teens, trying their hand at poetry, plays and prose and always aspiring to see their work in print.

After their first meeting in 1919, Georgette, Joanna and Carola met often to discuss their ideas and read their latest works aloud to each other. They were three clever, literate young women: all could have gone to university, taken degrees and carved out successful careers for themselves in academia. Carola's younger brother Charles went to Oxford, but neither she nor her sister Dulce was raised with any expectation of a tertiary education, despite their father's eminent position at the University. Similarly, Joanna did not think of going to Oxford, even though she had grown up amidst its colleges and 'dreaming spires'. Before the War, she had aspired to be an artist and, after leaving school, had gone to Paris to be 'finished'. She took art classes, fell in love with the city and hoped eventually to embrace the life of the Parisienne artist with a room in a garret and free love. The War put an end to her dream and in 1914 she returned to England to become a VAD nurse. After her marriage she began writing again and when she met Georgette was hoping to be published (like her sister May Cannan). Ironically, it was neither Joanna nor Carola who was to publish a novel first, but the youngest of the three, Georgette.

PART II

'FIRST CRACK OUT OF THE BAG'

1920–1930

4

Of course, if you're just going to do a grand romance, culminating in dark deeds in the ancestral house, with the maximum amount of wax candles, whispering brocades, & dying splendour, that's quite all right.

Georgette Heyer

Georgette had always loved making up stories. From an early age her imagined characters enlivened her childhood as she gave them life and a stage on which to strut in her games and storywriting. In her letter to Jane Aiken Hodge, the friend from her schooldays described how she used to spend Saturdays at Georgette's house where the two girls were free to make full use of the drawing room for their games and play-acting. The room 'was tacitly regarded as our private domain and there we acted play after play . . . all dialogue completely impromptu, of course, but the plots always produced by Georgette'. In later years, this friend would recognise a number of those early plots in Heyer novels, including *The Black Moth*, *The Masqueraders* and *Beauvallet*. Many of the characters and stories imagined in childhood stayed with Georgette throughout her teens, shifting and changing with their creator as she lived through the War years and gradually emerged from adolescence into young womanhood.

Partly because she grew up in an era in which letter writing was considered *de rigueur* for a well-bred person, and partly because of the War, the business of writing came naturally to Georgette. She had written regularly to her father while he was stationed in Rouen, and cultivated the art of writing as she spoke and penning sentences which exactly captured the mood of the moment. Her descriptions of daily activities, social encounters, her brothers' antics and her own thoughts and feelings helped her to develop her talent for dialogue and for re-creating humorous scenes from life which she hoped would make her reader laugh.

Georgette wrote mostly with a fountain pen and gradually developed a small, neat handwriting which sometimes became illegible when she was annoyed or in a rush. When she was young her handwriting was rounded and open; as she grew older it became more angular and idiosyncratic with lower-case 'e's that looked like 'a's and a tendency to run some of her consonants together. Not for the adult Georgette the affectation of green or violet ink for her letters; dark blue or black ink was her preference and she generally favoured small-sized writing paper. Although in her adolescence she must have been writing stories and essays for school and probably for personal pleasure, there is nothing to indicate where she wrote, at what time of day or night, or how often. Her father returned to his writing almost immediately after coming home from the War and was frequently to be found composing articles, essays, poems and short stories, all with a view to publication. He was an encouraging mentor and it is not difficult to imagine father and daughter enjoying their shared passion for writing, discussing points of grammar or Georgette's next story.

She was a natural storyteller, with the gift of knowing just how to please her audience and how best to create the intense desire to know 'what happens next?' She often told stories to her brothers and in her early adolescence she and Boris would sometimes join forces to create amusing plots or situations which they would then act out. They shared a similar sense of humour and, in the tradition of their grandfather George, would think up pranks to try out on their family and friends, or even on unsuspecting strangers. One of these was to travel up to London where they would board a bus and Georgette would take on the role of worldly-wise older sister escorting her young brother 'just up from the country' about town. He would ask about some building or other and she would deliberately offer an explanation that was rich in detail but totally incorrect. The game was to see how long it took before some 'officious but well-meaning fellow passenger' corrected her. Another game which they both enjoyed was to ride a London bus in the guise of two uninformed visitors who, upon being asked for their fare, would name a destination in the opposite direction and when told their mistake would descend from the bus in feigned horror while all the while trying not to laugh. As an adolescent, Georgette already possessed a robust sense of humour and often saw the ridiculous side of human nature.

The years following the First World War were a time of considerable change and upheaval, particularly for Georgette's generation. Many young people had lost friends and loved ones in the carnage, or experienced first-hand the horrors of the battlefield, and now wanted nothing more than to put the War behind them. For those who could afford it, the 1920s were a time to dance, drink and play; to throw off what they saw as the restrictions and restraints of the Victorian age. This was the era of the 'Bright Young Things' and the 'modern' girl who smoked, learned to type, took up secretarial or other work and moved out of the family home before she was married. For many, independence was key and 'free thought' its symbol, which found expression in raised skirts, bobbed hair, the Bohemian movement and in new ways of speaking and writing through the media of books, films and the theatre. Many earnest young men and women saw peace as a chance to build the world anew – to cast off old conventions like class and tradition and create a better society.

Although her contemporary novels show that she thought deeply about many of the ideas current during those postwar years, Georgette was not among those wishing to change the world. She was more inclined to mourn the passing of old traditions and to look back instead of forward to find that which would comfort her. The only known description of Georgette during the 1920s comes from an article in the New Zealand *Sun* newspaper written by a literary acquaintance of hers, the author, Jane Mander, who worked at Christy & Moore:

Smilingly, she called herself a sheltered daughter, and said she was glad of it. She has never been to a university and considers herself a Victorian. She hates Bohemians and studio parties, loves home life and country sports. She calls herself a reactionary and loathes the Freudians, and speaks slightingly of certain famous modern realists. She detests the average modern novel, and loves the old ones, particularly Jane Austin [sic] and Thackeray.

Although Georgette disdained many of what she perceived to be the quirks and poses of the postwar generation she liked being part of a social group and enjoyed going out with friends to the theatre, the opera and dances. At seventeen, she attended the Blue Ball at the Royal Albert Hall, a grand affair also attended by the famous stage actresses Fay Compton and Gladys Cooper. They made such an impression on Georgette that years later she wrote to a friend:

How Fay Compton was attracting all eyes–until Gladys Cooper turned up, when no one had any eyes for anyone else. She couldn't hold a candle to Fay Compton as far as classic beauty of nature was concerned – but her Eyes! They would have knocked anyone for six, not only because they were so large, & so lustrous, but because of the beauty of their expression!

Georgette also had lovely eyes. At eighteen she was considered striking – even beautiful. Tall at five foot ten, she was slender and elegant, with a 'cloud of hair' and a dusting of freckles on porcelain skin. She enjoyed clothes and always dressed well, keeping up with the latest fashions in frocks, hats and accessories and often wearing a long string of amber beads with matching earrings. Adulthood suited her, and friendship came more easily than it had at school. She had grown into her intellect and people understood and appreciated her humour much more readily, although she was not always tactful. Polite conversation, small-talk and trivia were never her style. She was far too down-to-earth and forthright to refrain from expressing her opinion among friends, who soon learned to expect the sharp wit and frank remarks.

Georgette would never seek the limelight or be a poseur – although she did fall prey to the fashionable pastime of smoking. In those days smoking was considered smart and elegant and she developed a taste for cork-tipped Virginia cigarettes, smoking up to two packs a day for the rest of her life. Georgette attracted attention. According to the Hodge biography, at parties 'young men abandoned everyone else and clustered around her "like flies round a honey-pot".' But Georgette was in no hurry to fall seriously in love. She enjoyed male company but was happy to have a man's friendship without the burden of romantic entanglement. From an early age she found that she often preferred men to women, liking their way of speaking, forthright manners and emotional restraint, in contrast to women who so often wanted to share their deepest feelings after only a few hours' acquaintance.

Georgette did have female friends, however, and not only Joanna and Carola. In the 1920s she had at least one other close girlfriend with whom she went out socially and who may have been the source of invitations to the sorts of weekend house parties, hunt balls and supper dances which she would write about in her contemporary novels. Dorothea Arbuthnot was the great-niece of the Duchess of Atholl and of Georgiana, Countess of Dudley. She had grown up in a stately home in Sussex with her two sisters and a retinue of servants. Known to her intimates as 'Doreen' this is what Georgette also called her when they got to know each other after the War. It is not clear when or where the two girls met, but by 1924 Georgette and Doreen were close friends and remained so until at least 1930.

Although Georgette was not presented at Court – being neither rich enough nor sufficiently well-born for that – she had certain qualifications for joining in at the fringe of upper-class society: she was unusual and articulate, intelligent and well-educated, with a father who was a graduate of Cambridge and an MBE, and a mother who was a graduate of the Royal Academy of Music. Georgette was not upper-class and would never be part of the élite inner circle, but she knew what was expected and how to behave and was well able to interact appropriately whenever she found herself on its periphery.

Georgette's entrée into the exciting social world of postwar London had not stopped her from writing and her experiences at events like the Blue Ball clearly fed her already active imagination. In late 1920 her literary efforts suddenly bore fruit. The previous February she had made up a serial story for Boris, who had been ill. The family had gone to Hastings for his convalescence and it was there that Georgette first devised the exciting adventures of Jack Carstares, the earl turned highwayman, 'to relieve my own boredom and my brother's'. Her father had heard some of the story, recognised the spark of the natural storyteller and 'insisted that [she] do some serious work on it with a view to publication'. Georgette finished the story, wrote it out in her best handwriting and sent the manuscript to Constable, the well-known publisher. She was only seventeen.

Soon afterwards Constable offered to buy *The Black Moth*. The contract was for both British and American publication with a £100 advance against sales. It was an extraordinary achievement for such a young writer and a thrilling experience to have her work accepted 'first crack out of the bag'. But Georgette did not immediately sign the contract. Instead she wrote to the Society of Authors. Established in 1884, the Society existed specifically to protect the rights of authors and assist them with advice regarding agents, publishers and contracts. On 28 March 1921 Georgette sent her contract to the Society and requested they give it their attention – 'especially Clause 17'. Three days later she received a comprehensive reply.

It is impossible to know the precise contents of the original contract for *The Black Moth* because Constable's archives were bombed during the Second World War. Georgette's correspondence with the Society of Authors makes some of its details clear, however, and her prompt and decisive reply is impressive not only for its clear-headed grasp of her correspondent's detailed advice, but also for her insight into her publisher's position:

Thank you very much for the advice on my contract. On most points I agree with you, but Clause 3 – concerning the American sales, I am leaving as it stands. Houghton Mifflin are collaborating with Constable's, and publishing my book in America. The profits of net sale are to be divided equally between Constable's and myself. As Constable's run a certain amount of risk in bringing out an entirely new author, I think this is generous.

When her correspondent told her frankly that 'I object very strongly to Clause 17, and should advise you to delete such clause,' Georgette calmly wrote back 'As to Clause 17 – concerning my future three books, I intend to ask that in the event of my second book reaching 10,000 sale, when I shall receive 20% on it, my third book shall start at that percentage.'

From the beginning she knew that there were more books to come, though she may not have known what they were to be about. She eventually thought better of asking for the higher starting royalty for the third (hypothetical) book in her contract with Constable as she had come 'to the conclusion that it was too much to ask, and I didn't ask it!' By the end of the correspondence, Georgette signed the contract for *The Black Moth* and joined the Society of Authors. She was still only eighteen.

Selling *The Black Moth* was the first of two pivotal events that took place after Georgette's eighteenth birthday. The second occurred in December 1920, when her father took the family to the Bushey Hall Hotel in Hertfordshire for a week's holiday. A vast neo-Jacobean pile set in verdant parkland, the Hall had been built as a private residence in 1865 and later converted into a hotel. It was popular with affluent middle-class families and the Heyers spent Christmas there. At the hotel's Christmas dance Georgette met George Ronald Rougier. Known as Ron or Ronnie, he was a serious-looking student of twenty in his second year of study at the Royal School of Mines and a member of the famous Harlequins rugby team. Georgette knew little about either mining or rugby, but Ronald was tall, handsome and intelligent, with the kind of dry sense of humour she liked, and she was amenable to learning about sport and minerals. They danced together that evening and he discovered that, despite her eighteen years, this tall, stylish, rather shy young woman had a formidable intellect with a sharp wit and direct way of speaking which aroused his interest.

Like the Heyers, the Rougiers were part of the comfortable middle class with aspirations to rise up the social ladder. Ronald's father was of French Huguenot descent and his mother was Scottish. The Rougiers had emigrated to England in 1686 and in 1794 they founded a horn-and-tortoiseshell manufactory in York. Ronald's father, Charles Joseph Rougier, was one of the fourth generation to work in the family business. In 1890 he had moved to the Russian seaport of Odessa where he worked as a shipbroker and ran an import-export business. It was in Odessa that he met Ronald's mother, Jean Crookston, whose brother John was a naval architect with the British Black Sea Fleet. Ronald's parents were married at the British Consulate in Odessa in November 1892. Ronald was born in Odessa in 1900, four years after his brother Charles Leslie Rougier (known as Leslie). The family lived near the harbour in a house in Torgovaya Street and remained in Odessa long enough for Ronald to acquire Russian and an enduring love of caviar.

As a boy Ronald developed an interest in ships and the sea. He would often visit Odessa's busy port to watch the many foreign vessels set sail. He and Leslie had an English governess, Hannah Atkins, but by 1908 it was decided that the boys needed an English education if they were to be properly prepared for their chosen careers in the Army and the Navy. The Rougiers returned to England, where Leslie became a boarder at Marlborough College in Wiltshire and Ronald attended Northaw Place, a preparatory school at Potter's Bar, about ten miles north of London. His parents moved into a house in Stevenage in Hertfordshire, not far from the famous Letchworth golf course. Ronald often rode his bicycle there on weekends and it was on the greens and fairways of Letchworth that he formed a life-long passion for the game of golf.

Ronald was a clever student who won prizes for Latin and Mathematics at Northaw Place. Early in 1913 he passed the entrance examination for the Royal Naval College at Osborne and in May began his officer training there as a member of the 'Exmouth Term'.

Ronald would spend the next two years at Osborne before progressing to the Royal Naval College at Dartmouth for another two years of training. He did well at both Osborne and Dartmouth, but the War changed everything. When hostilities broke out in August 1914, the entire College was mobilised and many of the Dartmouth cadets were sent straight to the Fleet. Although they still had another term at Osborne, Ronald and his classmates, including Prince Louis of Battenberg (later Lord Louis Mountbatten), were moved immediately to Dartmouth to complete their naval training as quickly as possible.

Every cadet knew that he would be sent to sea as soon as he was needed, regardless of whether he had finished his training, and that he would need to be passed fit before going into active service. Towards the end of his second term at Dartmouth it was discovered that Ronald suffered from defective eyesight and his naval career was brought to an abrupt end. It was a devastating blow after nearly three years of training. Deeply disappointed, Ronald began his education afresh at Marlborough, where he eventually became a prefect and captain of the rugby team.

In December 1918 he left Marlborough and the following year began studying at the Royal School of Mines in London. For the next four years Ronald studied mining, geology and metallurgy at the school's headquarters at the Imperial College in South Kensington. He had wanted to study law but his parents felt that reading for the Bar was too expensive. There had been a sharp downturn in the Rougiers' Yorkshire business in recent years (largely brought about by the dramatic shift in women's hairstyles after the Great War) which may have underpinned the decision, but years later Georgette wrote bitterly of Ronald's mother that she 'was a mean old cov-enanting Scot who wouldn't finance his Bar career though she could have'.

Ronald was a sociable young man and an engaging talker who only recently had ended a brief relationship with Marjorie Tanner, known as 'Tam' (she later fell in love with Ronald's brother Leslie and married him). Although Georgette was quite different from the lively and energetic Tam, Ronald found much to hold his interest.

That Christmas week at Bushey Park they were often together, for Ronald had also taken an instant liking to Georgette's father. He found George's ability to bring any subject to life, his enthusiasm for history and literature, his habit of quoting from the Classics, of talking about ideas and offering information without condescension, enormously endearing. Although Ronald loved his parents they were not interested in the kinds of things that stimulated him and he found great satisfaction in his friendship with Georgette's father.

Ronald soon became a regular visitor to the Heyer house. In the years after the War, the shortage of men meant that a young woman was expected to bring her own partner to a dance and Ronald became Georgette's reliable escort, riding his motor-bike to her house in order to squire her to parties, plays and dances. Georgette, in her turn, regularly watched him play rugby, taking the trouble to learn the rudiments of the game and braving the cold and damp to stand on the sidelines to cheer him on. He was a key member of the Royal School of Mines students' team and had debuted with the Harlequins in November 1919. In the world of English rugby, the only thing better than representing the Harlequins was representing England and Ronald was selected for the English team in 1923. He missed playing for his country only because of illness. He was a clever, courageous player who regularly represented the Harlequins alongside Adrian Stoop, a legendary Harlequin with whom Ronald and Georgette remained in touch for many years.

Ronald excelled at golf as well as rugby. He also played tennis – a game of which Georgette's father was fond and an obvious pastime for anyone living in Wimbledon. George and Ronald sometimes played tennis together while Georgette and Sylvia watched, and then the four of them would play bridge. Georgette enjoyed card games, especially bridge and solitaire. In later years she would play endless games of patience or engage in a complex jigsaw while working out the plots of her novels. She possessed an orderly mind and liked solving puzzles or engaging in anything that required skill and precision. She also had style and flair and it was this combination that was to prove such an asset to her writing.

In 1920 the postwar bubble burst. Both the Heyers and their friends the Pullein-Thompsons lost heavily on the stock market. It was always said in the Pullein-Thompson family that Georgette passed on her £100 advance for *The Black Moth* to her father in order to relieve the financial strain. George had resigned from the War Office earlier in the year after suffering a serious illness (possibly pneumonia). This was the second year of the devastating influenza pandemic which killed twenty-seven million people worldwide and left many war-weary families, whose loved ones had survived the carnage of the Front, unexpectedly bereft. Fortunately, George recovered from his illness and was officially demobilised in May, with permission to retain the rank of Captain.

For him, those first few months as a civilian were a challenging time. Like so many returned soldiers, George soon discovered that his years of service to his country did not necessarily count for much in the postwar world. Instead of the 'land fit for heroes', promised by the Government, unemployment was rife. More than a million men were out of work by 1920. George's own employment position in the months after leaving the War Office is unclear. Some of the difficulties he encountered in finding work are revealed in a humorous essay he wrote for *Punch* entitled 'Getting Fixed' – a satirical story about a well-educated man looking for a job after being demobbed.

The Heyers moved to Weybridge that year and it was there that Georgette must have dealt with the page proofs for *The Black Moth*. Her first novel tells the story of Jack Carstares, Earl of Wyncham, who has turned his back on his lands and title after being falsely accused of cheating at cards. Jack sacrifices his own honour to protect his brother Richard who, fearful of losing his heart's desire – the lovely Lady Lavinia – allows his brother to take the blame for his deception. The 'Black Moth' of the book's title is Lavinia's brother, Tracy Belmanoir, the Duke of Andover, also known to his intimates as 'Devil'. Jack and Belmanoir cross paths after they each fall in love with the beautiful Diana Beauleigh. *The Black Moth* came out in September 1921, with Georgette's photograph in a medallion on the back cover. The novel earned her her first reviews in both England

and America, including a short one in *The Times Literary Supplement* which concluded: 'Jack's easy-going smiling quixotry is almost excessive; but he makes a fascinating hero of romance; and it is a well-filled story which keeps the reader pleased.'

Georgette had included in the book most of the props, plot devices and conflicts expected of a 'cloak and sword' romance. There are enough sword-fights, gorgeous costumes, and daring escapades to entertain even the most jaded reader. Jane Aiken Hodge aptly described the book as 'a young girl's wildly romantic tale, and wildly readable', but it is more than that. Setting aside the inevitable melodrama of the costume romance, Georgette's first novel is a surprisingly mature work, which reveals a mastery of prose unusual in a seventeen-year-old and an ability to create characters that are sufficiently interesting and complex to give the book an extraordinary longevity. Ninety years after its initial publication *The Black Moth* is still in print.

5

Surely the writer of that must possess a lively mind?

Georgette Heyer

The Black Moth sold moderately well in its first year of publication and its success encouraged Georgette to begin work on a second, far more ambitious novel. She had always been interested in history, reading widely, learning from her father and even attending a series of history lectures given by Professor Forbes of Westminster College. She had no formal training in historical research, but her father's teaching and her reading had given her a general understanding of how to gain a sense of a period, its key players and events. By late 1921 she was busy researching and writing her new novel. Set during the Restoration, *The Great Roxhythe* was to be a story of courtly love and political intrigue in the reign of Charles II (1660–1685).

To bring it off Georgette needed, among other things, a detailed understanding of the nature and personality of King Charles II and the Prince of Orange, their courts, the intricacies of the Succession, the religious issues of the day and the ramifications of the English Civil Wars (1642–8). Into all of this she would weave the personage of the Most Noble Marquis of Roxhythe, an entirely fictitious character whose ideas, actions and conversation had to blend seamlessly with those of the historical past. The new novel was a more serious and in some ways less successful attempt at combining history with fiction than her first book. It was also a decided departure from the adventure and romance which had characterised *The Black Moth*.

The Great Roxhythe is a fervently patriotic book, typical of the postwar period, in which characters say things like 'nothing mattered so much as England' and 'he had the hatred of the average Englishman of the time for France'. Georgette read and wrote assiduously well into 1922 and by the middle of the year was ready to deliver the manuscript to her new publisher, Hutchinson.

It is not known why Constable published only the first of her novels. Her comments about Clause 17 in her original contract indicate that they had an option on her second and third books. Possibly her second novel was not what they expected from the author of *The Black Moth*. They may have decided to pass on *The Great Roxhythe*. Georgette had recently acquired an agent and it is also possible that he felt that a different publisher would manage her work better and had negotiated a better contract for her with Hutchinson.

Her new agent was Leonard Parker Moore, or 'L.P.' as Georgette would eventually call him. He became her agent in April 1922 – six months after the publication of *The Black Moth*. She was nineteen and he was forty-five and a partner in the literary agency of Christy & Moore. Moore's father was an agent and his brother Henry a novelist and Leonard himself had worked as a journalist before becoming a literary agent. He and his partner Christy (whom Georgette's father knew) ran their business from an office in London's Outer Temple. They were a middle-tier agency with a medium-size list which at different times included George Orwell, Carola Oman, Marco Pallis, Jane Mander and Catherine Cookson. Georgette would remain with Christy & Moore for nearly thirty years.

Her new contract with Hutchinson appears to have been for a two-book deal (the company's records for this period no longer exist) with no apparent proviso for style or genre, given that her second book with them would be a modern novel. Hutchinson had scheduled *The Great Roxhythe* for November publication and, in keeping with her personal work ethic of discipline and professional integrity, Georgette delivered the manuscript on time and in good order. Even at nineteen she was the complete professional who, on signing a contract, would do whatever was necessary to meet her deadline.

The Great Roxhythe came out in Britain on 10 November 1922 and in America in 1923, where Georgette had a new publisher in Small Maynard. The book was well received on both sides of the Atlantic with respectable sales and a number of good reviews. She came to dislike the novel quite early in her career, however, inscribing it 'This immature, ill-fated work' on the flyleaf of her own copy. She eventually sought to have the novel suppressed – though the reasons for this drastic act of self-censorship are not entirely clear. Towards the end of her life, Georgette wrote to an American fan, who had sent a polite letter asking about *Roxhythe*, telling him that 'this very jejune work, written when I was nineteen (and just the kind of book you'd expect from an over-ambitious teenager!) was withdrawn, at my own urgent request, from circulation years ago.' It is possible that one of the reasons for Georgette's growing dislike of the novel arose from a shift in the public awareness of homosexual love which had evolved by the Second World War.

The Great Roxhythe is the only novel in the Heyer canon that does not have a significant male-female relationship at its centre. The Marquis of Roxhythe cares for no one but his King, Charles II, while Roxhythe's young secretary, Christopher Dart, is passionately devoted to his master. One of the turning points of the novel is Christopher's devastating discovery that Roxhythe has deceived him and is, as he has been warned, a spy for the King. Chris's heartbreak is palpable but his passionate laments seem more suited to a young woman betrayed by her lover than from a secretary deceived by his employer:

"There's no peace for me in England, and no work. Always I think of Roxhythe, longing only to see him–to hear his voice–feel his hand in mine—" . . . "And he does not–care as I care. It is not to be expected. Lady Fanny–I am not–complaining, but–I loved him so greatly! I trusted him so! And he tricked me. It's–all over. I've to forget it all. I've to forget Roxhythe, and all that he meant to me. I must go right away, where I shall not be so constantly reminded of him." . . . "Since I have been with–Roxhythe–he has had all my love. He has it still. There will never be another in his place. I'm such a weak fool–but–oh, Lady Frances, I want him so much!" . . .

When *The Great Roxhythe* first appeared in 1922, this sort of conversation and the male focus of the book elicited no particular comment or criticism. In fact, the reviewer for *The Times Literary Supplement* complimented the author on her 'neat dialogue'. By 1951, however, when the book was reprinted for the last time (against the vehement wishes of its author), it is possible that some readers may have interpreted Georgette's youthful rendition of seventeenth-century courtly love quite differently from its author's original intention. When Jane Aiken Hodge asked Georgette's brother Frank whether *The Great Roxhythe* was intended to have a homosexual slant, he denied it, explaining that Georgette 'was totally square and would have disapproved of homosexuals if she had been aware of them when writing *The Great Roxhythe*'.

With *Roxhythe* completed by the middle of 1922, Georgette began casting about for a new project. She had ideas for several novels and by autumn had begun some preliminary work for a book about a protagonist named Smith. This was probably Sir Harry Smith, the Peninsular War soldier who later became Governor of the Cape Colony and about whom she would eventually write a book. But beginning a new historical novel meant waiting an indeterminate amount of time for her next advance and Georgette had discovered the pleasure of a publisher's cheque. She had also learned that a diligent author could reap a quick return writing short stories.

The postwar years were a golden age for short-story writers, as publishers sought to meet the demands of an increasingly literate public with an insatiable appetite for fiction. In Britain in the 1920s dozens of magazine titles were published each week, many of which depended on short stories for a large part of their content. The demand for short fiction made writing a viable occupation for numerous aspiring authors. Some of the best-known writers of the twentieth century began their careers composing short stories for periodicals such as *The Happy Mag*, *The Red Magazine*, *Everywoman's*, *Argosy*, *My Home*, *Good Housekeeping*, *Home Chat*, *Women's Home Pictorial* and, from 1927, one of the most prestigious of them all, *Woman's Journal*. Georgette's earliest stories appeared in the same magazines that published stories by writers such as Edgar Wallace, Richmal Crompton, Edgar Rice Burroughs, Edna Ferber, F. Scott Fitzgerald, Agatha Christie and Leslie Charteris.

Georgette's first foray into short-fiction writing was a light, contemporary romance entitled 'A Proposal to Cicely'. Published in *The Happy Mag* in September 1922 this was her first known attempt at contemporary romance. It is a readable story with some humorous dialogue and several well-drawn minor characters including a Pekinese called Chu-Chu-San and a bull-terrier named Bill: the first appearance in Georgette's writing of the breeds of dogs which she herself had owned or loved. The story is about a young woman fed up with modern life who, having steadfastly refused the regular marriage proposals of debonair, patient Richard Spalding, goes off to the country to show him that she can manage without a man. She befriends a local farmer who completely misreads her open, friendly manner and eventually makes what she considers unwelcome, vulgar advances. Though predictable, the story is interesting for its reflection of Georgette's youthful perceptions of class and etiquette, as well as for its portrait of Richard Spalding, with his calm demeanour and down-to-earth attitude to romance. His was the first appearance in her published fiction of the reliable, athletic hero who had so much in common with the real-life Ronald Rougier. The character type was to reappear in most of her short fiction, as well as in two of her contemporary novels and, though cast as a pragmatic, unromantic hero, he always proves the best choice for the heroine in the end.

Reading her early short stories it seems that Georgette's romantic ideal was not of a man who would sweep her off her feet or with whom she would fall in love at first sight. Her fictional heroes were often men prepared to wait for the heroine to know her own heart and mind. One of the consistent themes in her writing is that a successful relationship takes time and that true love requires mutual understanding and empathy and not mere physical attraction. Even in *The Black Moth*, where the characters and plot owe more to Baroness Orczy and Jeffery Farnol than to Jane Austen, Georgette depicted a variety of love affairs, not all of which fit the stereotype of the swashbuckling romance. In the book, love comes in several different guises and causes almost as much pain as it does happiness for a number of the characters. Although she was only seventeen when she wrote it, Georgette showed how perceptive she could be about the vagaries of love and the ways in which relationships can evolve, hearts can be broken or mended and how love can lead individuals to change.

The success of her first short story inspired Georgette to write a second and 'The Little Lady' appeared in the Christmas edition of *The Red Magazine*. In some ways the story is Georgette's most juvenile and sentimental work with its unhappy lovers and elfin-like heroine who inspires the hero to declare awkwardly that 'I thought you had stepped from the pages of Jane Austen.' Despite its contemporary characters and 1920s dialogue, the story has an unusual, almost period feel to it, with a blend of old and new and a central character who does not always convince.

After the ready acceptance of her short stories by *The Red* and *The Happy* magazines Georgette decided to try her hand at detective fiction. In March 1923 'Linckes' Great Case' appeared in *The Detective Magazine*. It was touted as a thrilling tale of how 'A mysterious leakage of Cabinet documents and the trust of a very charming young person gave Linckes the chance of his life.' This first effort in the detective-thriller genre is not a good example of Georgette's writing. Transparent plotting, stilted dialogue and an obvious ending make it probably the worst story she ever wrote. Only in its romantic moments does it really come to life and she did not repeat the experiment.

Instead, Georgette returned to the contemporary romance genre for her next three short stories. Between them, 'The Bulldog and the Beast', 'Acting on Impulse' and 'Whose Fault Was It?' demonstrate just how quickly she could pen the humorous, light-hearted love-story. But she could also write tragedy and in 1923 a short historical romance simply entitled 'Love' became her sole publication in *Sovereign Magazine*. It remains the only romantic story she ever wrote that tells of the bitterness of love's sacrifice, and ends, not with the happy union of two lovers, but with their separation and lifelong sadness.

These early publications are an interesting reflection of the young Georgette's romantic ideals. They demonstrate a depth of thinking about love that must be considered unusual in such a young writer. Her skill as a storyteller and the ease with which she produced new material are also apparent. Despite changes in period or genre her style remains consistently readable and she is able to bring even the most mundane subject to life. Georgette had the storyteller's gift from the beginning, and even in her least successful books and short stories, where the plotting may lack pace and the dialogue is not always convincing, she never fails to engage her reader's interest and hold it to the last sentence.

Between September 1922 and November 1923 Georgette had at least seven stories published in various London magazines.[2] She had no illusions about the literary quality of the pieces but the money was good and she benefited from the discipline of having to structure each tale within a word limit. In the autumn of 1923 she told her agent that 'If Mr Shand likes my story he must be mad. But, of course, if he really does want it he must pay for it! What are you going to ask for it? I'm getting horribly mercenary!' She was learning her craft in those early years and in many ways the short stories and one or two of the early novels represent her juvenilia. Georgette later decided that all but one of her early short stories (which had been published in translation) were best forgotten and she excluded them from her personal catalogue of her publications.

Georgette enjoyed having a personal income, especially after her father found work and she no longer needed to add her literary earnings to the family coffers. Earlier that year George had returned to his position as Appeals Secretary at King's College Hospital with a salary which had not only eased the financial strain of earlier years

---

2 It seems probable that Georgette published more than this but the actual number may only be discovered by trawling the magazines themselves, many of which do not have indexes and must be searched page by page. The main repositories of likely magazines are the collections at the British Library, St Pancras, and the Newspaper Library at Colindale in England where some titles exist in hard copy and others on microfilm. I have searched over 3,000 individual magazines to discover nine previously unknown Georgette Heyer short stories. I believe that there are others yet to be found.

but also enabled him to buy a house (they had always rented previously). No. 5 Ridgway Place in Wimbledon was an attractive, three-storey Victorian terrace house at the top of the hill, just two doors from the Oakhill Academy where Georgette had first gone to school (the houses in Ridgway Place were re-numbered after 1925 and the original no. 5 which the Heyers owned became no. 67). It was in their new home that over the next two years she continued to follow her literary whims, writing often, and always with an eye to publication.

Georgette was remarkably single-minded about her writing. It was never a question of whether she *could* write, but rather a question of *what* she would write. She was brimming with story ideas and her magazine writing had not stopped her producing novels. As well as working on 'Smith' through 1922 she had also begun an entirely new manuscript, about which she wrote enthusiastically to her agent. The as yet unnamed book was a return to the style and period of her first novel. In January 1923 Georgette sent her agent a copy of *The Black Moth* which she wanted him to read as an introduction to the new manuscript. As she explained to Moore:

> Here is *The Black Moth* – a very juvenile effort. I do hope you'll like it. At the risk of earning a dubious headshake from you, I will tell you that some time ago I began a sequel to it, which one day I shall wish to publish. The sequel is naturally a much better book than *The Moth* itself, and is designed to catch the public's taste. I have also tried to arrange it that anyone who reads it need not first read *The Moth*. It deals with my priceless villain, and ends awfully happily.

She was excited about the new novel's possibilities and proudly told Moore that 'Dad is as enthusiastic over it as he is over Smith – more so, in fact.' The manuscript was not yet finished but she assured him 'it will be one day'.

Georgette was unusually confident for such a young writer. She never seems to have doubted her ability to produce saleable works. The new manuscript was intended to be quite different from the more sombre *Roxhythe*. It had an original heroine and a fast-paced adventure story that would hold the reader's attention. She had a clear plan for the book's eventual publication, which she outlined to Moore: 'I'd like to make a success, then to get *The Moth* out of Constable's hands and to induce another publisher to reprint in a cheaper edition, and lastly to bring out the sequel!' Soon after writing this she put the unnamed and nearly completed eighteenth-century romance aside – although it remained in her mind and was an obvious influence on her next published book.

6

I can't possibly puff off my own work.

Georgette Heyer

In April 1923 Georgette's third novel appeared in the bookshops, although probably only her closest friends and family knew of it. For some unknown reason, she chose to publish the book under a pseudonym and with a publisher other than Hutchinson. The novel was *The Transformation of Philip Jettan* by 'Stella Martin' published by Mills & Boon. In the 1920s the name Mills & Boon was not yet synonymous with a specific genre of romance fiction. They were still a large general publisher with a broad list which included travel guides, cookery books, novels, biographies, plays, sporting guides and histories. *Philip Jettan* was just one of a hundred new Mills & Boon novels that year and 'Stella Martin' appeared alongside popular authors including Jack London, Gaston Leroux and Louise Gerard. Mills & Boon never actually published a novel by 'Georgette Heyer' and may not even have known that 'Stella Martin' was really the up-and-coming author of *The Black Moth* and *The Great Roxhythe*.

Georgette's decision to conceal her identity is puzzling. There are several theories as to why she might have chosen to publish this sole book under another name. *The Transformation of Philip Jettan* is by far her shortest novel. Written in just three weeks, she may have felt that such a hastily constructed book was best published without her name on its cover. She was already writing a contemporary novel for Hutchinson when struck by the inspiration which resulted in *Philip*

Jettan and may not have wished them to know that she was publishing a book with a rival company.

Georgette was trying her hand at different genres in those early years of her career and she may not have wanted to be identified solely with the swashbuckling romance. It is possible that her father suggested she write *Philip Jettan* under a pen-name. George had often written under a *nom de plume*, signing himself 'B.I.N.K.' in the Cambridge magazines *Granta* and *The Pheon*, and anonymously publishing his poems in *Punch, The Pall Mall Gazette* and *The Saturday Westminster Review*. He was also writing detective stories under a pseudonym and may even have been published by Mills & Boon himself.

Her father was a valued reader and adviser and a vital part of Georgette's writing life. He had a high regard for historical fiction, a topic in which he took a particular interest. In 1923 he gave a lecture to the Wimbledon Literary and Scientific Society on 'History in Fiction' in which he declared that 'the best historical novels rank with history, and serve as a valuable stimulus to the young.' George believed that the general reader gained 'much of their knowledge of the 18th century and early Victorian times from the work of the novelists'. In light of this it is not surprising that his daughter wrote historical fiction – although George's own literary ambitions lay elsewhere. He hoped to make his mark in the world of academic publishing with a translation of François Villon's poems. By using a pseudonym for his detective stories he could use his own name for more scholarly writing. As the writer of the more serious *Roxhythe* it is possible that Georgette also wished to conceal her identity as the author of the more frivolous, lightweight *Philip Jettan*. She eventually inscribed her father's copy of *Philip Jettan*: 'I beg your acceptance, Darling, of this elegant trifle' signing it 'Dordette' (her family's pet-name for her).

The Transformation of Philip Jettan was the only one of Georgette's books to be published by Mills & Boon. With the manuscript complete she returned to the contemporary novel to be published by Hutchinson in the autumn. The two books of hers published that year could hardly have been more different: *Philip Jettan* is a light-hearted romantic romp set in the eighteenth century and *Instead of the Thorn* is a sedate story of modern life. *Philip Jettan* is still in print (as *Powder and Patch*) while *Instead of the Thorn* was firmly suppressed by its author some fifteen years after its original publication. Her first attempt at a full-length romance set in her own era, she worked hard on it and made frequent visits to Joanna Cannan's home in nearby Marryat Road to talk about 'the fortunes of Elizabeth Arden' – the novel's naïve and troubled heroine. The title, *Instead of the Thorn*, comes from the Book of Isaiah ('instead of the thorn shall come up the fir tree') and refers to the journey of self-discovery which Elizabeth must undergo in order to develop into her true self. The novel explores some of the sorts of issues and ideas with which Georgette was grappling in those early years of her young adulthood. The long dedication to Joanna Cannan reveals that they talked a great deal about married life, men, sex and relationships. It was an unusual book for a single girl of twenty to write, with its central theme of a troubled marriage and a heroine who must work out the dynamics of the male–female relationship before she can live honestly and well.

Georgette's picture of Elizabeth Arden, who has been raised by her foolish, egocentric father and narrow-minded maiden aunt, also shows her struggling with ideas about a woman's place in the world and the effects of keeping women too much in ignorance – especially about sex. Elizabeth suffers as a result of her aunt's Victorian views and surfeit of sensibility which have been imposed on her since childhood. Her restricted emotional growth and the ingrained belief that she must speak and act according to other people's expectations lead Elizabeth to suppress her own thoughts and personality until she becomes enmeshed in a web of self-deceit. Early in the book she meets and marries Stephen Ramsay, a successful author, whose fame and upper-class credentials make him a 'suitable' husband, even though Elizabeth does not truly love him. Their relationship is tested when she enters the marriage knowing nothing of sex only to find that she is utterly unprepared for it. Horrified and confused by the physical and emotional demands which marriage brings, at first she tries to meet her husband's and her family's expectations but gradually discovers that this requires an even greater deception.

Eventually the marriage fails and Elizabeth must face the world alone for a time while she learns to think and act as herself. She gradually does and is greatly helped by a pragmatic farmer's wife who offers her 'stray scraps of her life's philosophy':

> "There's a deal of give and take in marriage, and girls don't realize it. The man takes and the woman gives. Leastways, I've always found it so . . . It comes more natural to us, you see, and a man's a great weak creature when all's said and done, without much more understanding than a baby. You're to humour a man. Lord, that's what we're here for! It's a poor woman who's got no man to manage . . . You see, dearie, a man's selfish. He can't help it; he don't have to bear what we bear. At the best he's stupid when it comes to understanding how we women feel. We don't really like him any the less for that."
>
> "Are men selfish?" Elizabeth asked. "All of them?"
>
> "More or less, mostly more. Because they don't understand. So the woman's got to be unselfish. Stands to reason she must be, or how would she fit in? A man doesn't fit, ever. He doesn't know how to."
>
> "It seems rather hard – and unfair."
>
> "My dear, don't you get to thinking this is a fair world for women, because it isn't. I'm not saying that if we could start all over again we wouldn't have things different, but seeing as how they are as they are, we've made the best of 'em, and we've learned to fit in as quickly as possible. You've got to put up with a lot, the Lord knows! but it's worth it in the long run."

Georgette's own experience of entering adulthood in a postwar world and her struggle to come to grips with the period's often conflicting views about men and women and their roles, found expression in each of the four contemporary novels she would eventually write. Between them, *Instead of the Thorn* (1923), *Helen* (1928), *Pastel* (1929) and *Barren Corn* (1930) offer a fascinating insight into her view of middle- and upper-class life in 1920s England. They are thoughtful books and well-written but without the pace or tight plotting of her other novels – although on one level *Barren Corn* is a gripping psychological study which has much to say about the worth of the individual and the power of class.

A theme common to all four contemporary novels is that of a young woman emerging from the world she has always known – usually her home and family – into a new world of handsome, debonair men and daring, modern women, all of whom appear to live life to the full. Georgette's heroines are intrigued by the devil-may-care attitude of many of the books' young 'moderns' and are drawn into their world as much by curiosity as a desire to belong to it themselves. Each of her contemporary heroines is a naïve, untried young woman who, on finding herself either married or in a relationship with a man, discovers that she has deceived herself and him about her real feelings and expectations. Georgette carefully constructed her protagonists' journeys of discovery and self-revelation and, in the first and last novels in particular, she shows considerable insight into the slow and often tortuous process involved in learning to know oneself.

Taken together, the value of the four contemporary novels lies mainly in what they reveal about Georgette's perception of her world in the 1920s and her depiction of postwar English life, with all of its contradictions and complexities. Her characters converse in the language of the day and through them she expresses many of the ideas and beliefs that were current at the time. In some ways it is as though Georgette is trying to work out her ideas on paper, to discover what *she* really thinks about women, class, relationships, and even sex. Some of the most interesting conversations between her characters are about the role of women in the 'new' society and whether or not females are as capable or even as intelligent as men. It is surprising to find so many of her characters – both male and female – express less than flattering opinions about women, and tempting to try to discern Georgette's own point of view in these discussions. In the end, her personal views remain tantalisingly elusive, but the novels show that she was thinking a great deal about such things.

Georgette celebrated her twenty-first birthday on 16 August 1923. Three weeks later she went into hospital for surgery (probably to do with her teeth, which were to trouble her throughout her life). From there she wrote to her agent. Georgette had received the proofs for *Instead of the Thorn* and consequently was 'full of energy'. Two weeks later she wrote again to say that the operation had been successful, though her face was still swollen on one side. She had talked to her 'charming surgeon about being photographed' and he had laughingly suggested she have a profile done. Although in later life Georgette grew increasingly resistant to having her photograph taken, in her twenties and thirties she sat for a new photographic portrait every few years.

The session which she had mentioned to her surgeon was an important one, for she had been accorded the honour of being photographed by E.O. Hoppé, then the most famous photographer in the world and a household name. By 1923 he had already photographed King George V and most of the crowned heads of Europe, as well as many of the great literary and theatrical luminaries of the day, including Thomas Hardy, Rebecca West, Rudyard Kipling, John Galsworthy, A.A. Milne, Henry James, George Bernard Shaw, Sir Edward Elgar, Anna Pavlova, Diaghilev and the entire Russian ballet, among others. When Hoppé photographed Georgette, she had published only three books under her own name but she must have been perceived as a rising talent to be photographed by the man Cecil Beaton dubbed 'the Master'.

In the autumn of 1923 Georgette attended Hoppé's studio in South Kensington. He always took time with his subjects and made a point of discussing with them their backgrounds and interests in order that he might capture the subject's true nature in his photographs. Hoppé's portraits of Georgette are unlike any others. Looking at them it is easy to see why, in those early years, Hoppé's photographs of women were, as Ainslie Ellis has said, 'considered too frank'. Georgette is utterly herself in the photos, without a hint of make-up, glamour or artifice. There is no pose: she simply sits, gazing forward or reading a book, a little shy, but completely composed and looking absurdly youthful despite her twenty-one years. There is a powerful impression that Hoppé captured her exactly as she was – in many ways a child still, but with a formidable intelligence and a reserve and an uncertainty that is balanced by the strength of her chin and the quiet poise of her frank, unshuttered face.

The five portraits – two of them in a fashionable hat and fur coat – appear to have disappointed their sitter for, despite the honour of being taken by Hoppé, Georgette seems not to have found the photos flattering and may well have found them far too revealing. Georgette's descendants never saw the photographs and within a year she had taken herself off to a photographer in the Strand for a new portrait. The new shots were much more glamorous pictures of her made-up, with her hair stylishly coiffed and wearing a modish evening gown and Chinese silk shawl. All trace of the child has vanished and the overall effect of these pictures is of a beautiful, striking woman.

Towards the end of the year, however, Georgette was not thinking about photographs or publicity but about Ronald's imminent departure for Africa. He had graduated from the Royal School of Mines in July and was keen to pursue his new career as a mining engineer. There were plenty of opportunities for eager young professionals in Africa during the 1920s and Ronald had secured a position with the Niger Company in northern Nigeria. It would take him away for at least a year. Georgette had grown used to his regular and reliable presence; he was a stimulating companion who engaged with her intellectually and she was not keen to see him go. But jobs for mining engineers were scarce in London, and Nigeria promised adventure to a young man who had once dreamed of a naval career and seeing the world from the deck of a ship. It was a wrench to say goodbye, for he was a good friend and they had 'enjoyed many feuds' in those early years of their relationship. Georgette would feel his absence very much.

On 20 October 1923 Ronald played his last game for the Harlequins and left the side having played forty-seven games in the First XV with an impressive 18 tries or 54 points. (A try used to be worth 3 points. At the beginning of the 1971/72 season it changed to 4 points and then for the 1992/93 season it became 5 points.) Eleven days later Ronald sailed from Liverpool on the S.S. *Adda* bound for the west coast of Africa and the Nigerian capital of Lagos.

7

I imagine the book will sell, because it is a Luv story.

Georgette Heyer

With Ronald gone, Georgette returned to her newest literary venture, a medieval novel with a heroic protagonist named Simon Beauvallet. *Simon the Coldheart* was to be her first attempt at the medieval period and her second attempt at a less swashbuckling historical romance – although the novel had neither the seriousness nor the more considered historical approach which she had applied to *The Great Roxhythe*.

Georgette had been reading Carola Oman's first novel in manuscript and was impressed by her friend's vivid portrait of the young Mary, Queen of Scots. Carola's recent marriage to Gerald Lenanton had not stopped her writing and she had finally achieved her goal of publication when Fisher Unwin accepted *The Road Royal* for their 'First Novel Library'. The novel told of Queen Mary's childhood in France, her dramatic reign and eventual downfall. It marked the beginning of a writing career which would see Carola go on to make her name as an eminent biographer as well as a historical novelist. Joanna Cannan had also continued writing after her marriage. Her first novel had been published by Fisher Unwin the year before Carola's. *The Misty Valley* appeared in January 1923 to good reviews and Joanna was already working on a second book, *Wild Berry Wine*.

The three friends met whenever possible to read each other's work-in-progress and talk about their writing. In her lengthy dedication in *Instead of the Thorn* Georgette acknowledged her debt to Joanna for her advice, for reading the book 'all in cold type', her 'sympathy in moments of depression' and for offering 'criticism that was careful, and shrewd, and very kind'. She and Joanna were close in those early years of their friendship. When Joanna and Cappy's first child was born on 3 April 1924, Joanna asked Georgette to be godmother. The baby was named Josephine and, not surprisingly given her literary heritage, she also became an author. Like her sisters, Diana and Christine Pullein-Thompson, Josephine wrote a series of much-loved pony books for children.

Georgette spent most of 1924 writing her medieval romance. It was set in England and Normandy during the reigns of Henry IV and Henry V with a scene at the Battle of Shrewsbury and a dramatic dénouement. This novel required more research than *The Black Moth* or *Philip Jettan* but less than for *Roxhythe*, for she had a general idea of the period through her reading of books and plays such as Shakespeare's *Henry IV* and *Henry V*. Georgette did not have the detail at her fingertips, however, and it was important not to undermine the story with obvious factual errors. Lacking formal training in history and research, she had begun to develop her own methods of rummaging in the past for material. For *Simon* she read mostly for ephemeral detail, making notes on language and vocabulary, customs, castles, costume, battlecraft, weaponry and etiquette.

Georgette never sought to understand the medieval period as a historian would and she never really came to grips with medieval life which, in its cultural complexities and world view, was so different from her own. Her minimalist approach to religion would prove a major weakness in those of her books set in the medieval period (and in the sixteenth and seventeenth centuries). These were eras in which the power of the Church was all-pervasive and religious belief an integral part of daily life. Yet in those novels Georgette offered only a perfunctory acknowledgement of the role of religion in her characters' lives – usually by way of a religious oath or a walk-on part for a cleric. Years later she acknowledged that 'between us and the Middle Ages there is a gulf that no historian has ever bridged, probably because it is bedeviled by enormous superstition engendered by a lack of scientific knowledge.' She was not altogether wrong, but what Georgette interpreted as medieval superstition was a profound, sustaining belief in God and the Church.

In her own life, Georgette had never been particularly interested in religion, although she knew her Bible well – especially the Old Testament of which her father had the appreciation characteristic of the Classical scholar. He could read the Greek of the Septuagint and the Latin of the Vulgate, while admiring the rich, sonorous language of the King James Version. George revelled in the drama of the scriptures and admired Job as 'an exquisite poet', but there is no sense that her father instilled in Georgette any form of religious belief. When she was a child, the Bible was a source of story and wonderful language rather than a literal text to be obeyed. As an adult, she showed little interest in attending church or in any form of organised religion. This lack of direct religious understanding and experience sometimes spilled over into her books.

Simon the Coldheart consumed Georgette for most of the year. Apart from one short story and Small Maynard's publication of *Instead of the Thorn* in America, she did not publish anything in 1924. The short story was a simple tale of love and luck entitled 'Chinese Shawl' and it appeared in translation in the Danish periodical *Tvidenskronder* in March. Georgette's decision not to publish a book in 1924 may have been partly due to her father's work translating François Villon's poems. He and Georgette discussed his work many times and when Oxford University Press published *The Retrospect of François Villon* in December George acknowledged Georgette's contribution to its success on the flyleaf of her copy:

Over and over again
      You were appealed to, Georgette,
"Comma before the refrain,–"
      Query:–delete it? or stet?

You were appealed to Georgette,
      Ready, it may be to groan
Query:–delete it? or stet?
      Pondering work of your own.

Ready, it may be to groan
      "This", you decided, or "that".
Pondering work of your own.
      Always you answered me pat.

"This", you decided, or "that".
      Whether you'd thought the thing through,
Always you answered me pat,
      Just as I wanted you to.

Whether you'd thought the thing through,
      Often you gave me a hint,
Just as I wanted you to;–
      Here is the outcome in print.

Often you gave me a hint,–
      Phrases of which you are fond,–
Here is the outcome in print,
      All of it carefully conned.

Phrases of which you are fond
      Jostle with some you disdain,–
All of it carefully conned
      Over and over again.

By now the teacher had willingly become the pupil. George not only recognised his daughter's superior literary talent, but was happy to seek her advice on points of expression, punctuation and syntax. Theirs had become a sort of literary partnership in which they read each other's manuscripts, discussed ideas and problems and shared thoughts about dustwrappers and advertising campaigns.

In 1923 Georgette had written an unequivocal reply to a query from her agent about whether her father might be able to assist with the advertising for *Instead of the Thorn*: 'About Daddy as an advertising factor (Good God, what a sentence! Are you convinced yet?) No, no. And again, No, No! For one thing he hasn't a moment to spare; for another, although he can do good advertising work, he hasn't the necessary influence with the papers.'[3] Two weeks later she wrote again to Moore to say that, while her father could not help with advertising, he did have some influence over distribution: 'If Hutchinson is willing to put the book on Smith's stalls, I think Daddy can do the rest. You see, he's closely in touch with the firm, and I think they'll do as he asks.' Her father was a vital factor in the early years of her career and Georgette knew it. Years later she acknowledged that she had inherited her 'literary bent' from George.

She finished *Simon the Coldheart* early in 1925 and it came out in America in May with a dedication to her friend Doreen Arbuthnot. For some reason Georgette had not yet secured an English publisher for this book. Her American publisher, Small Maynard, had previously published *The Great Roxhythe* and *Instead of the Thorn* in the USA. This latest novel received several good reviews in the States, where she was beginning to make a name for herself as a historical novelist. Almost from the first her novels stood apart from the usual offerings among historical fiction. As the reviewer in the *Boston Evening Transcript* wrote of *Simon the Coldheart*:

---

3 Calling her parents 'Daddy' and 'Mummy' was typical for a woman of Georgette's age, class and generation. Unusually for the time Georgette often called her father 'George'.

Historical novels are of two kinds. They show how things were
different in days gone by, or they show how they were the same.
Sir Walter's were of the first variety, Sabatini's of the second. A
few rare people accomplish the improbable, by showing us both.
This is why we claim a certain greatness for Miss Heyer's books,
despite the many conclusions with which it is possible to quibble.

Neither Georgette's youth nor her lack of formal training prevented
her from combining the two things which she had in abundance – a
natural flair for storytelling and a vivid sense of the past.

Ronald Rougier returned from Africa in the spring of 1925 and
lost no time in reacquainting himself with Georgette and her family.
His arrival from Nigeria after an absence of more than eighteen
months marked a new phase of life for Georgette, rich in emotion
and possibilities. She looked forward to renewing their relationship.
She was not someone who could speak about such things easily,
however, and so she did what she would always do when dealing
with intense emotion in her life, and that was to write about it.
Around the time of Ronald's return, Georgette composed one last
contemporary short story – a romance entitled 'The Old Maid'.

It is an unexpected tale, rather different from most romantic short
stories of the era. This one has an older, outspoken heroine whose
assumed veneer of femininity temporarily masks a decidedly
unromantic persona. A variation on Jane Austen's novel, *Persuasion*,
the story tells of the return, after many years overseas, of Maurice
Parmeter, the man whom the heroine, Helen, has always loved. She
is a successful author in her late thirties, renowned for her blunt
manners, direct speaking and sharp sense of humour – qualities which
she elects to hide during a week-long country house party at which
he is also a guest. By the end of the week, Helen is unable to go on
repressing her real personality and it bursts forth, to her great relief
and to Maurice's, who has spent the days wondering what has
happened to the woman he has always loved.

Reading 'The Old Maid' it is impossible not to see the direct
parallels between Georgette's own life and her fictional heroine's. It

is typical of her that she chose to write out something of her feelings at the time of Ronald's return, and also telling that she wrote the story under her old pseudonym of 'Stella Martin'. The certainty that her readers were ignorant of the author in the text liberated Georgette, giving her the freedom to express her emotions and explore her view of herself and her world. In her twenties, these were things about which she cared deeply and about which she would continue to write in the contemporary novels still to come. 'The Old Maid' appeared in *Woman's Pictorial* but, given Georgette's use of her pseudonym and the personal nature of the story, unless she told her family or friends about its publication, it is possible that no one but she ever knew that she had written it.

In May 1925 Ronald proposed to Georgette and was accepted. They did not immediately send an announcement of their engagement to *The Times*. Ronald had not been in England for long and had yet to find employment, while she was content to enjoy a long engagement and to get on with her writing. This was a happy time. Georgette had published five novels and at least nine short stories in less than four years. She was beginning to make a name for herself in publishing circles and had received a number of positive reviews from literary critics. She had enjoyed the social *cachet* of being photographed by Hoppé and was now engaged to a man who regarded her writing as worthwhile and of whom her parents approved. The future was bright, she had several ideas for new books, and time to plan her wedding.

The family was now comfortably settled in Wimbledon and her father's career at King's College Hospital was prospering. George had recently had great success organising a fund-raising dinner at the Savoy which had garnered nearly £20,000 for the new hospital, and he had plans for several future events. Georgette's brothers were also doing well, with Boris due to complete his studies at Lancing College in July while Frank would start there as a boarder in September. Sylvia, meanwhile, had all the excitement of her only daughter's wedding to look forward to. As for Georgette, she was thinking of moving to yet another publisher.

Wanting an English publisher for *Simon the Coldheart* Georgette considered giving the book to a new firm. Her experience with both Constable and Hutchinson had left her feeling dissatisfied and, while she had been happy to give Mills & Boon her hastily written pseudonymous romance, she had no plan to let them publish a 'Georgette Heyer' novel. She always had an eye for the market and was quick to note what she perceived to be poor publishing or advertising decisions. She had not been pleased with Hutchinson's handling of either *The Great Roxhythe* or *Instead of the Thorn* and they had incurred her resentment when they had advertised *Roxhythe* in the end-papers of Ethel M. Dell's latest novel, *Charles Rex*. Georgette loathed this form of advertising and a year later was still infuriated by it: 'I haven't yet forgotten the appalling thing they wrote on Roxhythe,' she told Moore. The 'appalling thing' was one of nearly ninety blurbs included at the end of Dell's book in which the publisher recounted the entire plot of *Roxhythe* and gave away the ending.

That spring Moore wrote to say he had found a publisher for the UK edition of *Simon the Coldheart*. Heinemann had offered a £50 advance with royalties beginning at 12½ per cent on the first 2,000 copies sold and rising through amounts of fifteen, twenty and twenty-five per cent on sales from 7,000 to 15,000 books. They had also taken an option on her next book. This, Georgette decided, would be the sequel to *The Black Moth* about which she had written to her agent more than two years earlier. At the time she had put the manuscript aside but now it seemed a likely novel for her new publisher. It was quite unlike *Simon*, but she thought it would please Heinemann. If the sequel were successful it was possible they would buy the rights to *The Black Moth* and reprint it – exactly as she had planned in 1923.

Although she thought of it as a sequel, in terms of its story, the new novel had no direct relationship to *The Black Moth*. Instead, Georgette took the villain and several minor characters from the first book and recast them in the second with new names and backgrounds. In a humorous acknowledgement to those readers who had read *The Black Moth* and who would undoubtedly recognise 'shades' of that book's characters and plot she called the new novel *These*

Old Shades. The title was also a reference to a poem by Austin Dobson (one of her father's favourites) which she included in the front of the book. It begins

> "What is it, then" some reader asks,–
>> "What is it that attaches
> Your fancy so to fans and masks,–
>> And periwigs and patches?"

And ends:

> Whereas with these old Shades of mine,
>> Their ways and dress delight me;
> And should I trip by word or line,
>> They cannot well indict me.

> But—should I fail to render clear
>> Their title, rank or station—
> I still may sleep secure, nor fear
>> A suit for defamation.

The nearly completed sequel was another eighteenth-century historical romance. It was inspired partly by *The Shepherd's Fairy* and partly by *Charles Rex*, an Ethel M. Dell romance which Georgette had originally read in serial form in *The Red Magazine* in 1922. Like thousands of other young women she was a fan of Dell's hugely popular angst-ridden novels with their breathless heroines and cruel heroes. In *Charles Rex* the heroine spends the first part of the book masquerading as a boy, in which disguise she is rescued by the hero, the cynical Lord Saltash. She becomes his servant and he takes her from Italy to England where she becomes a girl again and falls in love with him. There are at least half-a-dozen points of close similarity between Dell's book and Georgette's before the plots diverge and the two stories become quite different: where *These Old Shades* is a compelling historical novel, brimming with action and enlivened with humour and several enduring characters in Leonie, Rupert and the Duke of Avon, *Charles Rex* is a modern book heavy with description, with several false endings and a language and style that has not survived beyond the 1950s.

While Georgette clearly took inspiration from Dell's heroine-in-disguise, she also knew that, 'at the close of literally dozens of English Renaissance plays the cross-dressed page doffs her doublet and hose and reveals herself to be a woman – usually a well-born and marriageable woman.' Among Georgette's favourite Shakespearean plays were *Twelfth Night*, *As You Like It* and *The Merchant of Venice*. In each, the heroine masquerades as a male for part of the story. And the ruse was no less popular in twentieth-century literature: Dell was not the only contemporary author to use disguise, deception or masquerade to liberate her heroines from the social constraints of the day, or to find in such concealment the ideal opportunity for a grand transformation scene.

Young though she was when she began writing the sequel Georgette was well aware of the popularity of masquerade and how much readers revelled in finding that beneath their disguise the hero or the heroine was in fact well-born, rich, and destined for a life of happiness. As she explained to Moore in 1923, her unfinished sequel 'Deals with my priceless villain and ends awfully happily. Tracy becomes quite a decent person, and marries a girl about half his age! I've packed it full of incident and adventure, and have made my heroine masquerade as a boy for the first few chapters. This, I find, always attracts people!' Her assessment was extraordinarily accurate because *These Old Shades*, which was eventually published in 1926, remains a perennial favourite among Heyer fans and one of her bestselling books. It has never been out of print.

On 15 June 1925 Georgette signed the Heinemann contract for *Simon the Coldheart* and for a second book. The following day Ronald came to call, as he often did, to spend time with her before going to play tennis with her father. The two men returned to the house after the match and joined Georgette inside. George was glad to come indoors and rest, for he had been feeling unwell. There was no warning when his eyes suddenly glazed over, he lost consciousness and collapsed. Georgette rushed to his side but there was nothing she could do. Within seconds her beloved father was dead.

8

Writing oils one's wrist.

Georgette Heyer

Her father's death from heart failure was the great cataclysm of Georgette Heyer's life. She was never the same again. Completely unprepared for the finality of death and unable to express her feelings easily, Georgette struggled to come to terms with her loss. Throughout her life her father had been by her side, advising and encouraging her, her closest ally and the guiding light who would show her the way. Now the light had gone out and she found herself under a pall of unspeakable grief.

Two years later, in *Helen*, she would write of 'a grief so huge, so devastating, and so terribly dumb' that Helen became numbed and mute in the weeks following her father's sudden death. Like Georgette, the fictional Helen's temperament makes it difficult for her to talk about or show her innermost feelings. It is only when her closest friend, Richard, comes to comfort her that she finds some kind of momentary release: 'Suddenly, as though something had snapped within her, she seemed to collapse. "Daddy, Daddy!" she said chokingly. "He's dead! He's dead! I shall never see him again! Never, never, never! I can't, I can't . . ." She clasped her hands to her head; a rending sob broke from her. "He's gone–gone–gone!"'

Helen's histrionic outburst is brief, for she quickly regains her composure and forever afterwards endures her grief in private. Richard is one of the few people in the novel to comprehend her sorrow and even he admits that he 'never saw her break down again. What tears were shed, what agony was endured in the long night-hours he could only guess.' Helen's grief is not lessened by her apparent fortitude, it is rather that it becomes essential for her to hide her feelings from the world. This was the stoic attitude which, in Georgette's mind, was *de rigueur* for a well-bred English girl. A controlled response was the most important thing in the face of suffering and she clung to this principle when confronted with her own devastating loss.

In the real world, it was Ronald who understood her deep reserve and knew best how to respond to her suffering. He did not fuss over her but talked instead of ordinary things, just as he always had. He was a calm, rational and reliable friend who made no 'misplaced attempt to console' and demanded nothing more of her than that she should be comforted. A month earlier Georgette had agreed to marry him at some future date and he had been content to wait until he was better established and she was ready to leave her home and family. Her father's death changed everything. Ronald could see that the best thing for Georgette would be to begin a new life, removed from the home where her father's absence was felt most keenly, and separated from her mother, with whom she did not always get on.

Georgette's feelings about her mother at this time are not easy to discern, but what little evidence there is suggests that it was a complex and changeable bond which was affectionate enough in the early years but which became increasingly ambivalent as Georgette grew older. Her brother Frank described their mother as a 'Victorian puritan who instinctively thought it wrong to enjoy things', whereas Georgette loved to laugh and liked going out to the opera and the cinema or to dances with friends. Sylvia did have a sense of humour, however, and one which could be surprisingly ribald at times. Once she and Georgette had a hilarious conversation about Sylvia becoming an 'entrepreneur' and Georgette a call girl, an unlikely vision which made them both laugh uproariously. Such moments were uncommon, however, for Sylvia's tendency to pessimism led her family to christen her 'Mrs Gummidge' after the mournful character in Dickens' *David Copperfield*.

Sylvia was devastated by her husband's death. Quite apart from the emotional trauma, his death left her with limited finances and a daughter and two sons still dependent on her. She had neither the temperament nor the means to support her family. Although Boris was almost eighteen and now the 'man of the house', he would never be able to provide for his mother, brother and sister. He was not clever like Georgette and he suffered from mood swings which made him 'mercurial and unpredictable, one day a riot of fun, the next morose and silent'.

Frank was only thirteen when his father died. He had been three when George had gone to war and seven when he came home. Two years after his father's return from France Frank had gone to board at The Wick Preparatory School in Hove. He spent five years there and never got to know his father as Georgette and Boris had. Frank's recollection of George was of a stern parent – although Georgette always insisted this was their father playing a joke. Frank was in the next room preparing for the scholarship examination to Lancing when his father died. Whatever their relationship, it was hard for a boy to lose his father and at thirteen there was little Frank could do to help his mother. Sylvia would always make her children feel guilty about her loss. The comfortable life she had known with George ended abruptly when he died and it cannot have helped that for the rest of her life she would be financially dependent on her daughter.

In July Georgette and Ronald's engagement was announced in *The Times*. On Tuesday, 18 August 1925, two days after her twenty-third birthday, they were married at St Mary's Parish Church, Wimbledon. It was a quiet, simple wedding without bridesmaids or pageboys and with only their families and closest friends in attendance. Georgette wore an elegant square-necked dress, fur-trimmed cloak and a low-brimmed cloche hat with a swooping osprey feather. She carried an enormous bouquet of three dozen roses. Ronald was handsome in his morning suit with a silk tie, spats and a white carnation in his buttonhole. Georgette missed her father keenly on her wedding day and photographs show her looking sombre, despite the occasion.

After the ceremony, she and Ronald, with her mother and his

father, moved to the vestry where they each signed the register. Their marriage certificate records Ronald's occupation as 'mining engineer' but there is only a line through the box headed 'rank or profession' against Georgette's name. The omission may have been a reflection of her uncertainty about her future as a writer. A sense of ambivalence about her writing after her father's death would not have been surprising. Georgette's usual way of dealing with strong feelings was to write them down, to give them character and voice and let her fictional creations carry some of her emotion for her. But now she struggled to write for the burden of grief stifled light-hearted prose.

However, only grave illness or death would prevent Georgette from fulfilling her contractual obligations. Committed to Heinemann for a second book, she returned to *These Old Shades*, the unfinished manuscript she had put away three years earlier. It was difficult. Later, in *Helen*, she would describe her heroine's struggles to return to an unfinished novel after her father's sudden death: 'She unearthed the manuscript from the bottom of her trunk, and sat down to read it. It was very hard to do this; Marchant's pencilled corrections occurred again and again: more acutely than ever did she feel the need of him; she had to force herself to continue.' At first, Helen finds it difficult to write but she perseveres even in the face of 'spells of hopeless depression' and a sense of purposelessness in writing a book her father will never read. She gradually finds her ability is not lost, however, and that there is still joy to be found in writing: 'It was a different pleasure she had in it now, lacking the exuberance she had felt before, but she was relieved to find that there was still pleasure in the work.' Like Helen, Georgette rediscovered her enjoyment of writing and even the cruellest tragedy could not deprive her of her ability to write comedy.

Published the year after her father's death it has always been assumed that Georgette began *These Old Shades* in 1925 and that, as Jane Aiken Hodge put it, she was 'writing with an easy pen that first year of her marriage'. In the absence of evidence to the contrary it was a reasonable assumption – especially since the book is a riveting historical romance full of light-hearted prose. Reading *These Old*

Shades it is difficult to imagine its author beset by grief and struggling to write, but Georgette's pen was anything but easy in the difficult months after her father's death. 'I haven't started another book,' she confessed to her agent in November, 'but I'm trying to. I think it will be modern. I don't think I have the heart to write a period novel. But that's "slop", and I don't think you ought to be worried with it.'

The period novel would always be a form of escape for her; a pleasurable experience in which aspects of a world free from care could be remembered and relived and in which she could give full rein to her romantic imagination. Whatever the characters might endure within the pages of the novel, the happy ending was assured, whereas in real life tragedy and loss could not be eradicated with a pen-stroke. Georgette made only one public reference to her father's death and it was, appropriately, in a book. In October 1925 Heinemann published *Simon the Coldheart*. In the original American edition the book's dedication had been to Georgette's friend Doreen Arbuthnot. When the first British edition of *Simon* appeared, it had a new dedication. It read: 'To the memory of my father – this, his favourite.'

Georgette was not only wrestling with the return to her writing that autumn and winter, but also with other, more prosaic, challenges. Back in London after their honeymoon, she and Ronald moved into a flat in South Kensington at 27 Hogarth Road. After the wilds of Nigeria and months in a tent, Ronald coped easily with the more cramped quarters, but Georgette had only ever lived in a flat for the few months spent in Paris as a child, and it took her a little time to adjust. She also had to deal with domesticity for the first time on her own, planning the meals, doing the shopping and some of the cooking, managing the household accounts, and dealing with the daily 'help'.

Some of it was fun and she enjoyed the new independence which marriage brought; Ronald was a comfortable partner but their relationship was not without its occasional frictions and there were adjustments to be made. They were both strong-minded and forthright in their opinions and it was not always easy to learn forbearance and to be patient with each other's habits and idiosyncrasies. Money was another persistent pressure, especially as Ronald (who apparently had some form of income though its source is not known) was helping to support Sylvia and Boris. The Wimbledon house had been sold and Georgette's mother had moved into rooms at 130 Queen's Gate, just north of the Cromwell Road and less than a mile from her daughter's flat.

Sylvia found it difficult to settle into her new life. She moved to five different addresses in South Kensington over the next five years. She would spend the rest of her life living in hotels and rented rooms. Life for a genteel, middle-class widow with limited means and two sons to think of was not easy in 1920s Britain. A scholarship had ensured Frank went to Lancing in September but Boris was often unwell and would never be strong. His erratic moods also meant that (as one relative described him to me) he was 'like so many of Chekhov's characters, pretty useless at making a living'. Boris had taken a job at Bovril on leaving school but had not liked it and eventually persuaded his mother to let him give it up. Throughout his life, he would need some support and it was Georgette who took on this responsibility and assisted her brother whenever the need arose.

By January 1926, she was worrying about money to the point where she told Moore that the sale of an option on *Simon the Coldheart* to the Fox-Film Co. 'has become acute with me now! A lump sum would relieve the tension considerably, for two establishments are so expensive for poor Ronald!' The film deal did not materialise. She and Sylvia could have reduced living expenses by sharing accommodation, but Georgette's financial worries would never convince her to move in with her mother.

Towards the end of 1925 Georgette had begun to think about her writing again. On 1 December she joined the London Library, a private subscription library established in 1841 by the writer and historian, Thomas Carlyle. Located in the heart of fashionable London at 14 St James's Square, the London Library's modest façade still conceals an elegant Victorian interior with polished wooden desks and comfortable red leather wing-chairs set before the (now defunct) fireplace in the reading room. Portraits of past presidents line the walls and members thumb through the enormous guard book catalogues before entering the stacks. It was the sort of setting that exactly suited Georgette. She borrowed from the Library until December 1926, when she let her membership lapse because she and Ronald were planning to leave England for several years.

Ronald had not found it easy to find suitable employment in London and his experiences in Nigeria had made him keen to obtain work overseas again. A few weeks before Christmas Georgette wrote cheerfully to Moore about the possibility of Ronald getting a job in Mexico. She described the opportunity as 'rather fun, don't you think?' and told her agent that she would 'be able to write blood and thunder short stories!' Two months later she wrote again to say that, instead of going to Mexico, she was to be a 'grass widow'. Ronald had been offered a position with an American mining company and would be sailing for the Caucasus in a week. Georgette would remain alone in London until she could join him in Russia. It was a daunting proposition, but she faced it with her usual stoicism and wrote a long, positive letter to her agent telling him all about the opportunity.

Ronald's new job was with the British arm of the Georgian Manganese Company. The American firm had a twenty-year mining concession from the Soviet government to take manganese from the ore-rich canyons in Tchiatouri (Chiatura) in central Georgia. It was an excellent opportunity for a young engineer, though Ronald did not relish the prospect of a lengthy separation so soon after marriage. Georgette hoped to go to Tchiatouri in the autumn and wrote Moore a long letter describing the challenge of filling out innumerable forms in Russian and the censorship rules laid down by the Bolshevik government:

> My manuscripts would all be confiscated if I didn't first get them sealed here by the Soviet censor! Fancy having to get permission to take your own works out. God knows how I shall send them

<u>out</u> of the country. We hope that our firm will manage it for me. And it seems likely that you will have to address envelopes to me in Russian! . . . And as letters will probably be censored I shan't be able to tell anyone that the Bolsheviks are a filthy crowd, and no one will be able to ask me about the state of Russia, so I expect I shall have to stick to history. They won't mind that, but they might be very suspicious of a modern book. But what an experi-ence! I am greatly looking forward to it, as you may imagine.

Ronald sailed for Russia on 22 January 1926. The last stage of his trip began in Tiflis (Tbilisi) at midnight, and he endured eleven hours by rail and road to reach Tchiatouri. Despite the beautiful scenery, the final destination was beyond anything he could have imagined. Situated along the Kvirila River, more than six hundred metres up on the steep sides of the canyon, Tchiatouri was best known for its mud – described by one employee as 'unspeakably slimy and slippery'. Ronald soon learned that Tchiatouri was suffocatingly hot in the summer and freezing in the winter. By the time he had been there a month, the weather was changing daily from rain to snow to drizzle, and he, like others, had concluded that the place was 'impossible'.

Living conditions in Tchiatouri for the English personnel were adequate but limited and Ronald shared the only large house in the mining town with twenty British and American workers. New housing was promised for employees and their families but building had begun only recently and Georgette could not hope to join Ronald until there was suitable accommodation. She found it 'horrible to be separated' but was gradually returning to her writing. She had not started a new novel but her compulsion to write found an outlet in regular letters and in what she called 'young books...all about nothing' which she penned and sent to Ronald for his entertainment.

He returned from the Caucasus in June with no plans to go back. Even in its best months, Tchiatouri was a difficult environment and Ronald's time at the site had convinced him that it was no place for his wife. He had not given up on an overseas career, however. Soon after his return to England he decided to go back to Africa and seek his fortune as an independent prospector. He had heard that there were good mining prospects in the tin fields of Tanganyika (Tanzania). His earlier experiences in Africa encouraged him to think that he and Georgette might live quite happily there while he attempted to find a rich mineral strike and make their fortune. Ronald sailed for Tanganyika in the autumn of 1926 with plans for Georgette to join him there early in the new year.

She was fully occupied in those last few months of 1926 before her departure for Africa. As well as her writing, there were her mother and Boris and Frank to think of, the flat to be vacated, banking arrangements finalised and the packing completed. She had finished writing *These Old Shades* while Ronald was in Tchiatouri and it was published on 21 October. It had not been an easy year for publishers, with the General Strike in May and the continuing coal strike which had affected paper supplies and production until October, when the stoppage was finally ended. Carola Oman's new novel, *King Heart*, had come out the week before the General Strike began and her book had suffered badly from a lack of reviews and advertising. Georgette fared better with *These Old Shades*, which was published six months later, long after the General Strike was over (only the miners remained on strike), when the disruption was much less. The novel had an initial print run of 3,000 copies with an extra 1,500 copies for export to Australia, New Zealand and Canada.

The first indication that she had written something out of the ordinary came from Australia where the novel sold well from the first. An Australian librarian wrote to her to congratulate her on the book and to tell her she was 'a bonzer woman' and that 'all the girls who read the *filthiest* books like yours'. An unusual accolade, but with *These Old Shades* Georgette had brought something new to historical romance. She had created a female protagonist who was not simply a passive victim of adversity but an active, energetic force, determining her own destiny. Where other bestselling novels (including Dell's *Charles Rex*) frequently featured heroines as panting, tortured females doomed to suffer, Georgette's heroine, Léonie, is never cowed or broken down by the events that beset her. Throughout the novel she remains feisty, courageous and endearing, with an *espièglerie* and a sense of humour that enables her to behave in a manner quite unlike that of the traditional heroine, who was so often ready to faint in a moment of crisis.

In America the novel was Georgette's last publication with Small Maynard, but in Britain it was reprinted in November 1926 and again in January, May, August and November 1927. *These Old Shades* was Georgette's first decided success but, as her son explained years later: 'No one knew anything about her when she first made her name because she was abroad with my father.'

9

If he wishes to <u>praise</u> the book, what author yet failed to
lap up encomiums gratefully? Not this imperfect soul!

Georgette Heyer

On 18 December 1926 Georgette said goodbye to her mother and
brothers and sailed for Africa with her pet Sealyham terrier, Roddy.
It must have been something of a relief to get away after the emotional
upheavals of the past eighteen months. The weather was fine as the
ship took her east across the Mediterranean to the Suez Canal and
south to the Port of Sudan. She arrived in the Red Sea in time for
the new year and took photographs of the bustling ports and the
Arab dhows, which plied their trade between Africa and the Arabian
Peninsula. Everything was new and different. Shipboard life was
pleasant and uncomplicated, with no one to make demands on her.
Here she was not Georgette Heyer, up-and-coming author, but Mrs
Ronald Rougier travelling out to meet her husband in East Africa.
There was respite in this and freedom from the cares and responsi-
bilities which had been her lot since her father's death. She celebrated
Christmas and New Year's Eve on the ship and wrote enthusiastic
letters home to her family and to Carola Oman, describing the voyage
and the many fascinating sights.

When the ship arrived in Mombasa early in January Ronald was
on shore to greet her. It was a glad reunion and they spent some
time in the town to give Georgette a chance to acclimatise.
Everything around her was lush and green, with palm trees and dirt

roads and hills and mountains in the distance, all quite unlike the views at home. After a short break she and Ronald took the train to Nairobi where they stocked up on last-minute items – none of which would be available at their final destination. From Nairobi the train took them north and west to Jinja, a Ugandan port town on the northern shore of Lake Victoria. The train journey took several days but there was plenty to see and Ronald had time to tell her about the district of Karagwe, and about Kyerwa where they would live.

From Jinja they caught the lake steamer, *Nyanza*, to the small Tanganyikan town of Bukoba on the western shore. This was their last stop before the final plunge towards Kyerwa and the compound that would be Georgette's new home. They travelled there by lorry, mostly following the rhinoceros paths through the grasslands or the occasional bumpy dirt track through the bush. It was eighty miles from Bukoba to Kyerwa as the crow flies, but closer to one-hundred-and-fifty miles by lorry and Georgette experienced firsthand the exigencies of travel and the realities of a rough road. She may not have been travelling in a stagecoach-and-four but the small, narrow-wheeled truck buffeted and bruised its occupants as surely as any nineteenth-century stagecoach.

It is unlikely that anything could have prepared Georgette for her new home, as a greater contrast between it and her homes in Wimbledon and South Kensington could hardly have been imagined. Kyerwa was not only incredibly remote, it was also utterly different from anything she had ever known. Her house was a hut made of elephant grass. The local people used its bamboo-like stems to make the walls, tying them together with rope made from bark fibres. The roof was made from thick layers of dried elephant-grass leaves laid across narrow wooden rafters to overhang the sides of the hut as a kind of verandah. For a hut it was surprisingly roomy, with two doorways beneath the verandah roof leading into an area for sleeping and another for eating, where Georgette could also work during the day. With characteristic good humour she christened her new home 'the Manor House' and soon grew used to its earthen floor and rudimentary facilities. Theirs was one of a handful of huts in a small compound surrounded by a tall, elephant-grass fence – their only protection against the lions, leopards and rhinos which roamed the plains outside.

The view from Georgette's front door was of bare earth and straggly grasslands with an occasional tree in the middle distance and hills on the far horizon. The compound was staffed by local men, mostly from the Haya tribe, none of whom had ever seen a white woman before. Apart from Georgette and Ronald, there was only one other European living in the compound – a 'rough, Cornish miner' also prospecting for tin. As the only white woman for one-hundred-and-fifty miles and with Ronald away a good deal of the time, Georgette often found herself living a solitary life. She does not appear to have minded and, despite the isolation, the rough living and sparse conditions, seems to have been determined to adapt and give Ronald her full support.

There was a kind of freedom in living so far from civilisation and a certain pleasure in making do with no one to judge her or question her behaviour. Photographs taken of Georgette in Tanganyika show her wholly at ease, without make-up or accoutrements of any kind. This was the simple life at its most authentic, where the building of a new pantry out of logs and elephant grass was an event worth recording and the incursion of a rhinoceros into the compound at dawn exciting enough to make her leap out of bed and throw 'a coat over my pyjamas' before rushing out to see the intruder. In her little bit of Africa Georgette wore comfortable clothes, went for long walks, put up with all sorts of inconveniences, wrote her books, cheerfully accompanied Ronald on a twelve-day safari, and relaxed in a way that she probably never did again.

Georgette had a capacity to be completely self-contained and was content to be left alone. Her imagination was a constant source of creativity and entertainment and there was always her writing. She wrote regular letters home and got on with *Helen*, the modern novel she had mentioned to Moore in 1925. It was not one of her best books but *Helen* became an important outlet for her grief by allowing

Georgette to write her own private memorial to her father.[4] Ironically, when the novel came out in 1928 some of the reviewers criticised Georgette for having the father die so suddenly in the novel, with one calling it a 'cheap and easy device'. Understandably ignorant of Georgette's own tragedy, they missed much of what the novel was really about. Her brother Frank always said that *Helen* was Georgette's most autobiographical novel, and it seems also to have been her most cathartic.

Happily settled in Africa, Georgette began making plans for her first historical romance since her father's death. It was to be another high-spirited adventure story in which disguise played an integral part in the plot. She wrote *The Masqueraders* on her lap in the hut in Kyerwa, drawing on her prodigious memory for details of costume and eighteenth-century ephemera when her small library failed to give her what she needed. It must have given her pleasure and some amusement to describe the powdered wigs, splendid jewels, silk patches, dancing, duelling and elegant evenings spent among the *ton* while sitting in a grass hut in a remote corner of Tanganyika. Georgette clothed her heroine in perfectly cut velvet suits with gold trim and Mechlin lace and her brother, Robin, in gowns of pale blue taffety and rose pink satin, while she herself was dressed in plain khaki shorts and shirts. *The Masqueraders* is the only one of her novels in which it is raining in the opening scene and she probably enjoyed recalling the cold dampness of a rainy evening in England while writing in the equatorial heat of Africa.

Georgette spent more than a year in Africa before she and Ronald decided to try their luck elsewhere. Although he had enjoyed some success in his prospecting venture, Ronald had not found the really big strike needed for a substantial profit and early in 1928 they prepared to go home. Georgette had enjoyed many aspects of life in Kyerwa but she missed England and would not be sorry to return.

---

4 The only other memorial to her father is a plaque commissioned by the Board of King's College Hospital for the hospital chapel. It reads: 'In memory of George Heyer MA MBE (Mil). Appeal Secretary. Who entered into rest 16th June 1925. At the age of 56 years.'

They left Mombasa early in April and sailed to Zanzibar where they spent a day exploring the old city before sailing on to Port Elizabeth and Cape Town. From there they sailed on the S.S. *Usaramo* up the west coast of Africa, arriving back in London one week after the April publication of *Helen* – Georgette's first novel with Longmans. She now had two publishers: Heinemann, who would continue publishing her historical fiction, and Longmans, who had (for reasons unknown) taken over publishing her contemporary fiction from Hutchinson.

She was not destined to remain in England for long. Ronald had secured a position with the Kratovo Venture Selection Trust Ltd and by the time *The Masqueraders* came out on 30 August, he had gone to Macedonia and the lead mines near the Bulgarian border. Georgette sent an advance copy of *The Masqueraders* to him in Kratovo in September and days later received a telegram which read: 'Congratitations. Find Mahineroders excellent' [sic]. She was due to join him in Macedonia in December but before she left England Georgette finished writing *Pastel*.

This third contemporary novel continued the theme of a young woman who must learn to know herself and the differences between one's romantic dreams and life's realities. It was a tale of two sisters living in a thinly disguised version of Wimbledon in the 1920s: Frances, the heroine and the elder of the two, is 'pastel' – fair, sincere and a little dull, while the younger sister, Evelyn, is dark, vibrant and always the favourite. It is Evelyn who, unaware of her sister's feelings, marries the man with whom Frances has fallen in love. Later, Frances gives up her ideal of an ardent, romantic love and marries steady, stolid, athletic Norman (Frank Heyer later identified him as Ronald): 'He was not Romance, but he was her husband, and she did care for him. If she was not passionate that was the fault of her temperament. She thought of the man who might have meant Romance, and awaked passion obtruded for an instant. She banished it swiftly.'

Pastel appears to have been more of an outlet for Georgette's personal preoccupations than a riveting, plot-driven story. It is a plain, thoughtful book which is interesting mainly for its auto-biographical elements and account of middle-class life in 1920s England. One striking feature are the conversations in which the book's characters discuss relationships, marriage, the New Age and the place of women in it. Georgette has her characters say things like 'you all fall into the error of comparing the cleverest women with the dullest men' or 'if you take your greatest woman doctor and your greatest man doctor you'll admit the man wins in a walk', before giving the last word in the conversation to the book's aristocratic matriarch, who concludes: "'So silly to vie with men when our minds are so different. Positively a confession of inferiority. Why not stick to our own kind of mind instead of pandering to man's conceit by trying to acquire his? Ridiculous! Who wants to be like a man? So detached and tabulated! One thing at a time, which is very dull and sensible and successful.'"

Georgette was clearly interested in the contrasts between the sexes and *Pastel* appears to reflect many of her own marital experiences. The novel was also influenced by her reading of Rudyard Kipling's short story 'The Enemies to Each Other' – a re-telling of Adam and Eve's expulsion from the Garden of Eden. She and Ronald were great admirers of Kipling and his final scene where Adam and Eve laughingly recognise their mingled love and animosity for each other is echoed at the end of *Pastel* when Frances concludes that 'Life was bound up with Norman, whom she loved and whom she hated; who was so dear yet so exasperating; with whom she quarrelled and to whom she clung.'

Georgette dedicated *Pastel* to her mother and sent Sylvia a copy of the book from Macedonia with a tantalising inscription: 'Here is a book for Mummy, which is sent with love and the hope that She will like it. Some of it she may disagree with; some of it is designed to make her laugh; but whether she laughs or whether she frowns, this book should, on the whole, please her since it contains so much that is Really and Truly her.' (Georgette often capitalized words and phrases to express irony, for emphasis or to make a humorous point.)

If Sylvia is the mother in the book then Georgette depicted her as a kind, sensible woman who loves her husband, is affectionate and caring with her children, but who has a prosaic, pragmatic approach to love and relationships. The fictional mother, Mrs Stornaway, tells lovestruck Frances that she hasn't 'much faith in the lasting qualities of a grand passion' and that it is often 'the dull things [that] turn out to be the most satisfactory'. Neither statement makes her daughter feel any better about her own turbulent emotions. Towards the end of the book, Mrs Stornaway says of Frances that 'I used to think she was very like me, but she isn't. I don't always understand her.' Perhaps Sylvia, too, had finally realised that her daughter's hopes and dreams were not the same as her own.

Georgette had followed in her father's footsteps and not her mother's. This might not have been an issue if Sylvia had approved wholeheartedly of her daughter's writing, but it was to be some years before her mother expressed pride in Georgette's literary achievements. There must have been a degree of disappointment in the realisation for the gifted mother that she had produced a gifted daughter, but with a taste for literature rather than music. But there were stronger feelings too because, according to Frank Heyer, Sylvia's disapproval of her daughter's writing sprang from feelings of resentment and even envy that Georgette had succeeded in using her talent while her mother had not.

Soon after finishing *Pastel* Georgette left London for Macedonia. Before her departure she was 'interviewed' by the New Zealand writer Jane Mander who had come to know Georgette, Carola and Joanna through her job at Christy & Moore. During the 1920s she had developed a relationship with the three young women, which in 1933 prompted her to describe them as 'my own authors, since I read and advised on their early manuscripts before they were as well known as they are now'. Jane Mander was herself a published author who supplemented her small income by reading manuscripts for Christy & Moore and writing articles for the New Zealand *Sun* newspaper which touted her as one of their regular 'London Correspondents'. It was in her *Sun* article, 'Two Clever Women Writers: The Work of Georgette Heyer and Carola Oman', that she recorded Georgette's description of herself as 'a sheltered daughter' and someone who disliked 'Bohemians and studio parties'. Jane Mander also offered a rare glimpse into Georgette's childhood, describing her as 'an infant prodigy' who 'started to write as a child' and that it was her 'love of history [that] turned her writing ability to by-gone days'.

Although Jane Mander and Georgette certainly talked together it is not clear whether the New Zealander ever actually interviewed Georgette in a formal sense or whether she simply remembered things from their conversations and wove them into an article for the *Sun* after Georgette had left for Macedonia. A few years later, in January 1933, Jane Mander wrote a piece for the New Zealand *Mirror* entitled 'Women Writers I Have Known' in which she discussed each of Georgette's, Joanna's and Carola's personalities, lifestyles and literary achievements. Here she was pleased to inform her readers that, Georgette's 'sales mount steadily, and in Australia have reached the surprising figure of over ten thousand. But all this success had not spoiled Georgette Heyer. She is easily one of the most charming writers I know.'

There is no record of what Georgette thought of Jane Mander (although she disagreed with her criticism of Carola's 1931 novel *Fair Stood the Wind*). It is possible that Jane Pilbury, the governess in *Helen*, whom Georgette described as 'very shy and brusque' and 'something like Queen Elizabeth [I] as regards face and hair', may have been based on Jane Mander, with her red hair, patrician looks, shyness and honest, brusque manner. By the time Jane Mander's first article appeared in New Zealand, Georgette was well-established in her new home in Macedonia; the piece never appeared in the British press and it is doubtful if she ever knew of its existence.

Georgette travelled out to Macedonia by train, reaching Kratovo in a few days. Her new home was an old Turkish house in a small village with a water supply originally constructed by the Romans. Kratovo had long been a source of precious metals and when Georgette visited the mines she could still see the centuries-old names of slaves carved into the rock. As in Africa, she adjusted to her new

life without complaint and got on with writing her next historical
novel for Heinemann.

Beauvallet was to be a swashbuckling adventure story set in the time
of Elizabeth I with a hero (Sir Nicholas Beauvallet) whose courage,
daring and skill with a sword was undoubtedly inspired by characters
such as Baroness Orczy's Scarlet Pimpernel and Rafael Sabatini's
Captain Blood. Georgette also drew on her own earlier work by making
Beauvallet a direct descendant of the hero in *Simon the Coldheart*.
Ronald took a keen interest in her writing and she enlisted his help
as a researcher. After their marriage he was always her first reader and
critic. She valued his opinions and admired his knowledge of history
and his ability to hunt up elusive facts or bits of 'period colour' which
she could use. She eventually inscribed his copy of *Beauvallet*: '"To
Wonaldy-pet, Our joint effort"' signing herself 'George' – a name
reserved for use by only her closest friends and relatives.

Georgette wrote her first article in Macedonia. Entitled 'The
Horned Beast of Africa' it appeared in *The Sphere* in June 1929 – the
only time she wrote about her experiences in Tanganyika. The article
was mainly about the rhinoceroses she and Ronald had encountered
in Kyerwa and how Ronald had narrowly escaped death while
shooting an old bull rhino. Georgette rarely wrote about her overseas
experiences. She found little fodder for her fiction in the years spent
in Africa and Eastern Europe. She did weave the ghostly footsteps
she and Ronald sometimes heard in their house in Kratovo into her
first detective-thriller and a later mystery would feature a character
who spoke Serbian. But personal adventures – such as the time she
nearly died in the local dentist's chair in Kratovo after the anaesthetist
failed to notice a blockage in the gas-line and her face turned blue,
or the night the owner of the Kratovo cinema invited the whole
town to watch him burn the theatre down in order to collect the
insurance money – she did not consider good story material.

When not writing Georgette spent her days reading, taking walks,
horseback riding with Ronald or visiting the capital Skopje. There
was a small community of 'Britishers' there who would invite one
another to dinners and cocktail parties and often get together for

drinks at the only bar in town. David Footman, the British Consul in Skopje, became a friend. He later wrote a book of short stories about his time in the Balkans. Heinemann published *Halfway East* in 1935 and in a letter to her childhood friend, John Hayward, Georgette described the stories as 'very good'. Reading them it is tempting to think that Footman's depiction of one of the English wives was based on his memory of Georgette:

> Lorna Coote was thirty-three. She was tallish and slender, with blue eyes and dark brown hair. When you saw her in evening dress you thought she was rather pretty. Some people thought she was rather highbrow, and complained that she didn't have much to say for herself. That was because she generally refused a second cocktail and never seemed much at home among the noisy and drunken parties we sometimes used to have. She did not like crowds. She was always charming to everybody, and if she was ever nervy or depressed or bad-tempered she did not show it. She was fond of music and read a good deal. She used to have a lot of books sent out from England.

Georgette had re-joined the London Library after her return from Africa in 1927 and she also had books sent out to her from England.

She finished *Beauvallet* in Macedonia and posted the manuscript to Heinemann, who paid her £200 against royalties and published it in September 1929. The fourfold increase in the advance (she had received a £50 advance for *Simon the Coldheart* and for *The Masqueraders*) was indicative of her steadily increasing sales. Georgette sent one of her advance copies to her mother in England with a word of warning on the flyleaf: 'Darling Mummy with love from Dordette. A book she must be prepared to dislike!' Her inscriptions to Sylvia were often frank and humorous and they shed a little light on Georgette's sense of her mother and her need for her approval. In the first decade of her writing life she cared a good deal about Sylvia's opinion of her books. It was only later that she became intolerant of her mother's preference for certain kinds of her novels and often dismissive of her views.

Georgette was still in Macedonia when she began a new contemporary romance for Longmans entitled *Barren Corn*. It centred on a mismatched love affair between Laura Burton, an intelligent, lower-middle-class woman from Brixton, and Hugh Salinger, a handsome, selfish member of the upper class, who meet on the French Riviera one summer after the War. In it Georgette gave voice to some of her thoughts about sex, religious beliefs and life after death. Her most ambitious and compelling contemporary romance, it was also the only one of her novels to deal directly with the issue of class in English society. From the outset Laura sees the class difference between herself and Hugh as insurmountable, whereas Hugh decides that he can change her so that even his mother will 'forget the accident of her birth'.

An unusual book, *Barren Corn* remains a surprisingly empathetic novel which caught the attention of several reviewers in both Britain and America. In it Georgette examines the psychology of an enduring, dedicated love – a love so strong as to be utterly self-sacrificing – albeit for the wrong reasons. And, whether she meant to or not, in telling Laura's story Georgette demonstrated a deep understanding of aspects of the human psyche and the kinds of mental traps into which individuals can fall when driven by love or sexual desire. She sees the great class divide and explores its bitter consequences for Hugh and Laura after their marriage. *Barren Corn* is as much about snobbery as it is about the worth of the individual, and the book benefited from the kind of physical and emotional detachment from England which came from living as an expatriate overseas.

This was to be Georgette's final contemporary novel. Years after its publication, and despite several reprints, she informed Longmans (they had bought the rights from Hutchinson and re-published *Instead of the Thorn* in 1929) that she wanted each of her four contemporary novels permanently suppressed. Georgette could be a harsh critic of her own work and in later years was unstinting in her condemnation of these early novels, asking Louisa Callender of Heinemann to 'forget all about INSTEAD OF THE THORN,

PASTEL, HELEN, BARREN CORN. They aren't thrillers, and they stink, and I want them to be buried in decent oblivion.' She had her wish. The contracts with Longmans were cancelled and the books remain out of print to this day.[5]

---

5 In the 1970s due to a loophole in the copyright laws, a small American publishing firm reprinted the novels without permission but ceased production after copyright was reasserted.

PART III

A NEW LIFE: THE SUSSEX YEARS

1930–1942

10

I have always considered that one of the more important
points between Author & Agent is that each party should
understand the other tolerably clearly.

Georgette Heyer

Georgette and Ronald returned to England early in 1930 and in April
Longmans published *Barren Corn*. Having described her heroine as
like 'a Luini Madonna', Georgette was appalled by the book's dust-
jacket and wrote at once to Moore to protest:

> I never in my life saw a more – well, <u>blood</u>-stained wrapper! It
> nearly made me sick it up on the mat, so to speak . . . What
> malign spirit of inartistry prompted the – so-called – artist to plonk
> that ghastly, that <u>dire</u> woman on the cover? If he'd contented
> himself with the mimosa on a black ground it mightn't have been
> so bad. As it is – he ought to be put in a pot and boiled.

Her feelings of antipathy towards Longmans were not enhanced by
Willie Longman wandering into their flat one evening to tell her 'in
his usual rather vapid manner' that there were problems with
payments from Australia. After just three books with Longmans
Georgette was growing dissatisfied with his handling of her work and
'the methods of his blighted firm'. But she remained with the company
for another five years.

Georgette had no new novel for Heinemann in 1930. Instead they
published her pseudonymous Mills & Boon novel, *The Transformation*

of Philip Jettan, under the new title of *Powder and Patch* – this time with her own name on the cover. It may have been Georgette's suggestion to delete the original final chapter. When she wrote the book in 1923, she was young, single and relatively naïve; seven years later she was married and had experienced life in foreign climes. Jane Aiken Hodge wrote perceptively of the book's alteration: 'In the first version, he wins her and takes her to Paris, to become exquisites together. In the second, they will retire to Sussex and become a country gentleman and his wife, very much like the Rougiers.' By 1930, the emphasis had shifted from romantic extravagance to a practical, comfortable approach to life that more accurately reflected Georgette's own experience. She may have dreamed of reaching the heights of passion in her youth, but as she grew older her novels increasingly dealt in a quieter reality – still romantic, but more humorous, prosaic, and often far more lasting.

Back in London the Rougiers took a flat at 62 Stanhope Gardens, South Kensington, where Georgette began her twelfth novel while Ronald decided what to do next. There were limited employment prospects for a mining engineer living in London but he would not take another overseas posting. The return home from Macedonia was largely the result of their decision to start a family. This, Georgette had told Ronald, could happen only if they were settled in England. Although she could be reticent on some topics, there were others about which she could be quite forceful and outspoken: the decision to have a baby was one of them. For Ronald her resolve meant that, unless he was willing to embrace the solitary life of a married man working overseas without his family, he would have to find another occupation. Accordingly, he bought into a partnership in a gas, light and coke company in the Horseferry Road, but the business did not prosper and he was forced to think of something else. After several months in London, he and Georgette decided to leave the city and settle in the country.

Many things at home had changed during the years they had spent overseas. Like other Western countries, Britain was now in the grip of the Great Depression, with growing unemployment and hardship and privation for those unable to find work. For Georgette there were certain attractions in moving out of London. With a growing literary reputation and with at least two more books in mind, she wanted the sort of privacy that had been an intrinsic part of her life overseas. Africa had been an escape and a hiatus from grief which had given her space and time alone with few demands and a caring, empathetic partner in Ronald. In the wilds of Tanganyika, Georgette had returned to her writing and the deep wound of loss had gradually healed over. And in Macedonia, there had been a comforting distance from the life she had known when her father was alive.

Back in London there were constant reminders of George which, if they did not re-open her wound, made her all too aware of it. In leaving England, Georgette had willingly left the past behind: she had finished with the early chapters of her life and put them away for good. Carola Oman described how Georgette 'could put up complete barriers around certain topics which were then never discussed', and this is what she did after her return to England from Macedonia. From then on she chose not to discuss her childhood or her father; with few exceptions, she never again made reference to George's life or death and she shared her personal feelings with only her closest family and friends.

By October 1930 they had chosen Sussex as the ideal county in which to live. Ronald had been offered a lease on a business in Horsham, a market town about thirty miles south of London. They borrowed money from Georgette's Aunt Ciss and Aunt Jo (paid back over time with interest) and bought the Russell Hillsdon Sports Store at No. 9 The Bishopric in the centre of town. It was a good location, with rooms above the shop where Boris would live after it was decided that he, too, would leave London and help Ronald run the business. They were to move to Sussex in the new year, to allow Georgette time to finish her new novel.

This latest book was a much more ambitious attempt at recreating the medieval period than *Simon the Coldheart*. Georgette had decided to re-tell the story of William the Conqueror from his birth in 1027 to his coronation in Westminster Abbey in 1066. She immersed herself in the sources and once again enlisted Ronald's aid in the acquisition of useful bits of information – later recording his contribution in one of her characteristic tributes on the flyleaf of his copy: 'Here is THE CONQUEROR for Ronald, with acknowledgements for his watchfulness & care in all such matters as Bear-fights, Cavalry-charges, Distances, & Male-Etiquette and with love from George.' They took a holiday to Normandy to see the sites of William's battles and sieges and to gather material for the book. Fifty years later, Georgette vividly remembered: 'What a lot of work I put into it! And how difficult it was to correlate the various contemporary (and largely inaccurate) accounts of William's Life and Times.'

She finished *The Conqueror* late in 1930. It had not been an easy book to write, and halfway through she had felt a sudden anxiety about it, telling Moore:

> I have finished Part II, 60,000 words perpetrated already. I shall have to cut it a bit, shan't I? William has now married his Matilda, & I approach what I think is going to be the most difficult part of the five – "The Might of France". I don't know what Heinemann will say. Sometimes I think I've written a book heavy as lead; at others I don't think it's so bad. Carola likes it; Joanna Cannan says it is the most interesting historical novel she has read, but I fear she is partial and prejudiced.

Apart from Ronald and her mother, Joanna and Carola were Georgette's main readers and the three women continued to critique each other's work well into the 1930s. Despite Georgette's fears of bias, Carola and Joanna were both experienced authors, well able to read a manuscript with a critical, practised eye. They were neither of them as prolific as Georgette but they had both written consistently since 1923. In 1930 Joanna's sixth novel *No Walls of Jasper* came out in the same month as Georgette's *Barren Corn*, while Carola's seventh book *Fair Stood the Wind* appeared in July. *Fair Stood the Wind* was a mildly entertaining modern novel and Georgette's judgement that 'the first 100 pages want cutting' proved astute.

Far more compelling was Joanna's *No Walls of Jasper* about a

(*Above*) Baby Georgette and Sylvia
(*Right*) Georgette aged 18 months

(*Above*) Georgette aged 8 and Boris

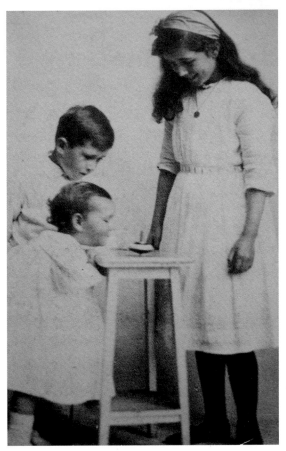

(*Right*) Georgette aged 12
with Boris and Frank

Sylvia Watkins and George Heyer

George Heyer

Sylvia on her wedding day 1901

Captain George Heyer circa 1915

Georgette's grandfather George Heyer

Georgette's grandmother Alice Heyer

Georgette's grandfather William Watkins

Georgette's grandmother Annette Watkins

(*Left*) Cecily, Annette and Josephine Watkins

(*Right*) Fairfield House

(*Above*) Georgette and
Grannie Watkins

(*Right*) Georgette with Boris
and Frank about the time
of writing *The Black Moth*

(Left) A photograph of Georgette possibly from *The Black Moth* jacket

(Right) *The Black Moth*
Constable 1921
(Far right) *The Great
Roxhythe* Hutchinson 1922

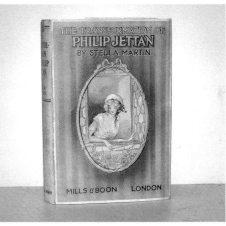

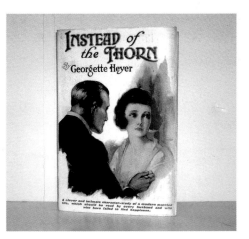

(Above) Georgette Heyer by E. O. Hoppé 1923

(Above right) *The Transformation of
Philip Jettan* Mills and Boon 1923
(Right) *Instead of the Thorn* Hutchinson 1923

(*Above*) Charles Joseph Rougier
(*Above right*) Jane Henderson Gray Crookston

(*Right*) Young Ronald Rougier

(*Below right*) Ronald Rougier, naval cadet
(*Below*) Ronald Rougier aged 22

(*Top*) Carola and Dulce Oman
(*Above*) Joanna Cannan
(*Above right*) Georgette Heyer
circa 1922

(*Right*) Georgette and Ronald's
wedding 1925
(*Far right*) George Heyer a few hours
before his death

(*Left*) Georgette
in Tanganyika 1927

(*Below left*)
Georgette outside
'the Manor House',
Tanganyika

(*Above*) Georgette and Ronald
in Kyerwa, Tanganyika

(*Left*) *Helen* 1928 the most
autobiographical novel
(*Far left*) *The Masqueraders*
1928 written in the grass hut

middle-aged married couple disillusioned by the realities of middle-class family life. Joanna dedicated the novel to Georgette, who read it and wrote to Moore to ask rhetorically 'Isn't her new book Good?' Reading Joanna's description of the fictional lady writer in the novel, Georgette must have recognised something of herself:

> Cynthia Bechler was a historical novelist; her "cloak and sword" romances were nearer to "best sellers" than anything to be found in the sober general catalogue of Messrs. Curtis, Fayre and Haydon. She was dark; not just brown-haired like Phyl, but strikingly dark, and very tall; fifty years ago she would have been ridiculed as a "maypole," and considered unmarriageable. She was not beautiful, not pretty; her nose was too large, aquiline yet lacking delicacy, and she had too full a mouth, too heavy a chin. But her eyes were beautiful, almond-shaped, tawny amber-brown, the lower, as well as the upper, lashes prettily curled; and she was admirably *soignée*…

While Joanna's description of her fictional novelist was mostly complimentary, her characters' take on Cynthia Bechler's work was less so:

> "I've been trying to imagine what it was like in the Middle Ages, but the people won't come human."
>   Martin reflected. "That's the fault of these wretched historical novelists – that woman your husband was speaking of – what's-her-name? They cloak and sword their characters and set them leaping about like Douglas Fairbanks, when they were really only poor mutts making a muddle of things like ourselves. I can't stand the tripe that woman turns out. She's got no respect for herself or her public or the past."

Georgette does not appear to have taken offence at Joanna's description, for their friendship remained robust throughout the 1930s. She was aware of the sort of licence that novelists sometimes took with people they knew or had met, writing them into their stories – never precisely as they were in real life – but making use of elements of their personalities, characteristics or mannerisms. It was something

Georgette herself had done when she wrote aspects of her mother into *Pastel* and which she would take great delight in doing with friends, family and chance-met acquaintances in future novels.

Georgette liked Joanna's contemporary books but she admired Carola's historical novels, of which the last two, *Crouchback* and *Miss Barrett's Elopement*, had been particularly successful. *Crouchback* was about Richard III, and Jane Mander recorded that Carola had 'spent over a year reading contemporary chronicles, and every authority, ancient and modern, on which she could lay hands, before she began it'. It was this approach to the serious historical novel that Georgette herself had used while writing *The Conqueror* and which had inspired her to dedicate that novel to Carola: 'In friendship and in appreciation of her own incomparable work done in the historic manner dear to us both.'

The doubts Georgette expressed to Moore about *The Conqueror* were an early sign of her burgeoning need for praise from people she respected. By the time *The Conqueror* was published in 1931 she had written twelve books in ten years and tried her hand at the contemporary novel, the serious historical, the swashbuckler and the light-hearted romance of manners and modes. She had been regularly reviewed in the major newspapers in both Britain and America, complimented on her 'pretty talent', her skill at creating amusing characters and situations and her ability to bring the past to life, and criticised for being old-fashioned, artificial and glib. She does not seem to have paid too much attention to her reviewers in those early years, choosing instead to follow her literary impulses and write where whim or fancy took her. This was unsurprising given that she had been published 'first crack out of the bag' at nineteen, never had a novel rejected and reliably sold several thousand copies of her books in their first year of publication.

She was not yet a consistent bestseller, however, and this may have been due in part to her eclectic publishing history. After six years and six novels with Heinemann and three years and three novels with Longmans, Georgette still had not settled to a single style or historical period. Her books varied considerably in terms of their seriousness, comedic elements and pace of plot. For those readers who had read and loved *The Black Moth* or *These Old Shades*, her medieval novels, *Simon the Coldheart* and *The Conqueror* made for rather different reading, while her four contemporary books may have been disappointing to anyone expecting the style or humour of *Beauvallet* or *The Masqueraders*.

In that first decade as a writer, Georgette was still learning her craft. She had yet to come to grips with the rhythms and cycles of the publishing industry. It took time to build a reputation and a readership, especially as she had so often changed publishers. Having a publisher she liked was vital to her. After several books with both Longmans and Heinemann she was still not altogether satisfied with either firm's handling of her work. Despite knowing Willie Longman of Longmans and Charles Evans, the Managing Director of Heinemann, well enough to both criticise and praise them, Georgette did not have the sort of personal relationship which she would have liked with either man. Although she appears never to have consciously acknowledged it, Georgette would always need the presence in her life of a charming, cultured and educated male (in addition to her husband) whose judgement she respected and who would respond positively to her work. In the years following her father's death, this role appears to have been filled by her agent, Leonard Moore, to whom she dedicated *Helen* in 1928.

The Conqueror came out in March 1931 as Georgette and Ronald were preparing to move to Sussex. They were due to leave London at the end of April and planned to stay at a hotel near Horsham while they looked for a suitable house. But on 18 April, their leave-taking was thrown into disarray when they learned that Ronald's father had fallen under a train at Down Street tube station and been killed. It was an appalling shock but worse was to come when, three days later, the Coroner, Mr Oddy, brought in a verdict of suicide while of unsound mind. (Down Street station lay between Green Park and Hyde Park Corner on London's Piccadilly Line. It was well known for suicides and was permanently closed the following year.) Ronald's mother was devastated and Georgette and Ronald were united in rejecting the judgement. 'No one who knew him believes that he was of unsound mind,' Georgette assured Moore, 'but it is a wicked, hateful thing to have said about such a dear, placid, cheery & level-headed man. He was a darling. It is like losing a second father.'

Charles Joseph Rougier was 71 and apparently in good health (though he had made his will exactly one month to the day before the tragedy). He had been a much-loved husband and father and Georgette had been especially fond of him. She and Ronald were convinced that 'from certain indications during the past six months', his father had suffered a stroke and fallen on to the rails. Whether the closure three months earlier of the Rougier family's factory in Yorkshire had any bearing on Charles Joseph's death is unknown. His financial position appears to have been sound, for he died leaving an estate worth £35,000, a very large sum in those days. The money (minus death duties) went entirely to his widow and did nothing to ease Ronald's financial worries.

The fortnight following his father's death was intensely busy for Ronald as he made the funeral arrangements, saw to the will and prepared to leave for Sussex. Georgette was busy organising the move but she and Ronald visited his mother as often as they could. Jean Rougier was not an easy person and Georgette had never been good at sympathy. Her mother-in-law had what Frank Heyer described as 'an acid, nagging tongue' and she had earned Georgette's disapproval by her perceived preference for Leslie, Ronald's elder brother. Leslie and his wife Tam managed Jean better, but as a career officer in the Lancashire Fusiliers Leslie was often away, so that the supportive role frequently fell to Ronald and by extension to Georgette. She was glad to be leaving London and had great hopes of their new life in the Sussex countryside.

A few days before she left the city Georgette wrote a hasty letter to Moore. 'I've done nothing about a modern book,' she told her agent. 'I don't think I can now, but I'll try & write some shorts. This appalling tragedy is too much on my mind. And that swine Oddy's verdict has just about finished us.' With Ronald between jobs she was the main source of income and the financial pressure was already beginning to build. Concerns about money were to become a recurring theme – partly because she never knew in advance just how much her next royalty cheque would be. Royalties were calculated twice a year in March and October, but the amount she received depended on the number of books sold and the price paid for them – something impossible to predict.

Georgette enjoyed solid sales for each of her titles and even after the initial burst of advertising and reviews had passed her novels continued selling steadily. A good writer could remain in print for years if a book sold several hundred or a thousand copies a year. In the 1920s and 1930s (before the advent of the paperback in 1935) publishers would start a book at 7/6 and within a year or two would offer a successful title in a cheaper 3/6 edition. Royalties were less for the cheaper books – at 10% just over 4d a copy. If Georgette's novels sold a thousand copies of each title in the cheaper edition annually (a possible 11,000 copies in 1931) her yearly royalties would have amounted to less than £200. This was not an insignificant sum in the early 1930s, but receiving it as she did in two separate payments six months apart made controlling day-to-day expenses difficult and she often found herself struggling financially. In April the receipt of her first royalty statement for the year prompted an anxious letter to Moore: 'Thank you for the cheque. I see the *Shades* still go on . . . I hope you'll get rid of the American rights in *Conk* [sic]. With no modern book I look like being broke.'

The financial strain that was to dog Georgette for most of her writing life was an inevitable consequence of spending her money faster than she earned it. This was partly because she was supporting her mother and Boris in addition to her own household. Sylvia had also decided to move to Horsham and had taken rooms at the Black Horse Hotel a few doors down the street from the sports store. Frank was now at Cambridge, having left Lancing the previous year. He had won the Bevan Exhibition to Pembroke College and although he was less of a drain on Georgette's finances he still required help occasionally. Even with an Exhibition, life at Cambridge could be expensive and there were several months of vacation each year when Frank came down from the University, shared the rooms above the shop with Boris, and had to be provided for. Georgette did not baulk at giving her family financial support, but the need to have a reliable income – something not likely to be supplied by the profits of a small sports store in Horsham – did put pressure on her to keep writing.

Georgette's relationship with Ronald does not seem to have been harmed by her role as the main family breadwinner. Nor does she appear to have resented the responsibility or even questioned it, although she did find it a burden at times. Ronald did his best to contribute financially and, although it was not where his ambition lay, had pinned his hopes on making a go of the sports shop. It cannot have been easy for a man of his class and social background to have to depend on his wife as the main source of income – particularly in a postwar world where men were assumed to have returned to their 'rightful' place as head of the home and family provider. That it was Georgette's earnings that largely supported them in the 1930s and that Ronald's response, so far from being resentful, was to assist her with her writing in whatever way he could, suggests a maturity in the relationship and a strength of character that helps to explain why their marriage endured for nearly half a century.

Georgette and Ronald understood each other well. His practical support of her writing, via his reading of her manuscripts and research assistance, also meant that he had a legitimate stake in her work, which must have made their dependency on her literary income somewhat easier to bear. Although she did not resent the demands on her creative powers or on her purse, Georgette felt them never-theless, especially as the move to Sussex, so far from saving them money, eventually proved to be a significant drain on their finances.

They left London on 30 April 1931 and moved in to a cottage called Swan Ken at Broadbridge Heath, near Horsham. Six months later they moved into a comfortable, two-storey house called Southover in Colgate, a tiny hamlet in Lower Beeding, east of Horsham. Southover lay at the end of a long, narrow lane deep in the West Sussex countryside, with only a handful of houses nearby and one pub, the Dragon. It was secluded and private, which entirely suited Georgette. For her, country living did not mean embracing community life. She did not wish to become involved in the parish church or join the Women's Institute and had no need of a large group of friends or a busy social life. Although she mingled with the local people and regularly went into Horsham to shop and sometimes went to the cinema with Ronald, Georgette preferred to remain out of the public eye and to safeguard her privacy. People knew who she was, of course, for a celebrity of any kind rarely remains anonymous in a small English village, and the postman was a reliable source of information about any newcomer. Word quickly got around. Although people sometimes exclaimed over her achievements or tried to talk to her about her books, they mostly left her alone. Ronald was more outgoing and his love of golf meant an instant entrée into the local community after he joined the nearby Mannings Heath Golf Club.

The Rougiers took Southover fully furnished for a year. It was a relief to be in their own place again. Their stay at the Swan Ken had not stopped Georgette writing, however, for she had begun a magazine serial story there which she told her agent was 'developing into a remarkably fine effort'. It was her first attempt at a detective-thriller, a departure from her usual writing but one which she hoped would make money. The detective-thriller had become hugely popular by the 1920s, thanks largely to the writings of Edgar Wallace, whose novels sold in millions. Georgette's first 'thriller' was called *Footsteps in the Dark* after the ghostly footsteps heard in their house in Kratovo. The story was typical of the genre with a haunted house, secret passages, a skeleton and several mysterious characters, one of whom turns out to be an undercover policeman. It is not a great piece of writing and lacks the wit of her later detective novels but it is good fun in parts and she obviously enjoyed writing it. In some ways it reflects her mood at the time: light-hearted, hopeful and with a promise of things to come. Georgette had discovered she was pregnant.

11

Thank you for these few kind words about my letters. I think they are rather peculiar. I write very few.

Georgette Heyer

Delighted to find that she was going to be a mother, Georgette wrote to tell Moore: 'We are expecting an addition to the family in February to my almost insane rapture, & Ronald's equally insane horror.' Her pregnancy was the fulfilment of a long-held wish for a child and her husband's 'horror' had more to do with their financial situation than with the thought of becoming a father. Since giving up his career as a mining engineer, Ronald had not enjoyed great success in business. They had lost their savings invested in the gas, light and coke company and had borrowed the money for the sports store; with a baby on the way Ronald must have felt an even greater pressure to provide for his family.

He needed a regular income. But the profits to be made from stringing tennis racquets, repairing guns or selling golf clubs were never going to be large in an English market town with a population of only 14,000. Ronald worked hard at making the shop a success but Georgette was moved to tell her agent: 'I MUST HAVE MONEY. Like that. All in capitals. I pray god to soften the heart of an editor unbusinesslike enough to pay me an extortionate sum for the privilege of producing the thriller.' In November she agreed to a £200 advance from Longmans who wanted to publish *Footsteps in the Dark* as a novel.

Spurred on by the need for money and the demands of a growing number of fans, even before she had finished writing the detective-thriller, Georgette was planning her next book. 'I've got something far more Amazing up my Sleeve,' she told Moore. 'What price a sequel to These Old Shades? Yes, I thought that'd make you sit up.' She intended the book to be like her earlier historical romances: with a hero the fans could adore and a heroine (originally named Helen) who would appeal to both old and new readers. She was excited by the new book and told her agent:

> It is a return to this author's popular manner, & – discarding hyperbole – is a sort of "Twenty Years After", for it is to be about Avon and Léonie's son, Dominic. He is going to be quite remarkably like his father, with a bit of Ma's hot temper thrown in, & her total disregard for human life. I haven't thought out the whole plot, yet, but he's to be a Bad Man (but Terribly Handsome and Attractive, of course) & he's to be a Famous shot. One of those impossible people who shoot as well Drunk as Sober. There will of course be an Abduction, a villain (neither handsome nor Attractive), a cross-country Chase, hair-breadth escapes, etc. And I propose to give Léonie, Avon, Lord Rupert, & Co. good fruity parts in the epic.

In the end she dispensed with her planned villain and made Dominic, the Marquis of Vidal, a more interesting and desirable character by casting him as both the hero and the villain of the piece. It is Vidal who abducts the heroine, Mary Challoner, and he who discovers soon after forcing her aboard his yacht bound for France that she is neither the trollop he first thought her nor the typical romantic heroine. Georgette deliberately turned several romantic stereotypes on their heads in this sequel and Mary Challoner was her first anti-heroine. Not for Mary the traditional scene where the aristocratic hero ravishes the fainting, helpless, but secretly enamoured heroine. Instead, Georgette built to a superb comic climax early in the book:

> "And now," said Vidal silkily, "and *now*, Miss Mary Challoner…!" Miss Challoner made a heroic effort, and raised herself on her elbow. "Sir," she said, self-possessed to the last, "I do not care

whether you go or stay, but I desire to warn you that I am about to be extremely unwell." She pressed her handkerchief to her mouth, and said through it in muffled accents: "Immediately!"

His laugh sounded heartless, she thought. "Egad, I never thought of that," he said. "Take this, my girl."

She opened her eyes once more, and found that his lordship was holding a basin towards her. She found nothing at all incongruous in the sight. "Thank you!" gasped Miss Challoner.

Georgette called the novel *Devil's Cub* in a nod to fans of *These Old Shades* and that book's much-loved hero, 'Satanas', the Duke of Avon (she had rejected as titles *The Son of the Duke*, *Wolf of Avon* and Boris's ironic suggestion: *These Old Shadows*). Georgette hoped to finish the sequel in time for spring publication but her writing was interrupted in mid-February by the arrival of her long-awaited baby.

At 3.40 p.m. on Friday, 12 February 1932 Georgette gave birth to a healthy eight-pound boy. She called him Richard, a favourite name which she had used in *The Black Moth*, several short stories and for the hero in *Helen*. Richard's second name was George, after his father, George Ronald, and his grandfather, George Heyer. Later in their lives the reverse initials of father and son became something of a family joke and Georgette would regularly refer to her son as 'R.G.' and her husband as 'G.R.'. Eight days after Richard's birth, Georgette wrote to tell Moore of her son's safe arrival, that the baby looked 'like a Gauguin picture, & has shoulders like his father's' and that she was 'in that sort of a Mood just at present when I am Affronted by receiving letters which do not mention Richard George Rougier.' She was a proud parent and a devoted mother, although her time with Richard would always be limited by the demands of her writing.

In a fitting reminder of her literary career Richard and *Footsteps in the Dark* appeared on the same day. Kenneth Potter of Longmans wrote to Georgette to say he hoped that the baby and *Footsteps* 'were going to be my two most successful works' (her earlier concerns about Longmans had been temporarily allayed by their prompt production of the detective-thriller). Some years later Georgette wrote of

Footsteps in the Dark as 'This work, published simultaneously with my son . . . was the first of my thrillers, and was perpetrated while I was, as any Regency character would have said, increasing. One husband and two ribald brothers all had fingers in it, and I do not claim it as a Major Work'. Richard, however, she described as 'my most notable (indeed, peerless) work' and 'my most successful achievement'.

Her son was now three months old and 'Lusty & Belligerent', but he had deep blue eyes with long lashes and she loved him. He had a nanny, of course, but Georgette gave Richard as much of her time and attention as she thought proper in the first year of life, and she often wrote at night instead of during the day 'so as not to disrupt family life'. Some days she would begin her work at nine or ten in the evening and sit up all night writing her manuscripts in longhand. She also had an ancient typewriter which Moore had given to her during his first year as her agent and sometimes she wrote on that.

Her relationship with her agent had become more important since the move to Sussex and she wrote to him often. In May she asked Moore if he 'could squeeze £300 out of Heinemann' for *Devil's Cub*. On receiving a rather terse reply, in which he assured her that she could 'safely leave the question of the advance' to him, she responded with one of her joking letters: 'I won't be sat on, so there!' After ten years of writing to Moore (it would be another year before she began calling him 'L.P.'), Georgette treated her agent as an affectionate niece would treat her kindly, old-fashioned, Victorian uncle. Moore seems not always to have known how to respond to her habit of poking fun at him and may have preferred a more conservative author-agent relationship. Georgette, however, like many authors, needed more than that and was swift to let him know whenever she felt neglected or out of touch. She visited him at his office when she was in London and when he failed to visit her at home in Sussex expressed her disappointment in typical fashion: 'How much we enjoyed your visit to us the other day! (HINT.) How nice of you and Mrs Moore to run down to see us, AS YOU SAID YOU WOULD. (sarcasm.).'

Despite her insistence that she wrote very few letters, Georgette was a prolific correspondent. She thought nothing of writing several letters in a day – even when she was busy with a new manuscript. She frequently regaled her agent with humorous excerpts from her latest book, descriptions of baby Richard, and stream-of-consciousness accounts of small moments in her daily routine. She had the ability to bring the least incident to life: the changing of the nib on her fountain pen, a bout of laryngitis or Richard's latest achievement, while the receipt of a 'very jammy' letter from a fan was an opportunity for a wry comment about the public taste and the worth of her own novels. Such moments of self-deprecation were rare in the first decade of her writing life, but in 1932 she wrote jokingly to Moore to tell him that 'One of these days you'll get had up for Obtaining Money Under False Pretences. And I shall be arrested as an Accessory & have to admit that I <u>did</u> write a series of worthless books for which you <u>did</u> obtain sums of money far greater than the said books were worth.' She ended the letter with a series of humorous postscripts:

> P.S. When I sat down to brighten your humdrum existence with a few deathless words from my pen, I thought I had something of importance to say. Isn't that funny? For on reading this prose poem through I find that I haven't said it.
>
> P.P.S. Careful as I am always to write to you in a spirit of decorum, & with the Respect Inspired by your grey hairs, I somehow feel that perhaps I should do well to head this note Private & Extremely Confidential. Then you'll get all-excited-like, & devour it in the hopes of Revelations of a Private & Shocking Character. Farewell!
>
> P.P.S.S. When some Admirer collects my letters & publishes them this'll make edifying reading, will not it?

Despite the derogatory remarks about her books Georgette hoped that her novels were better than she was prepared to admit publicly. By the late 1930s she increasingly wanted others to acknowledge their worth and the quality of her writing. Her suggestion that someone might one day want to collect and edit her letters or write her biography was an idea she mentioned several times. That Moore kept so many of her letters and was always careful to write her real name against her occasional humorous pseudonymous signature (Sophonisba Hawkins, Jemima Hopkins, Almeria Clutterbuck) indicates that he, at least, thought that she was someone whose work might endure.

At the end of May Georgette needed to 'have about 50 teeth pulled out'. Afterwards she would take a short holiday and try to finish *Devil's Cub*. She was maudlin and felt 'vile, & do not expect to live very much longer'. Over the next few years she would suffer several bouts of ill-health, and semi-humorous statements about death or suicide were not uncommon whenever she felt unwell, overwhelmed or under duress. What she could not say out loud Georgette said through the medium of writing. Her letters were a conduit for many of her ideas, thoughts and feelings – an essential outlet for her emotions which she expressed through humorous, ironic, or sarcastic comments about her domestic situation or her novels. Sometimes these were an unconscious reflection of frustrations or irritation felt at moments when life was difficult. Occasionally they were thinly disguised demands for attention.

Georgette rarely asked Moore or anyone (apart from Ronald) what they thought of her books and hardly ever suggested that they read them. She wanted genuine, spontaneous praise from people whose opinions she respected. Frustratingly, those who were best-positioned to tell her what she wanted to hear often did not read the signs or understand her need. L.P. Moore was one of these. When pressed, he would occasionally respond with an encouraging comment, but from his point of view she was a successful author who reliably produced a novel a year (and very often two), enjoyed solid sales, and received good reviews in all of the major papers. To him, her success was self-evident and even if he had discerned her growing need for recognition he was of a generation which did not hold with effusive outbursts of praise. Paradoxically, had he ever overcome his natural reticence and expressed himself in such a way, Georgette would have depressed such sentiments with all the contrariness of an author who yearned for praise but demanded privacy, and consistently resisted talking about her work.

Once she began writing again after Richard's birth, *Devil's Cub* was brought quickly to its satisfying and humorous conclusion. Moore had played his part and got the £300 advance from Heinemann, by which time Georgette had already begun her next book. Encouraged by the success of *Footsteps in the Dark*, which had sold out its first 5,000 copies in just three months (it was reprinted four times in its first year), she had begun a second detective-thriller in the hope of a quick financial return. Originally called *Half a Loaf*, the new book featured all the ingredients of the classic detective story with a murdered butler, suspicious heroine, debonair detective and the obligatory country-house party. Once again Ronald played his part in the writing: offering suggestions, reading the manuscript and helping with the kind of technical information Georgette needed – mainly to do with guns, cars and boats. He would collaborate on most of her detective novels and their son Richard later recalled that:

> At the time, Mother was writing both historical and detective novels. The latter were a form of mental exercise for her, but my father had a hand in them. He would work out how the crime was committed, but he was incapable of characterisation. One of my earliest memories is of my father starting off: "Now we have X who is third in line for a fortune which is at present in the hands of Y. The girl is Z and she and X plot to do this…" He had started outlining the plot when Mother interrupted saying: "Oh no! X wouldn't do that. He's not that kind of person." My father exploded, but she just couldn't help putting flesh on the bones.

A friend of the Rougiers told Jane Aiken Hodge that Ronald 'at this time was an immensely supportive husband, charming, friendly and always there when his wife needed him, if perhaps always a step behind. And he was a tower of strength when it came to reading proofs, where she relied on him to catch errors she was too close to spot.' *Half a Loaf* became *Why Shoot a Butler?* and Georgette acknowledged Ronald's contribution by dedicating the book 'To one who knows why'.

By the time Georgette's second thriller came out in February 1933, her first had sold almost 12,000 copies. It was an encouraging figure in an era when publishers were pleased to sell four or five thousand copies of a title. With royalties of fifteen per cent on the first 3,000 books sold, Georgette had earned back her advance in the first three months. Within a year *Footsteps in the Dark* had brought in nearly £800 – a substantial return considering a housemaid earned just fifty or sixty pounds a year. It also meant that Georgette could see clearly where the money was. Of her fifteen novels only her contemporary books sold less than 10,000 copies in their first four years of publication. The novels that had merited the most reprints were *These Old Shades* (25,000 copies in seven years) and *The Masqueraders* (22,000 copies in five years). Sales of *Devil's Cub* were also strong. Given the success of her crime and historical fiction it is not surprising Georgette gave up writing contemporary romance.

Soon after the publication of *Why Shoot a Butler?*, and possibly on the strength of her improving royalties, Georgette and Ronald decided to find a house with an extended lease into which they could settle long-term. They had been married for almost eight years and been in Sussex for nearly eighteen months. Country living suited them and once Richard was born they may have felt a desire for greater permanency. In May they left Southover and moved into the Sussex Oak Inn north of Horsham. From here they found the ideal residence.

Blackthorns was a large, two-storey brick house set in fifteen acres with a big garden and a wood in which nightingales sang. There was a stream and a pond where Richard could sail his boats, and a well from which their water was pumped each morning and evening. Set on the outskirts of a tiny hamlet called Toat Hill (toat being Saxon for lookout) in the parish of Slinfold, Blackthorns lay four miles to the west of Horsham. Like Southover, it was set well back from the road with a long driveway and a great many trees to shield it from public view, and was far enough removed from Horsham to ensure Georgette's privacy. She did not find it inconvenient, however, for they bought a car ('the Viper') and Slinfold had its own railway station with a train service that could get them to London in an hour.

About this time, Georgette joined the Empress Club in Dover Street in central London. Established in 1897 as a club for educated, professional women, the Empress provided an elegant, sophisticated environment which enabled Georgette to play host to her agent or friends whenever she visited the capital. On trips to London she often liked to 'drop in' on Moore and occasionally they met at the Empress for lunch. Georgette appears to have remained a member of the Empress Club until the War.[6]

It may have been through her association with Moore that during the 1930s Georgette gradually came to know a handful of other authors or 'fellow-inkies' as she liked to call them. One of these was another Heinemann author, Margaret Kennedy, whose 1924 novel, *The Constant Nymph*, had been a sensational bestseller. In later years changes at Heinemann saw Georgette's circle of literary acquaintances slowly increase to include other Heinemann authors such as J.B. Priestley, Graham Greene, Somerset Maugham, Eric Ambler and Clifford Bax. But, despite meeting them socially, it seems that Georgette never attempted to further the relationship beyond that of a friendly acquaintance and her only close writing friends remained Joanna Cannan and Carola Oman.

The upheaval of the move to Blackthorns meant that Georgette published only *Why Shoot a Butler?* in 1933. It was a moderate success with some good reviews, including one in *The Times Literary Supplement* and another in a smaller paper which amused Georgette immensely:

Somebody in the *Westminster Record* says that *Why Shoot a Butler?* ought to be on every shelf. Now don't burst into hoarse, mocking laughter. I'm taking myself very seriously. They talk about my "Art" in Horsham, & that sort of thing soon goes to one's head. They can't think how I make my people talk. They are sure they wouldn't know what to make their characters say, & they wonder how ever I think out a plot at all. So do I. So when I next brighten your dull life with one of my gracious visits, just remember that I've

---

6 The Empress Club survived until 1952 and closed for good in 1956.

got my Art, & can make my people talk, & ought to be on every shelf. No, I'm not sure that I like that last bit. After all, I <u>did</u> manage to lure Ronald into marrying me.

While she was always glad to know she was read and enjoyed, Georgette did not relish the type of gushing praise and incredulity which her writing inspired in some of her neighbours. Although she appreciated the local people within their context, she did not go out of her way to mix with them. She left it to Ronald to get to know them through the shop and his golf, and to shield her from anyone who sought to intrude into her writing life.

They lived at the Sussex Oak for some weeks before moving into Blackthorns. Georgette put the time at the inn to good use by writing the opening chapters of an eighteenth-century historical romance which she felt was 'going to be very good value'. She was so enthused by the new book that she wrote out several excerpts for Moore by hand and asked:

Now how do you like those choice excerpts? Pretty fruity? Would you like to hear my Dramatis Personae? No? Well, it's too late now, you've got to.

<u>Marcus Drelincourt, Earl of Rule</u>. Hero of the best type. Very pansy, but full of guts under a lazy exterior. Aged 35.

<u>Elizabeth Winwood</u>, lady in the best XVIIIth cent. tradition. Sweet & willowy. Age 20

<u>Charlotte Winwood</u>. Improving spinster. 19

<u>Horatia Winwood</u>. A stammering heroine, of the naïve & incorrigible variety. 17

<u>Pelham, Viscount Winwood</u>. Brother to above ladies. Young rake & spendthrift. Provides light relief.

<u>Maria, Viscountess Winwood</u>. Mother to all the above Winwoods. An invalid of exquisite sensibility.

<u>Edward Heron.</u> Lieutenant of the 10th Foot, invalided home from Bunker's Hill. Enamoured of Elizabeth.

<u>Louisa, Lady Quain</u>. Trenchant sister to Rule.

<u>Sir Humphrey Quain</u>. Her husband.

Arnold Gisborne. Secretary to the Earl of Rule.

Caroline, Lady Massey. I regret to say, Rule's discarded mistress.

Crosby Drelincourt. Cousin & heir-presumptive to the Earl of Rule. A Macaroni, & a nasty piece of work, taken all round.

Robert, Baron Lethbridge. Best type of villain. Fierce & hot-eyed & sardonic.

This sort of list was important, for her characters were often the starting point for her novels. She would first imagine an individual, then spend hours thinking about him or her while playing endless games of patience, fleshing the character out in her mind and devising a suitable name. Once created, a character's behaviour and dialogue followed naturally. Georgette found it impossible to force one of her creations to behave in a manner contrary to their established personality. When writing a book her *dramatis personae* lived for her to the extent that they frequently determined the course of the story. There were even times when she complained, as other authors have, that a character had taken her in a direction in which she had never contemplated going.

Once Georgette had created the cast for the new book she was able to give Moore a hint of things to come: 'All these people are naturally going to fall into a number of awkward situations, & I rather think Pelham has a duel with friend Crosby, while I am quite sure that Rule has one with Lethbridge. Lots of gambling. Horatia is a gambler, & I should imagine will get herself into a fairly sticky mess over it. But don't you fret – it will all End Happily.' Two weeks later she had made rapid progress:

I'm glad you like my excerpts. I'm thinking of calling it *The Convenient Marriage*. O.K.? Yes, isn't it sad about Caroline Massey? Not a Nice Woman at all, & do you know I'm afraid she's going to have a liaison with Lord Lethbridge as well as with Rule? I do hate promiscuity, don't you? Her husband was in Trade, you know, & of course that was a Grave Drawback, & she never got herself received in the very best circles, but she had a lot of money, & gave lavish parties, & people who liked deep basset used to go to her house a lot. She had a good cellar, too, which attracted people like Lethbridge.

One of the remarkable things about several of Georgette's manuscripts was the extent to which the first drafts were so often the final drafts. The excerpts which she wrote out for Moore from the early manuscript of *The Convenient Marriage* are almost word-for-word as they appear in the published novel. Once she knew what the book was to be about she was generally able to write quickly and easily, with minimal re-writing or re-working of the plot and only occasional 'sticks'. More than once in the first three decades of her career Georgette completed a manuscript in less than twelve weeks. She did get 'stuck' briefly while writing *The Convenient Marriage* and told Ronald about the problem. '"Ah! I've been waiting for that,"' he told her, before proceeding 'to enumerate all the Sticking places in all the books I've written ever since I married him'. Ronald assured his wife that she would overcome this obstacle as she had the others.

The difficult bit was in chapter three where the hero, Lord Rule, goes to visit his mistress, Lady Massey. As Georgette humorously explained it to Moore:

> Here I am, in Lady Massey's boudoir (all rose pink and silver, you know), & I can't either talk to her, or get away. The trouble is I've led such a sheltered life. It's a frightful drawback, & I do think young females about to embrace a literary career ought to get to know a few good demi-mondaines. Personally, I can't make out what Rule sees in that odious Massey. She seems to me a very ordinary woman. No S.A. at all. But you never know with Men, do you?

Georgette's description of Caroline Massey as 'ordinary' and having no sex appeal (S.A.) was based partly on her perception of the character as vulgar. Vulgarity was still the unforgivable sin in Georgette's world – both real and fictional.

Her notion of class and breeding underpins all of her writing and is crucial to understanding her view of the world. Although she held to the idea of a natural social hierarchy, she also recognised the capacity for vulgarity in any individual regardless of class, and frequently depicted dishonourable aristocrats alongside principled lower-class characters. Georgette's own view of herself was as someone who was well-bred and most comfortable in upper- and upper-middle-class circles. Ever class-conscious, in Horsham society she felt herself to be on the same social plane as those who moved in 'county' circles, despite the fact that she did not own an estate, hunt, or even farm her own land. A photograph taken of her with baby Richard shows her looking elegant and very 'county' in a tweed jacket and pearls. Georgette's particular kind of snobbery was rarely overt – she was much too private for that – but it is implicit in most of her public and private writing.

Although Richard was only eighteen months old when she was writing *The Convenient Marriage* Georgette told Moore that her son didn't 'care for the book. He does like a Womanly Woman, & thinks that a Mother's Place is in the Nursery.' As an observer of human nature and human relationships, Georgette could recognise all kinds of women: young, earnest, athletic types; glamorous, worldly wise girls; witty socialites; vamps, and even the 'angel in the house'; and all of them clearly and obviously 'womanly women'. Yet, Georgette felt herself to be none of these things. She knew what the female stereotypes were, but she could also see that she simply did not fit into any of these roles. It was not even as if the 'mother in the nursery' was a natural calling for her when, although she adored Richard and Ronald, her affection for them was far more cerebral than tactile.

Her wonder that the Earl of Rule should desire the 'very ordinary' Lady Massey may also have been because Georgette did not see *herself* as having sex appeal. Caroline Massey is a strong, forceful, ambitious woman – not unlike her creator – and yet Georgette struggled to see her as sexually appealing or desirable to men. In her own life sex was not a consuming passion. While Georgette obviously understood the psychology of romantic passion and was able to write about it convincingly, the physical manifestation of love made her uneasy. It was not merely that inter-war British society did not encourage the view of women as actively sexual beings; it was that she baulked at the physical act of intercourse.

This comes through most clearly in her earliest contemporary novel *Instead of the Thorn*, in which her heroine struggles with the realities of sex and its place in marriage. In the book Georgette shows herself acutely aware of the fact that many women of her generation had come to their first experience of sex completely unprepared for it. As the writer Vera Brittain reported in her famous autobiography, *Testament of Youth*, prior to marriage many women in that era had never seen a man naked nor had the least idea of what sexual inter-course involved. As a result, numerous brides (and some grooms) entered marriage without any notion of what it physically entailed. Even Marie Stopes, the author of *Married Love* (1918), had not known that sex was a necessary part of procreation. She had only made the startling discovery after two years of unconsummated marriage.

Georgette had read *Married Love*. She had also discussed sex with Joanna Cannan and Carola Oman when writing *Instead of the Thorn*. Her two married friends had told her enough to enable her to write perceptively about her heroine's struggle with the physical side of married life. Whether Georgette herself ever experienced an over-whelming urge for sex is impossible to know, although a close friend later described her as 'not terribly interested' in sex. She and Ronald only had one child and for much of their married life slept in separate beds, giving little or no impression that physical lovemaking was an intrinsic part of their life together. Georgette had her passions but they were not physical. Her marriage to Ronald was first and foremost a marriage of two minds.

While theirs was to be a long and happy relationship, Georgette gradually became completely conservative – even reactionary – in her views, and ambivalent about the role and place of women in society. She consistently criticised the feminist stance, and could be vehement in her condemnation of women in business, despite the fact that for most of her life she would be the main family bread-winner. While Georgette was never a feminist in ideology, she was in many ways a feminist by temperament: a strong woman who never questioned her ability or her right to succeed in a patriarchal world

– a modern woman in an Edwardian shell. It was this version of the female character that she was to develop most strongly in the novels yet to come.

Georgette returned to *The Convenient Marriage* and eventually got past the sticking-point by simply getting on with the writing. As she told Moore: 'I've something better to do than to write letters to you. There's that blasted widow, still sitting in the rose-pink and silver boudoir, & Rule's there too, & I ought to extricate him. You know, it's a bad business. He's gone & got engaged to the heroine, & now here he is messing the Massey (note the alliteration) about. I shall have to do something about it.' She always spoke about her literary creations as if they were real people. One of the reasons Georgette's characters live for her readers is that they lived so vividly for her.

12

Since I shall have been (I trust) extremely amusing on paper for a month, there should be little reason why I should not go on being extremely amusing on paper for another month.

Georgette Heyer

They moved into Blackthorns in the second half of 1933 and Georgette immediately began writing her third detective-thriller. *Murder on Monday* (later re-named *The Unfinished Clue*) proved rather different from her earlier mysteries, with tighter plotting and far less dependence upon external elements for excitement – gone were the secret passages, foggy nights and kidnappings. Instead, she wrote plenty of witty dialogue and created a cast of characters guaranteed to heighten the tension even in the calm setting of a country-house weekend. One of the highlights of the book is Lola, a Mexican dancer whose magnificent unconcern for anyone but herself gives rise to a series of funny scenes. The detective is a well-bred policeman whose charm and intelligence might have qualified him for the growing ranks of iconic fictional detectives if Georgette had not ended the novel with him giving up policing.

The Unfinished Clue appeared in March 1934 and Dorothy L. Sayers wrote a review of it in *The Sunday Times* which began: 'I said last week that good writing would often carry a poor plot, and here is a case in point.' She concluded with a paragraph which must have given Georgette particular pleasure – coming as it did from one of the greatest of all English detective writers:

> And yet, simply because it is written in a perfectly delightful light comedy vein, the book is pure joy from start to finish. Lola, the fiancée, by herself is worth the money, and, indeed, all the characters from the Chief Constable to the Head Parlourmaid, are people we know intimately and appreciatively, from the first words they utter. Miss Heyer has given us a sparkling conversation-piece, rich in chuckles, and all we ask of the plot is that it should keep us going until the comedy is played out.

Georgette was becoming known for the humour which would set her books apart and help to ensure their longevity.

Publication of *The Unfinished Clue* brought renewed concerns about Longmans. The firm had raised her ire when, after sending them the corrected proof pages, Georgette had received 'frantic and numerous telephone messages desiring me to inform them <u>where</u> are the proofs?' She hated this sort of inefficiency and once her displeasure was incurred it generally marked the beginning of the end. Georgette could be stubborn where her books were concerned. Although it could take her a long time to make a decision to change an arrangement, once the process was begun it was usually irreversible. She and Moore met at Georgette's London club, the Empress, where they discussed the matter. She left unappeased. A few months later she began writing *Death in the Stocks*. It was to be her last novel with Longmans.

Death in the Stocks was the only one of her detective novels written without Ronald's input and many people think it her best. In it Georgette gave her comic gifts free rein. This was the first of what she came to call her 'real crime stories' and the novel in which she introduced her detective, Superintendent Hannayside, who would re-appear in several of her later mysteries. Although a likeable character, he lacks the impact and idiosyncrasy of other detectives of the era such as Ellery Queen, Hercule Poirot, Miss Marple, Lord Peter Wimsey, Maigret, or Simon Templar ('The Saint'). Even with the later addition of an amateur psychologist in the form of Sergeant Hemingway, Georgette's detectives never attained icon status. *Death in the Stocks* earned her another commendation from Dorothy L. Sayers, however: 'Miss Heyer's characters and dialogue are an abiding delight to me . . . I have seldom met people to whom I took so violent a fancy from the word "Go".'

Georgette always noted her reviews. Though when Moore's assistant, Norah Perriam, wrote to make sure she had seen and kept them, she laughingly dismissed the idea: 'But my dear good creature, do you really picture me with a pot of paste and a pair of scissors eagerly sticking press cuttings into an album? I'm thirty-three & I've been writing for thirteen years – no, <u>sixteen</u> years![7] The day of such follies is over fast.' This did not prevent Georgette from telling Norah Perriam exactly which papers had reviewed her novel and where the best reviews had appeared! Although she often denied taking an interest in such things, she was always aware of where she was written up and by whom and her attitude to her publisher could shift according to the kind of press coverage she received for each new novel.

Longmans did not want to lose Georgette after the success of *Death in the Stocks* but in February 1935 she severed relations with the firm and signed her first contract with Hodder & Stoughton for 'her next four new and original "modern" novels'. Determined to maintain two separate publishers for her historical and contemporary books, she had great hopes of Hodder. Their list included some of the most successful writers of the day and the firm had built a strong reputation among readers with their trademark Yellow Jacket books. John Buchan, Baroness Orczy, 'Sapper', James Hilton and Leslie Charteris were all well-known Hodder authors when Georgette joined the firm. It was not only the firm's stellar list which impressed her, however, but also their ability to sell novels. By the mid-thirties, the firm proudly claimed 'There was not a bookshop that did not open its doors to a traveller [company salesman] with the Yellow Jacket list to sell.'

---

7 She was actually thirty-two for another three months.

Established in 1868, Hodder & Stoughton had a long-standing reputation for conservative values and reliability. For many years the firm had been run by Sir Ernest Hodder-Williams and his younger brothers, Percy and Ralph, all of whom were members of a Nonconformist family whose strong Christian beliefs permeated every part of their business. When Ernest died in 1927 Percy became head of the company. It was perhaps fortunate that Georgette had very little direct contact with her new publisher for she and Percy Hodder-Williams were far from being kindred spirits. He was well-known among literary agents as 'the last of the puritans' and, while she was herself undeniably conservative in many of her views, Georgette would not have approved of the type of moral censorship which Hodder sometimes applied to its authors' manuscripts. In 1924, Ernest had turned down Michael Arlen's bestselling novel, *The Green Hat*, on the grounds that its content did not comply with Hodder's policy that their Yellow Jacket books had 'nothing in them which would shock or harm any reader from ten to eighty'. Ten years later, Percy had similarly refused to publish a Leslie Charteris 'Saint' story called 'The Intemperate Reformer' because 'it was too much of an affront to the nonconformist conscience.' While Georgette was aware of Hodder's conservative editorial policy there was nothing to indicate that it would ever affect her and she signed the new contract without a qualm.

Within a week of finalising the Hodder deal, Georgette had also signed a contract with Heinemann for her new historical romance. For the first time since joining the firm in 1925 her contract included an option on her next three historical novels. Provided she could maintain the pace of writing which she had sustained over the past decade, between them the Heinemann and the Hodder contracts meant that she had guaranteed publication for her next seven novels. It must have been a huge boost to her morale. All she had to do was write them.

Three months later Georgette had a breakdown. Early in May she became ill with what she described as 'internal poisoning', which though not desperate was horrid. The condition quickly became serious, however, and she told her old friend John Hayward that she had 'succumbed to a Nervous Breakdown and been languishing ever since'. For several weeks she remained confined to her bed, unable to work, and with instructions from the doctor not to write anything until she had recovered. It was three years since Richard's birth and in that time Georgette had moved house twice, written six books, endured periods without domestic support, suffered several episodes of severe financial strain and committed herself to writing seven new novels. In some ways a breakdown does not seem surprising.

'It's only fair to warn you that I have had some sort of a collapse,' she wrote to Norah Perriam in late May, '& am under strict doctor's orders still. I'm getting better, but I doubt whether I could do any work. I find I can't even read for long without losing all power of concentration. The only thing to do is to obey orders, & hope for the best. I'm up – which means that I get up to lunch, lie on a sofa till eight o'clock, & crawl back to bed.' Ronald was to take her away for a full month's convalescence at the end of June, and, despite her weakened state, she had urgently requested that the proofs of her new historical romance be sent to her before they left for the north. These had promptly arrived – awash with errors. In spite of repeated requests that her books be typeset exactly as written, to her great chagrin Georgette found that Heinemann's printer had 'corrected' her spelling, punctuation, and capitalisation.

She had decided views about how her books should read and her irritation with Heinemann was only exacerbated by their habit of sending her a bill for excess corrections of the proofs. She laboriously amended the printer's 'corrections' of her work and then wrote a detailed account of her concerns which she asked her agent to 'convey tactfully' to Heinemann:

> They are not "bad" proofs; by which I mean that there are very few printer's slips. What is bad is that the compositor had throughout followed his own inclination where it has seemed good to him. Now, I think that after all this time I am not being unreasonable when I say that I expect Heinemann's printers to remember

& to respect my personal idiosyncrasies. For years I have spelled words such as Realize with a z . . . In every book of mine Heinemann have had of late years they have changed all my z's to s's, & I have been obliged to change them back . . . In every instance I have mentioned an inn, they have put the name between inverts, Thus we have:- The chaise drew up at "The Green Man" – till I could scream . . .

The proofs were for *Regency Buck* – her first novel set in the colourful, extravagant decade known as the English Regency (1811–1820), when George III was 'mad' and his eldest son, George, was appointed Prince Regent to rule in his stead. Georgette's reading and research for her eighteenth-century novels had led her to the Regency era, a rich repository of fascinating people, places and events. She 'raided' the London Library for books and spent hours among the sources soaking up information about life in the period. A year earlier she had written enthusiastically to Moore about her plans for the novel: 'I'm going to open *Regency Buck* with a Prize Fight – probably Cribb's second battle with Molyneux, at Thistleton Gap. I've read *Annals of the Ring* & *Pugilistica* – & I know a bit about it now, I can tell you. There will also be a bit of cocking, possibly a meeting of the Beefsteaks, certainly a coaching race to Brighton & a street mill. It ought to be a lovely book.'

It was 'a lovely book' in some ways, although it did not achieve the subtlety of plot or the brilliance of character which were to be the hallmarks of her later Regency novels. It is an entertaining story which offers a vivid introduction to upper-class Regency London and Brighton in 1811 and 1812. The book is not without its faults, however. Georgette's enthusiasm for the new period spilled over into the novel in a rare example of over-writing and there are moments when the ephemeral detail threatens to engulf the plot.

Carried away by so much rich material Georgette also made an uncharacteristic error. Towards the end of the book she sent her heroine, Judith Taverner, to Brighton – there to meet the Prince Regent at his summer palace, the Brighton Pavilion. In describing (in loving detail) the minaret-domed exterior and the magnificent Chinoiserie interior of the Pavilion, Georgette described a building which did not yet exist in that form. Judith's visit to Brighton took place in 1812. Yet the Oriental architecture and opulent interior which were to become such an iconic testament to the Regent's extravagance did not commence until 1815 and were not completed until 1823.

While it remains the fiction writer's prerogative to adapt history to suit the needs of a story, this had never been Georgette's approach. Her mistake in *Regency Buck* came from her reading of the limited source material (there were only four books about the Pavilion published before 1935) – in this case a careless reading of Brayley's 1838 *Account of the Pavilion*. Georgette made very few mistakes in her historical novels and the discovery of an error always caused her considerable distress. Some months later, while on a visit to Grantham, she was dismayed to find 'that the George Inn here, which I described in the *Buck* as Palladian, is no such thing. I have mixed it up with another.' She made no mention of her more major error, however, and like most of her readers it appears that Georgette never realised her mistake.

Whatever its faults, after correcting the proofs Georgette was pleased enough with the final manuscript to make a rare positive pronouncement about one of her novels. 'Have just been glancing through *Regency Buck*,' she told Moore, '& really it is rather a fascinating book!! I actually became lost in my own work! I do hope it sells. It's easily my best.' She also expressed something of her innermost feelings about her writing: 'If *Regency Buck* doesn't go big I will die – because I shall have lost my faith in human nature, my belief in myself, & all my secret hopes.'

One of her unspoken secret hopes was her growing desire for greater recognition. While the new Heinemann contract with its £500 advance (a significant increase on the £350 paid for *The Convenient Marriage*) had made her feel appreciated, Georgette also wanted to know that what she wrote was good. Although she always maintained a sense of humour about her writing in the 1930s, it had not yet acquired the rather cynical, self-deprecating tone that would emerge in the next decade. While she had a capacity for self-mockery, in the Sussex years it was of a gentler, kinder type which she occasionally expressed to Moore:

> When you write your memoirs I shall expect to figure largely in them. In fact, I think I'll insert all the bits about Me myself. I feel you might not do justice to the Grandeur of the Subject. I don't want to read that "Georgette Heyer was one of my more frequent visitors. I can see her now, seated in my office for long hours at a stretch, talking about her baby & Bigger Royalties." Yes, you may well blush. Well, you're not going to publish that bit. The bit you're going to insert will run on these lines: "Then there was Georgette Heyer, strange, incalculable creature, whose letters to me are among my most treasured possessions. Every one is a Prose Poem, even the one's [sic] about her publisher, & the exquisite refinement of her language, & the modesty of her sentiments baffle description."

Even when writing to Norah Perriam from her sickbed, Georgette managed to find humour in the situation: 'I toy with the idea of an expensive funeral & a book (by my spouse) entitled *Georgette Heyer As I Knew Her*. And of course my letters, all collected & published with notes supplied by a sorrowing editor. But if I've got an American publisher, perhaps I'll postpone it all.'

She had not had an American publisher since the 1920s when Houghton Mifflin and Small Maynard had between them published five of her early books. Although Longmans had also published a handful of her titles in the United States in the 1920s (her four contemporary novels, and two Heinemann titles: *The Masqueraders* and *Beauvallet*), it was nearly ten years since Moore had sold one of her books directly to an American firm. In 1935, Doubleday Doran bought *Death in the Stocks* and published it under the title *Merely Murder*. Despite her early success in America with her historical fiction, Doubleday turned down *Regency Buck*. In Britain, however, Georgette's historical novels were growing in popularity. In that year alone Heinemann had reprinted *These Old Shades* three times (13,000 copies), *The Masqueraders* (8,000), *Beauvallet* (9,000) and *Devil's Cub* had sold an impressive 15,000 copies.

Georgette was disappointed about the American response to *Regency Buck* but certain they would

> take Regency Buck one day. I've been going through it to see where it can be improved, & – modesty, as you know, is my long-suit – I am inclined to think it is a classic! I don't really know how I came to write anything so good. I do remember putting in a lot of work on it – And <u>how</u> I loved writing it! The characters in it say "Very true" & "Depend upon it" & Their spirits get "quite worn-down", & it is "long before the evils of it ceased to be felt". And as for the Earl of Worth –! Talk of "Heyer-heroes"! He tops the lot for Magnificence, Omnipotence, Omniscience, & General Objectionableness.

She never did re-write *Regency Buck*. But it was the first novel about which she was prepared to claim: 'It <u>is</u> the best I've done, you know. Actual writing, & technique, I mean.'

Georgette rarely talked about her abilities, but *Regency Buck* was one of a handful of her books which prompted her to acknowledge her gift for telling a compelling story, creating unforgettable characters and writing convincing dialogue:

> Kindly note Purple Patch (Clarence's proposal). Carola Lenanton [Oman] paid me the biggest compliment I've ever had by asking me whether I'd found it in some unknown memoir, & "lifted" it for my book. She said (though I shouldn't repeat it) that "not one word was false, or out of place." I knew it was a High Light, but so few people know enough history to recognize it as such!

Although Moore had not been able to sell *Regency Buck* to the Americans, he did manage to sell it as a serial story to *Woman's Journal*. Serials and short stories were the lifeblood of magazine publishing in Britain between the wars. Readers often bought magazines because their favourite author's name was on the cover. For writers, serialisation of a novel prior to publication was an effective way of boosting book sales and a lucrative source of additional income. *Woman's Journal* was the most influential of several magazines published by the Amalgamated Press (AP) in London. To have a book serialised in it was a feather in any author's cap. The magazine's editor was the formidable Dorothy Sutherland, who would prove to be a thorn in Georgette's side for the next thirty years.

Dorothy Sutherland was only a year younger than Georgette, but equally determined to make her mark in publishing. She had joined Amalgamated Press in the early 1920s, where her talents were soon recognised with appointments to the editorship of a number of AP magazines. In 1926, when she was just twenty-three, she had become editor of *Woman's Journal*, a new magazine with a staff which for a time included the aspiring novelist Pamela Frankau and Edgar Wallace's elder daughter, Patricia – then two ambitious teenagers in their first jobs. Over the next forty years Dorothy Sutherland became one of the most powerful editors in magazine publishing in Britain and a legend in the industry. Tall, slim, dark-haired and domineering, she was a stickler for detail, famous for her sharp tongue and her immaculate dress sense. A strong, decisive woman, who operated a divide to rule policy, Dorothy Sutherland did not suffer fools gladly and was said to 'work all the hours God made' while keeping her private life strictly private.

While the editor and the author had many things in common (a clear case of like repelling like) there were two aspects of the editor's life of which – if Georgette knew of them – she would not have approved: Dorothy Sutherland was illegitimate and a lesbian. Although the nature of her birth had been largely obscured by her mother's marriage (when Dorothy was five) to the journalist and editor, David Sutherland, her sexual preference was well known at Fleetway House, where her talents as an editor were always the prime consideration. Under Dorothy Sutherland's direction *Woman's Journal* quickly became the firm's most prestigious, popular and successful monthly publication. By 1935, the list of authors published in the magazine read like a *Who's Who* of English literature. It included such well-known names as John Galsworthy, Edna Ferber, A.A. Milne,

G.B. Stern, Rebecca West, H.G. Wells, Hugh Walpole, Daphne du Maurier, Evelyn Waugh, Agatha Christie, Vera Brittain and E.M. Delafield. In June Georgette Heyer joined the list.

She and Dorothy Sutherland appear to have struck sparks from the first. The editor had initially incurred Georgette's disapproval the year before when she had serialised *Footsteps in the Dark* and *Why Shoot a Butler?* in another AP magazine, *Woman's Pictorial*. Dorothy Sutherland had changed the title of *Why Shoot a Butler?* to *Woman in Danger*, without notifying either the author or her agent. Georgette was infuriated, but not nearly so annoyed as when she discovered the insertion into her story of words she had never written. 'Do you know they had the bloody cheek to make a character of mine use the vulgarism "la-di-da"?' she told Norah Perriam. 'I am still furious.'

The following year she was even more incensed by the discovery that Dorothy Sutherland had re-named *Regency Buck*, *Gay Adventure*, with a caption that read: 'Gay Adventure – in the Dare-Devil Days when Men were Men and Women Seductively Coy!' above an illustration that made her strong-minded heroine look exactly like the sort of insipid female she despised. Georgette found this sort of take on her work maddening, for she worked hard to lift her plots, characters and dialogue out of the rut of stereotypical and formulaic fiction. The impression of *Regency Buck* created by the magazine made it almost impossible to convince those who had not read her novels that she could be anything other than a writer of 'frippery romances'.

She wrote to her agent to express her outrage: 'That Sutherland woman had the neck to write to me again, that she quite agreed an agent should settle the business details, but other points, <u>such as discussing alternative titles</u> we ought to deal directly over! I am so furious I can't bring myself to reply. She chose that <u>filthy</u> title, *Gay Adventure* (it makes me sick to write it) without <u>one word</u> to me!' Nothing incensed Georgette more than interference in her work and Dorothy Sutherland's meddling was something she would not easily forgive. The two women did not actually meet for twenty years but Georgette always referred to the editor as 'that Sutherland Bitch' or 'the S.B.'.

Despite her abrasive relationship with its editor, *Woman's Journal* would eventually become an important cornerstone in Georgette's career. In 1935 Dorothy Sutherland bought *Regency Buck* and the following year she published three of Georgette's short stories. It was ten years since Georgette had written one but she had decided to re-visit the genre after staying with her old friend Carola Oman (now Mrs Gerald Lenanton) earlier in the year. Both Carola and Joanna Cannan had enjoyed a good deal of success in writing short stories for magazines such as *Good Housekeeping*, *The Illustrated London News* and *Britannia and Eve*.

The magazines paid well and were an effective way of gaining exposure and enlarging their audience. Earlier in the year (before her breakdown), Georgette had stayed with Carola at Bride Hall, the Lenantons' beautiful manor house in Hertfordshire, for a week, and enjoyed a much needed respite from domestic cares. She had recently lost her cook and had yet to find a replacement. Since the War it had become much harder to find and keep good, reliable servants and any upset in Georgette's domestic arrangements inevitably affected her writing – as she told Norah Perriam after returning home: 'How I <u>loathe</u> domesticity.'

Her return to short stories resulted in 'On Such a Night', which her agent sold to an Australian magazine (so far the story remains undiscovered, with no indication of what it was about or the period in which it was set). Georgette told Moore she would be happy to do lots more if he thought he could sell them. A second story planned as 'Incident on the Bath Road' was delayed by her nervous breakdown, however, and she did not write it until after she had recovered. Her poor health persisted into June. The pressure of dealing with the unsatisfactory proofs of *Regency Buck* had taken their toll and Georgette found that 'neither pen nor paper inspire me with anything but complete mental paralysis.' A request from Heinemann for a photograph and biography also met with a negative response: 'I am having no more done. I'm past the age for that sort of thing. As regards the biographical details, I don't care about this either. My life isn't of interest – my books (I hope) are. I'm sick to death of chatty bits about authors, & LOATHE this form of advertisement.'

Although she had not been averse to publicity in the early years of her career, after her return to England in 1930 Georgette had developed a decided dislike for sharing personal information with the press and the public. She was not convinced of the need for personal publicity to sell books and would cite the case of Ethel M. Dell, a renowned recluse, whose refusal to grant interviews had no apparent effect on her enormous sales. Georgette begrudgingly sent Heinemann a nineteen-word biography. To her annoyance, a few months later she received a similar request from Doubleday, who wanted author details for the publicity for *Merely Murder*. This time she was even more explicit:

I will give no biographical details, for this country, Australia, or the States, or, in fact, any other place under the sun. The main dates & landmarks in my life anyone can know: I don't mind, but I will not submit to any sickening sentimental rubbish on the lines of "From her earliest years Miss Heyer has always, etc, etc." Nor will I have the details of my private life broadcast, or used for the sorts of publicity I detest. I was born in August 1902, & my literary bent was inherited from my father, whose translation of Villon appeared in 1925. I was educated at numerous high-class seminaries; I did not go to College, nor did I pass Matriculation or any other kind of examination. I attended History lectures given by the late Professor Forbes, who was (I believe) the history-professor of Westminster College. I wrote my first novel when I was seventeen, & published it at the age of nineteen, in 1921. In 1925, aged 23, I married G.R. Rougier, & in 1926 accompanied him to East Africa, where I remained until 1928. At the end of 1928 I went to Yougo-Slavia, [sic] where I lived for just over a year. I rather think we returned to England in 1930. My son was born in 1932. I live in Sussex, extremely quietly, have a rooted objection to personal publicity, & own two dogs & a cat. And you can embroider that as you please, but I'll be damned if I'll supply material for the sorts of nauseating soul-throbs dear to the American public.

On the last day of June, to Georgette's great relief, she, Ronald, Richard, his new nurse and Ronald's white bull-terrier, Jonathan Velhurst Viking, better known as 'Johnny', left for a fortnight's holiday at the Victoria Hotel, Bamburgh in Northumberland. They spent two glorious weeks walking, paddling, shrimping and exploring Bamburgh Castle. Determined 'not to do one stroke of work during July' Georgette had left her writing at home. Free of responsibility, she found herself growing stronger by the day.

She and Ronald spent the third week touring the Scottish Highlands with the bull-terrier, while Richard stayed behind in Bamburgh with his nurse. It was Georgette's first trip to Scotland and she told Norah Perriam that she had 'every intention of "going-all-Jacobite" so the Spouse & I will probably get a divorce before we're through'. In the end they had a glorious week travelling from St Andrews (where Ronald indulged in 'an orgy of golf') to Inverness and down the Great Glen to Fort William and Skye. They saw Loch Ness and visited Lochaber where Georgette 'mourned over the dead past' and Glenfinnan where 'Charles Edward raised the Standard'. It was to be the first of many happy holidays in Scotland. By the end of the trip she was completely recovered and ready to start a new book for Hodder.

13

With all due respect to Miss Sutherland, & without wishing
to appear unduly conceited, I do not think she can teach
me much about the <u>technique</u> of a murder story.

Georgette Heyer

A month after their return from Scotland Georgette had made a
rough start on the new detective novel. A request for a title and an
outline sent her to a favourite source for inspiration: 'Here I laid
down my pen & wandered over to the bookshelves, & took down
the Concordance to Shakespeare. I am now in a position to offer
H. & S. two titles. My own fancy is "Behold, Here's Poison". *Pericles.*
An alternative, but not so good, I think, is from *Romeo & Juliet*, V3.
"Timeless End."' She added a short synopsis and suggested that Hodder
'concentrate on my humour – that's what I'm getting a name for, &
I can assure you there's going to be plenty of it.'

She set *Behold, Here's Poison* in a fictional version of Wimbledon
and wrote most of the book while living in temporary quarters at
Broadbridge Heath. The family had moved out of Blackthorns after
deciding to renovate. Georgette found it impossible to write amidst
the continual noise of builders, painters, plasterers, carpet-layers, and
the sorts of interruptions from the housemaid ('"A-Gentleman-from-
Vi-Spring-to-see-you-ma'am"') guaranteed to prevent lucid prose. She
did manage to write the promised short stories before moving,
however, and her agent had no trouble selling 'Incident on the Bath
Road' and 'Runaway Match' to *Woman's Journal*. Georgette had

instructed Norah Perriam that under no circumstances should they be offered to 'the cheap "popular" magazines such as *The Red* & *The Happy*'. It was more than ten years since she had been published in those short-lived periodicals and Georgette knew how far she had come in a decade.

The disruption affected her writing, however, and nearly nine months after signing the Hodder contract for *Behold, Here's Poison* she was still labouring over the novel. It was unusual for Georgette to struggle with a manuscript but illness, domestic upheavals and a problem with her chosen murder method had all combined to delay its completion. Renewed money troubles only made things worse. In October she had taken out an overdraft of £400 to help pay for the house renovations and now she urged Moore to sell a film right to offset the cost. Georgette had always wanted her novels to be made into films but so far the various proposals from film companies had come to nothing and she knew she could not depend on a film sale to solve her immediate financial problems.

The sale of another short story, however, encouraged her to think that these might be a way out of her pecuniary difficulties. 'If I do one a month could you sell them?' she asked Norah Perriam. The stories were quick work for ready money, but the need to complete the book for Hodder and write a new one for Heinemann was also pressing and in the end Georgette could not maintain the pace. As she explained to her agent:

I'm glad Amalgamated Press like the new story, but don't divert my attention! How can I send you more when you keep on yelping at me to get on with this Sanguinary Novel? If I thought I could sell 6 short stories off the reel & cash in On the Nail I'd chuck the book & write the stories, because this furnishing racket is Awful, & I shall soon be at my wit's end for ready cash. Things mount up in the most ghastly fashion, & my damned Bank would only give me an overdraft for £400 instead of £500, which puts me in the soup. Why the blazes not one of those stinking film companies can see what a Super-film *Regency Buck* would make beats me. I despair of films – I expect Fate is going to be ironic, & I shall sell them when it doesn't really matter much.

A few weeks before Christmas Georgette finally had a breakthrough with *Behold, Here's Poison*. She had been feeling 'thoroughly depressed and unhopeful about the book until a Funny Bit flashed into my head, & looks even funnier when set down in black & white'. Her sense of humour had come to her rescue and by Christmas Eve she had done a 'Solid Wog [Georgette's word for wodge] of Good Matter'. Once she hit her stride Georgette usually got the words down quickly. She never had an editor and by the mid-1930s neither her agent nor her publisher read her manuscripts all the way through, or even at all, prior to publication. The draft she sent to her publisher was the book they published – usually without reference to a third party or professional reader (only in the last years of her life). Once the proofs had been dealt with and the book was on its way to the printer Georgette would destroy the original manuscript and start thinking of her next novel.

Blackthorns seems to have been conducive to writing. Over the next five years there Georgette would produce twelve books. Life in Sussex meant a large, comfortable home, at least two servants, a garden, fresh air, and dogs. Georgette had always had dogs and they were to be a feature of life in the country. Her pet Sealyham, Roddy, who had been with them in Africa, had died not long after Richard's birth and Ronald had acquired their pure-bred white bull-terrier instead. Johnny was an intelligent animal who ruled the roost at Blackthorns. Although he disliked other dogs, he liked people and adored Richard. As a toddler Richard would sometimes take his nap with Johnny beside him and Georgette once found her son fast asleep 'firmly clasping the large & grim-looking bull-terrier in his arms. How unhygienic, but such a nice picture!'

The family was back in Blackthorns in time for Christmas. Ronald's brother Leslie, his wife Tam and their two young sons, Michael and Jeremy, were to spend Christmas week with them. Georgette was fond of Leslie (now a Lieutenant-Colonel in the Lancashire Fusiliers) and Tam, though they did not have a lot in common, but she was not a fan of the festive season. Visitors for Christmas, new financial worries ('which doesn't mean Poorhouse, but cost of Drawing-Room Carpet, which is in some ways worse') and the need to finish *Behold, Here's Poison* only made the holiday a 'time of Unparalleled Stress'. The one bright spot was her acquisition of an Irish wolfhound puppy named Misty Dawn. Johnny the bull-terrier and Puck the Siamese cat deigned to accept the newcomer and Georgette told her family jokingly that she thought she 'would look well with a stately wolf-hound at my feet'. The new dog would also be a playmate for Richard. He was nearly four and his mother had already discerned a literary bent:

> My son is proving that there's a Lot in Heredity. He now tells us Stories, and I can assure you they abound in the professional touch. It is not enough for him to say: "The cow said...." He styles it thus: "Oh!" said the cow. We also have Thrilling Bits, such as: "<u>Suddenly</u> . . . he heard a Voice! And what do you think it said?" ME: "What?" – "It said Fee-fi-fo-<u>fum</u>!" ME: "Good Heavens, how awful!" –"Yes. And what-do-you-think-happened to him <u>then</u>?" – "I don't know: what?" – "He was all SHWIVELLED UP!"

Christmas came and went. She returned to *Behold, Here's Poison* and apologised to Hodder for not finishing the manuscript in time for their planned February launch. Since her nervous breakdown Georgette had found that she 'daren't sit up all night writing any more, 5.30 a.m. is now my limit, and that means early bed the next night'. A few hours sleep were usually enough to restore her energy, however, and she was always up in time to see Ronald and Richard in the morning. From 1928 this gruelling regimen enabled Georgette to write an average of two books a year for more than a decade.

But even this prolific output could not prevent them falling deeper into debt. By February Georgette was faced with more than £300 of unforeseen bills and no clear idea of how she was to pay them. She toyed with the idea of asking Ronald's mother to put up the securities needed to guarantee them an overdraft but as she and Mrs Rougier did not always get on this was a last resort. A few months earlier she had considered selling the copyright in one of her novels to Heinemann. She had fixed on £250 as a reasonable price but done nothing about it. She thought of writing a series of eighteenth-century short stories or 'hurriedly writing the Waterloo book, in the hope of serial rights', but a novel about the Battle of Waterloo was not the sort of book to be written quickly. She assured her bank manager that she would deposit 'substantial sums' into her account as soon as she received her latest advance and wrote despairingly to Norah Perriam: 'I don't quite know what happens next. Bankruptcy, I think. Something unpleasant, anyway.'

Georgette finally delivered *Behold, Here's Poison* to Hodder in February. Still smarting from her unsatisfactory experience with Heinemann's printer over *Regency Buck*, she insisted that Hodder print the book exactly as typed. The novel was scheduled for May publication but Georgette hoped she might earn some extra income from its serial sale because 'You never heard anything like the way the wolf is howling round our doorstep.' Determined to stave off financial disaster she returned to the short-story genre in the hope of a quick cash sale and within a day of finishing the Hodder novel had written 'Hazard' which she described as 'Quite too thrilling for words . . . Glorious drunken gambling scene with wicked step-brother staking his sister.' Two more short stories followed, but by mid-March Georgette had capitulated and written to her mother-in-law asking her to guarantee an overdraft of £700.

Despite having made over a thousand pounds the preceding year, Georgette was again spending her income faster than she earned it. She and Ronald had spent over £800 renovating Blackthorns (which they did not own). This, she confessed, 'out of income, takes some doing'. Even with the best estimates her earnings for the next six months would not exceed £1,200 and she was unable to see how this could be stretched to cover the household expenses, provide for her mother and Boris, meet her next tax bill and whittle down the overdraft. Georgette's calculations included the £500 advance for her next (as yet unwritten) Heinemann novel and £300, if Moore sold the first serial rights for the book. But this was hypothetical income; if she was to earn it she had to keep on writing. The stark financial reality was not made any easier by Ronald's decision to chuck in the shop and become a barrister.

Ronald had done his best to make a go of the sports store but by Christmas 1935 he could see that both the income and the long-term prospects were always going to be limited. He was not shy of work, but it had needed a considerable mental shift to switch from being a mining engineer living and working overseas to running a shop in a small country town in England. After a few years in the business, Ronald had begun to think seriously about pursuing his long-held ambition of reading for the Bar. He and Georgette talked about the possibility but they were never a couple who worked things out quickly. Major decisions took time, and from early in their relationship Georgette made a point of deferring to Ronald on financial matters. She was aware that she earned far more than he did and possibly always would. As a result she felt an unspoken obligation to accord him a degree of deference in matters which, in reality, she was quite capable of handling herself. Georgette cared deeply about Ronald, about his happiness and his well-being. When, early in 1936, he decided to take the plunge and pursue a legal career she fully supported his decision – despite the considerable cost involved. Accordingly, for the next four years, the burden of providing for their family came to rest squarely on her shoulders.

To become a barrister in England in the 1930s meant forgoing an income for at least three years while the candidate qualified. There were also admission fees, lecture fees and term dinners to be paid for, the cost of a wig and gown, and the expense of obtaining and keeping a place in an established chambers. Because a candidate could not accept briefs or be paid while reading for the Bar, the system effectively precluded anyone without a private income from becoming a barrister. Ronald applied for admission to the Inner Temple in the spring of 1936 and Georgette wrote to Norah Perriam to say, 'If you can think of any way whereby I can raise ready cash by my pen, pray tell me of it!' She had abandoned the Waterloo book and decided 'to write a light, saleable Regency novel which I rather think I shall call "Corinthian".'

She planned to set the novel in the same period as *Regency Buck* 'so that I need not waste time reading for it', and thought she could finish it in six weeks. A serial sale to *Woman's Journal* would mean a quick £300. So desperately did Georgette want the money to pay off her overdraft and release Mrs Rougier's securities that she was even 'toying with the idea of playing Hodders for a big advance on my period stuff'. But Ronald was 'dead against it. Says it is mortgaging the future, & I should not leave Heinemann without good reason.' She was feeling strained because her idea for 'Corinthian' had not crystallised and she could not think of anything else.

Having given up on 'Corinthian' she was beginning to despair of *ever* thinking of a suitable plot for a new historical novel. 'After several days brain-racking, during which time it appeared to me that I had Written Myself Out & couldn't think of any plot at all, a Wholly Glorious Novel burst upon me in the space of twenty minutes,' she told Norah Perriam triumphantly. 'Three hours work filled in the rough sketch, & the result is the accompanying synopsis, which I hope may convey something to you . . . Unless I've lost my gift for the Farcical, which I do <u>not</u> think, I'm going to perpetrate one of my more amusing & exciting works. The title is *The Talisman Ring*.'

Six weeks later she delivered the first half of the book to Moore. He easily sold the serial rights to *Woman's Journal*. Georgette had already forwarded the early chapters to Dorothy Sutherland, when Richard fell ill and required surgery. His needs naturally took precedence over her writing, but Georgette assured the editor that she would receive the rest of the book in time for publication. The moment Richard recovered she went straight back to her writing.

The Talisman Ring proved an ideal novel for serialisation: fast-paced and with plenty of the ironic comedy and unsentimental romance at which Georgette excelled. She set the novel in 1793 in the familiar countryside around Horsham, introduced an intriguing murder mystery and created an engaging cast of period characters to solve it. The first instalment appeared in *Woman's Journal* in August, with illustrations which gave Georgette 'a hearty laugh. Two ladies in full Victorian ball-dress in the middle of a winter's morning & staying in a country inn!' It was an amusing *faux pas* but it also reinforced her poor opinion of Dorothy Sutherland; Georgette cared a great deal about historical accuracy.

On 19 June 1936 Ronald was admitted to the Inner Temple and began his training for the Bar. He had sold the lease on the sports store and, despite the increased financial responsibility for Georgette, was relieved to be rid of it. In July, the family took rooms for a fortnight at No. 3 The Wynding, an Edwardian terrace house situated behind the dunes at the foot of Bamburgh Castle. This time Georgette took her typewriter, though she had no expectation of using it.[8] She spent the days on the beach with Ronald and Richard, 'sitting on the sands, or visiting Places of Interest', and letting her brain lie 'wonderfully fallow'. But even in this tranquil setting she could not escape her money worries.

Ronald's mother was becoming increasingly concerned about her still unreleased securities and Georgette wrote to Moore from Bamburgh urging him to wrest the money for *The Talisman Ring* serial from Amalgamated Press. Not even a £325 royalty cheque had sufficiently reduced her overdraft and an American proposal to produce *Merely Murder* for Broadway seemed a vain hope. Georgette could only conclude that she and Ronald would 'have to start thinking of a new detective story' as soon as they got home. It must have been a continual challenge: finishing one book only to have to almost immediately start the next. As Georgette expressed it to Norah Perriam: 'What a life!'

Home from her holiday, she was back at work by the end of August. She called her new detective novel *They Found Him Dead*, another Shakespearean title, this time from *King John*. Georgette hoped the book's 'general atmosphere of mystification and Fear' would convince

---

8 It is not entirely clear how much of her manuscripts Georgette actually typed and how much she wrote in longhand. In the late 1930s it appears that, regardless of how she wrote them, she paid a typist to type the final draft.

Dorothy Sutherland to buy the serial rights. She sent the first eight chapters to Moore and suggested that he remind reluctant editors 'why E.M. Delafield sells so well! – Because she draws lots of absurd & well-known types, & we all love laughing at people we know. That's what I've done.'

In *They Found Him Dead* Georgette took great delight in poking fun at various relatives and chance-met acquaintances. She had a knack for detecting a person's foibles and frailties and of writing them into her fictional characters. The new novel included 'a thumbnail sketch of a woman I met at Bamburgh this year; two Striking Portraits of my brother-in-law & his wife; one middle-aged Female Explorer ("Out in the Congo one gets used to facing danger"); one schoolboy with a strong predeliction for American gangster films.' And she clearly had Ronald in mind when she had Hannayside tell his sergeant that:

> "You think that if a man plays first-class football, and gets into the semi-final of the Amateur Golf Championship that he can't be a murderer!"
>
> The sergeant blushed, but said defiantly: "Psychology!"
>
> "Rubbish!" said Hannayside.

Georgette even took a satirical swipe at her own imperfections and domestic situation through the fictional Rosemary Kane:

> You see, I know myself so frightfully well– I think that's my Russian blood coming out . . . My grandfather was a Russian . . . I know I'm selfish, capricious, extravagant and fatally discontented . . . I wasn't born to this humdrum life in a one-eyed town, surrounded by in-laws, with never enough money, and the parlour-maid always giving notice, and all that sort of ghastly sordidness . . . I'm the sort of person who has to have money . . . you can say what you like, but money does ease things.

With her mother-in-law now 'agitating ceaselessly' for the return of her securities, Georgette knew only too well how money eased things. The lack of it was almost driving her to distraction with the result that her 'whole aim and object is to be free of this obligation'. Although she had succeeded in considerably reducing her overdraft and there were no longer renovations to pay for, general household costs had not abated. The uncertain nature of her income made it difficult to budget, and unforeseen expenses had made it impossible for her to completely clear her debts. She was only a few hundred pounds short of balancing the books: 'Once I'm straight I think all will be plain sailing, as I seem to be making a fair income, one way & another. That's why I'm so mercenarily minded at the moment, & lie awake praying for the American play to be a success, & for Fox Films to buy *Talisman Ring*.'

Despite her initial scepticism, *Merely Murder* was to be staged on Broadway. The writer was A.E. Thomas, a New York playwright whose play *No More Ladies* had been made into a film starring Joan Crawford and Robert Montgomery. Thomas regularly sent Georgette drafts of the *Merely Murder* script, but they did not impress her. She felt that he had veered down the vaudeville path and inserted into the story what she considered to be 'low comedy'. She asked Moore to inform Thomas that 'Wit & custard-pies don't mix. If he tries to introduce "mad situations" he will fall between two stools.' She also wanted the producer, Mr Blatt, reminded that 'the original reason for dramatizing the book lay in the quality of the dialogue', the characters' personalities and in the reader's uncertainty about Kenneth Vereker's guilt or innocence.

She would have liked to go to New York and collaborate on the play but felt it to be impossible. 'This play is not going to be as good as I could make it,' she told Moore, 'to correct by correspondence is very difficult, as I don't wish to hurt Mr Thomas's feelings. The ideal thing would have been for us to have worked together – he to plot the sequence, me to write the necessary dialogue. Reading this 2nd version has made me more than ever determined to do *Behold, Here's Poison* myself.' Georgette could see how easily just one successful script or screenplay would provide instant relief from her financial embarrassments. But her plan to turn *Behold, Here's Poison* into a play was short-lived because she was soon distracted by other, more pressing, concerns.

By the end of 1936 Georgette had grown concerned about Heinemann's handling of her books. She had given them nine novels in twelve years, none of which had needed discussing, editing or rewriting. If she was not yet an *instant* bestseller, her cumulative sales ran into the hundreds of thousands. Yet she felt there was little active interest from Heinemann in either her or her writing. She might have put up with what she saw as personal neglect if she had felt that the firm was doing its best to sell her books. But Hodder's successful promotion of *Behold, Here's Poison* seemed a stark contrast to Heinemann's approach: 'I notice that I have been dropped from Heinemann's advertisements,' she told Moore, 'I think this premature.' Nor was she happy with the presentation of her latest work: 'The wrapper to *Talisman Ring* is held on all sides to be cheap in execution & I very much object to having other books advertized in the end pages of mine.'

Burdened by her overdraft and strained by her efforts to produce enough work to clear the debt, she wondered if a change of publisher might not solve her money troubles. She knew Hodder were eager to acquire her historical novels and would pay handsomely for them. When Georgette discovered that she had again been left out of Heinemann's advertising, she put the idea of a change to Moore:

> My ire has once more been roused by the noticeable omission of my name from Heinemann's list in today's *Observer*. I don't know whether I wrote strongly enough to you on this subject in a previous letter, or whether you may perhaps have thought that I was merely suffering from a spasm of irritation. I'm not. I doubt very much whether you will succeed in getting me to sign a new contract with Heinemann. I don't deny that they are good publishers. What I feel more & more is that they are only concerned with their high lights. If you think it over, what is their utter unconcern over each book of mine but apathy? It is sometimes annoying to be badgered by your publisher for a synopsis of your new book, but at least it shows a keenness which seems to me to be lacking in Heinemann's organization.

My complaints against them are several. First, they apparently regard me as a certain seller up to a certain number of copies, & see little point in trying to push sales beyond that maximum. Second, they do not advertize me. Third, they seem to be unable to get the book reviewed . . . As regards the advertizing I do not wish to be told by C.S. Evans that he does not believe in advertizing. No such disbelief seems to deter him from billing continuously works by Dunsany, Somerset Maugham, Maurice Baring, & Masefield. Well, those are big names, but my point is that if Evans is only concerned with these he is not the publisher for me . . .

I've been with Heinemann for a number of years now, & I don't really want to change, but I wonder whether I've been with them too long? They don't care <u>what</u> I produce. Had they written to me that they didn't think *Talisman Ring* quite up to the mark these doubts wouldn't exist in my mind. But they didn't. They probably haven't read it. And I feel certain that the comparative failure of *Regency Buck* is attributable to their apathetic handling of my work. It was "another Heyer" to them, cast out to sink or swim like the rest. But had Hodder handled it might it not have rivalled David Murray's *Regency*? [This moderately successful novel about a woman named 'Regency' and three of her identically named descendants has faded into obscurity.]

I want you to think the situation over carefully, and to glance at my contract. Am I tied up past this book? And I'm not a bit interested in the slow increase of sales. I have just seen what Hodder could do with a book like *Poison*, as against what an inferior publisher did with a far better book, *Death in the Stocks*. And a prejudice against Hodders, a liking to be amongst Heinemann's authors isn't going to weigh with me if once I am convinced that Hodder would put me over bigger. How much do Hodder want my romances, and what are they prepared to pay for them?

Moore conveyed the gist of her letter to Heinemann who did not respond. It did not help that there was no one at the firm specifically responsible for her. Georgette would have liked a more personal relationship with someone at Heinemann, but it was difficult. She did not like the Chairman, Charles Evans, and, unlike other Heinemann authors, she did not make a habit of calling in at the firm's headquarters at 99 Great Russell Street to discuss her work or check on the progress of her latest novel. Although other successful Heinemann writers, including J.B. Priestley, Somerset Maugham and Francis Brett Young, expected – and received – a good deal of personal attention and support from the firm, this had never been Georgette's style.[9] She was mostly content to remain in Sussex and write.

Busy with her work, she put her concerns to one side and got on with correcting the proofs of *They Found Him Dead* and the script for *Merely Murder*. Things were not going well with the play, which was depressing for she had counted on the income from the production. Without it Georgette could see herself being in 'just the same financial muddle next spring as I've been in this year'. She was also depending on *Woman's Journal* buying *They Found Him Dead* and was endeavouring to meet Dorothy Sutherland's request for cuts and changes.

Georgette hated doing this sort of abridgement and ended by giving the editor permission to insert whatever 'drip' she considered necessary to achieve a greater 'stress on the love interest'. She still did not really trust Dorothy Sutherland to handle her work appropriately – especially after the editor had altered her short story title 'Pharaoh's Daughter' (after the card game Pharaoh or Faro) to 'Lady, Your Pardon'. Georgette thought this 'lousy'. Her only comfort was that she did not have to read *Woman's Journal* and that the money for the serial rights for *They Found Him Dead* would go a long way towards clearing her overdraft: 'By my own Herculean efforts I've

---

9 One of Heinemann's stars, Francis Brett Young was 'not an easy author. More than once, when he felt his books had not been given enough publicity or some minor thing went wrong, he threatened to find another publisher, but his large and regular sales ensured that he was treated as a VIP, being allowed the use of the private flat at the top of Great Russell Street.' He also expected Evans to closely read his manuscripts and to discuss in detail his plans for his next novel.

paid off £800 overdraft – & now to be faced with a new one is too dispiriting for words! Ora pro nobis!' [Pray for us!]

But her prayers went unanswered for in December King Edward VIII abdicated to marry Mrs Wallis Simpson. The change in the Succession meant a change in *Woman's Journal* editorial policy. Dorothy Sutherland felt that a murder mystery was not wanted in an edition about the abdication and the Royal family and consequently had decided not to serialise *They Found Him Dead*. Georgette received the news in mid-January and immediately wrote to Norah Perriam:

> I think Miss Sutherland might well be jolted. She really is not treating me at all fairly. When you consider that I rushed the book on so that she might receive it early in December, & further made alterations in the story at her request, & handed them in three days before Christmas, her dilatoriness is not only inconsiderate but extremely rude into the bargain. I do not wish to hear from her that the altered succession is to blame . . . Saving your presence, she is treating me to a startling example of the folly of Woman at the Helm. A bigger example of incompetence than this going into a flat spin would be hard to come by.

The cancellation of the planned serial left Georgette with a gaping hole in her finances. It was too late to sell the serial elsewhere, for Hodder were publishing in May.

Incensed by Dorothy Sutherland's dilatory rejection she instructed her agent that, in future, 'If Miss Sutherland refuses the M.S., or postpones its publication in serial form to the prejudice of H. & S's publication of it in book form no further MSS of mine are to be offered to her.' Georgette had begun a new book which, though 'not precisely a sequel', followed on from *Regency Buck* (successfully serialised in *Woman's Journal* eighteen months earlier). She was sure Dorothy Sutherland would want the new manuscript for her magazine – though she would get it only if she 'pulls herself together and sends you a cheque', Georgette told Norah Perriam. 'If she finds it incredible that I should be prepared to sever relations with her you can, if you choose, tell her that her handling of my work has from start to finish been an annoyance to me; her criticisms always seem to me illiterate, & her alterations even more so. Accompany these compliments by any rude gesture that suggests itself to you.' But no cheque was forthcoming; Dorothy Sutherland apparently wanted neither *They Found Him Dead* nor the new book and it was to be ten years before Georgette again had her work published in *Woman's Journal*.

14

Like Brummell, I am <u>very</u> good at Depressing Pretension.

Georgette Heyer

By March 1937 Georgette's concerns about money, serials, play-wrights, *Woman's Journal* and her publishers' inadequacies had vanished before the 'welter' of material she had gathered for her new novel about the Battle of Waterloo. She was even more enthusiastic about the book than she had been about *Regency Buck*:

> My whole attention is centred upon Waterloo, so that nothing else has much reality. I even had a dream wherein I argued absurdly with Ronald about who was in command of the 1st Brigade of Guards. I was right too! I have now "gutted" 26 works dealing with the campaign, the soldiers, the officers, etc, & could draw you, with tolerable accuracy, a detailed plan of the battle, placing the brigades with exactitude, & a great many of the regiments. The house's littered with huge sheets of 3-ply, to which are pinned maps, plans, & god knows what. Poor dear Ronald has Waterloo for breakfast, lunch, tea & dinner.

She could already 'see heavenly bits' and, although 'There's not a speck of adventure (in the style of the *Talisman Ring*)', she was convinced that she could carry the story off with 'only the triangle of one girl and 2 men, & the crashing climax of Waterloo'. The girl was to be Lady Barbara Childe, a direct descendant of characters in *These Old Shades* and *Devil's Cub*. Although Georgette acknowledged that the novel was 'not precisely a sequel' and later admitted 'that Dominic couldn't have had grand-children of mature age in 1815', she felt that the characters' popularity was such that her readers would forgive a little poetic licence. (Georgette's son later explained that his mother never intended it as a true sequel to *Devil's Cub*. Rather, that she gave Mary and Dominic Alastair parts in the novel 'as a sort of friendly wave to previous readers'.)

It was April before Georgette lifted her head from her Waterloo research but when she did, it was to fire another shot across Heinemann's bow. She had been stirred to anger about the firm again by a local bookseller friend ('A woman of brains and education, she worked for many years at the F. O. [Foreign Office], so is to be respected') who had raised concerns about the absence of Heyer cheap edition titles from Heinemann's spring list. Her criticisms reminded Georgette that Charles Evans had not replied to her last letter and she suggested to Moore that he 'have a shot at forcing a quarrel with Heinemann'.

Evans's silence was unusual, for he had a close working relationship with most of the firm's well-known authors. As John St John observed in his history of Heinemann, Evans was seen as a man who 'understood and liked authors and in turn they liked him'. Except for Georgette. For some unknown reason she and Evans did not get on. While he was not the kind of cultured, charming, handsome man she liked, he inspired great affection in most of those who knew him and was famous for his ability to recognise talent and spot the potential bestseller. It was Evans who had signed John Galsworthy, Somerset Maugham, Margaret Kennedy, J.B. Priestley and Francis Brett Young to Heinemann and he may even have signed Georgette in 1925. Evans was admired by many in the publishing industry and he had a special gift for recognising 'potentially successful "broadbrow" fiction' – exactly the sort of book at which Georgette was proving so proficient. It is possible her books were not to his taste and there may have been an element of social snobbery on both sides.

Whatever the cause, by June Georgette had heard nothing from

Evans or anyone else at Heinemann, and she wrote again to Norah Perriam:

> I am so dissatisfied with the firm that at the back of my mind there lurks a half-formed resolve to write my Waterloo book, & then to put it by. Any rubbish will do for Heinemann. Unless I get some sort of satisfaction out of Evans I'll see him dead before he handles my new book. If, as I begin to suspect, he has no longer any interest in my work, would he perhaps like to tear up the existing contract? I know what your arguments are against forcing Heinemann to pull their weight, but I don't think I entirely agree with you. If there were but one more book due to them I should hesitate to hot them up. But I'm tied up for two more, & frankly I see little sense in sitting by while they do their best to see that my works are still-born. If they want to keep my name on their list they will presumably put their backs into the job of selling me. Provided they do this I'm prepared to stay with them. But I can see no harm in either you or L.P. telling Evans what my feelings are in the matter. I hope that in "Colonel Audley" I am going to turn out something a great deal better than anything I have yet achieved. But if Evans is looking for 'another of Miss Heyer's entrancing romances' it won't do for him. Either he does what he can to put it over big, or he doesn't get it.

Feeling she had dealt satisfactorily with her publisher she returned to her writing.

After four months of intense research, Georgette had filled several notebooks with detailed information about the Hundred Days – from Napoleon's escape from Elba to his final clash with the British, Belgian and Prussian armies at Waterloo. She made careful notes about every aspect of the campaign: from weaponry and uniforms to topography and troops. She created a detailed chronology, wrote biographies of the major historical figures and made notes on all of the contemporary accounts of the battle she could find. She also drew several large, detailed maps of the Battle showing the movements of the French, British and Prussian regiments throughout the day (these maps still exist and have been preserved along with Georgette's remaining notebooks and private papers by the Heyer Estate).

The Duke of Wellington was a major focus and she read all his letters and dispatches, making copious notes and lists of his sayings and speeches. Her study of Wellington eventually caused her to change her original opinion of the man: 'I came to curse & stayed to praise. I set out disliking the Man Wellington very cordially, but by God, you have to hand it to him after all! He is going to loom very large indeed, as is proper.' She made a point of using his words wherever she could throughout the novel, drawing repeatedly on the twelve volumes of his dispatches and telling her readers in an Author's Note that, although it meant Wellington's words were at times chronologically inexact, she had felt impelled to use them because they were far superior to anything she could have written.

Initially 'scared to death of Wellington', she had 'finally brought him on with a trembling pen. But no sooner was his hook-nose well into the book than he seized the pen from my hand and practically wrote himself.' She eventually suggested to her agent that:

> If Heinemann want to make a "point" in their blurb they might hint gently that I've done Wellington a fair treat. I think I have. This is not as conceited as it sounds . . . I do feel that wherever I may have failed it is not with the Duke. He simply slipped out of my pen on to the paper. I felt all the time he was right. He dam' well ought to be – I couldn't tell you how many books I've read dealing with him!

Georgette had written almost half the book when she finally received a detailed letter from Charles Evans addressing her concerns. But his response only irritated her more and in a seven-page reply she told her agent exactly what she wanted communicated to Heinemann:

I have read Evans's letter three times, & each time I read it, it annoys me more. I want certain things quite definitely brought to his intelligence. The first point I wish to make is that during the many years of my having been with the firm I have not troubled them with vain complaints. To the best of my recollection I have <u>never</u> before complained that they were not doing their best for me. When *The Conqueror* only sold moderately well, & caused no comment at all I blamed myself, not Heinemann. I think I was right: it wasn't a seller. But I then wrote *Devil's Cub*, & in so doing hit on a manner that suited me, & which the public seemed to like. Since that date I've turned out 3 swiftly moving &, I think, amusing romances. My sales have increased as one would expect them to. If they had <u>not</u> I wonder how long Heinemann's [sic] would have kept me on their list? My point is that my publishers, seeing that I'd found my right style, sat back (so far as I have been permitted to see) and said: "Isn't that nice? I wonder whether the next will increase too?" They didn't see in me a "rising market", & thrust me on for all they were worth. They continued to push the books out just as they always had, selling them quite adequately & never brilliantly.

I used to blame myself but having had experience of H. & S.'s methods I've now changed my mind. No one will make me believe that I <u>really</u> write terribly good thrillers, but H. & S. are making the public think so, & have shown me clearly what <u>can</u> be done in the way of increase of sales. If Evans should say, Ah yes, but modern books are easier to sell, he might be told that H. & S. would pay heavily to get my period stuff.

Regency Buck, though Mr Evans may not know it, was a darned good book. It was accurate down to the smallest detail, & had popular appeal as well. The firm handled it <u>damnably</u>, & allowed Murray's book, *Regency*, a lot of which was cribbed from mine, to get well ahead . . .

When I review my dealings with the firm during the past five years at least, I realize that every year I have sent them a book, into which I quite honestly put the best of which I was capable. I have never received from any member of the firm the slightest hint either of appreciation or of disappointment. I have no reason to suppose that my books are even read. If I am late with delivery no inquiry is made. No one bothers me for a synopsis for the purposes of advance advertizing. Such an apparent apathy has the firm in its grip that I wonder sometimes whether any one would notice if I missed a season. I don't know whether the firm likes my humorous stuff, or my more ambitious essays. They have never told me. I sent them *Talisman Ring*, which I knew wasn't quite up to standard. They didn't tell me so. Was it tact, ignorance, or apathy?

Since I have been with H. & S. I have noticed certain outstanding differences between them and Heinemanns. Long before I have set pen to paper H. & S. want a synopsis of my new book. Annoying? Yes, maddening, but at the same time I realize that they're putting their back into the job. When I deliver the MS to H. & S. they take the trouble to write a pleasant little note about it. It may mean nothing, but it is a pleasant change from the Trappist silence brooding over Great Russell Street.

Without wishing to dig up old bones, I should rather like Mr C.S. Evans to cast his mind back to the publication of *Devil's Cub*. If he has forgotten I have not that no one in his firm realized that that book was the sequel to the *Shades* which I'd so often been asked for. <u>You</u> told them so, but not until we'd kicked up a row did they make the slightest capital out of it. Ever since that date I've had a mistrustful feeling about the firm. Nothing that has been done by the firm since has allayed that feeling.

Evans wants to have a talk with you, I see. Well, please let it be snappy! What I <u>want</u> is to terminate the contract. I can't do it, but I should be delighted if he would. I don't want him to handle my Waterloo book. Perhaps it won't be very good – I don't know, but I'm sure it won't get any help from Evans, who will publish it in the same old style, & think how nicely he's handled it if it sells a couple of thousand more than *The Talisman Ring* did. That sort of increase might be satisfactory were I today writing my third or fourth book instead of my twenty-third.

In conclusion I object strongly to the tone of Evans's letter & I hope you do too. His lawsuits are no concern of yours, & I fail to see why they should be offered as an excuse for inattention to business. An air of injured dignity pervades the letter. It is not for him to feel injured. That is my prerogative. My last book was dropped from their lists very early in its career; Norah wrote several letters to Evans which were all of them ignored; my name did not occur in the Spring Booklet; *The Marriage* (or is it *The Buck?*) was not brought down to 3/6 on publication of the new book as has been the rule with all my others – & then Evans has the infernal cheek to write that he doesn't understand what I have to complain about. Well, lack of courtesy will do to begin with, & this I am unable to ascribe to anything but lack of interest.

For your private ear, I am increasingly uneasy about the firm. Have you seen their new list? It is shocking. My bookseller friend is ordering only one Heinemann novel this season – and I may say she keeps a goodish stock in her shop. All the old authors seem to be gradually drifting otherwhere. I know Margaret Kennedy left because she was fed-up with them. I shall be the next.

My standpoint is that if Evans puts his back into the Waterloo book – à la H. & S. – & I am satisfied that he really did do his best for it I shall have no reason to leave the firm, whether the book sells well or ill. I think it should be put to him quite clearly that as far as I'm concerned the Waterloo book is the crux of the matter. I may have to give Heinemann one more – but if they make me feel that another firm would have sold more of Waterloo I can assure them that I shall put no extraordinary pains into the final book for them.

Four days later she had made rapid progress with her Waterloo novel and wrote a chatty letter to her agent with several entertaining extracts from the manuscript. She told Moore about Wellington, explained that her hero had fallen in love with Lady Barbara ('a pity, but can't be helped') and ended by suggesting to her agent that he tell Evans 'What a Noble Work the book is'. This apparent turnaround in her attitude to Evans – albeit temporary – was typical of Georgette. The truth was that she hated confrontation.

It was one thing to voice her anger and indignation in a letter to Moore and to ask him to 'have a shot at forcing a quarrel' with the firm, and quite another to actually engage in the argument herself. However strongly worded, Georgette's letters were nearly always one step removed from their intended target. She expected her agent to absorb the full force of her displeasure, distil her comments, and ultimately take responsibility for their communication. She repeatedly left it to Moore to decide how much and what part of her grievances should be conveyed to her publishers and, whether he liked it or not (and there were times when she clearly made him very uncomfortable), she expected him to be a buffer between her and those she chose to criticise. It was not a courageous stance, but it was generally as close to direct confrontation as she was prepared to get with anyone outside her small, safe circle of friends and relatives. Georgette's ability to express her feelings on paper gave her an outlet, and she sometimes lashed out with her pen in a way that she never would have done in person.

That summer the Rougiers went to Cornwall for a month's holiday, taking Richard and his governess, Miss Butler, with them. This time Georgette also took her manuscript. While Richard and Miss Butler swam at Kynance Cove, played, explored and went sailing with Ronald, Georgette got on with her writing. She joined her family on some of their expeditions around the peninsula but confessed that she was 'too busy to see much of it'. She was working

> knee deep in maps, despatches, roll-calls, & a welter of notes, & spend frenzied periods searching for a forgotten piece of information. I've never done anything that required more work, & have to make notes for each chapter – first, the political events; 2nd, what I wish to quote from Despatches; 3rd, what the fictitious people are to do; 4th, which real characters must drift through again. My hair will shortly be white, I expect.

She had yet to write the Battle chapters and still had not settled on the book's title. She had so far rejected *Colonel Audley, At Waterloo,*

Loud Sabbath, Sepoy General, The Crowded Hour, Doubtful Battle, But Still in Story, A Damn Nice Thing, Unless With Victory and *Arm, Warrior, Arm.*

She managed to complete the first fourteen chapters on holiday. With the manuscript written in longhand she begged Norah Perriam to find her a typist 'Who will come to my house, complete with machine, & take the book at my dictation.' It meant having a stranger at Blackthorns but Georgette explained that 'It wouldn't be for many days, & if she was of the typist-class she could consort with my governess in the evenings. If not, it wouldn't matter.' In the end, Norah Perriam found her the ideal person. Sylvia Gamble stayed at Blackthorns for a fortnight while Georgette read aloud, 'complete with punctuation', from her manuscript which Sylvia took down in shorthand before typing it up.

It was obvious to Sylvia that Georgette took great pride in her subject, and she later described her as having 'a beautiful brain' and an 'ordered intellectual apparatus' which liked nothing better than to be immersed in meticulous research. Georgette had taken great pains over her Waterloo book and frequently found herself struggling with the 'welter of contradictory information' which made it 'difficult to know what was accurate and what not'. After months of hard toil, however, she felt able to declare: 'I have done my best: at all events I can quote chapter & verse for everything I say of the <u>real</u> part of the story.'

The book was almost finished when she suddenly found the title: 'Whoopee! I've got it at last, & it's a Peach! You needn't bother to hunt around for any more suggestions; this is Final. <u>Forgive, Brave Dead!</u> It comes out of that beautiful Scott poem, the *Field of Waterloo*.' She was delighted with the flash of inspiration and felt that it was just the sort of title to 'catch the eye; it has a ring; & it disarms criticism from all these who feel inclined to say, who are <u>you</u> to write about Waterloo?' She was well aware that some of her readers and reviewers might feel that she did not have the credentials to write a book with so much military history at its heart. But her ability to combine history with story was one of Georgette's great skills and her account of the Battle of Waterloo (the final ten chapters) would eventually become recommended reading at the Royal Military College Sandhurst. She had become very protective of her Waterloo book, rating it much higher than any of her previous work and she desperately wanted it to be a success: 'I hope that the book will be liked. I am too close to it to have a very clear idea of it. All I know is that it has entailed a tremendous amount of work, & I have loved doing it, & feel a bit shattered by it.'

With the manuscript finished she hoped that her agent or someone at Heinemann would read it and give her a professional opinion. When Charles Evans's joint managing director took an interest in the novel she was delighted. He even had decided views about its title. Georgette was no longer sure of her choice of *Forgive, Brave Dead* and had offered her publisher an alternative; she was pleased to discover that the director's choice 'coincides precisely with <u>my</u> preference!' His name was Alexander Frere-Reeves and the preferred title was *An Infamous Army*.

15

Presumably, if you continue to hand over the goods your sales are bound to increase a bit.

Georgette Heyer

Frere-Reeves came into Georgette's life at a time when she was predisposed to like anyone at Heinemann who would respond positively to her books: 'I was extremely pleased to find, from my conversation with you [Norah Perriam] this morning that Mr Frere-Reeves is inclined to take this book of mine seriously.' She sent him a detailed summary of the plot and several suggestions for the cover design and was gratified to receive from him a rough sketch of the proposed dust-jacket. 'I find it an excellent design,' she told him. 'It is very much "in period".' For the first time Georgette felt that there was someone at Heinemann who understood and appreciated her work. But Frere-Reeves's interest in her work at this time was only temporary, for it would be another year before he took a permanent role in her writing life and she still had several unresolved grievances against the firm.

'Anxious to hear an unprejudiced opinion' of the new book, Georgette gave one set of proofs to her bookseller friend and another to her mother (although Carola still sometimes read her manuscripts, Georgette no longer sought Joanna's input). Sylvia often read her daughter's novels in draft, but in recent years Georgette had found that she no longer valued her mother's opinion as she once had and tended to dismiss her views if they did not concur with her own. In the end neither reader gave her the response she wanted: 'My book-seller friend thinks I shall bore my schoolgirl public – which I don't mind – and says she personally longed for more "Wellington bits." My mother – quite the man in the street – is now reading it, and is uninterested in the Wellington-bits (I think bored, too) but seems to like the romance – which I think rather poor.'

Disappointed, she begged Moore to read it: 'I wish – if you've a spare reading-evening anywhere – you'd take one of the proof-copies home, and read it. I want a professional opinion badly.' But neither Moore nor Frere-Reeves nor anyone else at Heinemann apparently read *An Infamous Army* prior to its release. While it was a measure of her success and reliability as an author that neither her agent nor her publisher felt the need to read her manuscripts, in this instance Georgette felt badly let down. She was obliged to wait until publication to see how the book was received.

An Infamous Army was due out in November. In the meantime she had promised Hodder a new detective novel. They were keen to receive another thriller from her for *They Found Him Dead* was selling well and Georgette's reputation as a crime-writer was growing. She had written a general outline for the new book but was waiting on Ronald who was 'largely responsible for the plot'. This usually meant explaining to Georgette how the murder was committed and leaving her to tell the story. But Ronald was busy with his Bar exams and she could not give Hodder a synopsis until after they were over.

She had received several good reviews for *They Found Him Dead*, but not everyone admired the novel. A young tobacconist's assistant wrote demanding an apology for a speech uttered by the fictional hero's mother (who has just met her son's fiancée for the first time):

> "Jim tells me you are going to be married. I should think you'll suit one another very well. It's always been my dread that he might marry something out of a tobacconist's shop so you can imagine what a relief it is to me to know he's had the sense to choose a really nice girl. Not that I'm a snob, but there are limits, and young men are such fools."

Georgette's reaction to her reader's letter was frank: 'I can see not the slightest reason for encouraging her,' she told Norah Perriam. 'I don't write for that kind of person, after all, & if she chooses in future to ban me from her library list it's all the same to me. What is more, there is nothing to be said. I should regard it as a major tragedy if my son were to marry a tobacconist's assistant.'

But the reader's letter was a reminder that there would always be those who read her contemporary novels and related them to their own lives and circumstances. Several years after the tobacconist episode Georgette received a complaint from a solicitor whose name she had unwittingly given to an unattractive minor character in another of her thrillers. In neither book had she deliberately set out to offend her readers – she was writing fiction after all – but the incidents did emphasise the advantages of setting her novels in the historical past. No one could take offence at the snobbery and injustice inherent in the social hierarchy in Regency, Georgian or Medieval England. Georgette could write with impunity about such things as the perceived inferiority of the lower classes, the disastrous consequences of an ill-judged marriage or the moral hypocrisy of the aristocracy, sure in the knowledge that her readers could not object to behaviour, ideas or attitudes that were a matter of historical fact.

In October came the news that Doubleday Doran were thinking of publishing *An Infamous Army* in America. Though pleased by the interest in her cherished novel, Georgette thought that 'On a pure matter of policy, it would be a mistake.' She worried that allowing Doubleday to bring out her Waterloo book when they had already turned down *Regency Buck* ('to which this new book is almost a sequel') would not necessarily enhance her reputation in the United States. Her fears proved unfounded. Doubleday did a splendid job with the novel, and the American reviews were excellent. Georgette's uncharacteristic anxiety about the potential American reaction to one of her books reflected her feelings about *An Infamous Army*. She thought it her finest novel to date – and held great hopes that it would be well received by the British critics.

When *An Infamous Army* came out in early November, Georgette pounced on the newspapers and was devastated when no review of it appeared the first Sunday after publication. She instantly wrote to Moore to tell him of her 'failure':

> I suppose you've seen that both the Sunday papers have ignored *An Infamous Army*. It may be my fault for having failed, but nothing will ever convince me that I should have fallen so flat with another – any other – publisher. I think the newspapers must dislike Heinemann, for how is it that Longmans & H. & S. never fail to get their books reviewed? The blurb that Heinemann wrote of the *Army* makes me sick – but what could I expect, when the man whose business it is to write blurbs sent me a specimen with the cool information that he had not been able to read the book? I am feeling so dispirited, that the grave seems the only tolerable spot to be in.

Her reaction was premature. Within a week reviews of *An Infamous Army* appeared in all the major papers and the one in *The Times Literary Supplement* must have pleased her:

> Here is a romance of which the historical details are presented not merely with astonishing care and accuracy–bibliography and maps all complete–but with a comprehension of the essential features of the Waterloo campaign even more unusual, and which yet holds from first to last our keen interest in the fate of the principal personages . . . The meaning of the opening moves of the campaign is better grasped than in some historical accounts, and there is even a sound criticism of Wellington's strategy . . . For Waterloo we take our places on the field as spectators, and if a battle has ever, in fiction, been more vividly and accurately described from the point of view of a staff officer hurrying from one part of the line to another, one cannot recall an instance. The ordinary reader will find these episodes good, but he will not realize just how good they are.

The *Daily Mail* was even more enthusiastic: 'One of the clearest and most balanced accounts in the English language of the Hundred Days . . . A brilliant achievement.'

Unfortunately, Georgette's original view that Heinemann had not done its best for *An Infamous Army* prevailed, and she found herself dreading her future with the company. Within a day of the reviews appearing she wrote to Moore outlining her 'burning grievance against the firm'. Her perception was that Heinemann made 'just enough money to make it worth their while to stick to me while they can – but not enough for them to think it worth their while to push my work'. She thought the firm could have done a lot more to promote *An Infamous Army* and Georgette's diatribe was directed mainly at Charles Evans. The chairman's apparent indifference to her concerns was surprising from a man who was renowned for his shrewd and energetic handling of so many popular authors and their books. Evans had been ill, however, and he may have thought her complaints trivial and unwarranted (although he had frequently taken the time to soothe other writers' ruffled egos). Whatever the cause, his perceived indifference to her writing prompted Georgette to shelve plans for the serious historical book she had been intending to write about Princess Charlotte, the Prince Regent's ill-fated daughter. Georgette's bitterness over what she saw as Heinemann's neglect of her endured for over a month as letters passed back and forth between her and Evans via Moore to the satisfaction of neither party.

What Evans had failed to perceive was the degree of Georgette's emotional involvement in *An Infamous Army* and that in giving Heinemann the novel she had 'handed them the best of which I was capable. I put my whole heart into that book, and I did expect my publishers to put some of theirs into its production.' She now felt this had been 'touching but misplaced confidence', for not only had the head of the editorial department, Arnold Gyde, failed to read her book before writing its blurb, but 'some meddlesome and illiterate' person had also taken it upon himself to change her spelling and punctuation after she had passed the proofs for publication. This was intolerable: 'What I cannot stomach is an intellectually conceited person tampering with my work without so much as a by-your-leave. One would have thought, moreover, that the perusal of my book, and its bibliography, would have made him a little chary of interfering with the work of one who obviously had made a fairly profound study of her subject.' To Georgette, these egregious actions by members of Heinemann's staff were not to be borne.

Had he been involved in the correspondence, Frere-Reeves might have been able to smooth things over and allay her concerns – something which Georgette herself acknowledged:

> In justice to Mr Frere-Reeves, I should like to say that while he was in charge I had nothing to complain of. Whether he was interested or not, he at least assumed an interest, and by his tact and courtesy, and his way of answering letters immediately without any moan about being too harassed by libel-cases to attend to anything else, did much to reconcile me to my fate in having to give another book to a firm which prides itself on being able to say that my sales have not actually dropped-off.

If he ever saw it, Frere-Reeves would have derived a good deal of satisfaction from this letter, for he and Charles Evans had been adversaries from their first meeting in 1923. Then Evans had been manager of the firm and Frere-Reeves a Doubleday protégé. In 1927 Frere-Reeves was made a Heinemann director and in 1933 he was appointed joint managing director of the firm. Evans strongly resented what he saw as an incursion into his territory and there had developed a mutual dislike and a rivalry between the two men which had not abated over time. Georgette's complaints against Evans aroused Frere-Reeves's interest and he deliberately set out to succeed where his rival had failed. It cannot have been a difficult undertaking. Georgette's resentment was palpable and she was ripe for attention and a sympathetic ear.

On 3 December 1937, *Merely Murder* opened on Broadway at the Playhouse Theatre. Three performances later it closed. For Georgette, it was a disappointing finale to a long drawn-out series of re-written scripts, renewed options, changing playwrights and producers. She was not surprised by the play's failure and it only increased her scepticism of similar proposals for adapting her work for the theatre. She had already been discouraged by Frank Vosper's play script for *Behold,*

Here's Poison in which he had 'cut out the wit & added nothing to replace it'. Neither Thomas nor Vosper had succeeded in conveying the inherent humour in her novels and Georgette herself declared 'if a success is to be made of me I must be treated in my own vein – that of broad comedy.' She and Ronald thought of writing a play themselves but never made the time for it. Instead she put her comedic gifts to work on a new detective-thriller.

By the second week of January she had produced 20,000 words of draft, 'some of it quite funny,' she told Norah Perriam. 'You'll be glad to hear that the corpse is discovered on the first page, & there is no assembly of characters to be sorted out.' A month later she delivered the completed manuscript to her agent. She originally thought to call it *Blue Murder* but on finding the title had been used changed it to *A Blunt Instrument*. It is, in some people's estimation, Georgette's masterpiece among her detective novels and even 'Torquemada' of *The Observer* called it 'the best, and for want of a better adjective – the truest of Miss Heyer's detective novels' (Georgette confessed that she 'almost let it go to my head!'). Her creation of Malachi Glass – a dour, evangelical police constable given to uttering reproving Old Testament scriptures to anyone he meets – certainly set the book apart.

Within hours of completing *A Blunt Instrument* Georgette was planning her next novel. Renewed troubles with her cash flow had also prompted her to consider writing some short stories for *Woman's Journal* 'to frighten wolves with' and she hoped to sell the serial rights for *A Blunt Instrument* to Dorothy Sutherland as well. Her interest in serial rights had been re-ignited by the sale of *An Infamous Army* to the *Australian Women's Weekly*.

Georgette was becoming increasingly popular in Australia, where her historical novels had been successful from the first. Her 'colonial' market included Australia, New Zealand, South Africa and Canada and reliably brought in several hundred pounds annually. A few years earlier Georgette had sold her rights in those and her European markets to her mother 'for a token sum – persuading her that by buying them she was really doing me a favour, and saving me from Sur-tax demands!' It was a generous act which gave Sylvia financial independence and saved her from the indignity of having to ask her daughter for money. Although Georgette often found her mother frustrating and difficult she loved her and was genuinely concerned for her well-being.

That spring Georgette signed a new contract with Heinemann for her next three historical novels. In recognition of both her selling power and her improved relations with her publisher the terms were better than in previous agreements with a significantly increased advance of £750 for each book. Frere-Reeves had taken over management of the author and her novels and he responded to Georgette's writing in a way that made her feel valued by the company. At a time when the world around her was becoming increasingly uncertain and insecure, this meant a great deal.

16

Let me tell you (for my biography) that neither by training nor by temperament am I suited to Domesticity.

Georgette Heyer

Across Britain there was talk of war and concerns were felt in many quarters about Hitler's intentions in Europe. Since the mid-1930s, Britain's response to Germany's increased militarisation had been appeasement: a policy of acceptance in the interests of peace – of conciliation rather than confrontation. Georgette herself had recognised the anti-war mood in England when, nearly a year earlier, she had suggested possible dust-jacket designs for *An Infamous Army* and told Moore that 'It may be felt that a battle scene would not be popular in these pacifist times.' She was a regular reader of *The Times* and the *Morning Post*, and liked to keep abreast of politics. A lifelong conservative and decided Tory voter, she was also one of many in Britain who approved of Prime Minister Neville Chamberlain's policies – believing that a plan for peace was better than a declaration of war.

The idea that war was impending pervaded British life throughout the late 1930s and each of Georgette's historical novels written between 1936 and 1939 was about war. After *An Infamous Army* was published she decided to write the story of Charles II's escape from Cromwell's England following the Battle of Worcester in 1651. Once again, she read avidly and set about visiting every house and inn at which Charles had rested or hidden during his perilous flight to

France. Sylvia Gamble returned to Blackthorns at Georgette's request and accompanied her on several of these expeditions which she later described as 'immense fun'. In April Georgette ended a hasty letter to Moore: 'No time for more. On the road to White-Ladies, & the dawn at hand.' It was to White-Ladies Priory that Charles II had fled after the Battle of Worcester.

Once she had her material in hand, Georgette began writing with her usual verve and speed. The early part of the book came together quickly. In May, at her request, her agent forwarded the first eight chapters to Dorothy Sutherland in the hope of a serial sale. The editor had already turned down *A Blunt Instrument* on moral grounds (an explanation here would spoil the plot), but Georgette refused to be discouraged. That summer she insisted that each new batch of *Royal Escape*'s chapters be sent to Dorothy Sutherland for consideration. But the editor did not think the book a promising serial (the *Australian Women's Weekly* disagreed; they successfully serialised the novel the following year). Georgette finished *Royal Escape* in four months and dedicated it to Norah Perriam, who had recently left Christy & Moore due to ill-health and would not return. With Norah gone, Georgette returned to her old habit of writing regular letters to Moore. She told him that she hoped *Royal Escape* 'will not be a long, dull book!' But his concern was the timing of its publication.

By September 1938, Hitler had intensified his demands for the Sudetenland and Britain was desperately and rapidly re-arming. Chamberlain flew twice to Germany to negotiate peace but Hitler would not alter his demands. War seemed inevitable. Air-raid trenches had been dug, gas masks issued, and Heinemann's London headquarters evacuated when Chamberlain signed the Munich Agreement on 30 September. He flew home to proudly brandish the Accord and declare 'Peace in our time.' Georgette expressed the feelings of many when she told Moore: 'What a relief! If only we haven't ceded too much!' Like others she was unhappy about the British government's conciliatory response to Germany's territorial aggression and was far from convinced that war had been avoided. For the moment, however, it was a welcome reprieve, although she could not help regretting the ill-timed release of her 'poor, unfortunate book': *Royal Escape* had appeared on the bookstands four days before the Munich Agreement was signed.

Although subscriptions were up on those for *An Infamous Army*, Georgette was not optimistic about *Royal Escape*'s success in a time of war. Not even Arnold Gyde's enthusiasm for the novel (this time he assured her he had read it) nor his promises of publicity encouraged her. 'What's the use of publicity now?' she asked Moore. 'This ghastly European situation will kill my book as surely as anything could.' But the novel's success or failure was a minor concern in the circumstances and Georgette was 'too much occupied with this ghastly situation and necessary precautions' to think about her work – although she assured her agent that she would carry on writing if war began and requested a meeting with Hodder to discuss the sort of book they would be wanting if the peace did not hold.

Hodder & Stoughton were delighted with sales of Georgette's thrillers, but what Percy Hodder-Williams ('Uncle Percy') really wanted was her historical novels. While this had been a possibility during her tussle with Charles Evans, the advent of Frere-Reeves into Georgette's writing life marked the beginning of a change in her relationship with Hodder. She had found in Frere-Reeves a mentor, whose kindness and 'unsolicited sympathy' over *Royal Escape* had been a soothing balm after her previous experiences with Heinemann. A month before that novel's publication she had lunch with Frere-Reeves in London – one of her earliest meetings with him – and afterwards had told Moore that 'I find him quite a Man & a Brother, & he seems to understand me when I speak, which C.S. [Evans] never did.'

It was after that lunch with Frere-Reeves that Georgette first expressed concerns about Hodder's handling of her detective novels: she felt they were taking too long to bring out her books in the cheaper 3/6 edition and 'deprecate[d] very sharply their keeping my thrillers hanging on at 7/6 long after they have virtually ceased to sell'. The criticism was a very different take on the firm which, only a few months earlier, Georgette had held up to Charles Evans as an example of the ideal publisher whose management of her books was infinitely superior to his own. Frere-Reeves was a clever advocate for Heinemann. Once he became aware of her, like Percy Hodder-Williams, he quickly recognised Georgette's value to the firm and could not regard her continuing relationship with a rival publisher with complaisance. He also realised that to have Georgette Heyer writing exclusively for Heinemann would not only be a feather in his publishing cap but also a point scored against his rival, Charles Evans.

A keen chess and bridge player, Frere-Reeves was a born strategist who, once he had an agenda, liked devising ways and means of achieving his ambition. In this he was not unlike Georgette herself and as their relationship developed the two of them found that they had a good deal in common. He was well-read, cultured, and keen on golf and cricket – both Rougier passions – and he had a charm which she found very appealing. Frere-Reeves was also a Cambridge graduate, a past editor of *Granta*, and had served in the Great War. In those things at least he must have reminded Georgette of her father. His exclusive address in Albany in Piccadilly, his distant connection to John Hookham Frere (a British diplomat during the Napoleonic Wars), his sense of humour (described by one of his editors as 'bitchy') and his understanding of the various pressures besetting Georgette, all combined to make Frere-Reeves a very desirable new friend. At the end of that first lunch together he had set the seal on Georgette's approval by gallantly escorting her to Miss Lennox-Carr's 'Registry Office for governesses' and telling her of his own two children. It was the beginning of a friendship which would endure for more than thirty years.

Georgette was trying to ignore the 'depressing political situation' and get on with her new detective novel when the new governess arrived (Miss Butler had left suddenly to care for her ageing parents). Richard had grown used to Miss Butler's lively ways and the change was an adjustment. Now six, he was an energetic little boy with a vivid imagination and the sort of sense of humour which came from living mostly amongst adults. Although his parents spent time with him when they could, there was always a nanny or a governess to take care of him while Ronald was studying for the Bar and Georgette was writing.

Richard grew up in an era when the British middle- and upper-classes believed that good manners included physical and emotional restraint. In many families it was usual for fathers and sons to shake hands and for hugs and kisses between parents and children to be low-key, controlled and kept to a minimum. Georgette herself appeared not to believe in public displays of physical affection. The Rougiers were not a tactile family and neither Georgette nor Ronald the sort of parents to engage with their son in rough-and-tumble games or other childish activities. As Richard grew older they encouraged him in the sorts of pastimes that they enjoyed: Ronald taught him to fish and play golf and gave him clubs to practise with on the lawn; Georgette read to him and praised his attempts to write stories of his own, and they both taught him to play bridge and other card games.

It was not an unhappy childhood, but Richard was often lonely. He spent much of his time outdoors, playing in the garden with the dogs (whom he adored) or exploring the woodland near the house. Ronald sometimes collected him from a kindly neighbour on his way home from work. Mrs Towse lived at the end of the drive and remembered Richard telling her that he was 'lonely, as Mummy is busy writing' – a complaint echoed by Georgette's mother who sometimes caught the bus from Horsham to visit her daughter at Blackthorns. Driven by persistent financial pressures and her own compulsion to write, Georgette did not always confine her writing to night-time hours. Richard was proud of his mother though and from a very young age remembered her talking to him about her novels. He once asked Mrs Towse: 'Do you read her books?' When she explained she had just finished *These Old Shades*, he told her: 'Mummy says, "I could have written it much better."'

Early in 1939 *Royal Escape* appeared in America. Despite feeling 'dreadfully depressed' about the book and doubtful that it would appeal to American readers, Georgette was pleasantly surprised by the enthusiastic reviews in *The New York Times*, *The New Yorker* and *The Saturday Review*. British sales also exceeded her expectations. Frere, as she now called him (in July, he would drop the Reeves and change his name by deed-poll), showed her 'some nice-looking figures': in just three months *Royal Escape* had sold nearly 8,500 copies in Britain – 1,500 more than *An Infamous Army* and 3,000 more than *Regency Buck* – and the figure did not include the Christmas sales.

They lunched together again and Georgette found that she 'like[d] Frere more the more I know him'. It helped that he knew exactly how to encourage her:

> He was awfully tactful about the *Princess Charlotte*, & did not ask me if I was writing her! He assumed (correctly) that I was working on a book for Uncle Percy, & merely inquired, in a voice of resignation, whether I wanted to miss a season. I assured him not, so he said as long as I didn't hand him the book on 1st Sept. for autumn publication, all would be well. We had a talk about advertizing & he told me how he has advertized *Royal Escape*, which seemed to me a good way. He also told me it was easy to sell me to booksellers, & why. So I purred gently.

As much as Percy Hodder-Williams wanted her historical novels, Frere wanted Georgette's detective fiction. While he was resigned to her continuing with Hodder if that was her preference, his first priority was the Heinemann list. Frere made a point of telling Georgette about Heinemann's policy of 'bringing out a cheap edition of the last book at about the same time as they publish the new one.' The following day she again questioned Moore about Hodder's policy of delaying the release of her novels in the cheap edition: 'I feel most strongly that to keep a book lingering on at 7/6 long after its sale is exhausted is wretched business . . . People wait for my books to come down to a cheap price, & I know that they are continually asked for. But if one delays too long, I think one runs the risk of the public's forgetting that particular book.' As Heinemann's star gradually rose in Georgette's eyes, so Hodder's began to fall.

17

I've made every conceivable kind of muddle over my income.

Georgette Heyer

By early spring Georgette had written well over half of *No Wind of Blame*. Although she thought the new thriller very good fun she doubted 'whether it will please Uncle Percy'. She was aware that Percy Hodder-Williams's religious views were likely to be a stumbling-block and she ruefully told Moore that in this latest book she had created

> One of the grandest comedy-situations I've handled yet. But I won't pretend that it's quite nice, because it isn't. I never write smut, nor have I a liking for prurient minds– preferring the broader, Elizabethan style! I can only tell you that some of the sallies have made Ronald shout with laughter – but they have also made him wonder "what-Uncle-Percy-will-say." One good thing is that Uncle Percy can't say much, because if he turns it down Frere would snap it up.

The novel was another of her Hannayside and Hemingway mysteries, though with Hannayside now in a minor role allowing the newly promoted Inspector Hemingway to take over the case. The plot featured a 'highly technical' murder devised by Ronald which Georgette described as 'so obscure that although several vital clues are presented to the reader right at the start, I think it will be an exceptional reader who (a) recognizes them as clues, & (b) grasps their significance'.

Explaining Ronald's ingenious murder method was not easy and the book reflects some of the drawbacks of their collaboration. Most of her detective novels were the sum of ideas from two quite different minds and her vision did not always mesh successfully with his. This was especially true in *No Wind of Blame*, about which Georgette later confessed: 'I DID know, broadly speaking, how the murder was committed, but I didn't clutter up my mind with the incomprehensible details. Ronald swears that he came home one evening when I was at work on the final, explanatory chapter and that I said to him: "If you're not busy, could you tell me just how this murder was committed?"'

While Georgette did not regard her thrillers as 'her real work' (and sometimes described them as potboilers), according to Richard his mother enjoyed writing them in the same way she enjoyed 'tackling a crossword puzzle – as an intellectual diversion before the harder tasks of life have to be faced'. Some of her reviewers disapproved of the humour in *No Wind of Blame* (not being in keeping with the genre) but the novel still sold well. At a time of growing political tension many readers welcomed the entertainment value of Georgette's books.

By February she was desperate to get the novel finished and receive the £300 she hoped Dorothy Sutherland would pay for the serial rights. Georgette was facing a growing financial crisis of the sort she had described a year earlier in *A Blunt Instrument*: '"There's nothing more uncomfortable than not having any money, and being dunned by tradesmen. Receiving To Account Rendered by every post, with a veiled threat attached, and totting up the ghastly totals–".' She had herself been holding off her creditors (including her mother-in-law) and 'shelving bills until I've cashed in!' and was desperate for the Hodder royalties and the *Woman's Journal* payment. It was a blow when the Hodder cheque was less than expected and Dorothy Sutherland turned down the detective novel.

Worse still was a letter from Moore warning her of possible problems at Heinemann. She instantly replied:

The news you convey about the bad season is most disquieting. Are you trying to prepare my mind for a drop in Heinemann's royalties? If that happens, I'm done, & I quite honestly can't see any way out of the mess. To have sold the serial rights well in the new book would, I think, have saved the situation for the moment, but I see little chance of that now. I'm by no means sure that there ever was a chance. As the thing stands, the advance on the new book, the American royalties, & the Heinemann cheque will leave me about £150 overdrawn at the bank – with debts of about £300 to pay. It just doesn't add up, does it?

With Ronald and her extended family still dependent on her, the financial problems which had haunted Georgette ever since the move to Blackthorns now threatened to overwhelm her. She had written nine novels in five years but was still beset by mounting bills and seemingly endless debt. It was intolerable. With a royalty income many authors would have envied, Georgette knew her financial situation should have been different:

It must seem odd to you that I __am__ in this mess. The fact is, I borrowed from the bank to furnish this house, & have never been able to get straight since, on account of the heavy expenses that have crashed on our heads, over Ronald's bar training, & other such things. This is between ourselves of course. My overheads are pretty heavy, as well, but if I gave up this house, which I may be forced to do, & moved into a villa somewhere, & did with one maid & no governess, I question whether I should ever be able to keep up my literary output. As you know, I find it a bit of a struggle as things are now. It's this blasted monetary worry. If I were a great artist, I should flourish under adversity, but alas, I'm not, & when I'm going round & round in my vicious circle, wondering how to acquire the next penny, my mind refuses to work on paper.

Paradoxically, her only means of alleviating the financial burden that prevented her from writing, was to write. Georgette struggled to come to grips with her dilemma:

I expect to finish the new book within the next ten days, & will bring it in as soon as the last word is typed, & trust to you to wring the advance out of H. & S. in record time. I will then start to work for the Heinemann book, but I am troubled by the few months at my disposal, & wonder whether I must yet once more shelve *Charlotte*, & do something easy. And yet that's such bad policy – oh dear, how difficult life is! And all the time there's a book in my head that would be terrific – & would take me a year to do. I do wish my useless mother-in-law would die. Things would be so simple then! Wouldn't Frere, & the public, & every one else just gulp down an Elizabethan book – not high life, but Alsalia,[10] [sic] Abraham-man, mariners & that fascinating London life of the period? Oh, L.P. I've had it in my head for years, & never found the time to study for it yet! It's a grand story, too, & in the richest of backgrounds – not food for babes & sucklings, but I think really big – very long, of course.

Georgette wanted literary kudos. If she could not write Princess Charlotte's biography she thought perhaps a grand Elizabethan novel set in Alsatia (the area of London where criminals could legally claim sanctuary until 1697) would impress the critics. Her ambition had veered towards the serious novel – though she would never allow herself the freedom from either financial or family cares to pursue it properly.

Her unfeeling remark about Ronald's mother was indicative of the stress she was under as well as the strain she sometimes felt caring for her extended family. Nor did it help that she still had not managed to release her mother-in-law's securities. She had reduced the overdraft but not enough and she felt the weight of the debt very much. A few years earlier Jean Rougier had moved to Sussex to be nearer her son and daughter-in-law and the closer proximity had not enhanced relations between her and Georgette. Age had not diluted the acidity of Jean Rougier's tongue and as she grew older she needed increasing amounts of care and attention. A good deal of this responsibility fell to Georgette and there were times when she resented it – particularly when it interrupted her writing.

---

10 Georgette meant Alsatia.

Alleviating the financial pressure meant producing books in fairly quick succession. To write the serious novels she envisioned meant a long delay between advances and this she could not afford. Georgette's talent had become both a source of pleasure and a burden and sometimes she found herself wishing that: 'I were a Victorian Little Woman, & not a wage-earner. It is a vicious circle, you know, if I were to devote a month to the writing of shorts, I should be late with the Heinemann book, & that would be fatal. Oh well! I suppose one day I shall look back & smile at these agonies.' But her financial woes were set to continue for some time.

Her concerns about money prompted her to query again Hodder's handling of the cheap editions of her detective fiction. Since the advent of the 6d Penguin paperbacks in 1935 and the success of Gollancz's 2/6 hardback editions, with their eye-catching yellow wrappers, competition in the cheap edition market had become fierce. Yet, despite her objections, Hodder insisted on selling their cheap editions at the uncompetitive price of 4/. Georgette urged Hodder at least to match the Gollancz price of 2/6 but they refused. Their slowness to act shook her confidence in the firm and she told Moore that she would 'retire from public life before I let H. & S. get their talons on my real work'.

Her real work was her historical fiction and she returned to it in mid-March. She had been lent Sir George Scovell's (1774–1861) unpublished diaries, and his account of his experiences in the Napoleonic Wars re-ignited an old ambition. She had first thought of writing a book about 'Smith' in 1922 and now she began gathering material for a story about Harry Smith, the famous soldier of the 95th Rifle Brigade who became governor of the Cape Colony (the South African towns of Harrismith and Ladysmith were named after Harry and his wife). This time there would be no need for a fictional romance, for Harry had met and married his aristocratic young Spanish bride, Juana, on the battlefield after the fall of Badajos. Once again, Georgette immersed herself in the contemporary sources and set about weaving the Smiths' adventures into the daily drama of battlefield life. She drew heavily on Sir Charles

Oman's 'monumental' *History of the Peninsular War* and would later thank Carola's father for his 'kindness in searching for an obscure reference on my behalf'.

Georgette had written 25,000 words of the new novel in just three months when family demands again interrupted her work. Richard was unwell and her mother-in-law was becoming increasingly incapable, with a form of dementia then called cerebral anaemia. Mrs Rougier needed regular attention, and Georgette admitted 'I shan't be able to do much this month, what with mother-in-law, & then Richard's operation.' The local shops were demanding payment and she urged Moore to 'wring the royalties out of all publishers' as the latest cheque would 'settle a few outstanding accounts, but only a few'. In May Ronald had been formally admitted to the Bar and was beginning to get briefs, but it was a slow business and it would be some time before Georgette would feel that the burden of financial responsibility was no longer hers alone. She was a little cheered by her first appearance in *Who's Who* in 1939, but these were difficult times both on the home front and abroad, and Georgette could not help thinking that her new book was 'the only bright spot in an otherwise god-forsaken existence'.

The situation on the Continent had worsened through 1939 as Hitler had pushed further into Eastern Europe. In March Chamberlain had pledged Britain's defence of Poland in the event of a German invasion. Georgette did her best to ignore the gathering storm clouds and get on with her writing. In mid-August she sent the first few chapters of *The Spanish Bride* to Moore with a detailed outline of the book. She was pleased with her progress and thought 'the story would serialize very well. It will be all incident, & love-stuff.' She hoped Dorothy Sutherland would buy it. She had also been asked to write a modern serial for a new magazine and, needing the cash, had agreed to do it under a pseudonym. She had thought of 'the nucleus of a nice story for the serial, but haven't worked it out yet. Sort of paraphrase of *Regency Buck*, in modern dress, & much shorter.' But she could not write it until she had finished *The Spanish Bride*.

Faced with what she saw as a dire financial situation, Georgette sought advice from Moore:

The bank is getting very restive, as the overdraft is over £1000. I've explained to them about not being able to finish my book, & thus pay in £750, but meanwhile I must reduce the thing to reasonable proportions, & have said that I'll do so. I want £500. £300 to bring the overdraft within limits of my securities – at least, my <u>mother's [in-law]</u> securities; £170 to pay 2nd instalment of Income Tax, overdue; & £119 to pay an outstanding account . . . It seems to me that if we are to anticipate royalties I must cover that, or find myself in a worse mess next year. If you could sell the *Bride* as a serial for £300–£350, & get me £300 for the pseudonym work, I should have done it – but how chancy! I honestly don't know which way to turn, & it's fast getting me down. My head begins to swim, always a bad sign. It would be awful if I went in for another of my nervous breakdowns. I try not to let myself think too much, but it's difficult when letters come from the bank, demanding instant attention.

To add to her woes, her domestic arrangements were in disarray and she was having to cope with 'no servants, except one daily help, very rough – I spend my time cooking.' Ronald was working in London most days and Richard's imminent operation meant at least three weeks of convalescence at home when he would need her attention. With the advance for *The Spanish Bride* looking increasingly unlikely before the new year, Georgette struggled to think of some other way to bring in some money. Heinemann had recently sent *Royal Escape* to Alexander Korda, the film director, and she had a brief hope that Korda would buy it. But it was not to be, and Georgette was left to ask Moore: 'Will you let me know what you propose doing? I'm dreadfully sorry to be such a nuisance to you, & there's no sort of reason why you should be bothered with my idiotic affairs. It is nice of you to help me.'

A fortnight later, her personal anxieties faded before a much greater concern. On 1 September 1939 Germany invaded Poland. Two days later the British Prime Minister announced that the deadline for Germany's withdrawal had passed and that 'consequently, this nation is at war.' In Britain people expected an immediate start to the fighting and bomb shelters were built, defences laid, and city children evacuated to the countryside before the combatants settled into what became known as the 'Phoney War'. For months little happened as both sides attempted to negotiate an end to the war. Some people were lulled into believing that the crisis had passed, but Georgette remained sceptical.

The declaration of war was the worst in a series of events that left her feeling low. 'I'm too tired & dispirited to think of another [story],' she told Moore. 'I suppose I shall have to try & finish the book, & must start night-work again. It won't be ready for anything earlier than January publication, if that. I wish some German would come & drop a bomb on me. It would solve all my problems.' Her money troubles seemed set to continue and when Dorothy Sutherland turned down *The Spanish Bride* on the grounds that it was too heavy for her readers Georgette was not surprised. Richard's operation had meant putting the novel to one side anyway and the only writing she had done during his convalescence was a light-hearted Regency short story entitled 'Pursuit' for *The Queen's Book of the Red Cross*. Georgette was one of fifty 'distinguished authors and artists' asked to donate their services to Queen Elizabeth's (later the Queen Mother) special fund-raising anthology.

Georgette picked up the threads of *The Spanish Bride* again in November, however, and at a lunch at the Heinemann headquarters at Kingswood was able to report good progress. Kingswood was the home of Heinemann's Windmill Press. Opened in January 1928 it was located in rural Surrey just outside Greater London and had a printing press, bindery, warehouse, offices and a staff of 150. Heinemann had evacuated to Kingswood after war was declared, leaving just a skeleton staff at its London office. Georgette did not often go to Kingswood but she enjoyed her day there that autumn: 'We got along very well, though it was tacitly accepted that Frere has the handling of my work. But the party – Evans, Frere, Oliver,

Hall,[11] & myself, was most cheery, & everyone was flatteringly full of interest in the Smiths.' Gratified by their response to *The Spanish Bride* she returned to Sussex delighted to know her novel was being taken seriously.

The Kingswood lunch further consolidated her friendship with Frere. Afterwards he gave her a copy of Antoine de Saint-Exupéry's recently translated account of his experiences as an aviator in the 1920s. Two days later Georgette wrote to Frere directly to 'thank him' for *Wind, Sand and Stars*:

> Damn you for giving me a book like that on the very day that you urge me to finish my own by Christmas. To start with, one can't put it down, & to go on with it puts one out of conceit with oneself, & convinces one that one's (the deadly snare of "one" I observe!) own book ought to be thrown into the dustbin. But it's quite lovely, isn't it? The most elusive, fragile piece of work. Both R. & I are entranced by it. Oh dear! It's a real book, & what in hell are the rest of us playing about at? What's it like in the original? What a power of phrase the man has! . . . Talk of purple patches! Why, Frere, you can open it anywhere & find a passage that leaps to your eye! Well, I'm quite disgruntled, & I can't think why I ever embraced the profession of scrivener. Was it really as effortless as it seems? No, I think not. <u>Surely</u> only rigid pruning could have achieved that perfection. You will say, there speaks the journeyman writer.

She was unsure about pruning her own *Spanish Bride*, which at 160,000 words was to be one of her long novels. Although Georgette got 'the horrors from time to time, & am cross with one or two chapters', she thought it 'definitely Nice Work'. She enjoyed breathing life into dry historical documents and teasing out the human qualities in iconic historical figures: Wellington was already 'making a nuisance of himself, & trying to steal the stage'. Thinking he might be concerned about the book's length, Georgette reassured Frere that:

---

11 B.F. Oliver and H.L. Hall were Heinemann directors.

The worst book I ever wrote – the sort of book that makes you wake up shuddering in the night was 160,000, & you ought to know that it still sells hotly. I wish to god it wouldn't. Do you think that one day we could consign everything to the literary dustheap that I wrote before *The Masqueraders*, & change all the awful inversions in <u>that</u> one? My god, I had occasion to look something up the other day, & I'm damned if it isn't a Come-April [sic] book.[12] Oh, I'll let you keep on with those damned *Old Shades*, just because I need the characters again. [Going by the word count and considering only those books written before *The Masqueraders*, the 'worst book' she ever wrote appears to have been *The Great Roxhythe*.]

She also promised him that: 'If (bribe coming) you can send me any information about Richard B. Frere, gazetted 1st lieut 21 Aug. 1810, in 1/95, I'll not only feature him, but I'll dedicate the book to his illustrious descendant!' She finished the manuscript a week before Christmas, kept her promise and dedicated it 'To A.S. Frere'. She was sorry to see the end of the novel, for she had found real satisfaction in writing it. Between them, *An Infamous Army* and *The Spanish Bride* had kept alive her dream of one day writing a grand historical novel. But the world was at war and events were in train which would shift the direction of her writing and change many things forever.

---

12 It is not clear what Georgette meant by 'a Come-April book'. I have tried various avenues of research, including a query to the Oxford English Dictionary, but have been unable to find the phrase or its meaning.

18

I now have a very definite & over-mastering desire to throw
off a Regency trifle – a <u>bubble</u> of a novel: romantic, improbable, & – we hope – a little sparkling.

Georgette Heyer

The new year brought fresh challenges. Georgette's plan to write
the new Hodder thriller and the pseudonymous magazine serial had
not come off. She felt uninspired and by February still had not begun
either the thriller or the serial. Ronald did his best to help her
through her difficulties. Aware that financial pressure had prompted
her to accept the magazine proposal he tried to offer a more considered view, advising against the pseudonym story, which he felt would
not do justice to her talents, and urging her to concentrate on the
Hodder book instead. Georgette gave up the pseudonym serial reluctantly for she had wanted the money badly. Instead, she decided
that as soon as the Hodder book was done she would concentrate
on 'turning out a *feuilleton* [serial], or some shorts, or start work on
Henry V, or pass out'.

The idea for a book about Henry V had been in her mind for
some time. She was a great admirer of Shakespeare's historical drama
King Henry V, with its themes of patriotism and English bravery
and its memorable speeches: 'Once more unto the breach' and 'We
band of brothers'. The play had always been popular in times of
national crisis. In the current clime Georgette felt that a novel (to
be called *Stark Harry*) about the English victory at Agincourt would

be well-received. Her agent was less convinced and she felt compelled to reassure him: 'My dear L.P.! I do hope you will rid your mind of the idea that Henry V will be as faulty a work as *The Conqueror*! I never was more depressed than when I read your grim prophecy. And if it isn't a damned sight better than the *Army* (which has always filled me with a sense of satisfaction) it is time I packed up.'

Money troubles meant that the detective novel took precedence over *Stark Harry*, however, and life became increasingly fraught as Georgette tried to start the new novel and deal with increasing debt, renewed health problems and the inevitable consequences of war. Although rumours of a German invasion had so far come to nothing and Hitler had not yet launched his attack on the west, it was expected that hostilities would soon begin in earnest. Boris had already enlisted, Frank was intending to join up and Ronald had begun considering ways and means of getting past the eyesight problems which had kept him out of the Great War.

Although Georgette would not have attempted to dissuade her menfolk from fighting, their decisions to do so only added to a strain already exacerbated by a lack of domestic help and a general feeling of malaise. 'I can't remember when I've felt so utterly finished,' she told Moore. She felt ill and tired, with no resistance: 'If any one sneezes near me I at once develop a cold; the slightest draught gives me neuralgia; & a stupid companion makes me so irritable that I can scarcely contain myself.'

Dealing with the proofs of *The Spanish Bride* was also demanding: 'After reading it nine times I can scarcely like it, but there is one point about which I was doubtful: the timing is good. Nor is it, as I feared, just one dam' battle after another . . . Frere says he knows it is a good book – but I suspect him of trying to cheer a lady whom he knows to be practically moribund.' The only bright spot on the domestic horizon was the possibility of a cook. It would be a great relief to have that particular burden lifted from her, although Georgette was proud of her efforts to keep things going at home during such a difficult time: 'Considering the state of my blood-pressure, it hasn't been bad going, has it? I've done all the cooking, looked after my young, & written a hugely long & intricate book.' Increased rationing had not helped. Petrol, butter, sugar, bacon and meat were already rationed, with tea, margarine, cooking fats, cheese and fruit to follow. But even more disturbing from Georgette's point of view was the announcement of paper rationing.

With publishers' paper allocations set at just sixty per cent of their consumption in the twelve months before the War, paper rationing was a grave concern for the industry. Once rationing began it was the unenviable job of Heinemann's management to work out which books to publish and which not. As John St John explained in *A Century of Publishing*:

> Evans, Hall and Oliver were faced each week with difficult decisions over the allocation of the paper quota, so as to preserve a reasonable balance between the old and the new. The annual number of new titles dropped from a yearly average of 181 in the 1930s to an average of 55, *viz*: 1940–98; 1941–63; 1942–53; 1943–36; 1944–38; 1945–45. Among books by the established stalwarts were *The Corinthian* and *The Spanish Bride* (1940) by Georgette Heyer.[13]

Georgette had less to fear from paper rationing than many writers, for as a well-known, popular author she was virtually guaranteed publication. But paper rationing affected more than just the number of books and authors published. To maximise paper usage margin widths, fonts, and book sizes were all gradually reduced. Headings disappeared and cheaper, lighter paper and softer cardboard covers with plain utilitarian jackets became the order of the day. Three of Georgette's wartime books would appear with plain wrappers.

But this was for the future. In early 1940 these stringent

---

13 Some publishers, such as Macmillan and Penguin, had a much easier time during the War because their sales in the previous year had been so large. In 1938/39 Penguin had sold millions of copies of their Pelican and Penguin Specials editions while Macmillan benefited from the enormous sales of Margaret Mitchell's bestseller *Gone with the Wind*.

restrictions were yet to be put in place – although for Georgette they were just one more anxiety:

> I am pretty worried at the moment, on various counts. I don't think my husband will find it easy to raise a loan in these days, from what we can discover, & I have been creditably informed that my heart is very weak, & my blood pressure lower than ever before. I shall write two more books, because I must write them, but I am hag-ridden by fear of collapse. My head plays me up as soon as I put pen to paper . . . If I crack up, god knows what will be the end of it all . . . Could I, do you think, raise money "on my own recognizances"? I am aware that this merely adds to the load of debt, but somehow I've got to struggle through this year, & if I am going to suffer a physical breakdown, I must at least straighten out this mess first . . . I'm under doctor's orders . . . but I don't seem to get much better. I wake tired, & am exhausted by tea-time – having done almost nothing . . . You can imagine what a perfect blank my mind is, as regards literary output.

She had hoped to write two new books but the Hodder novel had languished and she could think of nothing suitable for Heinemann. Nor had her perception of Hodder's handling of her books improved and she told her agent not to accept another contract from them until they had discussed it.

Fed up with trying to cope with so many seemingly insoluble difficulties, Georgette decided to take action. Blackthorns had become expensive, impractical and impossible to staff reliably. Ronald was working in London and petrol rationing limited car travel to just two hundred miles per week. A move seemed the logical solution and Georgette told Moore:

> What we wish to do is to get rid of this place, spend the summer vacation cheaply in the west, & move into the Temple in September. But to get out of this place I must settle up all debts. It seems like a vicious circle. Perhaps the best way would be for me to let go, & retire into a Home for Nervous Wrecks! I <u>do</u>

sometimes feel inclined to throw in my hand, but I expect I shan't. I can't cut down any further while we remain here: already the strain of looking after Richard, & overseeing indifferent servants is getting to be too much for me.

Her irritability was only exacerbated by her apparent inability to get on with her writing – always a vital outlet for her emotionally, quite apart from being essential for their financial survival. By April, she had managed to forward only a synopsis of the new thriller to Hodder and had barely begun the writing. She called the novel *Christmas Party* in a vain attempt at comic irony. But Georgette felt anything but funny and as the weeks went by, she found it increasingly difficult to write. Not even the release of *The Spanish Bride* on 6 April excited her. Her bookseller friend had read it in draft and liked it but had predicted that it would not 'appeal to the true Heyer-friends'. Georgette's mother had not liked it and consequently Georgette had convinced herself that her novel was 'almost unbearably dull and certainly ill-timed'.

It was unfortunate timing, for the situation in Europe was worsening and the Netherlands was already in a state of siege. Hitler's armies appeared to be preparing for a major offensive and the only relief from the tension was having Boris home on a week's leave. He also read *The Spanish Bride* in proof but, unlike their mother, was enthusiastic about the book and assured his sister it would do well. He was right. Sales were good and the *Sunday Times* described it as: 'One of her best historical romances.' But Georgette was again disappointed by what she saw as the absence of either a critical response or an enthusiastic buying public for her more serious novels.

On 9 May 1940 Hitler ordered the invasion of Denmark and Norway. The following day he launched his mass offensive and invaded Holland, Belgium, France and Luxembourg. Code-named 'Operation Yellow', the German action was fast, lethal and effective. Within a week Holland had surrendered. At home in Britain, the news from the Continent was all of heavy fighting and casualties. Ronald's brother, Leslie, was in Belgium commanding his battalion, and Boris had rejoined his unit in France. Living less than twenty miles from the south coast of England, out in their garden Georgette and Ronald could hear the faint, frightening sounds of battle from across the Channel.

As the anxious days passed they waited apprehensively for news of Boris and Leslie. The strain affected her writing and Georgette told Moore that she would manage to write only one book that year – and she wasn't sure how she would even get that done in light of events in Europe and her own problems at home:

> I don't seem able, at the moment, even to get on with *Christmas Party*. To be facetious in the face of the present situation is beyond me. I don't know what will happen to me now. There isn't a way out, & that's the plain truth. My health continues obstinately poor. This wouldn't matter, if it were not for my wretched blood-pressure, which makes my head such an unstable member. I was disappointed that you had not, apparently, been able to clear the American cheque. It now becomes a question how much longer the local shops will allow my credit to stretch. I don't feel there is anything else to say: at the moment my mind is preoccupied by every kind of worry – not the least of them the whereabouts of my brother. We have not heard from him since the 11th May.

Two weeks later Georgette and Ronald received the news that Lieutenant-Colonel Charles Leslie Rougier had been killed in action. He had died on 22 May from a shrapnel wound to the head while commanding his battalion at Tieghem Ridge in Belgium. It was an appalling blow.

Georgette was deeply shaken by the tragedy. The news of Leslie's death, the horrific assault on Belgium and France and the desperate evacuation of Dunkirk, were shattering, and it was weeks before she thought of her writing. When she did, it was to tell Moore that she could not possibly complete *Christmas Party* in the current circumstances: 'The very creation of modern people, talking modern slang, immediately makes me think of what is really happening to the young men today, & I feel real nausea at my own attempt at flippancy.'

Aware that she had promised Hodder the new thriller in time for spring release, she had tried to get it written and fulfil her commitment, only to find that 'Every time I try to cope with *Christmas Party*, I find my brain either dwelling on the war, or weaving the details of a preposterous Regency romance.' She did not want to let Hodder down, but she knew that if she persisted with the thriller she would end by 'writing nothing at all'.

She decided to put off the Hodder book and begged Moore to assure Uncle Percy that she had 'no intention of abandoning him'. Georgette needed a diversion: her writing had stalled and the reality of war made it impossible for her to write contemporary fiction: 'There is no escape in it: my gorge rises at it, in fact. As I sat today, trying to spur up some interest in it, I found myself thinking: "if this were only a period book!" well, why not? At this rate I shall get no book written at all, which would be catastrophic. But I think perhaps I could write "Corinthian".' Originally conceived as a short story, *The Corinthian* now seemed the ideal choice for her next novel:

Because (a) it would be a comforting book to write, all about a very different age; & (b) it is far more important to write the Heinemann book, because those are the ones I shall <u>always</u> write. Perhaps – since use is half the battle – I shall be in real writing swing by the time I've finished it, & then I could pick up *Christmas Party* again . . . I suppose the trouble is that I never <u>do</u> like writing detective stories, & all the clues & things bother me at the best of times, & I feel the whole thing to be fatuous, & quite shudder to think of having to <u>read</u> such a book. At the moment, I seem to be struggling out of a dreary period of ill-health: I feel better, but deadly tired & worried, & to have to wrestle mentally with a murder mystery merely makes me want to cry, with a feeling of sheer inability to cope. I shouldn't (I think) feel like that about *Corinthian*. I shan't have to have any blasted clues or suspects, & I needn't be funny if I don't feel like it. All I have to do is write a light, cheerful romance, as remote from this hellish war as possible . . . I might even contrive to enjoy writing an airy piece of froth – & I <u>do</u> do that sort of thing well, don't I? I can't <u>not</u> be interested in a period, once I get deep into it.

Georgette had no clear idea of what the historical romance was to be about but assured Moore that 'the wisps floating through my head promise well'.

Percy Hodder-Williams's reaction to her temporary defection was to urge her to give *The Corinthian* to Hodder as a substitute for the postponed thriller. But his argument that she owed his firm her next novel regardless of genre (because otherwise Heinemann would 'be getting two books running') fell on deaf ears. Georgette had no intention of letting Uncle Percy have her period romances. She hated letting him down but was certain that, unless the situation in France forced her to evacuate from Blackthorns, she would eventually finish *Christmas Party*. Georgette had recognised that there were limits on her ability to cope: she was convinced that if she were to continue writing through the War then she would need to follow her literary instincts.

She was right. A fortnight after beginning *The Corinthian* she had written nearly 30,000 words of the new novel and was 'proceeding fairly fast'. The book was the escape she needed and it is no coincidence that the plot revolves around a hero and a heroine fleeing from the restrictions and demands of civilised society. It was also Georgette's last cross-dressing novel and she liberated her young heroine, Pen Creed, from social constraints by disguising her as a boy. The Corinthian of the title was one of her most debonair heroes to date and, with her tongue firmly in her cheek, Georgette built a plot around the pair which included a stolen necklace,[14] a murderous aristocrat, a pair of silly lovers and a thief whose presence gave her the opportunity to use her burgeoning vocabulary of nineteenth-

---

14 This was a humorous tribute to P.C. Wren's sentimental bestseller *Beau Geste* (1924), in which the theft of the famous Brandon family sapphire – although meant as a chivalrous gesture – brings tragedy and the eventual revelation that the jewel was only paste. In Georgette's story a different Brandon necklace is stolen, but its theft is quite dishonourable and the fact of it being paste becomes a source of comedy rather than tragedy.

century thieves' cant. She had a glorious time poking fun at romantic stereotypes in *The Corinthian* and passing subtle judgements on the social mores of the day:

> "I see now that there is a great deal in what Aunt Almeria says. She considers that there are terrible pitfalls in Society."
> Sir Richard shook his head sadly. "Alas, too true!"
> "And vice," said Pen awfully. "Profligacy, and extravagance, you know."
> "I know."
> She picked up her knife and fork again. "It must be very exciting," she said enviously.

By the end of July the book was finished and Georgette declared: 'It's very good fun, I think, & goes swiftly, & sparkles quite nicely.' It had also been a welcome respite from the War and from the news that Ronald was taking steps to enlist in the Royal Navy. He had written to the Admiralty and sought Moore's assistance with letters of reference and recommendations to influential men.

Although Georgette put on a brave face at home she told Moore that, while it was nice of him to help Ronald, he could not expect her 'to overflow with gratitude . . . Quite apart from the anxiety about his safety, it appears to me that I am now to face the music alone – the bankruptcy music. That will be very jolly.' She was convinced her pecuniary affairs had reached the point where she 'had got to do something drastic' to save herself from ruin. That her agent held quite a different view of her financial circumstances and wished that she 'wouldn't worry so much about money difficulties' suggests that her situation may not have been as dire as she supposed.

It is unclear whether Georgette's financial fears were reasonable or whether she was the sort of person who would always worry about money no matter how much she earned. Her father's death had unexpectedly made her responsible for her family's financial security when she was still a young woman – fifteen years later they still relied on her as the primary breadwinner and she could see no sign of the pressure easing. It did not help that, although she had a good understanding of their income and expenses, neither Georgette nor Ronald seemed capable of controlling their expenditure or maintaining a proper cash flow between royalty cheques. They regularly exceeded their income which meant drawing on their overdraft. They could have lived more economically – although Georgette recognised that doing without domestic support would inevitably affect her writing and by extension her earnings. Giving up other luxuries such as regular holidays, tailored clothes and private school for Richard was apparently not an option, even in the face of severe financial strain.

Despite the fact that she had reliably produced an average of two books a year for the past twelve years, Georgette never felt that there was enough money to prevent anxiety. Whether it was true or not, the fact that she *felt* herself to be near bankruptcy made it a reality and she could not accept Moore's assessment that she had nothing to worry about. Though he was well-informed about her money troubles (having been told of them in detail for years) and had faith in her ability to go on selling, Moore would never convince Georgette that her financial fears were groundless. From his point of view, she was a guaranteed seller whose royalty income showed no signs of diminishing, but he also had the luxury of a long-term perspective at a time when she was concerned solely with surviving in the short-term. Moore did his best to convince Georgette that her future was secure, but she always found it difficult to believe that anyone could understand or appreciate her situation better than herself. Consequently, she often resisted advice, deeming herself the only person who could solve the problem. In 1940 she decided the solution to her financial troubles was to sell the British and Commonwealth copyrights in three of her bestselling novels.

She had thought of selling a copyright to Heinemann as early as 1935, when her pressing overdraft had forced her to consider ways of raising a lump sum. At that time she had told her agent that she 'would accept a Mere Pittance (£250) for any other [than *Regency Buck*] of my noble works, not excluding T.O.S. [*These Old Shades*]'. Five years later she still felt that £250 would be reasonable compensation for one of her copyrights. Moore tried to persuade her against taking such an imprudent step and advised a different approach. She appeared to agree with his suggestions and in late June assured him that in putting her proposal to Frere she had 'said nothing of copyright, but used the phrase underlined in your letter' (none of L.P. Moore's letters to Georgette have survived). Whatever her agent may have suggested, ten days later on 8 July 1940, Georgette sold the British and Commonwealth copyrights in *These Old Shades*, *Devil's Cub* and *Regency Buck* to Heinemann for £750. The contract also included a clause giving to Heinemann fifty per cent of any film rights in *These Old Shades* and twenty-five per cent of the film rights to the other two novels (in 2000 Random House voluntarily agreed to cancel the 1940 contract and return full rights for the three novels to the Heyer Estate).

£750 was a paltry amount for the rights to three books that would continue selling long after she was dead, but this was a time of war and England was under threat of invasion. It was almost impossible to imagine a future without worry or fear or to think that anything might endure. Most people lived in the here-and-now and Georgette rarely allowed herself to believe that her books might last. Ironically, the War created a demand for her novels that saw sales far outstrip peacetime figures as blackout conditions, rationing, constant tension and tragedy made people eager for books. In 1940 Georgette could not know that the War would last nearly five more years and that sales of her future novels would reach into the millions.

19

I've coincided, so far, with a Printers' Strike, a General
Election, & the Invasion of Norway, & I can't say I think
these distinctions desirable.

Georgette Heyer

Two days after Georgette had signed over her copyrights to
Heinemann, the Battle of Britain began as the Luftwaffe attempted
to wipe out Britain's ships and defences and pave the way for Hitler's
invasion force. In Horsham great ditches were dug and a long barbed
wire fence erected across gardens, allotments and fields. Ronald sent
off his application to join the Navy and told Moore:

> Very many thanks for your activities on my behalf. With such
> backing some result of value shall crown my application. I can
> only hope that the Admiralty will act promptly & not leave me
> kicking my heels too long, but with all the French fleet to man
> perhaps things will move.

Denied his chance at active service in the previous War, Ronald was
eager for a second opportunity to defend his country. Georgette
remained stoical but she was not happy about his plans for war service
– or Frere's, who was leaving Heinemann 'to become Mr Bevin's
Public Relations Officer'. Winston Churchill had appointed former
trade unionist Ernest Bevin to the Ministry of Labour, and Frere was
to assist him in ensuring the support of a heavily unionised workforce
for the duration of the War. Georgette was concerned at what Frere's

departure would mean to her but was comforted by his assurance that he would always be available for her to 'unburden myself to him if I want to!' Frere would retain his position as joint managing director (on a half salary) and for the duration of the War he would never be completely out of touch. He also reminded Georgette that Charles Evans knew all about *The Corinthian* and would look after her.

Towards the end of July Ronald learned that his application for active service had been turned down. 'The secretary to the Royal Navy, (may his bones bend!) has intimated to me that my slightly deficient eyesight is a complete bar to the acquisition of my services,' he told Moore. 'Now we shall lose the war! Still very many thanks for your potent efforts on my behalf.' Georgette was relieved not to be losing another of her menfolk to the fighting but Ronald was bitterly disappointed. Striving to make the best of things he joined the Home Guard instead.

As the Battle of Britain continued Georgette took to fire-watching and tried to get on with *Christmas Party* for Hodder. It was a struggle, for she was again feeling tired and depressed. Frere had asked her to write another romance but she worried that she was producing too many books and told him that she would prefer to read manuscripts for Heinemann. She desperately needed an interest outside her writing: 'The trouble about this bloody war is that there's nothing to do but work, if you live 5 miles from anywhere as I do. You can't go out much, even if you feel inclined, & hens don't take up <u>all</u> one's time!' Frere took her at her word and arranged for her to be employed as an occasional manuscripts reader for the firm – paying two guineas for each report. He quickly discovered that Georgette was a discerning reader with an eye for a saleable book.

She found plenty to distract her when the Blitz began on 7 September. Since July, the Luftwaffe had targeted RAF airfields, radar stations and other strategic defence sites, but now they began a concentrated attack on London. For 57 consecutive days and nights German planes bombed the capital, killing thousands, destroying homes and buildings and setting parts of the city ablaze. But it was not only London that came under fire, for Hitler was intent on destroying public morale. For the next nine months, towns, cities, docks and industrial sites across Britain were bombed and many rural areas – including Sussex – were hit. A week after the Blitz began Georgette confessed that the German assault made it difficult to work: 'Too many stray bombs falling within a mile of us, & although I shouldn't worry for myself, I have to be on the *qui viva* [alert] at night, because of Richard, peacefully sleeping in his bed. We are situated on a positive rat-run here. They come over every night. That doesn't matter: it's when they come back that they unload their bombs, & shake us to our foundations.'

Bombs fell on Horsham and Colgate in September. Three men were killed when a bomb exploded outside St Saviour's, where Richard had been christened. In October, Ronald's office in Middle Temple Lane was hit by an aerial torpedo. His chambers had long since lost all the glass from their windows but this latest bomb did considerable damage. On 29 December London's main publishing area around Paternoster Road was destroyed by enemy action: over a million books were burned and entire company archives lost. Several major publishers, including Longmans and Hutchinson's, took direct hits. When the Blitz finally ended six months later in May 1941, over 43,000 civilians were dead, a million homes had been destroyed and more than twenty million books had burned in the conflagration.

Georgette was more fortunate than many authors, for the Heinemann press at Kingswood remained remarkably unscathed, with only a single bomb causing minor damage to the buildings. The press came into its own during the War, for the huge public demand for books meant the firm's sales were limited only by paper rationing. Production was still difficult, however, and *The Corinthian's* release was put back a week while they worked to produce enough copies. The delay did not prevent the book from being reviewed, however, and in late October 1940 Georgette declared Frank Swinnerton's review in the *Observer* 'balm to my hurt soul (I have sustained a great deal of well-meaning family praise, extolling this frippery piece of work at the expense of my more serious books, & I don't relish it).' Swinnerton declared himself 'one of Miss Georgette Heyer's admirers' and his light-hearted account of *The Corinthian* concluded: 'The result, highly unconvincing, is happiness for all, including the reader.'

By the end of the month, Georgette and Ronald had renewed their resolve to move out of Blackthorns and divest themselves of a house and garden which neither of them had the time or inclination to keep up. A move to London was no longer practical while the nightly bombing-runs continued, but Georgette thought that a flat in Brighton might meet their needs. Ronald could easily commute by train to London and Richard was going to boarding-school in the new year; Georgette and Ronald had decided to send him away for both educational and safety reasons. The Elms was a boys' preparatory school deep in the Worcestershire countryside and an unlikely target for German bombers. Established in 1614 it was a small school with fewer than seventy boys but with a reputation for academic excellence. Although it would be a wrench to see Richard go, Georgette wanted him to have the best possible English public school education and with this in mind she handled the approaching separation with her usual calm stoicism.

Richard was now nearly nine and unfazed by the War which, like many children his age, he saw as an opportunity for adventure. Much to his mother's dismay he and a band of evacuated boys roamed the countryside looking for bits of 'defeated German planes' and coercing members of his father's Home Guard patrol into giving them souvenirs 'in defiance of all regulations'. Richard had thought Georgette very mean for 'refusing to let him rush to the scene of an exploded Heinkel' and had thoroughly depressed his mother by informing her that he wanted to be a commercial traveller when he grew up. But he had a literary mind, and liked writing stories, poems and plays. Georgette was also encouraged by his having already read several of her books 'not in the expectation of enjoyment, but because he says he feels a fool not to have read any'. She was proud of her son and had great hopes of him. In his turn Richard loved his parents, although there was always to be a degree of emotional reticence among the three of them. They were not a family who talked about feelings very much and Richard's thoughts about being sent away to school were not a topic for discussion. His upbringing was of the type that not only compelled him to accept his parents' decision but also made it impossible for him to tell them how he felt about it.

Georgette began the enormous task of packing up the house. Although she always destroyed her manuscripts and rarely kept correspondence of any kind, over the years she and Ronald had acquired a great many things which could not be got rid of so easily. By the time she had finished packing she had fifteen large trunks and cases to go into storage that were full of 'Awful Things, like the embroidery one bought in Skoptya & doesn't quite know what to do with, & the Arab Knife spouse acquired by low barter at Dar-es-Salaam'. There were a few pangs at parting but it was mostly a relief to be leaving Blackthorns and to throw off some of her domestic cares. The War was not going well and although Georgette believed that the Allies would eventually prevail she felt that there were 'too many people suffering from easy optimism & thinking we're going to win this war by faith'. Her view was that it was going to be 'a bloody business' and that the outlook for Europe was bleak. It did not help that Boris, home after Dunkirk, would soon be returning to active duty or that Frank (now 'Gunner F.D. Heyer') was due to begin Officer Cadet Training by Christmas and would eventually go to Europe to fight.

They left Blackthorns in December (taking Johnny the bull-terrier with them) and spent a week at Heathfield House, a boarding house in Horsham, before moving to Brighton. By Christmas they were settled in a service flat in Steyning Mansions at King's Cliff with views of the beach (now closed and mined) and the famous Brighton pier (partly demolished to prevent use as a German landing-stage). It was not salubrious accommodation but with rents from thirty-one shillings a week it was cheap and Georgette did not have to cook. She saw Richard off to school in January and, relieved of several cares, was finally able to make rapid progress on the book for Hodder. No longer called *Christmas Party* she thought of calling it *Death Before Dinner* – although she didn't really 'think it matter[ed] two hoots what Georgette Heyer calls her new book'.

By February the title was *Imperial End* and after reading through the first 20,000 words she thought it 'not at all too bad', although she doubted whether she had 'ever created a ruder, more objectionable lot of characters!' Eventually she decided that *Imperial End* was too obvious, briefly called it *Without Enchantment* (from Ecclesiastes), before instructing Moore: 'Hold everything! Get hold of Uncle Percy, & tell him "Envious Casca". Isn't that a Wow? It doesn't matter that only one person stabbed Nathaniel, do you think? And the quotation is so well known that it needs no explanation.' The title was from Shakespeare's *Julius Caesar* and it was typical of Georgette to assume a readership familiar enough with Shakespeare's plays to recognise it. In fact, her books were read by a broad cross-section of society, including men and women of different ages, classes and backgrounds, from the tobacconist's assistant to the Attorney General, Lord Somervell, who would later become a Lord Justice of Appeal and a Law Lord. When he died in 1960 he bequeathed his entire collection of Georgette Heyer novels to the Inner Temple Library.

Georgette finished *Envious Casca* in April, almost a year later than originally planned. Even before she had written the last chapter she told Frere that he could have a 'Nice Romance for Heinemann's to publish this autumn'. The bombing had temporarily forced Frere out of Albany so Georgette only saw him occasionally. She had taken a particular interest in Mr Bevin since Frere had joined the Minister and now decided that Bevin was the 'only gentleman who gives signs of constructive post-war thought'. She also liked Churchill, although she baulked at the thought of him as 'Peace Minister'. Given her conservative upbringing and lifelong Tory beliefs, her support for the Labour element in the coalition government was remarkable. Even Georgette recognised the change: 'Am growing pinker & pinker, & shall end up bright Red. One thing you may take as certain: I am not a Conservative any longer.'

Frere spent several days with them over Easter and recounted to Georgette his years with Heinemann and his plans for the company's future after the War. She enjoyed these sorts of confidences and Frere was adept at telling the kinds of tales she liked. 'These days of close

companionship quite confirmed my belief that F.'s a very nice creature,' she told Moore. 'I felt that if a bomb dropped on your head
(which God forfend!) I could go straight to Frere, & say, What do
I do now? & that he would see to it that I wasn't eaten by sharks.'
This was comforting for, after nearly twenty years, Georgette's relationship with her agent was beginning to wane.

The first intimation of a breach came after Moore's office was
damaged in the Blitz and he decided to move his business out of
London to his home at Gerrards Cross in Buckinghamshire. While
she understood the need for a new office, Georgette could not see
why Moore should remove himself to the outer suburbs. She wanted
her agent in the city, at the centre of things where she could call
on him and be taken out to lunch. 'Nothing you can say will ever
reconcile me to your removal to Gerrards Cross,' she scolded.

> Carola Lenanton [Oman] & I were only talking about it the other
> day – The point is that often & often one thinks one will look
> in and talk over some small point with you. Not the sort of thing
> important enough to justify your coming up from Gerrards Cross.
> So one writes – or jettisons it altogether. Of course, it may be
> better for you <u>not</u> to have authors drifting in on frivolous business
> every day of the week, but I <u>do</u> think you're bound to get a little
> out of touch with us.

She still depended on Moore and had asked him to be one of the
trustees of her will, but the advent of Frere into her life had prompted
a slow shift in her perception of her agent. Moore was getting older
and he had never known precisely how to handle her. He was practical and kind and conscientious, but he was not charismatic and,
like Charles Evans, he did not understand her humour as Frere did.
In the early part of her career none of these things had mattered.
Now, however, she had a publisher and friend who was clever, witty
and actively interested in her. When compared with Frere, Moore
simply could not compete.

20

Oh, blast! Written too much, & feel queer.

Georgette Heyer

It would be some years before Georgette became completely disillusioned with her agent, however, and – along with Ronald and Frere – he was still an important sounding board. Early in May she told Moore of her plans for her new Heinemann romance:

> Do you recall a short I once wrote, & you or Norah sold to Woman's Journal for a pittance? Well, it was a poor short, but it has the makings of a novel, & it is going to grow into a lovely romantic bit of froth for Heinemann. Title will remain the same – *Pharaoh's Daughter*. <u>Not</u> Moses' girl-friend, but a lady addicted to gaming.

Her eagerness to start the new book was tempered by her difficulties in finding someone locally who could type up *Envious Casca*. The war situation made it too precarious to send the manuscript to London and on finding that 'no one in Brighton has ever heard of typing a novel in under a month' Georgette decided to type it herself. She thought it 'a great bore, & such a waste of time, when I might be working on *Pharaoh's Daughter*' but to her surprise she managed to type the entire manuscript in just over a week, revising as she went. Her success in typing *Envious Casca* marked a new beginning. Henceforth Georgette would type her own manuscripts and in later years any new typewriter would be fitted with special keys to suit her particular needs.

She dealt quickly with the *Envious Casca* proofs when they eventually arrived, only stopping when she found that someone had put a query against the word 'bloody'. Infuriated by what she saw as interference in her work, she told Moore: 'I require no one to censor my language, thank you. The word stands. I shall make a point of introducing it several times in my next book.' Georgette was about to begin her thirtieth novel: the notion that anyone should know better than she about her writing or that anyone other than Ronald, Moore or Frere would have the temerity to suggest corrections or alterations beyond ordinary typographic errors made her blood boil. Having dealt with Hodder to her satisfaction, Georgette returned to *Pharaoh's Daughter* and 'the most entrancing books . . . all about gamesters' borrowed from the London Library.

After two months she still had not put pen to paper. Instead she confessed that 'While I was meditating on *Pharaoh's Daughter*, a wholly unwanted saga about a preposterous family called Pendean, who live at Cressy Hall, crept into my mind, & grew, & grew, & grew.' She became obsessed with the story and told L.P. 'I don't know yet all the details, but Ambrose Pendean was murdered, poisoned, & he was a roaring, Rabelaisian old man, a real patriarch, with roaring Rabelaisian sons, & two who are Lilies of the Field, & a brother who has soft white hands, & collects jade, and a widowed sister with a wig, & foul language, trailing dirty skirts through the vast spaces of Cressy Hall.' Another two pages of detailed description led her to conclude that:

> The thing is called *Family Affair*, & possibly set in Cornwall . . . It will be long, obviously, & more of a problem in psychology than in cold detection. Next time Uncle P. gets restive, tell him that this thing burst on me, willy-nilly. I even dreamed about the Pendeans last night! I shall have to keep a note-book for them, as fresh imbroglios keep cropping up, & mustn't be forgotten . . . Tell Uncle P. that this will be a combination of murder-story & family saga. It might sweep the board. The family is preposterous enough.

As pressing as she felt the new book to be, Georgette forced herself to put it aside and get on with *Pharaoh's Daughter*. She had promised

Frere an August delivery, but by June still had not written a word. She was in a state of flux: distracted by the Cornish saga smouldering in her brain, impatiently waiting for the overdue advance for *Envious Casca* and irritated by a recent radio script of *The Talisman Ring*. Georgette could be a stern critic of other people's writing as well as her own and her wide reading often resulted in pithy critiques of recent publications. After hearing E.M. Forster on the BBC give his 'pick of the books of 1941', she told Moore:

> You never listened to such tripe, & if you could have <u>heard</u> his "pick"! there are just three books which rise above the rest head & shoulders – *The Silver Darlings*, by Neil Gunn, for beauty of prose, & sheer gift of story-telling; *Parents & Children*, by Compton-Burnett, for brilliance of wit & satire; & the *Story of J.M.B.* by Mackail, for originality of treatment, & complete mastery of his subject. Mr Forster mentioned none of them. He also talked some rubbish about the day of the professional writer being over. God knows what he thought he meant. He was very pleased with himself. He said "It is so" & "It is not so" – not admitting possibility of mistake in judgement. The words, "I think" or "in my judgement" were conspicuous by their absence. He was Mr Forster, & he KNEW.

Georgette was often intolerant of writers (whom she still referred to as 'Inkies') – and disliked those who prated on about 'My Public and My Art'. She found laughable the kinds of conceits that led Francis Brett Young to read his manuscripts aloud to Charles Evans or that prompted Margaret Kennedy to tell her that the 'film-people, when dealing with *Escape Me Never*, "left out some very beautiful bits"'. It was this sort of pretension that led Georgette to declare that 'all Inkies ought to be incarcerated.' The War had made her more impatient than ever of self-important behaviour. She saw it as the writer's duty to get on with producing books that would keep the populace occupied and entertained, not go about seeking acclamation.

 Like everyone else in Britain, Georgette had had to learn to live with death and disaster. This she did, making a point of never showing fear regardless of what was going on in her head. Each evening she saw Ronald off on his Home Guard patrol fully alive to the possibility that he might not return. They did not speak their fears aloud, but Richard always remembered the feeling in the flat that summer and how he would say goodbye to his father with a knot in his stomach. Ronald was a leader in 'C' Company and also, as Georgette humorously explained, 'now Gas Company Instructor, Bombing Instructor, & No. 1 Sniper. In the event of invasion, he will retire to the grave he has himself dug, a rifle in one hand, a Mills bomb in the other, & a piece of blotting-paper between his teeth.'

They were not entirely happy in Brighton and by mid-summer Georgette was thinking of moving again. She and Ronald hoped to find rooms in London after the War and in July they visited Frere at his chambers in Albany. He had lived there since 1932 and thought the place might suit Georgette. She had never been inside Albany before, but she knew from her reading that the grand old building had been home to many famous writers, artists, actors and politicians. The apartments (known as 'sets' or chambers, never flats) were not large, but the location – just five hundred yards west of Piccadilly Circus, across the road from Hatchard's bookshop and Fortnum & Mason, and near the London Library – was very appealing. 'I rather fell for it,' Georgette confessed to Moore. 'If we could get a large set we might consider it, as it isn't expensive, & it's wonderfully cloistral. Frere has Macaulay's chambers – very nice, but not quite large enough for us.'

Unlike the Freres (who had a house in the country and mostly lived in Albany during the week) the Rougiers wanted a permanent residence. Georgette was cheered by the possibility of Albany, though she would not set her heart on it, realising that 'there may be some snags, like No Children or Dogs.' Richard was not yet ten and children under the age of thirteen were not allowed to live in Albany. He was home from The Elms for the summer holidays, having slowly adjusted to boarding-school after a difficult beginning. All his life Richard remembered arriving at the station and having to drag his trunk through the snow to the school. He found the discipline harsh and the food unappetising – as his mother discovered on reading a letter from him explaining why he had not written the previous week: 'I did not write to you because we have been having that toad in the hole & I was feeling seedy & I couldn't wright [sic] very well & I am out of energy.' Georgette thought this a superb explanation for not putting pen to paper and told Moore that he could expect a similar excuse from her regarding *Pharaoh's Daughter*.

She had continued making notes for *Family Affair* through June but by mid-July still had written nothing of the new romance for Heinemann. 'Such trouble as I have been having over that wretched girl, *Faro's Daughter*! Or *Pharaoh's Daughter* – which do you like?' she asked Frere. She had plenty of ideas for the book but still had not 'unraveled' the plot. She did have a new sort of hero though, and confessed: 'The schoolgirls won't like his being a Mere Commoner, but I'm so fed-up with writing a lot of wash about improbable dukes and earls. He's fabulously rich, however, but he dresses all anyhow, and hasn't got a quizzing glass, or any graceful habits.'

Attempting to get past her 'obstinate Muse' she wrote Frere a long, amusing letter about her struggles, regaling him with several pages of stream-of-consciousness prose. She wrote a great many letters in this style but the personal ones to Frere show her at her most relaxed. She could write to him unhindered, 'speaking' on paper as if he were beside her and she was having to answer his constant (imagined) interruptions to her description of *Pharaoh's Daughter*:

> Because naturally it's a very fine work, and immensely entertaining, absorbing, witty, scintillating and erudite. Well, what I mean is, it <u>will</u> be, when I get around to writing it. No, then, I <u>haven't</u> started it, since you <u>must</u> know. Though what it's got to do with you – well, not <u>much</u>, anyway. Don't let's argue about that! Let me SPEAK! Badgering me like this. Pestering me for the thing. Not giving me a moment's peace. And just look at that set of somnambulists down at Kingswood! Do I ever get a letter from any one of them, asking me about my new book, and wanting to know when they can start advertising it? Oh, dear me, no! . . . And

why on earth you should instantly assume that you won't get the book in time to publish it this autumn I entirely fail to understand. Nothing I have said could possibly have given you that impression, so why you must needs get in such a temper about it – Do calm yourself! All I ever said was that from one cause and another – NO! Shut up! I am not going to explain what the causes were. Don't be such a fool! Can't you realize that if I were feeling inventive I should be writing the book, instead of this letter?

By the time she had given him an outline of the main plot points and characters, Georgette suddenly had a 'Eureka!' moment and the book fell into place. She thanked Frere for 'listening' and added: 'I really think that's done it. After weeks of fretting around in a sort of Hampton Court maze, too!'

She immediately began writing, with the story so clear in her mind that she was able to type it straight from her head on to the page (single-spaced because of the paper shortage). A month later the book was finished and Georgette triumphantly sent it to Moore. Despite her initial reservations about typing it herself (she only used three fingers) she was able to report that 'it was a howling success, and I went on and on and on, with only one hitch, lasting for an hour, when I sat back, and wondered what was going to happen to the various persons assembled in the book!' *Faro's Daughter* was another improbable 'bubble' of a novel that would prove popular with wartime audiences and it earned Georgette a welcome £750 advance.

The financial pressure had eased a good deal since leaving Blackthorns. With the advances for *Envious Casca* and *Faro's Daughter* and an unlooked-for £200 legacy from her Aunt Ilma Heyer (who had died in February) in hand, by September Georgette claimed she had not felt herself 'to be sitting prettier' in her life. Buoyed up by the successful completion of *Faro's Daughter* she thought she might 'perpetrate as soon as possible a mystery (with love-interest, God damn it) for Uncle P. to publish in the spring'. But the Cornish saga was also 'seething' in her brain begging to be written. Unable to dispossess herself of the idea for the book, Georgette repeatedly wrote to her agent about the novel, admitting that 'the thing is getting hourly more *Cold Comfort Farmish*'[15] and that she would have to get some 'fruity' books on Cornwall because 'that is where it all happened. I don't have much say in the matter. This appallingly vital family has things exactly as it likes, and haunts me if I try to alter anything.' The Pendeans had now become the Penhallows and Cressy Hall had become Trevellin. The characters swarmed in her head, but it would be another six months before she wrote their story.

In September Georgette and Ronald moved to Hove, a few miles west along the coast from Brighton. They had leased a small service apartment at 27 Adelaide Crescent, one of a curving row of three-storey white terrace houses with views across the sea. There was no kitchen (which suited Georgette perfectly) and she soon became great friends with the landlady, Mrs Isabella Banton, who brought their meals up to them. There was a garden in the centre of the crescent where Richard and Mrs Banton's daughter would play when he was home from school. Laryngitis had delayed Richard's return to The Elms that summer and it was mid-September when Georgette finally took him back to school before going on to stay with Carola Oman in Hertfordshire.

Although her contact with Joanna Cannan had dwindled in recent years, Georgette's friendship with Carola remained close. They wrote to each other often, visited whenever they could and continued to share confidences about their work. Carola had asked her to correct the proofs and create an index for her latest book, *Britain Against Napoleon*. Georgette was delighted by the proposal. She thought Carola's latest work 'magnificent' and 'pre-eminently a book for the well-read'. She returned home from Carola's in good spirits only to be immediately cast down by the news that the Inspector of Taxes was investigating the sale of her copyrights to Heinemann the previous year. Georgette had declared the £750 as a capital sum and therefore not taxable, whereas the Inspector deemed it income and subject to

---

15 *Cold Comfort Farm* was Stella Gibbons' 1932 bestselling novel.

tax. Having only recently cleared her overdraft Georgette was appalled by the thought that the Revenue 'may demand some huge sum from me'. Ronald did his best to allay her concerns and promised to deal with the case but Georgette was not optimistic and felt sure she would eventually have to pay.

Taxation demands would always be a sore point but for now she seemed resigned to her fate at the hands of the Inland Revenue. She had recently signed a new contract with Heinemann and knew that, provided she kept on writing, her income was guaranteed for several years ahead. The contract was on the old terms, for she had told Moore not to 'try to force up the advance: my books are just ticking over, I think, and I am thankful that Charlie doesn't suggest a smaller advance'. Typically, Georgette continued to underestimate both her value to the firm and her ability to earn back her advance – something she always achieved within the first twelve months (or sooner) after publication. She made no protest when Heinemann introduced a new clause into her contract exempting them from paying the 25% royalty 'so long as the high costs resulting from war conditions prevail'. She was far more concerned by the suggestion that Heinemann were prepared to publish her books without having read them.

Georgette strongly disapproved of this policy and told Moore she could not 'see why any publisher should be obliged to produce an inferior work, no matter whom it is written by'. So far from being flattered by the firm's apparent view of her as infallible, she did not want Heinemann to assume that everything she wrote was worth publishing: 'The more I think about it the less I like it. I don't want to be published on terms like that. In a more practical spirit, it is a maxim of the house that Heinemann publishes authors, not books. They won't turn down my first flop, but I hope to God they would turn down the second.'

In October Georgette was frustrated to discover that Hodder were planning to release *Envious Casca* the same week that Heinemann were publishing *Faro's Daughter*. 'They have had time to bring the book out twice over by now,' she crossly told Moore. '*Casca* was in their hands before I had even thought out the plot of *Faro's Daughter*.'

But Hodder were themselves 'feeling aggrieved', believing that they had an unwritten agreement with Georgette that her detective novels and period romances should alternate. She had no recollection of any such arrangement and insisted that she 'should have deprecated such a suggestion, foreseeing the possibility of my not wishing, at some future date, to write a modern novel'. Although she felt it her 'right to work on whatever sort of book I feel inclined to tackle', she assured Moore that her next novel would be *Family Affair* which Hodder could publish in the spring: 'if obsession counts *Family Affair* ought to be among my best books.'

21

Why, why, Frere, do all these people who think it is rather easier than falling off a post NEVER WRITE A BOOK THEMSELVES?

Georgette Heyer

Family Affair languished through November and December 1941. Georgette had been afflicted with a skin condition and the prescribed treatment of increasing amounts of arsenic had only made her worse: 'I cannot describe to you the horror –!' she told Moore. 'I have been in bed for a week, wholly unable even to sign my name. Better now, having jettisoned the cure.' She remained ill for some weeks, however, 'suffering from Aftermath, which includes such oddments as weakened heart, abnormally low blood-pressure, and blurred sight'. To make matters worse, Ronald's mother's mental condition was deteriorating and in November they had been forced to move her from Horsham to a nursing-home in Hove. On 31 December, after three anxious, difficult weeks, Jean Rougier died.

Although she had not always got on with her mother-in-law, Georgette felt the strain of her slow, painful passing. Ever since her son Leslie's death, Jean Rougier had become increasingly ill and frail and, despite her own poor health, Georgette had given her as much time and attention as she could manage. The final days had been particularly hard as she and Ronald had kept a bedside vigil. Georgette had felt 'worn to shreds with the anxiety, and the strain of waiting for an end which was inevitable from the start'. Afterwards she described Jean Rougier's death as 'a most merciful release and no occasion for mourning'.

By mid-January Georgette was feeling better and planning a serial for *Woman's Weekly*, who had offered £500 for a light modern romance. Her agent was enthusiastic about the commission and suggested that the story might do for her next novel. She found the suggestion irritating: 'You are getting a little out of touch with this author, Mr Moore! I am going to write a book about the Penhallows: just bear that fact in mind, and we shall get along fine.' But her Cornish saga was again delayed when Richard fell ill with whooping cough. Georgette found it impossible to write with her son at home and in such poor health. When, in mid-February, Ronald succumbed to tonsillitis and she came down with a cold she decided to give up 'the unequal struggle' and take the family to a favourite haunt of theirs at Cleeve Hill in Gloucestershire where there was nothing 'but a golf-course & lovely walks; & we expect to be thoroughly braced.'

It was not to be. So far from recovering, Richard spent the entire holiday 'in bed, running an erratic and incomprehensible temperature'. His parents brought two doctors in to attend him but blood tests proved inconclusive. His mother was anxious and his father concerned (though they both continued – in typically British style – to refer to their son affectionately as 'the brat') and Georgette got no writing done. Desperate to get on with the Penhallows she planned to engage a tutor for Richard on their return to Hove so that she would have mornings free to write. She had also revived her ambition to write *Stark Harry* (her proposed book about Henry V) after receiving a letter from Frere:

> He will publish whatever I want to write, & thinks well of my suggestion that I should do something more worth while than these frippery romances. He says good books are selling better than bad ones, & tells me Macmillan has <u>subscribed</u> over 10,000 of Miss West's new magnum opus![16] Isn't that a cheering thought?

16 *Black Lamb and Grey Falcon* by Rebecca West was about the causes of the Second World War.

Anyway, Frere says, Write what you feel like, & take as long over it as you want to, & throw off the 'tec novel & the serial in between whiles. He says "you can do them on your head" – little recking that at the moment I couldn't even do them the right way up. So it may well be that I shall have a stab at *Stark Harry*. What do you think about it? (Don't you like the spurious diffidence with which I consult you & Frere about what I've really made up my mind to do anyway? But in these bad times I really <u>would</u> be amenable to reason, if you both advised me against any dire course.)

Georgette longed to write a serious book and still had plans to write a biography, but her ambitions were postponed by their decision to leave Brighton.

Ronald was now well-established in London and, although he enjoyed the daily train journey (during which he and three friends played bridge at a reserved table in the first-class carriage), after nearly six years of commuting he felt he wanted to live closer to his work. Georgette, too, was tired of never seeing her friends and had concluded that Hove did not agree with her. Early in 1942 she decided that they were both 'sick of being homeless. So, provided we don't get invaded or blitzed this spring or summer, we think seriously of setting up house again, this time in London.'

But there could be no move until Richard was well again. Further tests had indicated that his 'blood seems to be in a very rotten state, and he has to be fed up, given as much sunlight as possible, and kept from getting overtired'. Georgette found it difficult to write with her son ill at home though she longed to get on with *Family Affair*: 'The Penhallows are seething in my brain, and if only I could have a month's peace and quiet I could get them down red-hot onto paper. What Uncle Percy will say about them I don't know, and shudder to think.'

Aware of the firm's Nonconformist views, she was concerned that an arch-conservative like Percy Hodder-Williams would look askance at any novel that began 'Jimmy the Bastard was cleaning boots.' Nor was he likely to admire a cast of characters that included several illegitimate children, a daughter who was 'obviously a lesbian (I shan't actually say so, but anyone would have to be soft-headed not to grasp it)', a number of lusty sons with a propensity for getting the female servants pregnant, another son with 'pansy boy-friends' and a weak second wife who would eventually murder the novel's tyrannical, foul-mouthed patriarch. But Georgette was obsessed by their story: 'It's no use begging me not to write this book: these astounding people have been maturing in my head for months.'

Contrary to Jane Aiken Hodge's suggestion that the book was written 'at a bad time in Georgette Heyer's life, the nearest she ever came to a breakdown', Georgette was now in excellent health and enthusiastic about the new novel. She began writing in earnest in March and within a fortnight had written 40,000 words. Her landlady, Isabella Banton, always remembered Georgette 'sitting at the side of the fire writing on her lap and living with real people'.[17] These were the Penhallows, so utterly alive to Georgette that they poured from her pen. She revelled in the intensity of the writing, which frequently overflowed into long letters about the book to Frere and Moore. As the novel took shape and Adam Penhallow's domineering personality filled its pages Georgette recognised its difference to her other books. 'It would be a subtle thing to lead Uncle Percy to expect the worst,' she told her agent:

> Then, when he reads the book, he will experience natural sensations of relief that it isn't as bad as you had led him to believe, and he will very likely publish it in a moment of reaction. Tell him that he would be very unwise to let me slip from his clutches, as this peculiar work is merely an erratic fit or start on my part, and I shall undoubtedly perpetrate many more of the light trifles he admires.

Not long afterwards she realised that she 'ought to have given it an eighteenth-century setting, and have ruled out the element of detection, but I can't do it now: these people ARE, and it's not a bit of

---

17 Based on the limited information available to her in 1983, in *The Private World of Georgette Heyer* Jane Aiken Hodge concluded that Georgette had written *The Spanish Bride* on her knee in the flat at Adelaide Crescent. The discovery of Georgette's early letters, however, has revealed that the book was actually *Penhallow*.

good trying to alter them to fit another period'. The more the book took hold of her, the more she worried over its publication: 'I don't think that the book will be obscene, because I doubt if I could be obscene myself. It will be a bit outspoken here and there, but Uncle Percy must try to be his age.' Ronald's initial view was that Percy Hodder-Williams would not get past the first sentence, let alone the first chapter. Reading on, however, he changed his mind. Although he agreed that it was 'a bit coarse here and there', he did not think that Hodder would turn it down.

Ronald was a comforting counsellor and Georgette felt greatly reassured by his certainty that the book was a good one. He was also doing his best to shield her from the worry and distraction of their continuing fight with the Tax Commissioner. She expected to 'go down' when the case was heard in the Horsham Court and was doing her best to ignore it. Her days were taken up with the Penhallows and Richard. His health was slowly improving and Georgette had taken to reading Dickens aloud to him in the afternoons. *Pickwick Papers* was 'going down very smoothly' with the ten-year-old, and she intended to 'try him on David Copperfield next, believing that you can't get on to the classics too early'. Richard developed a lifelong affection for Dickens' novels.

By May, Richard was almost well enough to return to school and Georgette's saga was nearly complete. She was typing up the manuscript and was 'not interested in anything outside of Trevellin. I am, in fact, completely rapt, and rarely leave this bloody machine.' After much discussion with Ronald (apparently his only input into the book) and Richard she had decided to call the novel *Penhallow* – a simple title that had 'the advantage of indicating pretty clearly that it isn't one of my usual murders'. She often puzzled over the book, uncertain of what to make of it, where it had come from and why it obsessed her. She described it as 'a very peculiar, long and unorthodox story' and wondered 'Why on earth did I have to write this disturbing book?' There was no clear answer, only the conviction that even if it was a mistake she had 'got to write it'.

Years later, Richard would speculate that *Penhallow* was a 'catharsis of her family' (meaning her extended family), but the only hint in Georgette's letters of what the novel might have meant was her conclusion that 'Penhallow was a dreadful person, but he did hold the family together, and everything goes to pieces when he dies.' The fact that she was nearing her fortieth birthday may also have been a factor given the sorts of emotional crises and aberrations that so often come to men and women as they approach the mid-point in their lives.

Notwithstanding its humorous moments, *Penhallow* remains a grim, fierce book full of angry, frustrated characters simmering with repressed emotions and silent suffering. It is not difficult to imagine it as a release for Georgette's own unexpressed thoughts and feelings. She rarely gave voice to the deeper emotions in her personal life; she could articulate the more fleeting feelings of irritation, amusement or frustration easily enough, but candid expressions of profound emotion such as pain, grief, joy or love were much more difficult. Her outlet for these was almost always her writing.

She finished the book at the end of May and sent it to Moore. Richard had suffered a relapse and his return to school was indefinitely postponed. Georgette was anxious about him and worried about Hodder's reaction to *Penhallow*. In almost every way, this book was unique among Georgette's novels and she fussed and worried over its publication as she had never done before. She begged her agent to read it. She thought the novel 'A bit of a *tour-de-force*, but I may be wrong! Let me tell you that with the exception of a handful of passages first jotted down in pencil in a rough note-book, as you see it, so it came out of my head.' Five days after receiving the manuscript Moore told her that it was indeed a *tour de force* but that 'he couldn't see Uncle Percy touching it with a ten-foot pole'.

Georgette's emotions ran high as she tried to work out *Penhallow*'s fate at the hands of her publishers. She agreed with Moore that 'it isn't a Hodder book at all, is it?' and finally decided 'The more I think of it, the more I feel sure that we oughtn't to hand *Penhallow* to H. & S. at all . . . I think that if we could honourably, & without giving offence, withhold Penhallow from H. & S., & send it up to Heinemann in the ordinary way, it would be good policy.' The idea grew and she encouraged her agent to convince Percy Hodder-Williams of the idea and to 'hold out a tempting vista of bigger & better Hemingways to the old man! I'll do him a lovely, sparkling one, without <u>any</u> bloodys at all!'

Frere knew all about *Penhallow* and had written to say that 'the very least you can do is to send me a set of proofs so that I can get at it before the reviewers start annoying me.' Georgette had given him 'first refusal of the epic if Uncle P. decided it was too hot for him to handle'. When Percy Hodder-Williams turned down *Penhallow*, she was elated and instantly wrote to Frere to tell him 'It's all yours! Percy was shocked, & when he had the bait of a Hemingway 'tec novel held invitingly out to him he gave L.P. back the MS, mourning gently over my fall from grace.' Revelling in her temporary release from Hodder she sent the manuscript to Frere in Albany with instructions to tell her 'whether it's any good, or whether I am kidding myself. And if you think it isn't any good, for God's sake say so! I don't say I shan't offer it elsewhere, because I've got a Thing about it, and I undoubtedly shall.'

A week later Frere confirmed all her hopes for the novel:

You made me see that roaring old man with his beak nose & unquenchable eye. Of course it was right for Faith to do it & get out of it on all counts in the way she did . . . a triumph, Miss-detective-storywriter-Heyer, & completely credible – including a timely & satisfying vignette of old-Phineas . . . From all of which you may deduce, dear Madam, that I liked your book More than Somewhat . . . Your best? Don't ask silly leading questions. You know it is. If Perc had published it I should have given up publishing altogether & become a permanent civil servant. Tomorrow I have an appt. with C.S. Evans & propose to deliver *Penhallow* to him with suitable words & phrases. He'll eat it. You['ll] see. Thank you, Miss Heyer, you have written the novel of your not unsuccessful career. There's no blemish on it.

Frere's reaction was everything Georgette wanted: for the first time he had written to her at length about one of her novels and raised her hopes high by telling her that it was 'a can't-put-it-down book'.

Jubilant about *Penhallow*, Georgette still felt a 'moral obligation' to Hodder. She had no desire to leave the firm and planned to write a real Hemingway novel for Uncle Percy as soon as *Penhallow* was safely in Heinemann's hands. She had removed her Hodder detective from the book and replaced him with a one-off character in Inspector Logan. But relations were soured when Percy Hodder-Williams, still keen to get hold of her period romances, decreed that he must have her next book regardless of genre. Georgette was incensed:

> Did you say that H. & S. "stipulated" that they should have my next book, whatever it was? I believe you did . . . But what infernal cheek! It seems to me that they'd better take a look at my contract. Technically, I am now released from any obligation to hand them any further books, so I should like to know where Percy gets his "stipulation" line of talk from? I don't choose to leave his firm, but there's nothing to stop my handing Heinemann three – or four – or five – straight off the reel. Seriously, I don't think a lot of Uncle Percy's business-sense. It is most unwise to pan authors whom you wish to keep with you. And what a lot of nonsense, to run a publishing business on Sunday-school lines!

But Georgette was wrong about her contract. The agreement which she had signed in 1938 was for four books of which *Envious Casca* was the first and *Penhallow* should have been the second. Although she could choose what she wrote and when, Georgette still owed Hodder three more books. She had no wish to leave the firm but Percy Hodder-Williams's renewed attempts to get hold of her historical novels upset her at a time when (despite her bravado) she was deeply disappointed by his dislike of *Penhallow* – a feeling thrown into sharp relief by her mother's and Frere's reactions to the book: 'My mother has read *Penhallow* in typescript & says Percy is mad. She likes it better than anything I've done. Frere says he might achieve a *succes fou* – but "what times you do pick to write your best books!"'

Praise from those whose opinion mattered to her inevitably raised her expectations, not only of good sales and popular success, but also of the yearned-for critical response. When Charles Evans declared his dislike of *Penhallow*, Georgette was devastated and wired Frere who immediately telephoned to ask, 'What the hell C.S. [Evans] was up to <u>now</u>?' '"He's trying to grind my face,"' she told him. On describing Evans's reaction to *Penhallow*

> Frere said, "He hasn't read it." I said I thought he had, & had been quite polite, but thought it "an unpleasant book". To which Frere replied "Good God!" After that gratifying expression of stupefaction, he became once again The Perfect English Publisher, & said, "Look, dear, don't worry! Lunch on Friday at the Escargot, & tell me just what Charlie's been doing." So I shall no doubt be given some Good Eats & Drinks, & shall end up by practically <u>giving</u> *Penhallow* to the firm.

Frere assured Georgette of *Penhallow*'s merit and reminded her that Evans had recently lost his youngest son in a night raid over Bremen and was taking it badly. Within weeks, Heinemann had bought *Penhallow* for £600 and scheduled the book for October publication.

Satisfied at last that her precious novel would be properly handled, Georgette took Richard to London to see his godfather, Dr Harris, the child specialist. He greatly relieved her concerns about her son's indifferent health, telling her not to worry any longer but to send Richard back to school, '& refuse to let him see any more doctors'. It was an enormous weight off her mind. She was also cheered by the possibility of a London apartment.

She and Ronald had been looking for some time, and had become quite disheartened after viewing a number of service flats and finding them too expensive. Georgette still wanted to live in Albany and in September had found a set 'which we definitely want . . . Up two flights of stairs, but with the most superb sitting-room, panelled in old pine, & with a huge bow-window.' But getting chambers in Albany was a complicated business. Alterations and permission for a new kitchen would be needed before A.11. would be ready to move into. In the end it proved too difficult and they got F.3. Albany instead. They were to move in at the end of November, but before that would come the long-awaited publication of *Penhallow*.

By early October, Georgette was on tenterhooks. Her hopes for a big success with *Penhallow* had been buoyed by the Heinemann Sales Director, Leslie Munro, who had written her a 'gratifying letter':

> He was awfully glad to have the selling of it ("it is a damned good book") & [said] that I needn't worry: it would beat all my records, in his judgement. That he was overjoyed to learn that I had a second Penhallow book in my head, & that if Jimmy the Bastard was responsible for the book's having come to Heinemann, "Here's to Jimmy!"

Ten days before publication she learned that the first 12,500 copies had sold out and *Penhallow* was being reprinted. She wrote ecstatically to Moore: 'is this good, or is this good?' His response was dampening: he did not think the pre-sales so exceptional given that *Envious Casca* had subscribed 14,000 copies. Nor did he think booksellers would be encouraged by Jimmy the Bastard.

Georgette was now in a 'deplorable state of nerves over this book' and told Moore:

> I expect to see some notices of *Penhallow* on Sunday – & dread seeing them. Oh, how absurd it is, after all! I have never been so stupid about any of my books before, not even the *Army*. I can't think what's the matter with me. Frere says he never knew a self-critical author who didn't suffer from irrational jitters, but it's no use, nothing serves to soothe my alarms. And yet I don't really care what any of you think. Perhaps this is the decay of a once noble intellect. Or did Percy saying it had no sparkle get under my armour?

Although she had poured herself, heart and soul, into *An Infamous Army* and *The Spanish Bride* (for which she had also craved acclaim),

Penhallow had taken something more and Georgette desperately wanted the reviews to reflect this. It was not the first time that she had found herself assailed by self-doubt in one moment, then re-assured by her own view of a book in the next, but the *Penhallow* experience was different – it was unique – and it would prove a turning-point in her career.

Towards the end of her letter to Moore Georgette suddenly cast all doubt aside and told her agent exactly what the book meant to her: 'How dared you say *Penhallow* was "a grotesque"? Carola Oman calls it my "Lear", & says my characterisation is "brilliant". So damn you! You'd better not say anything at all about *Penhallow*. You don't know anything about it. Nobody knows anything about it. You couldn't any of you say the right things about it.' She never wrote in this way about one of her books again.

Penhallow came out on 26 October 1942 and *The Times Literary Supplement* printed a good review of it five days later. Sales were also good. But it was not enough. The fact that *all* of her novels sold well, that nearly all of her titles were still in print, that her sales ran into the hundreds of thousands and that she was consistently well reviewed in all the major papers in both Britain *and* America was not enough. Georgette wanted more: she wanted critics, academics and the *literati* to sit up and take notice. The books that mattered to her most – *An Infamous Army*, *The Spanish Bride* and now *Penhallow* – all received positive and, in some cases, glowing, reviews. But still she was not satisfied. The critical recognition she craved continued to elude her.

Georgette had nurtured great hopes for *Penhallow*, and its recep-tion from reviewers was a huge disappointment. In the *Observer*, Frank Swinnerton was blunt: 'Miss Georgette Heyer, who usually flies in good spirits, falls in "Penhallow".' Though there were several positive reviews none of them judged the book the *tour de force* she, Frere, and Moore had thought it. She had hoped that *Penhallow* would be the novel that would finally enable her to shift the focus of her writing:

The end may possibly be in sight – the end to having to write detective novels, I mean. Once Ronald gets firmly established – & if I should do really well with *Penhallow* – I shall close that chapter in my life – & with what thankfulness! The truth is that I cannot keep up the two-novels-a-year pace. I think I never have kept it up. *Penhallow* knocked me up – just as the *Army* did, & the *Bride*. If I liked writing detective stories, it might be better; but I don't, & that means that they are a strain on what I sometimes feel to be an ebbing vitality. Ronald asked Frere which of the two classes he, as my publisher, would like me to write – Historical or *Penhallow*, Frere replied, *Penhallow*, of course. But I said, One day I shall write a biography, all footnotes. Will you publish that? To which he replied, simply: "Yes". Now, that is something to dream about! What fun I should have – sh<u>all</u> have! such <u>leisured</u> fun! Not a selling proposition at all, just a wish fulfilment.

She never did write the biography, for *Penhallow* marked the beginning of a change in her writing life. The novel passed into Rougier family legend as her Hodder & Stoughton 'contract-breaking book' and in time she accepted (possibly even encouraged) this re-telling of *Penhallow*'s creation. But it was not the truth. She meant to go on writing for Hodder and was even considering a sequel to *Penhallow* – 'Bart's book'.

But Georgette would never write for Hodder & Stoughton again. The breach caused by *Penhallow* proved irreparable and her association with the firm gradually dissolved. Percy Hodder-Williams attempted to restore relations by taking her to lunch at the Ritz, but Georgette found him pompous and patronising and left feeling aggrieved. It also rankled that Uncle Percy's view of *Penhallow* – so diametrically opposed to her own – was shared by others. In December 1942 the Irish Censorship of Publications Board banned *Penhallow* 'in all its editions' on the basis that it was 'in its general tendency, indecent' (the ruling eventually expired in 1967). Georgette's writing had been censored before, but where there was a kind of kudos in being 'banned by the Nazis' (she thought that 'Grand!'), she found none in being banned by the Irish.[18]

Georgette did not write for over a year after *Penhallow* and 1943 was the first time in fifteen years in which she did not publish a book. She seems to have been unwell for much of the year. In August she and Ronald went to Cornwall for six weeks. They stayed at the St Enodoc Golf Hotel, which Georgette thought the ideal spot to 'laze about till I can't laze any more'. Richard, now eleven, went with them; he no longer needed a governess and increasingly his parents were finding pleasure in his company. Georgette took him to see a local production of *As You Like It* and was stunned when, on seeing the throng of people ahead of them 'Richard said casually: "What a crowd! You'd think it was a second crucifixion!"' She told Frere: 'When I had got my breath I thought it well to say that I didn't find that funny (which was a lie, because I <u>crowed</u> inwardly!).'

The only blight on her lovely holiday was having her fellow guests discover her identity after Heinemann inadvertently forwarded a letter to her at the hotel: 'With "Georgette Heyer" emblazoned on the envelope. So all the inmates here Know, & O God, O God, O <u>God</u>! Frere, without exception they LUV *These Old Shades*. It's true. And if I write a letter, they say archly: "Hard at work?"' Ten months after the publication of *Penhallow* she wrote to Moore from Cornwall to say: 'Health better, pen still idle.' A fortnight later she wrote again: 'I return to town on Wednesday, & must then apply myself to literary production – if I haven't forgotten how.'

---

18 It is not known which of Georgette's novels were banned by the Nazi Party.

PART IV

ALBANY: THE GOLDEN YEARS

1942–1966

22

Well, isn't that splendid? I feel quite elated, & have decided
not to die after all.

Georgette Heyer

Georgette returned to London in September 1943. She and Ronald
had moved into F.3. Albany the previous year. After eleven years in
Sussex they found that town life suited them very well and that Albany
was their ideal home. Since its inception in 1803 as bachelor quarters,
Albany had been a much sought-after address. A unique haven in the
heart of London, the aim of the Trustees who administered it was to
ensure residents' privacy and maintain Albany's longstanding tradition
(described by former resident Jonathan Ray) 'as a discreet bastion of
the Establishment and as a refuge for the unconventional'.

The Rougiers' chambers were on the second floor, up two flights
of narrow concrete steps (seventy in all) leading to a handsome front
door with a brass knocker. Though two storey, the set was not especially large, but it had an elegant dining room and a spacious sitting
room (in which Georgette had her desk and her library) on the lower
of its two floors. Their bedroom and bathroom were also on that
level, but the kitchen was rather inconveniently located on the next
floor via a narrow, winding staircase. There were also two tiny
bedrooms upstairs for Richard and for Boris or Frank, should either
of them come home on leave. Georgette had, in addition, taken a
lease on F.1. Top, a tiny attic room with its own front door, a sloping
ceiling and one window which looked out over the Rope Walk (the

main walkway inside Albany) and Vigo Street; it would become Richard's quarters when he was older.

There were rarely children in Albany and in 1945 a new bye-law was introduced which allowed Richard to stay there during the holidays (it read in part 'Children under 13 may stay but not live in Albany'). It was a lonely place for a child and he later told a friend that his one confidant there was 'the part owner [of Albany] known as the Squire of Piccadilly who had been a bright young dog of the late Victorian age'. This was William Stone, a bachelor and life-long resident in Albany who owned many of the building's sets. On his death in 1958 Stone left the freehold of 37 of Albany's sets to his *alma mater*, Peterhouse College, Cambridge.

Albany was also the London home of the Freres (they had a house in Kent where they spent weekends). They lived in E.1. on the ground floor, the set made famous as the home of the great nineteenth-century English historian, Thomas Macaulay. However, it was in F.3. – Georgette's new home – and not E.1. that Macaulay had written his famous bestseller, *The History of England*. His ghost was said to haunt F.3. but Georgette always said that only Johnny the bull-terrier took any notice of it. Albany was home to a number of writers when the Rougiers moved there, including J.B. Priestley, G.B. Stern, Graham Greene, Margery Sharp and Harold Nicolson. It was not with them, however, that Georgette formed a bond, but with Frere's wife, Patricia Wallace. Pat or Miss Wallace (as her friends called her) had been in America with her two small children during the early years of the War and so Georgette did not meet her until after her return to England in 1942.

Pat Wallace was a journalist, book reviewer and theatre critic who had grown up in the literary and theatrical world. As Edgar Wallace's daughter she was used to mixing with famous writers and film people. In her youth she had worked for a time for Dorothy Sutherland at Amalgamated Press but had disliked the editor and resigned. For Georgette, her new friend's antipathy towards the despised Dorothy Sutherland was just another point in Pat Wallace's favour. Already predisposed to like Frere's wife, Georgette soon discovered that they had a good deal in common: Pat Wallace was strong-minded, intelligent and witty. She also had a keen sense of humour, understood writers and writing and admired Georgette's novels. At a deeper level, each woman had lost her father in her early twenties and, although Georgette rarely spoke of it, that shared understanding came to mean a good deal to her. Frere had encouraged his wife to befriend Georgette and in a little more than a year the relationship had blossomed: Pat Wallace had been deemed a kindred spirit and admitted to Georgette's small circle of confidantes.

Georgette never sought to be part of a large social group. She was happiest in her own company, with Ronald, or with a small group of intimates (Richard described his mother as 'very, very shy' and 'to hide this, she would talk nineteen to the dozen to strangers'). Although she was interested in people it was more often as an observer of human nature than as someone who wished to befriend them. Those, like Pat Wallace, who penetrated her outer reserve found her a kind, caring and generous friend, but to the rest of the world she could appear grand and formidable – someone who could hold people at a distance with a word or a look. This was one way of maintaining control. Georgette found a certain safety in her reclusive lifestyle and in keeping her circle of friends small and manageable.

Back in London after her holiday Georgette felt refreshed and ready to start writing again. Within weeks of her return she was well on the way to creating what was to become her own personal favourite among her many novels. She originally called the new book *Cophetua* but neither Frere nor Moore considered it a 'selling title' and preferred her alternative: *Friday's Child*. By November she had written 55,000 words and was enjoying herself. The novel 'is very lively indeed', she told Moore:

> a laugh on every page, & people ought to lap it up. I have a new sort of character in George, Lord Wrotham, who amuses me tremen-dously. He is a beautiful & turbulent young man, always trying to call his friends out to fight duels, & never succeeding. He's in love in a very romantic & despairing way with the Beauty, & I've got him well & truly embroiled in the Heroine's affairs too.

Once again she wrote out a dozen excerpts for Moore's amusement.

She finished *Friday's Child* in December and optimistically prepared a copy for Dorothy Sutherland. At 135,000 words, Georgette thought it probably too long for serialisation but suggested Moore tell the editor that 'this is the book for which all my feeble-minded fans have been waiting a year, & pestering me to write. It should increase the sales of *W.J.* hugely, in fact!' Surprisingly Dorothy Sutherland turned down *Friday's Child* and incurred Georgette's wrath by writing to tell her 'what was wrong with the book & how it could be improved!' But this time it was Dorothy Sutherland who was wrong. Readers loved the new novel. Within weeks of its release in July 1944, Georgette had her first instant bestseller.

Friday's Child quickly sold out its first 25,000 copies. A fortnight after publication Georgette reported that 'Harrods have sold [out], & say they could sell any number more, & are sick & tired of telling people they have no longer got it. Isn't that fine?' The numbers continued to climb and she was delighted to learn from Frere that, even with the novel's dull wartime jacket and smaller size, 'he could have sold 75,000 of my book merely by filling the orders; & 150,000 by exerting himself a little.' Within the next three years, *Friday's Child* would sell nearly a quarter of a million copies. And this time it was not only the readers but also the critics who were enthusiastic.

Georgette could not ignore the huge difference in the public response between *Friday's Child* and *Penhallow*. She had found a style of book that eminently suited her and which allowed her to use her vast fund of historical knowledge. *Friday's Child* was a sparkling romp of a novel with a cast of characters that also let Georgette fully indulge her Austenesque sense of humour. The love affair between her unlikely hero and heroine and the various imbroglios created between them and their three foolish but endearing friends also brought something new to historical fiction. An achievement which Georgette wryly acknowledged to Moore: 'Careful perusal of this work leads me to the ineffably conceited conclusion that No One can do this sort of thing Quite Like Miss Heyer. It's an Art, L.P., that's what it is.' Her self-mockery was characteristic, but in fact she was right.

Georgette never admitted her particular genius – but she came close with *Friday's Child*, telling Louisa Callender at Heinemann:

> You'll be quite safe to tell your travellers to spread the glad tidings that it will not disappoint Miss Heyer's many admirers. Judging from the letters I've received from obviously feeble-minded persons, who do so wish I would write another *These Old Shades*, it ought to sell like hotcakes. I think myself I ought to be shot for writing such nonsense, but it's unquestionably good escapist literature; & I think I should rather like it if I were sitting in an air-raid shelter, or recovering from 'flu. Its period detail is good; my husband says it's witty – & without going to those lengths I will say that it is very good fun.

Twenty years later she still thought the novel 'the best I ever wrote. Perhaps because it wrote itself. Perhaps because it contains Ferdy Fakenham, who not only stole it, but inspired me, years later, to write *Cotillion*.'

Georgette's gift for storytelling, her ironic wit, and her passion for historical detail found the perfect outlet in her Regency novels. *Friday's Child* marked a watershed in her life: for the next thirty years – with just two exceptions – she would write only Regency novels. And with those twenty-two books she would create a genre.

23

When you have a free morning you should invite me to lunch with you, and when I have eagerly accepted this invitation, should devote several hours (or days, according to your imaginative powers) in thinking up all the ways in which I am a superb novelist, an asset to your firm, and Just As Good As Ever I Was.

Georgette Heyer

The success of *Friday's Child* made it clear where the money lay – always a primary consideration for Georgette. Although the financial pressure had eased a good deal in recent years, she still found it difficult to relax about money and she and Ronald resented the ever-increasing taxation demands. In 1944 they finally lost the tax case over the sale of her copyrights and were required to pay over £1,000 in taxes and court costs. It was a bitter blow. The High Court ruling reinforced their view of the tax man as their enemy and the taxation system as one which unfairly penalised hard-working and successful people.

Concerned about the possible implications for other writers of the judgement against her Georgette wrote to the Society of Authors to request their help with an appeal. The Society's reply was courteous but bluntly realistic: 'In our opinion, given an accurate statement of the present legal position, there would be no hope of [t]his decision being reversed.' Georgette took the response as a perfunctory dismissal of her concerns and did not write again. Four years later she instructed her agent to terminate her Society of Authors membership.

Apart from the disastrous tax ruling, 1944 had begun well for the Rougiers. In January, despite the cost of the court case, Ronald had decided to fulfil a long-held ambition and bought 'a magnificent Rolls, Hooper-body-&-all'. In February Georgette had rejoiced to learn that Frere was returning to Heinemann. Evans was unwell and Frere had been running things at the firm while still working for Ernest Bevin. His return to the helm was good news, but even better was hearing that Boris was safely back in Britain: 'I am treading on air just now,' Georgette told Moore, 'for at 12.45 a.m. two nights ago my telephone rang, & Scotland wanted me. And while I was thinking what-the-hell . . . a voice said "Is that you, Sis?" & it was my elder brother! Just landed, with his battery . . . He'll be home on leave in about a week's time'.

Boris was soon installed in the upstairs bedroom at F.3. Albany. He had done well in the military. Army life suited him. Georgette rejoiced to see him again and was encouraged to think that Frank, too, might soon be home. By the middle of the year it was apparent that the tide of war was turning in favour of the Allies. The D-Day landing began on 6 June and brought renewed hope that hostilities would soon be over. 'The Powers that Be are terribly pleased with Monty's wedge,'[19] Georgette observed in July, '& everything is going a treat.' Although it was winding down, the War continued to make life difficult, however. Rationing was still stringently enforced and there were regular power outages across London. Ronald was busy with the local Home Guard and sharing duties with the other Albany residents, including J.B. Priestley who 'wandered in for air-raid duty last night, in an odd-looking tin hat, & saying that he felt like something left over from the Thirty Years War!'

When bombing began in the capital again Georgette responded with characteristic stoicism and good humour, refusing to allow even the advent of the German V1 Flying Bombs to perturb her: 'We had a doodle-bug in Regent Street today. No glass blown here, but a bit

---

19 General Bernard Law Montgomery (Montgomery of Alamein) was commander-in-chief, ground forces, for the Allied invasion of Normandy.

of plaster fell down, & it was one of Those Moments.'[20] The bombs killed thousands and occasionally Georgette and the other Albany residents were compelled to withdraw to the cellars (where the great stage actress and fellow resident Edith Evans would sometimes entertain them with a selection of dramatic turns). Both Moore and Sylvia wanted Georgette to leave London, which annoyed her. Irritated by her agent's earlier departure from the city she eventually lost patience with him: 'Oh, do stop girning [sic] at me about leaving London! I get so tired of it. The latest is from my mother, who thinks it would be nice if I moved into a different flat. Useful! I daresay the bombing will have an effect on me. So what? Maybe the war will have an effect on the men who are fighting it, too. You never know, do you?'

Wartime tragedies had become an intrinsic part of everyday life and Georgette usually took a fairly pragmatic approach to life and death. There were occasions, however, when she was reminded of her own loss and the grief she had so sternly suppressed after her father's death. In May 1944 Pat Wallace's brother was killed in action. He was only twenty-seven. News of the tragedy prompted Georgette to write to her friend:

> Frere has just told me about your brother's death, & although I think letters at such a time are perhaps worse than useless, I couldn't but write to say how dreadfully sorry I am, & how very deeply I feel for you. I know what it is to care very much for a brother, & the thought of what you must be going through now makes me feel quite sick. Which sounds silly, but you'll understand. The best thing I know about death is that one never forgets. It would be too awful if one did. And that sounds silly too, but again you'll probably know what I'm trying clumsily to convey. I don't expect you to answer this, & I beg you

---

20 Also known as Pilot-less planes, Doodlebugs or Buzz Bombs were terror weapons capable of killing large numbers of people and causing massive damage to homes and buildings over a large area. Between June 1944 and March 1945, flying bombs killed over 6,000 people in Britain.

won't. It's only to tell you how deeply both Ronald & I sympathize with you.

Charles Evans also died that year – he had never recovered from the death of his youngest son or from his experiences in war-time London. His death was a loss felt by many in publishing. In a *Times* obituary J.B. Priestley described him as 'one of the most influential publishers of our time' and someone 'to whom hundreds of thousands of readers owe a great deal'. Evans had discovered and nurtured some of the greatest literary talents of his era and he would long be remembered in publishing circles.

But Frere was also a force to be reckoned with. The famous literary agent Lawrence Pollinger once described Frere as 'the cleverest man in London' and he now had sole command at Heinemann. Frere had left Bevin in July and as the War slowly came to an end he began making plans for a future without paper rationing. Georgette was elated to discover that he intended to re-issue all of her earlier novels in order to 'cash in on them'. Frere was convinced that her sales would not lessen after the War. Her only proviso was that he 'drop *Roxhythe* and *Simon* out of the list' for re-printing as 'they never did very well & they're the worst books I wrote.'

Georgette wrote nothing in the second half of 1944 and, owing to the severe paper shortage, Heinemann did not press her. She was busy with domestic matters and had suffered a recurrence of her old dental problems earlier in the year that meant the extraction of several teeth. A photograph taken of her in early August at Dmitri and Dorothy Tornow's wedding (Dmitri was Ronald's cousin) shows her looking gaunt and frail. Soon afterwards, she and Ronald took Richard for a fortnight's holiday to Aberdovey in Wales followed by another fortnight at their favourite Hotel in Cleeve Hill near Cheltenham. She returned home in better health and to increasingly positive War news.

In September the Allies finally silenced the cross-Channel guns and after three long years Britain's southeast coast was at peace. Three months later the King told the Home Guard 'You have fulfilled your charge,' and the entire volunteer force was formally stood down. Increasingly busy in his legal practice, Ronald relinquished his Home Guard duties with some relief. He was now attending Quarter Sessions in places as far apart as Walthamstow in north London, Bury in Lancashire and Ipswich in Suffolk. He would eventually make use of his knowledge and experience as a mining engineer and specialise in utilities law with a particular interest in water.

Georgette was ill again in the new year and it was April before she pronounced herself 'a good deal better . . . though still not in very robust health.' She had been cheered by an invitation from Peter Watt, the literary agent (and grandson of A.P. Watt, the founder of the world's first literary agency), to lunch at his club. Watt's father, 'a Heyer-addict' would also be there and hoped to discuss the Duke of Avon's family tree with her. Georgette was flattered by the invitation, and wondered if it might not 'be a plot to lure me' from her own agent. There was no hint of it on the day, however, and afterwards she was able to tell Moore that there was 'not a word uttered you could Take Amiss!'

This may have been a disappointment, for Moore was growing old and Georgette was increasingly frustrated by her agent's continuing absence from London. 'I hope you're coming back to town now that the war is as good as ended,' she told him. His refusal prompted a frank letter:

> If it is progressive to carry on a literary agency at a distance from London I have certainly learnt something new . . . The very fact that a call to your office necessitates the utterly wearisome & daunting business of dialling TOL, & hanging on for anything up to ten minutes (when you give it up) . . . makes your continued sojourn at Gerrards Cross a Class A bore . . . if I want to see you I have to make a date with you at least a week ahead . . . the number of times I've thought, "I'll go & ring L.P. up, & ask him . . ." & then decided that I wouldn't bother, or would ring Frere instead.

Even the arrival at Christy & Moore of a new, younger man in John

Smith had not halted Georgette's growing dissatisfaction. Yet, despite knowing Peter Watt, she appears not to have considered changing agents. Instead she turned more frequently to Frere and by extension to his wife.

Georgette and Ronald often invited Frere and Pat Wallace up to their set for dinner or a drink and enjoyed many reciprocal invitations. They and the rest of Britain celebrated on 8 May 1945, when the war in Europe officially ended and Victory in Europe (VE Day) was proclaimed. Adjusting to the peace took time, and a month later Georgette's pen still lay idle. It was nearly a year since *Friday's Child* had been published but for once she seemed unperturbed by the long gap between books. The end of the War meant so much and she wanted time to absorb the fact that both her brothers had come through unscathed, her family was safe and there would be no more blackouts or bombing raids.

There were still hardships, however, though Georgette and Ronald were fortunate in being better-placed than many to withstand the postwar deprivation. Rationing would continue in one form or another until 1954 but Georgette's growing income meant they could afford to shop regularly at Fortnum's and Harrods, eat at the Savoy or other restaurants or dine at Ronald's club. Although most of the population suffered from the shortage of things like butter and oil, Georgette thought it wrong to complain about a lack of food. She had the added advantage that Richard's adolescent appetite was mainly catered for at school.

He had turned thirteen in February and was due to finish at The Elms in July before going to board at Marlborough College. Although his mother had occasional concerns about things like his spelling – 'I asked him for the measurements of his trousers, & this is what I got: "Waste (loosly) 27"' – and sometimes wondered if she had 'bred an illiterate', Richard was intelligent with a prodigious memory and a taste for literature, poetry and music. Georgette proudly told of one occasion when 'my mother asked me if I remembered a play, saying: "Do you remember *The Great Lover?*" Richard looked up and said: "Oh, quite one of my favourites! You mean, 'There you have loved'?".' When Georgette finally began writing again her new book had an engaging character in the hero's adventurous adolescent brother. She would dedicate the novel to Richard.

But, as she confessed to Pat Wallace in June, she had not begun a new novel yet. Her friend was in a nursing-home impatiently awaiting the birth of her third child and Georgette had written her a long letter after telephoning Frere for the latest bulletin. She had received an 'acid, over-wrought, & generally jaundiced discourse' from the expectant father and told Pat Wallace 'you have all my sympathy. I had little for Frere. I told him it was far worse for you, & he uttered a sound which I should write down in a novel as Ha!' After four pages of humorous 'nothings', Georgette asked:

> You are wondering (Dear Miss Wallace) why I do not apply my energies to the task of writing a book for Frere instead of drivel to you? I wouldn't know. It's just one of those things. Besides, he doesn't advertise me enough, & puts other authors above me, & doesn't give me all his paper, which is so unfair. And I daresay, if we only knew, he doesn't really appreciate me. From which you will gather that I have lately sustained a conversation with a fellow-inky. True. I am firmly of the opinion we should all be incarcerated. In parenthesis, this is a terrific gambit, & one that has not previously occurred to me. Apparently you "get a feeling" that your publisher is "out of sympathy" with your work. Under these conditions it becomes impossible for you to "give of your best." I can't think why, but then I've never been a very sensitive plant.

She closed the letter: 'I look forward to visiting you, & seeing the new Frere. It's a long time since I had anything to do with an infant, & it will be nice to see one again.' The Freres' third child, a son, was born six days later.

1945 was the year of the General Election and the only time Georgette ever voted Labour. She was not the only Tory to contribute to the Labour landslide that year by casting her vote contrary to her usual political inclinations. Many among the British populace had moved to the political left during the War and, despite Churchill's popularity as a war leader, did not consider him the best person to lead the country in a time of peace.

Georgette had an abiding interest in politics and was never shy of expressing an opinion. A year before the election she had read *Your M.P.* by 'Gracchus',[21] a ferocious diatribe against National-Liberal and Tory M.P.s and their acquiesence in the policy of appeasement before the War. The book had provoked a furore, sold 200,000 copies in its first month and prompted one of Georgette's blunt epistles:

> I seem to remember wildly cheering Labour & Socialist M.P.s at the time of Munich; while as for the decade before Munich, no party can afford to throw any mud. In fact, I think I am right in saying that it was Labour which raised the biggest outcry against any form of armament. Of course I rather loved parts of the book, because he went for people I detest, like Hoare, & Simon, & Wardlaw-Milne, & Baldwin . . . I suspect him of belonging to that illiterate mass of persons who apparently believe that the Government can always produce money out of a sort of a conjuror's hat. His remarks about the opposition to the Beveridge Plan betray a bland ignorance of the most appalling fact now facing us: that We Are Broke – broke beyond anything he can imagine, & perhaps irremediably. He, like *The Times* . . . would like to bleed the Upper & Middle Classes white – he, because he thinks it would solve everything & do no harm, *The Times* because it thinks by doing this we can stave off ruin for perhaps 30 or 50 years . . . In all, it was quite good fun, & very shocking, & bits were true, & bits were not.

With the election over she thought she might at last begin a new book. But Richard was home for the long vacation and Georgette had never liked writing in the hot summer months. She was also busy reading another manuscript for Heinemann. They had continued

---

21 Gracchus was Tom Wintringham, a former commander of the British Battalion of the International Brigade; he was also one of the founders of the Home Guard.

to employ her as a reader through the War and her latest report was for an unpublished book entitled *In Me My Enemy*. Georgette's frank advice and suggestions for improvements reflected her astute understanding of what a successful novel entailed:

> Well, you can't handle it. It's all very difficult, but I do seem to be sure about that. I think she has got something. She can tell a story, she has a gift of phrase, & the fact that she can't spell or punctuate doesn't really matter. What does matter is that here is a huge inchoate mass of a book, without rhyme or reason, overweighted & degenerating, in its last third, into a melodrama . . . At present she's undisciplined & she doesn't seem to see her story as a whole, or to know how to balance it. Nor does she understand that if you set out to write an immensely long book there must be more substance to it than the chronicle of various lives, leading us to no particular goal, positing no moral, working out no problems.

Georgette's final counsel was succinct:

> "Don't be too ambitious!" is impossible advice to give to a young author, but it is the right advice here. The girl has the makings of a romantic novelist, not of a great gloomy, introspective sagawriter. I would advise her to put this book in a drawer; to think out a good, close-knit plot with plenty of wild deeds and dark passions, & a nice, fat climax; to limit herself to 100,000 words; not to stray into the bog of psychology – & to get on with it!

24

While I like to have the fact of my having written a new book made known to an eager public, I cannot bear, and will not consent to any of the more blatant forms of self-advertisement.

Georgette Heyer

In October 1945 Frere sought Georgette's advice on a more serious project: Heinemann's publication of Richard Aldington's biography of the Duke of Wellington. Aldington was a great friend of Frere's and a prolific writer famous for his novel *Death of a Hero* (1929). Highly regarded in literary circles, Aldington's Wellington biography had already been published in America as *The Duke* and Frere now suggested re-publishing it in Britain as *Wellington*. He sought Georgette's advice on the best illustrations for the new edition and she read the book with interest, made a detailed list of possible pictures and wrote a letter suggesting some minor amendments and corrections to the text. Doubtful as to whether these should be forwarded to Aldington, she told Frere:

> Here is my letter to Aldington, & my suggestions for the illustra-tions. You had better read both, & if you think it won't do, don't send it. I tried it out on Ronald, asking: "Is that offensive, do you think?" He said: "Oh no!" Then I said: "I don't want to sound unbearably know-all, – but on the other hand I don't want him to think I'm offering a lot of criticism on insufficient information.

Do you think he'll realize that I really do know a good deal about the subject?" He replied gravely: "I think it will be irresistibly borne in upon him." Now, I regard this answer with the most profound suspicion. I do not like that word "irresistibly." Have I been insufferable? One so often is on one's own high horse.

But Frere did not think she had been insufferable. He told Aldington he had given *Wellington* to 'a deeply read authority on the subject, one Mrs Rougier, who writes under the name of Georgette Heyer, who knows the period backwards' and forwarded Georgette's notes. Aware that Aldington might resent interference from an unknown commentator, Frere explained that Georgette 'is a very great friend of mine' and also 'a great friend of Charles Oman's and by way of being a pupil of his'. He also explained that she 'has taken a great deal of trouble with suggestions for illustrations', before warning Aldington: 'She has one or two scholarly points to raise with you about this and that, and particularly your piece on Waterloo. She is enthusiastic enough about the book to not wish to give a pedantic reviewer a handle, but she is extremely diffident of making any suggestions. I have assured her that you are the last person in the world to resent such a thing.'

But Frere was wrong. At first glance Aldington's reply appeared sanguine for he thanked his publisher for sending Georgette's letter and corrections. He quickly explained, however, that he considered her suggested amendments (which he ignored) as having come from a writer with an ambition to write her own book about Wellington. The consequence of his unexpected reaction meant Frere had to tread a fine line between his two friends: shielding Georgette from Aldington's ire, while ensuring that Aldington was not deterred from completing the project. Letters and cables flew back and forth between the two men and Frere wrote Georgette a short, diplomatic letter which included several out-of-context sentences from Aldington's latest epistle:

Richard Aldington has cabled asking me to put off *Wellington* indefinitely, and he has followed up with a letter in which he says your points can only be answered in detail and at immense length . . . He goes on to say: "I can't tell you how much gratitude I owe you for sending those notes along." To which I would add my own special measure of gratitude. Personally, I don't mind how long he holds it up if the net result is as good as it can be.

This was a most satisfactory response to her annotations and Georgette was 'relieved and gratified'. She remained blissfully ignorant of Aldington's cursory dismissal of her scholarship and was delighted when he (somewhat ironically) decided to use both her proposed list of illustrations and her design for the book's jacket. *Wellington* came out in September 1946 with a cover which featured – as per her suggestion – 'the centre of the great gold shield, presented to the Duke after the Battle of Waterloo'. There is no mention of her small contribution anywhere in the book and Georgette never knew that her efforts had been misconstrued.

In September she told Frere: 'There is a book going round in my own head like a borer beetle, but it hasn't yet chrystalised [sic].' She soon worked it out, however, and early in the new year it was finished. 'I expect you will like my next book,' she told a young Australian fan, 'which is to be published this spring under the title of *The Reluctant Widow*'. Thirteen-year-old Rosemary White had written to Georgette from rural Australia after learning about the drastic food rationing in Britain (which in 1946 included bread for the first time). Worried that her favourite author might be starving and unable to write, Rosemary offered to send her a food parcel. Deeply touched and a little amused by her concern, Georgette wrote to reassure her: 'It is very kind of you to want to send me a parcel of food, but I think you had much better save the money to buy my next book! Then we shall both benefit! Things are difficult in England, but not desperate.' Despite her assurances, the promised food parcel arrived. Appreciating the gesture, Georgette sent Rosemary an inscribed copy of *The Reluctant Widow*: 'which I hope you will enjoy'.

Rosemary thought *The Reluctant Widow* delightful. A parody of the Gothic novel it was made even more amusing by its heroine's awareness of having fallen into an improbable adventure. Nearly fifteen years later Ronald was forcibly reminded of the novel in court. On 4 February 1959, at a session of the Water Bill Committee Hearings in the House of Commons (in which Ronald was acting as counsel for the Committee), the Chairman, Major Legge-Bourke, made a speech to the opposing counsel:

> The Chairman: Perhaps I might say to you, Lord Vaughan, that while you were using the wedding-metaphors I could not help but be reminded of something with which Mr Rougier is, perhaps, more familiar, from *The Reluctant Widow*, by Georgette Heyer: "I have spent a great deal of my life listening patiently to much folly. In my sisters I can support it with tolerable equanimity. In you I neither can nor will. Will you accept my hand in marriage, or will you not?"
>
> Lord Vaughan: Mr Rougier has matrimonially the advantage!

Georgette was widely read in the legal profession and in both Houses of Parliament. As Lord Keith once told her in relation to the House of Lords: 'as far as he can discover the better part of its inmates are my firm fans.'

The Reluctant Widow was also published in the United States where G.P. Putnam had taken over publishing her novels (they had also brought out *Friday's Child* in 1946). Georgette had not had an American publisher since ending her relationship with Doubleday in 1942 and her experience with them had made her a little cynical about her chances of success with the new firm: 'Putnam's say they are very excited about *Friday's Child*. It doesn't take much to excite an American.' She did not think much of Americans *en masse*, although she liked them individually. Her typically English view of Americans as uncultured and excessively gregarious was not enhanced by Walter Minton's (the head of Putnam) effusive response to her novels or by his empty promises of publicity and enormous sales.

The Reluctant Widow also caught the attention of a film company. This time the deal went through and Georgette was able to tell her young Australian fan that the novel was 'being filmed in technicolour next year!' With a film in the offing and the possibility of additional income from a successful production, Georgette and Ronald finally took steps to improve their financial situation and employed a new accountant, Mr J.M. Rubens. He advised them to set up a limited liability company and to have all of Georgette's future contracts and copyrights assigned to it. As the company's Chairman and Director, Georgette and Ronald would receive annual bonuses and dividends. The company would also pay Georgette 'for her services'. On 29 October 1946 they held the first annual meeting of their new company, Heron Enterprises Limited. For the next twenty-two years Heron Enterprises would own the copyright in Georgette's novels.

Her first book for Heron was *The Foundling*. In May 1947 Georgette wrote to Frere to say: 'Imagine! – L.P. has sold *The Foundling* to the S.B. for £1000 – on the strength of the first third of the book, which stinks anyway.' Her pessimistic view of the novel did not last and although she deprecated Dorothy Sutherland's handling of *The Foundling* ('the story is being embellished with some of the most appalling illustrations'), its sale marked a turning-point in her rela- tionship with *Woman's Journal*. It was twelve years since they had serialised *Regency Buck* as *Gay Adventure*. Over the next twenty years Georgette's serialised novels would become almost an annual feature of *Woman's Journal* and Dorothy Sutherland soon discovered that £1,000 was a small price to pay for an author whose stories guaranteed that the magazine sold out. Years later she told Jane Aiken Hodge that 'men snatched it from their wives to read the next instalment.'

Georgette took a break from *The Foundling* when Richard came home for the holidays. He was doing well at school and his sporting achievements and academic prowess seemed to his mother 'of far more importance than Widows or Foundlings'. She was also pondering the direction of the new book: 'Unless I do something about Harriet', she told Frere, 'this will be a novel without a heroine, for no one could call the ravishing Belinda a heroine. And whether I shall let it stand as it is – a leisurely, long book – or whether I shall ruthlessly cut & re-write I know not. I think it lacks sparkle.' Her view of *The Foundling* was probably not helped by Ronald – generally her most loyal supporter – who was advocating a return to a more serious style of novel:

> Ronald wants me to jack up the Regency & do a worth-while book again. He says I have it in me: I don't think I have. Says also that it was *The Army* which put me on the map, & why not start a big book? This is easily answered: it looks too much like work! I became Grand & Aloof, & talked about Writing only the Book one <u>wants</u> to write. To which he replied mildly that he had had the impression that I felt no particular urge to write *The Foundling*.

The suggestion that she write a 'real' book was one that would trouble Georgette throughout her life, with both Frere and Ronald intermittently prodding her to write this apparently elusive tome. That both men were probably taking their cues from her and telling her what each thought she wanted to hear was irrelevant: Georgette needed those she loved and trusted to tell her that what she was doing was meaningful and important.

Her continuing wish to be recognised as a serious writer was one reason why Ronald encouraged a return to a more historical book, but he may also have been trying to relieve the pressure on her to always write a 'seller'. Ronald was now earning, if not a large income, at least a reliable one and Georgette's royalty income alone was consistently bringing in over £1,000 a year (the equivalent of £22,000 in 2009). She also received a sizeable advance for any new novel and now there were to be regular payments from *Woman's Journal*. With their rent costing them only £350 a year they were comfortably situated. If Georgette had really wanted to, she could have put the Regency aside and written the 'worthwhile' book she so often talked about.

The fact was, she was already writing 'real books'. Her best novels were those in which she could give full rein to her comic genius and her passion for historical detail – the Georgians and the Regencies. These were the novels for which her readers clamoured. And, however much she scorned them or protested their worth, in her heart they were what she wanted to write. As Jane Aiken Hodge astutely observed: 'To write romantic comedy supremely well as she did, she must have enjoyed it.' Years later, Richard would assert that his mother was 'a compulsive weaver of stories' and that it was 'just talk to say she had to write another Regency to pay tax'.

25

Heyer-addicts just ARE (& some of them are quite sensible people!), & they don't mind What It's About.

Georgette Heyer

Georgette finished *The Foundling* in time for the first instalment to appear in *Woman's Journal* in September 1947. Her attitude to the novel had improved on completion and she told Rosemary White that she hoped she would like her new hero, the Duke of Sale: 'He isn't tall, or handsome, or dominant, but I rather love him myself.' Rosemary and her mother had sent another food parcel and Georgette had written a long, surprisingly frank letter (Rosemary was not yet fourteen) in reply:

> And what, pray, can I possibly send you in return, from this impoverished island? I know you would like a new book by Me, but I can't send you that, because it won't appear until March. It is coming out in serial form in *Woman's Journal* – one of those horrid monthly magazines which request you to "turn to page 175" after the first few paragraphs. For reasons which I don't pretend to fathom, the editor has altered my title, which is "The Foundling", to "His Grace, the Duke of Sale." Apart from the really awful snob-value of this, I believe the dictum laid down by my son at the age of twelve is correct: A Five-Word Title Won't Do!

Richard was now fifteen and in August his parents took him on an extended trip to Scotland. It was his first time 'over the border' and, like his mother (who as a supporter of the royal Stuarts thought of Scotland as her 'spiritual home'), he fell in love with the Highlands. They toured the countryside for several weeks, with Richard quoting *Macbeth* and the *Lays of the Scottish Cavaliers* and singing the *Skye Boat Song* as they went across to Skye from Kyle of Lochalsh. He and Georgette were both forced to quell Ronald's 'tendency to flip-pancy' at such moments.

The family also visited East Lothian where they discovered Greywalls, a former gentleman's residence designed by Edwin Lutyens with gardens by Gertrude Jekyll. It was now a country-house hotel with magnificent views across the Firth of Forth. Greywalls backed onto Muirfield, the world-famous golf course of the Honourable Company of Edinburgh Golfers (of which Ronald later became a member). For Georgette and Ronald there could be no more perfect place, and Greywalls soon became their favourite holiday destination. Georgette was so satisfied with their 'heavenly tour' of Scotland that she felt moved to declare that 'even if we have to go to some horrid watering-place next year, in a crowded train, at least we had fun this year!'

A much less successful trip was their Christmas holiday in Ireland. Georgette went as far as Killarney, but told her friends: 'as far as I'm concerned you can have Ireland!' They returned to London just after the new year to discover a Christmas parcel from Rosemary White in Australia. Georgette felt a great kindness towards this young fan and again tried to assure her that: 'Here, in England, nothing much is lacked' – a generous statement given that Britain was enduring the longest, cruellest winter for decades and she was 'anxiously calculat[ing] how long the coal-ration will last!' But Georgette's letters to Rosemary were always kind.

She could, when she chose, be dismissive of fans who wrote to her praising her novels, asking for sequels ('I wonder what more they think there is to say about them?'), posing 'fatuous questions' and even, in one instance, suggesting that a statue be erected to her. She did not always reply. When she did her answer usually depended on the nature of the question and her perception of the writer's intel-ligence. Often gracious and charming, she could sometimes write the sort of answer that 'seems to daunt them a bit!' Georgette had even been known to tell a fan who had pointed out an error in one of her novels that she would be better off to refrain from opening the book again.

The Foundling came out in April 1948 and Arnold Gyde, the head of Heinemann's editorial department, wrote to congratulate her and – remembering previous blunders – to explain the blurb he had recently written for the book:

> I do hope the present one is not particularly obnoxious. What struck me privately about your book was that you had developed a sense of comedy, latent in most of them, into a really flowering success. I wrote, in my poor way, much to this effect. "For heaven's sake", cried Frere, "do you want to give the impression that this is the first time she has achieved a comedy?" Of course, I meant nothing of the kind. What I really did feel was that you had developed this ingredient inherent in your work to a charming extent in this last book.

Gyde was right about *The Foundling*. Georgette had written a very funny novel with several new character types and a clever, pacy plot. Echoes of Jane Austen pervade the book and Georgette's creation of the pliable and dim-witted Belinda – the foundling of the title – was surely inspired by Harriet Smith, the foolish foundling in *Emma*. Although *The Foundling* as a whole bears little resemblance to *Emma*, Georgette took pleasure in writing her own version of the sorts of jokes at which Austen excelled. In *Emma*, Harriet Smith asks: 'Will Mr Frank Churchill pass through Bath as well as Oxford?' on his way from Yorkshire to Surrey. Georgette created her own 'geography joke' in *The Foundling* by having her hero spend the day searching the town of Hitchin for Belinda's protector, only later to hear Tom Mamble tell Belinda:

> "I daresay she doesn't live at Hitchin at all, but at Ditchling, or – or Mitcham, or some such place."
>
> Belinda looked much struck, and said ingenuously: "Yes, she does!"

The Duke was in the act of conveying a portion of braised ham to his mouth, but he lowered his fork at this, and demanded, "Which?"

"The one Tom said," replied Belinda brightly.

The Foundling had a first printing of 40,000 copies. Foyle's Book Club also published the novel, selling 220,000 copies in less than a year. Book clubs were hugely popular in postwar Britain. *The Foundling* was Georgette's third book with Foyle's, who had enjoyed tremendous success with *Friday's Child* and *The Reluctant Widow*. Book club royalties were considerably smaller than for her UK and foreign editions but what she lost in percentage Georgette made up in volume and book club sales soon became a valuable addition to her royalty income.

Ronald had continued urging her to begin a serious novel and she had finally 'yielded to the persuasions (some might call it nagging) of Husband and Publisher & am now committed to what Frere calls a Real Book'. But in September she was interrupted by sudden inspiration and wrote to ask Frere: 'Do you mind if I revert to an old idea, and write the story of George, Lord Wrotham, who figured in *F's Child*? It doesn't matter if you do, of course, because I think I'm going to, & I've got lots of good bits, in my head, though no particular plot yet. Ferdy will figure largely, and altogether I think it will be fun.'

Though there is a variation of Ferdy in the novel (in the character of Felix Scunthorpe) Georgette appears to have (temporarily, at least) discarded her idea of writing Lord Wrotham's story. Her new book was *Arabella* and by October Georgette had written nearly 20,000 words. She described her eponymous heroine as 'a nice wench, and giving me a lot of fun' while, 'as for Mr Beaumaris, the fans will fall for him in rows, because he's their favourite hero.' Georgette occasionally described her heroes as either Mark I: 'the brusque, savage sort with a foul temper' and 'a Know-All', or Mark II: 'enigmatic or supercilious' and 'suave, well-dressed, rich, and a famous whip'. *Arabella*'s Mr Beaumaris was the 'no. 2 model'.

She finished the book in just over a month and Moore easily sold it to *Woman's Journal*. Heinemann forecast it as a big seller and Arnold Gyde advised the recently appointed head of Heinemann's new Australian office, Clem Christesen, to prepare for a first Australian print run of 15,000 copies. 'Spare no efforts with this book', he told Christesen, 'as not only is Georgette Heyer an excellent seller in Australia but she personally is a great personal friend of Mr Frere the Chairman, and nothing will be better than to be able to show him the largest subscription a Heyer book has ever had in Australia.'

Australian readers were avid Heyer fans. *The Foundling* had sold 10,000 copies there on publication and 18,000 in its first six months. Christesen was not to 'make any mistake about her selling qualities in Australasia' but he did not need convincing. He was already preparing Australian reprints of *Friday's Child*, *Regency Buck* and *The Masqueraders* in what was becoming an increasingly lucrative market for Georgette's mother, who still received her 'colonial' royalties. Georgette's novels and short stories were often published in the country's most popular magazine *The Australian Women's Weekly* (circulation 725,000). As early as 1937 they had touted her as 'the greatest writer of the romantic historical drama'.

Georgette had recently returned to the short-story genre, publishing a whimsical Regency tale entitled 'Full Moon' in November's *Woman's Journal* and another Regency, 'Snowdrift', in *The Illustrated London News*. She was glad to have the extra money from the shorts, because her brother Frank was getting married in March and Georgette was paying for the reception. She had almost despaired of seeing either of her brothers wed and was delighted when, after taking a job as Classics master at Denstone College in Staffordshire, Frank had met Joan Peacock-Price. Joan was an attractive widow in her thirties with a young son. She was a vibrant, athletic woman and a first-rate tennis player (she had played mixed doubles at Wimbledon). Georgette and Joan would never be close (especially as Georgette was given to announcing proudly that she 'took no exercise and played no ball-games') but she was happy to see her brother married and to welcome Joan into the family.

Sylvia was also pleased to see Frank married. Georgette's mother had returned to South Kensington after the War and taken rooms at Courtfield Gardens, a short ride on the underground from her daughter. Georgette worried about her living alone and tried to persuade her to engage a companion. Sylvia refused. Her sisters, Ciss and Jo, were now in their eighties and resiliently active. Even after Jo had suffered a slight stroke, Georgette found her aunt as fiercely independent as her mother. Her ageing relatives were another reason why Georgette still struggled to relax about money. For twenty-five years she had been her family's financial safeguard – no easy task during the Depression and the War – and yet, despite the anxiety it often caused her, it was not a responsibility she chose to relinquish. She had a great affection for her aunts, who had known her since birth and who were strong-minded, forthright and amusing, and she had a genuine concern for their well-being.

Despite her independent attitude, Georgette's mother did need her support, although this was sometimes a thankless task. Sylvia had a tendency towards depression (it was said in the family that Boris had inherited his manic depressive condition from his mother). Although Georgette herself was not always easy, she sometimes found her mother difficult to the point that she later admitted: 'When Mama is at her worst she makes me ill – do what I will I <u>cannot</u> overcome this!' Nevertheless she continued to care for Sylvia and also, whenever necessary, for Boris. Self-sufficient during his army years, now that the War was over, Boris struggled to find a suitable occupation. Aware of the difficulties caused by his extreme moods and mercurial temperament, Georgette did what she could to smooth his path financially. Although her family was sometimes a burden Georgette felt a strong duty of care. If she occasionally complained about her mother and aunts, in practice she was unshakeably loyal and supportive.

Early in 1949 the injection of cash from *Woman's Journal* for *Arabella* created enough of a hiatus between novels to enable Georgette to at last begin working on her 'serious' book. By April she was 'lost in the fifteenth century'. She called the book *Fettered*

Eagle. Its subject was John, Duke of Bedford, younger brother to Henry V. Georgette's vision was of a grand medieval novel which would take a year or two of research and writing and be the sort of book to make people 'sit up and take notice'. She had learned a great deal in the twenty years since *Simon the Coldheart* and *The Conqueror* and while she was not entirely unhappy with *The Conqueror*, she loathed *Simon* condemning it (along with *Roxhythe*) as her worst work which she wished only 'to smother, remainder, and destroy'.

The new medieval book was to be quite different and she was excited by its prospects, even taking a research trip to France with Ronald that year to see the places where John of Bedford had lived and ruled. They visited Orléans, where Joan of Arc had led the French army against the English, and Rouen where they saw John's tomb. Georgette spent time trying to decipher early French while Ronald worked at translating Latin inscriptions. That first trip was only a beginning, but it was enough to convince Georgette that '*Fettered Eagle* is going to be grand!' By September, however, she had put the medieval novel away and begun writing a new Regency. *Fettered Eagle* would need time for both the research and the writing, whereas Georgette could pen a witty period novel in a few months. It also helped that these were the books her readers wanted to buy in ever-increasing numbers.

Frere fulfilled his promise to begin reprinting her novels that year. They were to be issued in a Uniform edition with new dustjackets which he assured her were 'going to sell <u>such</u> a lot of books'. Philip Gough would do the artwork for the Uniform series, for *Arabella*, and for the Foyle's Book Club edition of *The Foundling*. The wrappers were tasteful and stylish, and a welcome change after the plain jackets of the War years. Georgette was delighted with them, declaring 'each picture more charming than the last. If I have a preference, I think it is for *The Foundling*, which is utterly Stubbs!' She also liked Gough's design for *Arabella* – although she felt compelled to tell Frere: 'there is an error in it. For a few moments I couldn't think what was wrong, and then it dawned on me! The lady's stance! Even in my mamma's youth, any lady crossing her legs would have been torn right off the ship.' However, she deemed it a great improvement on the cover of the paperback edition of *The Corinthian*, her first-ever Pan title, published the previous year: 'Have you ever seen such a vulgar-looking job? What I particularly admire is the come-hither look on the heroine's face: you may see the same any evening in Burlington Gardens!'

Georgette hated any sort of salacious take on her work, but worse was to come, when in November 1949, she received the advance publicity for the film of *The Reluctant Widow*. A few moments' perusal was enough to convince her that her story was being advertised as a kind of bodice-ripper:

> I feel as though a slug had crawled over me. I think it is going to do me a great deal of harm, on account of the schoolgirl public. Already I'm getting letters reproaching me. They have turned the Widow into a "bad-girl" part for Jean Kent, and this week's *Illustrated* carries two pages, headed "Jean Locks Her Bedroom Door". Also seduction scenes 1 and 2 . . . I should like a notice to appear in every paper disclaiming all responsibility. At all events, I think I can get my name removed from the thing, and I shall. It seems to me that to turn a perfectly clean story of mine into a piece of sex-muck is bad faith, and something very different from the additions and alterations one would expect to be obliged to suffer. If I had wanted a reputation for salacious novels I could have got it easily enough. The whole thing is so upsetting that it is putting me right off the stroke.

Georgette was no prude, but she found it difficult to have her book torn apart and put back together with only the faintest resemblance to her story and not even a vestige of its original wit or humour. It was an unpleasant interruption to her writing, especially as she was trying to finish her latest novel before Christmas. She had already written 70,000 words of *The Grand Sophy* which 'My brother says is most amusing. But I have bought a large bottle of disinfectant.' She wrote Frère a long, satirical advertisement for the book and appended a witty, self-mocking summation of her personal principles for successful novel-writing:

1. Induce your publisher to hand over at once a sum of money grossly in excess of what the book is likely to be worth to him. This gives one a certain amount of incentive to write the thing, and may be achieved by various methods, the most highly recommended being what may be termed as The Little Woman Act.

2. Think out a snappy title. This deceives the publisher into thinking (a) that he is getting the Book of the Year; and (b) that you have the whole plot already mapped out. The only drawback lies in the fact that having announced a title you will be slightly handicapped when it comes to hanging some kind of story on to it.

3. Brood for several weeks, achieving, if not a Plot, depression, despair, and hysteria in yourself, and a strong desire to leave home in your entourage. This condition will induce you to believe yourself to be the victim of Artistic Temperament, and may even mislead you into thinking that you really are a Creative Artist.

4. While under this delusion, jab a sheet of paper into your type-writer, and hurl on to it Chapter I. This may give you an idea, not perhaps for the whole book, but for Chapter II.

5. Introduce several characters who might conceivably be useful later on. You never know: they may take matters into their own hands.

6. Assuming that he has been properly trained, read over what you have done to your husband. His extravagant enthusiasm may lead you to think you've perpetrated something good and this will inspire you to churn out a bit more.

7. Think out a grand final scene, with the maximum number of incongruous characters massed together in some improbable place. Allow your sense of farce full play. This will, with any luck at all, make the reader forget what the rest of the book was like.

8. Try and work out how and why these characters got together remembering that it is better to "gloss over", by technique (which

if you haven't learnt in thirty years you ought to have learnt), than to put your head in the gas oven.

9. Book a room in a good Mental Home.

Finally, a few things to be avoided while engaged on this work:

1. The thought that you are enduring this agony only to enrich the Inland Revenue.
2. All thought of the book that has obsessed your mind and soul for the past six months.
3. Any rational thought whatsoever. To indulge in this can only mean that you will stop dead, realizing that you are writing unmitigated rubbish, and would have done better as a charwoman.

I might, with propriety, append a few Phrases for Husbands – Copyright by Mr G.R. Rougier.

Your hand has not lost its cunning.
Strange that you should write anything so lively when you are not in the mood.
What "happened", pray, in FRIDAY'S CHILD?
I shouldn't worry.
I am sure Frere will love it.
I think it is most amusing, and/or most interesting.
Haven't you got anything more to read to me?
You always feel like this when you write a winner.
Just carry on.
It will come to you in a flash. (Cite examples from the past.)

Three weeks later, despite 'labouring under all the disabilities of Sinus Trouble', Georgette finished *Sophy* and wryly declared that it did 'not perhaps stink as much as at one time I feared it might'.

26

I must confess that I resent having my novels used, jig-saw fashion, to provide others with material for their stories. I can bear with tolerable equanimity the indignation of my readers at what – to quote the latest letter I have received – they call "gross plagiarism", but not the accusation, several times endured, of publishing shoddy stuff, under a pseudonym.

Georgette Heyer

Georgette's regular self-deprecation was to some extent a defence mechanism. Well able to recognise that her books sat outside the canon of great literature, she could also see that what she wrote was a good deal better than many of the novels on offer to an increasingly literate audience. She rarely spoke about her research or her writing and, on the few occasions when she did mention such things in her letters, the references were usually brief and sardonic. It was not until she learned that her burgeoning popularity had encouraged one imitator to overstep the boundary between inspiration and appropriation that Georgette finally mounted an energetic defence of her work.

She was first made aware of the possibility of plagiarism in May 1950, when a fan wrote to inform her of an author who had been 'immersing herself in some of your books and making good use of them'. She was referring to Barbara Cartland who had recently published her first three historical novels.[22] *A Hazard of Hearts* and *A Duel of Hearts* (1949) were the first and second books in a 'Georgian' trilogy of which the third novel, *Knave of Hearts*, had just been published. Barbara Cartland was a socialite with connections to the 'best circles', an occasional columnist for the *Daily Express* and the author of several works of non-fiction, three plays and some thirty moderately successful modern romances. She had written *A Hazard of Hearts* after a woman's magazine had commissioned her to write her first historical romance.

Georgette had never heard of Barbara Cartland and an initial, cursory reading of Cartland's first two historical novels left her inclined to dismiss the author as no more than 'a petty thief' of names, characters and plot points. Among Cartland's more obvious 'borrowings' were several names from *Friday's Child*, including Sir Montagu Revesby, altered to 'Sir Montagu Reversby'; Hero Wantage, now 'Harriet Wantage'; Viscount Sheringham was 'Viscount Sherringham', while Lord Wrotham remained 'Lord Wrotham'. Georgette identified many additional 'lifts' from this and others of her novels, including *The Corinthian*, *The Reluctant Widow* and *The Foundling*:

> On perusing the first two novels of Miss Cartland's trilogy, I was astonished to find that my informant had underestimated the case in so far as the number of identical, or infinitesimally altered names and titles is concerned. I also found what might best be described as paraphrases of situations I had created, and a suspicious number of Regency cant words, or obsolete turns of speech, all of which I can pin-point in several of my books, and all of which I have

---

22 Plagiarism can be a notoriously complex issue and is often difficult to prove. It must be pointed out that no official judgment has ever been made in relation to these books. To anyone familiar with Georgette Heyer's historical novels, however, Barbara Cartland's *Knave of Hearts* does strike a great many chords in terms of plot, characters, setting and dialogue. Georgette never brought the case to court, though she did brief her solicitor, who sent a formal letter of protest to Miss Cartland's publisher. Georgette's main aim was to put a stop to the 'borrowings' and, if possible, to see the books withdrawn from sale. In 1971, *Knave of Hearts* was re-issued under a new title, *The Innocent Heiress*, with a heading: 'In the Tradition of Georgette Heyer.'

acquired during fourteen years' study of the period. The facts that no word or phrase I have <u>not</u> yet used appears in Miss Cartland's works, and that she shows a strange ignorance of the meaning of some of those she does use also seem to me to be significant.

Having cited several of Cartland's errors, Georgette concluded with what she considered a clincher: 'One slang phrase which appears in her book, *Hazard of Hearts*, I got from an unpublished source.' This, she explained, was 'a privately printed book, lent me by a descendant of Lieut. Gawler, because the owner had enjoyed *An Infamous Army*. I don't think I have met the expression elsewhere, and I am sure Miss Cartland has had no access to my sources.'

Aware that there 'was no copyright in names' or in Regency parlance, Georgette's initial thought was to write a strong letter of protest to Barbara Cartland. But on reading *Knave of Hearts*, she changed her mind and wrote to her solicitor instead:

> Miss Cartland – possibly emboldened by my having taken no notice of her previous lifts – has now gone very much further. The conception of THE KNAVE OF HEARTS, the principal characters, and many of the incidents, derive directly from an early book of my own, entitled THESE OLD SHADES, and first published by Messrs William Heinemann in 1926.

A complete reading left Georgette in no doubt that in writing *Knave of Hearts* the author had lifted far more than characters and incidents: 'For her main theme Miss Cartland has gone solely to THESE OLD SHADES, but for various minor situations and other characters she has drawn upon four of my other novels.'

She carefully worked her way through Cartland's third historical novel and her own relevant books, annotating as she went. When she next wrote to her solicitor Georgette not only sent a cross-indexed copy of *The Knave of Hearts* in which she had 'ringed all names and period phrases, in red ink, and indicated in black ink, giving title of my own book and page of passage, all situations identical or too like mine, and all paraphrases', but also a ten-page list of the main points of similarity between the novels, with examples of Cartland's historical and linguistic errors. It was not only Regency dialogue which her imitator appeared not to understand but also Regency fashion, as Georgette pointed out:

> From *Hazard of Hearts*, pp.68, 69. 'He was in riding clothes, with boots of Hessian leather fitting perfectly over tight breeches of the latest shade of yellow, his coat of a rich shade of brown had been cut by the great Stultz himself.' From *Friday's Child*, p.4. 'The long-tailed coat of blue cloth, made for him by no less a personage than the great Stultz, sat without a crease across his shoulders; his breeches were of the fashionable pale yellow; and his top-boots were exquisitely polished.' Strange that Miss Cartland, so well-informed on such details as the most fashionable colour for breeches, and one of the most fashionable tailors of the day, should fall down on the ABC of Regency dress. Hessians were worn with pantaloons, never with breeches.

But even worse to Georgette's mind was Barbara Cartland's 'travesty' of the characters which 'she had done her best to model on mine' and 'a certain salacity which I find revolting, no sense of period, not a vestige of wit, and no ability to make a character "live"', besides a decided 'melodramatic bias'. The 'whole thing makes me feel more than a little unwell,' she told Moore. 'I think I could have borne it better had Miss Cartland not been so common-minded, so salacious and so illiterate. I think ill enough of the *Shades*, but, good God!, that nineteen-year old work has more style, more of what it takes, than this offal which she has written at the age of 46!'

Her detailed appraisal of Barbara Cartland's writing and research was the first time Georgette had comprehensively acknowledged her own very real pride in her research, her grasp of the era, her erudition and her ability to make characters and period 'come alive' – something which, in her estimation, Miss Cartland had totally failed to do. She was appalled by the author's palpable ignorance of the period and her apparent lack of historical integrity. In Georgette's view, writing historical *fiction* did not lessen an author's responsibility to the reader to provide an accurate and convincing account of her chosen slice of a particular period:

> With regard to the idioms, cant terms, and certain descriptions of costume, a novelist who showed throughout her books the erudition that one might have supposed to be necessary for the employment of these, could successfully claim to have culled them, as I did myself, from original sources. But no novelist who had found, through research, the rather recondite bits of period colour (so to speak) could possibly have fallen into the gross errors that bespatter Miss Cartland's pages. She is not only slightly illiterate: she displays an almost abysmal ignorance of her period. Cheek by jowl with some piece of what I should call special knowledge (all of which I can point out in my books) one finds an anachronism so blatant as to show clearly that Miss Cartland knows rather less about the period than the average schoolgirl, and has certainly never read enough contemporary literature to put her in possession of the sudden bit of erudition that every now and then staggers the informed reader. I am firmly of the opinion that if she were asked to state the source of any one of the archaisms, or recondite details, which she inserts into her books she would be unable to do so – since it is unlikely that she would cite me as her authority.

Georgette could see 'no reason why I should permit her to cash in on either my ideas, or my research' and told her agent bitterly that: 'I would rather by far that a common thief broke in and stole all the silver.' She resented the time needed to read Barbara Cartland's novels and the distraction from her own medieval book. She thought that the case might come to court but what she really wanted was for *Knave of Hearts* 'to be withdrawn from circulation, the offending names in her previous works altered, and a profound apology made to me'. There is no record of a response to her solicitor's letter to Barbara Cartland but Georgette later noted that 'the horrible copies of my books ceased abruptly'.

27

Frere says I have no business sense.

Georgette Heyer

In September *The Grand Sophy* appeared and Georgette had another instant bestseller. At Heinemann the book had been forecast as a 'runaway' and the finance director, H.L. Hall, described it as 'the best Heyer for a long time' and 'a Heyer to really stand up to the Heyer reputation'. *Sophy* was also a hit in Australia, where it sold 40,000 copies in its first five months. Although it did less well in America, where Georgette felt that Putnam's made a poor job of selling her, *The Grand Sophy* received several enthusiastic reviews in the States, including one from the *Chicago Sunday Tribune* which read in part:

> Once again Georgette Heyer has demonstrated her amazing ability to make English life in the late 18th century [sic] as real as today's news, flavoring it well with that spirit of that earlier day, and making the whole a piece of delectable entertainment. If this is not the highest art, it is certainly a relief for the reader, jaded with novels that try to deal significantly with sordid elements of life in our times, whether their approach be sound or sensational . . . There is more to this than superb entertainment, for Miss Heyer's art is a facile and limber one. It is no small feat to make Regency London come to life, and to make its characters speak and act as did the people of that time and place, without too much quaintness or strangeness of manner.

Although Georgette was pleased by the book's success, her reaction to the news that *Sophy* was 'selling between 400 and 800 copies a day' in Britain was to tell Frere that 'This spells RUIN' and to ask Louisa Callender acidly how she was to pay the tax on it. With the highest tax rate at the time set at nearly 85 per cent the demands of the surtax were oppressive and Georgette had begun writing her first detective story in ten years in order to raise additional funds to pay it.

The new novel featured the return of her erstwhile detective, Hemingway. One of Ronald's colleagues, Tony Hawke, had asked for the book and suggested that (given his years in the force) Inspector Hemingway should be made a Chief Inspector. Georgette had complied. The book was called *Duplicate Death* and Tony Hawke was one of 'certain members of the Bench and Bar' to whom it was dedicated. Its hero was Timothy Harte – the irrepressible fourteen-year-old in *They Found Him Dead* and now a handsome young barrister unwittingly embroiled in a murder mystery. Like her own son, the young men in Georgette's novels were growing up.

Richard had now left Marlborough, where he had done well, and in 1951 was awarded an exhibition to Pembroke College, Cambridge. He delayed going up to university, however, in order to complete his eighteen months' compulsory National Service. Richard joined the 2nd battalion of the King's Royal Rifle Corps, a choice of regiment which gave his mother particular pleasure, for the Rifle Corps had its origins in the 95th Regiment of Foot – the regiment in which Harry Smith of *The Spanish Bride* had served.

But Georgette's pleasure in Richard's achievements was tempered by the discovery that Heinemann had scheduled reprints of *Simon the Coldheart*, *The Black Moth* and *The Great Roxhythe* in its Uniform edition. She liked the new series which had 'figured handsomely on the latest royalty statement', but did not want her early books reprinted. 'PLEASE, PERLEASE don't do this!' she begged Frere.

> I thought we were agreed that, with the exception of the SHADES, over which I have no control, everything prior to the MASQUERADERS should be allowed to sink into decent oblivion.

CORINTHIAN, yes. The other three, ten thousand times, NO! why on earth have you chosen to do these lethal and immature works when the CONVENIENT MARRIAGE, TALISMAN RING, ROYAL ESCAPE, and PENHALLOW still await attention? When these are on the market again, I should prefer to see them reissued rather than those childish and utterly frightful books put out again. Include in this category, if you please, POWDER AND PATCH! I hope so much that it may not be too late to stop this. It will embitter my life!

Despite Frere's assurance that the unloved titles had been included without his knowledge and would 'remain in limbo as long as you want them to', nothing was done to stop publication. The books (Georgette described them as 'badges of shame') appeared against her wishes – the last publication of *The Great Roxhythe* and *Simon the Coldheart* during her lifetime.[23] While the early novels were naturally not as mature as her later work there was nothing in them of which to be ashamed and many readers enjoyed them. But Georgette found their re-issue excruciating.

Her latest Regency novel was a welcome distraction from the unpleasant news. For once she did not 'altogether dislike' the new book, thinking it superior to *Sophy* and even telling Frere it '*has* got a plot'. *The Quiet Gentleman* had another of her unlikely heroines, whose calm, practical demeanour ('try as I will I *cannot* be romantic!') was a perfect foil for the histrionics of Georgette's own favourite, the Dowager. Georgette enjoyed writing *The Quiet Gentleman* 'except when I remembered that its proceeds are destined for the National Drain'. She and Ronald had already paid £4,000 to 'the sharks' (as she described the Inland Revenue) that year, and in April she learned that once they had paid another £2,000 they should have 'cleared off all the back-surtax and shan't get

---

23 *Simon the Coldheart* was eventually reprinted in 1978 after Georgette's death in 1974. Richard Rougier approved its republication after being 'persuaded to read the book once more'. He subsequently decided that, 'in this instance at all events, her judgement had been too harsh.' *The Great Roxhythe* remains out of print to this day.

any more demands until June–actually!–when there will be P.A.Y.E. for Heron!'

The apparently endless tax demands were unavoidable in 'an epoch when not the largest fortune was permitted to yield its owner more than five thousand pounds yearly'. Five thousand pounds was a lot of money, however, and even with the heavy burden of the surtax, Georgette could still see how substantially her Regency novels had increased her net income. Characteristically, she expressed her feelings about the tax system in a novel. When *Duplicate Death* was published it included several cutting remarks about the Inland Revenue.

In April Georgette finally took the plunge and, 'not without difficulty' after nearly thirty years' association, gave her agent six months' notice. She had become increasingly dissatisfied with Moore's handling of her books and, after dealing directly with an American publisher, had decided she could dispense with his services. Moore's response to the news was to write a long 'sorrowing' reply to her letter which did not move her at all.

Although Georgette could take a long time to alter an opinion or decide on change, once her decision was made it was usually irrevocable. This aspect of her personality also meant that over the course of her life, her estimation of people she had once genuinely liked and admired could gradually alter until her judgement of them was almost the opposite of her original view. It was not always a conscious response but it sometimes meant that her later attitude to a particular person or her account of an event (as with *Penhallow*) was not an accurate reflection of her original feelings or experience. Mostly, Georgette was fiercely strong-minded and courageous, but she did not cope well with emotional adversity and when confronted with it tended either to return a vociferous response or disengage completely – sometimes to the point of glossing over or even re-imagining past realities. There was rarely any middle-ground.

Frere's response to Moore's sacking was to suggest that Heinemann act as Georgette's agent. She queried the idea – not on account of the potential conflict of interest, but because she worried that such an arrangement might bring upon you some unforeseen horrors. I don't mean you personally, but some unfortunate stooge ... How long would it be before you told me to go to hell if I started ringing you up to demand Why you hadn't sold my second Australian Rights (serial) and What you were doing about my Promising Swedish Market? And what about my rare excursions into the Shinies, with odd short stories; and selling the first serial rights in the new book to the S.B.? [Dorothy Sutherland] I can't cope with that sort of Sordid Stuff myself.

These were genuine concerns. Georgette advised Frere to think the matter over and not rush into a decision. But even before her contract with Moore had expired she had accepted Frere's offer and turned to Louisa Callender for support.

Louisa Callender had originally been secretary to William Heinemann himself and no one knew more about the firm. She was a formidable personality and extremely competent, with a no-nonsense, commonsense approach to the business and a vast knowledge of the company's contracts and rights. She had been made a director of Heinemann during the War and from 1943 had occasionally corresponded with Georgette. Theirs was a cordial relationship: by 1946 Georgette's letters had shifted from 'Dear Miss Callender' to 'Dear Louisa'. Now that Louisa Callender was to manage her foreign rights Georgette's letters became longer and friendlier as she increasingly looked to the Heinemann director for attention and advice. Louisa Callender did her best to respond in kind but she did not always find it easy to deal with Georgette's particular vernacular. Not everyone was comfortable with the author's manner, and her habit of writing as she spoke and confiding personal details could sometimes be disconcerting to a professional like Louisa Callender. She liked Georgette and her own letters mostly included sufficient personal commentary to be friendly, but she always signed herself 'L. Callender'.

In October, a week after her contract with Christy & Moore expired, Georgette wrote the first of many letters to Louisa Callender as her new agent: 'I've had no word from C.&M., thank God! I don't mind if Smith rings me up, but I funk poor old L.P. When you've known a man of his age since you were nineteen, & he <u>still</u> looks on you as a struggling young author, the situation is apt to be difficult. Having enjoyed the disadvantages of an Upbringing, I <u>cannot</u> be rude to old men!' Her relationship with Moore ended neither justly nor compassionately. The years of affectionate letter-writing, of involving him in her personal life, telling him her troubles and turning to him for advice, effectively forgotten. A few days later Georgette sounded the death-knell of their long association in another letter to Louisa Callender:

> I don't know what the effect was on you of L.P.M.'s letter, but it has made me feel basin-sick. My <u>father</u> entrusted my work to his care? Christ! What a vision this conjures up of the dowdy schoolgirl and the careful parent! My father at one time had some dealings with old Christy, and through him was casually acquainted with Moore. I certainly got him to make a third at a luncheon-meeting with Moore. And I can well believe that, the agreement having been sorted, he told Moore, in his genial way, to Do his best with my stuff. As for the implication that my work was more or less in my father's hands, and that he and Moore just sorted things between them "for the poor child", it makes me seethe with fury! Enough to make my father haunt Moore, too! Rest assured, I was <u>not</u> encouraged to be weak-minded, nor had my father any real parental instinct! I adored him, but he was far more like a brother than a father . . . Incidentally, if [Moore] regarded me, for thirty years, as a sacred bequest, I hope he feels he fulfilled his obligations. I don't. I think <u>I've</u> been keeping the wolf from <u>his</u> door.

While Georgette might have prospered even more with a different agent, Moore had, in fact, done a good job in protecting her interests. How good would only become clear the following year when Georgette signed the first of her contracts to be drawn up by Heinemann. Having an agent meant having an independent nego-tiator whose responsibility it was to secure for his client the most favourable contract, sell the rights to her novels in as many forms as possible, pay her royalties and protect her copyrights. Moore had fulfilled each of these roles to the best of his ability. As her career had progressed, with each new novel he had sought a bigger advance and better royalties. As early as 1929 with *Beauvallet*, he had brokered terms which gave Georgette 25% on all hardbacks sold above 10,000 copies. By 1946 and *The Foundling*, he had secured a royalty of 20% on the first 7,500 copies and 25% on all other copies unless 'the high costs resulting from war conditions prevail'. These were excellent terms.

When Georgette signed her first new book contract with Heinemann in June 1952 – having dispensed with her agent – her royalties were significantly reduced. The new agreement gave her only a 15% royalty on the first 15,000 copies and then 20% on all copies thereafter. All mention of 25% had been expunged and, even taking into account Moore's 10% commission which she no longer had to pay, the Heinemann contract left her nearly £300 worse off. Astonishingly, Georgette made no objection to the new terms. Even Ronald did not appear to notice the change – although he was quick to pick up an incorrect date.

It took some time to wind up her association with Christy & Moore and all Georgette's dealings were now with the younger partner in the firm, John Smith. They had corresponded through July and August over the sales of options on *The Grand Sophy* (to be produced as a stage play), and *The Corinthian* (to be adapted as a BBC radio play). Despite her distress over *The Reluctant Widow* film Georgette was still happy to sell a cinema or a stage right to her novels in the hope that someone might eventually produce a version she liked. She remained sceptical, however, and *The Grand Sophy* script proved to be another disappointment. John Smith was pleasant to deal with and, although Georgette's hackles went up at times, they generally worked through the issues. There were wrongs and rights on both sides in her relationship with Christy & Moore and a year later she seemed more able to recognise the fact and could write to Smith to say: 'I hope that you & L.P. are both well. Give him my love, please.'

28

I don't think this new book is going to cause me much
bother. I started to write Chapter I without any of the
usual false starts & erasures, & that augurs well.

Georgette Heyer

Georgette's thirty-eighth novel came out in October 1951. *The Quiet Gentleman* would be the last of her books for which Christy & Moore would receive commission. By now fans had come to expect the almost annual 'Heyer' novel and it had a first printing of 50,000. Georgette described the book to Pat Wallace as 'the latest example of a Tried Recipe'. One fan disagreed and wrote to ask 'where is the light-hearted gaiety and nonsense of *The Talisman Ring, Friday's Child,* and *The Corinthian?*' and was their author feeling 'older, sadder and depressed?' Greatly amused, Georgette wrote ruefully to Louisa Callender: 'Echo answers, Where? . . . but I shouldn't have thought it depressing, would you?' Several other fans wrote to question her use of 'son-in-law' instead of 'stepson', a point on which Georgette refused to budge: 'although to alter in-law to step might lay me open to the criticisms of SOME, an emendation would draw upon me the far more important strictures of OTHERS – who would accuse me (rightly) of having introduced modern terminology into a Regency book.'[24]

---

24 Although Dr Johnson's *Dictionary* indicates that 'stepmother' was in use in 1755, Georgette was quite correct in her use of 'son-in-law' to describe her hero in *The Quiet Gentleman*. Under Canon Law, 'in-law' was a term used to describe a relationship created by marriage – including the child of a husband or wife from a previous marriage. The replacement of 'in-law' with 'step' did not come into common use until the mid-nineteenth century.

She was a stickler for accuracy and resented anyone telling her she was wrong when she knew herself to be right. She was further irritated by a review in the *Daily Telegraph* in which John Betjeman claimed that 'my picture of Regency England is no more like the real thing than he is like Queen Anne'. She retorted: 'He best knows whether he is like Queen Anne, but what the hell does he know about the Regency?' But Betjeman was partly right, for Georgette's Regency world is a selective reconstruction which drew as much on her own Edwardian ideals and prejudices as it did on the history of the period.

Despite her prodigious historical knowledge, in retreating into the early nineteenth century she could not avoid bringing with her a twentieth-century sensibility. Her values may have had their roots in her Edwardian childhood, but Georgette had lived through two world wars, witnessed the emancipation of women and (unwillingly) participated in the rise of the Welfare State. These things inevitably affected her and her writing and in many ways her period novels were a welcome escape – for both their author and her readers – from some of the realities of modern living.

There were many aspects of twentieth-century life which Georgette did not enjoy. As the postwar years passed she became increasingly intolerant of what some people called 'progress', deprecating changes in education, the incursion of television and radio into people's lives (although she enjoyed sporting broadcasts) and in particular the economic changes which she felt so adversely affected her life. It was these things that would sometimes prompt her to denounce the modern world and declare, 'Oh Christ, why did I have to be born into this <u>filthy</u> age!'

By mid-November *The Quiet Gentleman* was already outselling *The Grand Sophy*, and Frere returned from a trip to the Antipodes to report that 'booksellers had begged him for more Heyer'. Her strong sales prompted the firm to pursue the rights to her earlier detective novels and re-issue them in a special Heinemann Uniform edition. Longmans were willing to relinquish their rights, but at Hodder & Stoughton Ralph Hodder-Williams was not immediately inclined to co-operate. Percy had retired in 1947. The firm had not re-published her detective novels for some years but they assured Louisa Callender (who had rung to enquire incognito) that they intended to reprint *Envious Casca* in the new year. Georgette was unimpressed by their assurances; they had originally promised to republish *Casca* three years earlier.

Heinemann did eventually secure the rights to the detective novels but it took time and cost Louisa Callender a great deal of effort. Aware that Georgette's affairs would not get any less complicated (or the author any less demanding), and knowing that she was due to retire in a few years, Louisa Callender proposed a meeting with Joyce Weiner, an American literary agent with several years' experience. Reluctant at first, Georgette agreed to lunch at The Ivy to discuss the proposition. To Louisa Callender's relief she approved of Joyce Weiner, who would henceforth manage her foreign and short story rights while Heinemann continued to look after her British rights.

The new year brought Richard home on embarkation leave and a 'week of ceaseless parties' left his mother exhausted. Soon afterwards he was posted to Munster from where he made her 'rage with descriptions of rump steaks, 9d, and gin at 4d a time!' Georgette enjoyed a glass of gin (she also still smoked heavily). In February she confessed: 'I keep going on gin and Dexedrine.' Commonly prescribed for cold and 'flu symptoms Dexedrine was, in fact, a powerful amphetamine which had the effect of keeping a person awake and the potential to increase energy, brain activity, memory and confidence. Georgette had discovered that a dose in the evening enabled her to write all night and still feel inspired in the morning. A number of her novels were written under its influence, including her latest Regency.

Originally entitled *Quadrille*, it would prove to be one of her funniest books, with an unexpected hero (initially named Felix) and one of her best endings. This was the book inspired by Ferdy Fakenham, the foolish young man in *Friday's Child*, which she had originally planned to write four years earlier but had produced *Arabella* instead. Although Ferdy remained the inspiration for the new novel, Georgette felt compelled to admit that 'when I got down to brass tacks I found he was just a little too foolish, and so changed him into Freddy Standen.'

Despite a few early challenges, which included her mother fainting in the middle of the Cromwell Road and taking to her bed, the 'leaving without notice of my Daily Obliger', having to 'wrestle with housework', and getting her heroine to London only to 'wonder what happens now', by early March she had written almost half the book. *Woman's Journal* were keen to serialise and Georgette suggested to Louisa Callender:

> If the S.B. rings you up, bleating about my new book, you will say:
> It is Terrific.
> It has reached the halfway mark. (After all, it will probably have done so by the time you get this.) It is a classic Heyer. (This means that it is a lot of froth about nothing, but you don't have to tell her that. Really, Louisa, how CAN you be so silly?)
> It is EXACTLY what the Fans like.

By now the title had changed from *Quadrille* to *Chicken Hazard* and finally to *Cotillion*. Georgette was pleased with the novel, which had proved to be a 'riot of absurdity', and was satisfied that she had not let a severe attack of sinusitis:

> Stop me being quite humorous in COTILLION, so probably I <u>am</u> one of these people like Keats and Bizet, who flourish under adversity, after all. Or maybe it's just due to Dexedrine, with which (and gin, of course) I keep myself going. If ever there was a flimsier story than COTILLION, I have yet to see it, but that, dear Louisa, is the secret of My Art. On no account must the story be About anything in particular, or hold water for half a minute.

Almost before she had finished *Cotillion*, Frere informed Georgette that he had 'scheduled a detective novel by Me for this autumn'. Although she had laughed at the suggestion Georgette was not averse to the idea. She had recently read several of John Dickson Carr's detective novels to see why he was so popular and told Frere: 'I didn't think any fictitious detective could set my teeth on edge quite as badly as Miss Ngaio Marsh's creature, but I find I was mistaken.' She did acknowledge Carr's ingenuity with a locked room (for which he was famous) but her dislike of his stories ultimately ensured that her next detective novel was 'a plain case of shooting . . . no locked rooms, or mysterious weapons, or any other trimmings'. The new thriller would be her last.

Boris announced his engagement in April and Georgette set about writing a couple of short stories in order to pay for his wedding reception. Her most recent effort, 'A Husband for Fanny', had been published in the *Illustrated London News* and she now dashed off 'Bath Miss' and 'Pink Domino' for *Good Housekeeping* and *Woman's Journal*. If she could think of a plot she also planned to write 'Cold Dawn'. The stories earned her upwards of £200 each and were easy money for a few hours' work. She could have had the £3,000 advance for *Cotillion* just for the asking but told Frere she wanted him to hold on to it until the autumn: 'I'm all right at the moment, but I expect I may be feeling the draught a bit by October!'

Georgette was now firmly established as one of Heinemann's star authors and she and Ronald were among the guests at the grand opening (by Somerset Maugham) of the new Windmill Press at Kingswood in June. She enjoyed the party and had her photo taken with Frere and Pat Wallace for *Tatler*. Although she looked her elegant best in a tailored suit, hat, gloves and pearls not everyone recognised her. Arnold Gyde of Heinemann remembered having

> a ghastly time recognising those who thought I knew them very well . . . "Who's that fine looking woman?" asked Noel Baker. So I introduced him. I was exhausted. I confused him with Black of *The Daily Mail* and said:
>
> "May I introduce you to Mr Black – Lady Jones, whose pen-name is Enid Bagnold."
>
> "Well," she replied, "I am not Enid Bagnold."
>
> "Nor am I Mr Black," said Noel Baker.
>
> It was Georgette Heyer!

. . . So this was a terrible moment. What was I to do? Run away into the bushes?

"Well," I said, "This is surely game and set in the Memory Stakes."

After this the old girl was very courteous and queenly . . .

A month later, Boris married his 'charming widow', Evelyn Lyford. Georgette thought Evelyn ideal for her amusing, affable, but often ineffectual younger brother. The reception was held at Albany and Georgette footed the bill. A week after the ceremony a raft of additional expenses – including a 'ghastly' dental bill and 'a hideous P.A.Y.E. demand of £1200' from the Inland Revenue – forced Georgette to call in *Cotillion's* advance. She had hoped 'to rush off *Detection Unlimited*' as well as a commissioned short story for the Coronation edition of *Good Housekeeping* to offset some of her expenses, but had yet to write them.

King George VI had died in February 1952 and his elder daughter, Elizabeth, had been proclaimed Queen (to be crowned in June the following year). Georgette considered it an honour to be asked to write the lead story for the magazine's special edition. It was September when she finally sat down without 'an idea in my head' to write what eventually became 'The Pursuit of Hetty'. In that same month, for the first and only time in her life, Georgette consented to meet a journalist.

29

*You know, the extraordinary thing about Miss Heyer, who
writes those Wonderful Books, is the way she <u>manages</u> –!*

Georgette Heyer

Coral Craig was a reporter for the *Australian Woman's Day*, working
in their London office. She had approached Heinemann about a
meeting with Georgette, only to be told Miss Heyer 'isn't interviewed'.
Somehow Georgette learned of the request and quite uncharacteristi-
cally invited Coral Craig to Albany for a drink. Although the ensuing
article contained no information about Georgette's novels, writing
habits or technique, it did offer readers a rare account of 'one of the
most widely read authors in the world'. Describing her as 'a tall,
dark-haired, distinguished woman, a charming hostess and certainly
the shyest of personality publicity I have seen', Coral Craig had found
Georgette unexpectedly friendly. The famous author had 'tossed the
conversational gambits back and forth across the centuries, discussing
in a most definite manner any subject except her own work . . . She
isn't interviewed. She made it quite clear, with a subtlety conveyed
neither by word nor gesture, that this was a social occasion and no
questions, please.'

Georgette had made her guest an 'excellent dry martini', told her
about Albany, claimed that she did not read reviews of her books,
and that on her son's advice she had not seen the film version of
The Reluctant Widow ('Don't go, mother. You would hate it.'). She
also 'spoke of poets', especially Elizabeth Barrett and Robert Browning,

and told Coral Craig: 'I never travel without the Browning Letters.' Some weeks later, after reading the draft article (entitled 'Georgette Heyer – the Shy Best-seller'), Georgette wrote to say: 'I am hugely flattered by your description of me–and shall take good care it never comes under the eye of my irreverent family.' But the article was a great success in Australia where it appeared in *Woman's Day* in October.

In January Frere pronounced *Cotillion* as Heinemann's first publication for 1953 and a novel which 'set a fine standard for the rest of the year'. Georgette had dedicated the book to Carola's husband, Gerald Lenanton, who had died suddenly in October. His death had left Georgette and Ronald 'feeling pretty shattered . . . Gerald was one of the nicest people we ever knew, and we shall miss him terribly.' Gerald had read *Cotillion* in proof and enjoyed it tremendously. As had William Watt, the senior partner at A.P. Watt and an avid collector of Heyer novels. Since 1943 Watt had regularly rung Heinemann 'to know if there isn't another Georgette Heyer coming'. On receiving *Cotillion* he had written to Louisa Callender:

> Thank you very much indeed for – once again – so kindly sending me the proofs of the new Georgette Heyer. I am sure that I shall enjoy it very much and I hope that it will have a sale as big as even you would like. I am glad to see that it is a good long one and I shall quite unashamedly revel in escapism. After all I have Mr Maugham on my side – you remember the broadcast?

Georgette may have heard Somerset Maugham's broadcast on books and writing for she often listened to the radio and would eventually own a television. She enjoyed listening to (and later watching) the cricket, show-jumping and horse-racing and always had a bet on the Grand National, which she considered her 'lucky race'. In the early 1950s, however, television was still in its formative years and when Joyce Weiner rang to say she'd been offered £250 for the 'recording rights in *These Old Shades*', Georgette told Frere: 'I didn't think you'd object to this recording thing.' He assured her that 'we have no interest at all in the "recording rights" (whatever they may be) in

These Old Shades, so you may tell Joyce to go to it and good luck to all concerned.'

On 2 June Elizabeth II was crowned Queen in the first-ever televised coronation. Having always 'held to the true Stuart line', Georgette was not a fan of the Hanoverians. She had been furious when baby Charles was christened, stamping her foot and declaring that 'the bloody silly German princess had given the heir a Stuart name to which he had no right!' – though she really rather liked the earnest young Queen. Most of Britain was swept up by coronation fever and Georgette was relieved to get away in July for three weeks' holiday at the Ailesbury Arms Hotel in Marlborough. She had finally finished the detective-thriller for Frere and needed a rest; she was also glad to escape the 'pile of bills awaiting attention' and which had caused her to call in the advance for *Detection Unlimited* early.

'Thanks largely to the antics of my accountant, my affairs are now in a chaotic state,' she told Louisa Callender, 'My own account being overdrawn, and Heron's overweighted by a huge balance I dare not touch until the Commissions of Inland Revenue (whom God assoil!) shall have decided a new Thing – of course against me. I hope to God you manage to sell the serial-rights.' But Dorothy Sutherland decided: '*Detection Unlimited* just isn't serial material.' It was a blow, for Georgette had been banking on the extra £1,500 from *Woman's Journal*. 'I only wrote the thing for sordid gain,' she explained to Louisa Callender before urging her to try elsewhere. But nobody wanted *Detection Unlimited*.

Georgette received the bad news at Greywalls where she and Ronald had taken Richard for a September holiday. It was the only blight on an otherwise perfect stay. They had grown to love Greywalls, with its quiet, elegant rooms, tasteful furnishings and excellent food. Despite feeling strapped for cash, they did not consider a few hundred pounds too dear for a month's holiday there. Ronald and Richard spent most days on Muirfield playing golf and Georgette sometimes walked the course with them. She spent the rest of the time knitting or reading by the fire in the drawing room, playing bridge or just sitting quietly enjoying the view. The news about *Detection Unlimited* was a reminder of what awaited her back in London. She pessimistically concluded: 'It is a great bore about the new thriller, and I can see the Bankruptcy Court looming. I can also see my mediaeval book fading into the far distance. I must think out a Typical Heyer romance for instant sale.'

Within weeks Louisa Callender was asking for an outline of the new book for Heinemann's spring list. But Georgette insisted that she had barely made a start: 'Are you trying to be funny? Tell you about my new book indeed! How can I, when I haven't yet worked it out for my own information?' She then proceeded to tell her that 'The title will be *The Toll-Gate*', that it was another Regency, set after Waterloo and its hero was 'a huge young man who has sold out of some dreary cavalry regiment or other because he doesn't fancy the army in peacetime.' A lengthy description of the book's characters, general plot and several likely scenes followed. 'It may sound a bit nebulous to you,' Georgette explained, but 'it will make a splendid serial'.

A week later she reported that she had 'got it pretty well taped now, thanks in some measure to my Life's Partner who suddenly uttered the cryptic word "specie!"' She had thought to embroil her hero in a smuggling ring or a bullion theft but Ronald had demurred and suggested an alternative: 'Having a pachydermaton's memory he recalled, out of the blue, that I once read him a long spiel about coinage after Waterloo, when, for the first time in years, we issued new gold and silver coins, and – which is important – minted the first sovereigns and half-sovereigns, calling in the guineas. So what could be better?'

In mid-November a partial manuscript and a synopsis arrived on Louisa Callender's desk with a note warning her that the novel 'might not work out quite like that'. After failing to sell *Detection Unlimited* as a serial, Georgette was keen to ensure that *Woman's Journal* bought *The Toll-Gate*. She had also been recently jolted when Dorothy Sutherland had informed Louisa Callender that she had 'bought another historical romance which she would begin in July of next year, and may not want to run two consecutively'. The editor had offered space 'in another of her magazines' with an assurance that 'it would be a magazine of high standing', prompting Georgette to ask: 'What high-class periodical, other than *Woman's Journal*, does A. Press run? I suspect the S.B. is going to ask us if we'd mind coming out in that frightful weekly paper of hers – *Woman's* Something or Other. It's far from high-class, but as I don't think Persons of Taste and Refinement read <u>any</u> magazines, I don't much mind – provided she pays the same price as she would for the *Journal*.'

The price was £1,500 and Dorothy Sutherland planned to run the serial through the summer with an October publication for the book. But to this Georgette could not agree. If *The Toll-Gate* missed Frere's proposed July publication date she would fall a book behind and create a gap in her income that she simply could not afford:

> You see, I fell into this trap once before in my career, and I know that the effects, not immediately visible, are cumulative and far-reaching. It is snatching at two birds in a bush instead of holding tight to the one in your hand. Even if you were to say to me, Detective fiction is different: do another for the spring! It wouldn't solve the difficulty. Initially these books earn exactly half what my "real" books earn; after the first royalties, nothing approaching half. I regard them as a pleasant addition to my income, that's all. And I find them damned hard to write. My object in having written TOLL-GATE was to get ahead of myself (so to speak) so that I could with a quiet mind return to my big mediaeval book for the best part of next year. To do that I must make sure of royalties rolling in steadily.

She lay awake through the small hours thinking about the problem and finally concluded: 'If the S.B. likes to go straight ahead, and serialize in time for a June publication, I should be perfectly content to accept £1500 . . . If she doesn't – well, I'm sorry, I shall perhaps find things a bit awkward in the immediate future, but I shall know that they'll be fine by the time I receive the royalties you pay me in the autumn.'

To her surprise, Dorothy Sutherland agreed. 'Please tell the S.B.

that I am most grateful to her for meeting me halfway,' Georgette told Louisa Callender, 'and have done what I can, by way of a quid pro quo, to meet <u>her</u> wishes with regard to the story itself. I have eliminated the succession, and the wicked cousin, and have reduced the book to more reasonable proportions.' Only a month earlier, Georgette had been 'thrilled' in being told by aspiring author Christopher (Kipper) Landon, that Dorothy Sutherland found her '"terribly hard", and "<u>hell</u> to work with!"' Now, the editor's graciousness softened her a little and she did her best to accede to her suggestions for the story.

She delivered the manuscript two weeks before Christmas, having finished it 'against the odds' which included a skin condition, liver trouble and her sole surviving aunt's broken femur. Aunt Jo had died a few years earlier and Aunt Cicely was now eighty-eight and 'A Holy Terror'. Georgette found it impossible to 'remain aloof from these events as I could wish'. It was not all bad news: *Detection Unlimited* came out in December and Georgette had her short story, 'The Quarrel', published in the Christmas edition of *Everywoman*. But far better was their departure for Rye, where they would spend Christmas with celebrations that would largely consist of 'Golf for the boys and a Rest for Mother!'

Richard often joined his parents on holiday. Having completed his National Service he was now up at Cambridge studying Classics and Law. He had turned twenty-one the previous February, was as tall as Ronald and shared his father's passion for golf and bridge. From his mother he had inherited wit and a flair for a well-told story. Richard had his own gift for writing, but had recognised at an early age the difficulties attached to being the progeny of an international bestseller. Consequently, he deliberately chose never to attempt becoming a published author (Richard was an accomplished letter writer and at one time expressed an interest in writing about the *Belle Époque*, but never did). Instead, he developed his skill as a raconteur and frequently amused his friends and family with his gift for mimicry and his ability to tell a good joke (undoubtedly inherited from his Heyer ancestors). Georgette adored her son and had a pride in his achievements which no amount of mockery, assumed indifference or pretended disdain could hide.

She returned home from Rye to mixed financial tidings. The good news was that her Book Club editions were selling in ever-increasing numbers and she was now being published by both Foyle's *and* Odhams. With a membership between 150,000–175,000 each the book clubs offered an enormous guaranteed sale to their selected authors. Royalties were usually only 2d a copy, but the huge volume ensured that Georgette received over £1,000 for Odhams' edition of *The Quiet Gentleman* and even the Foyle's edition of *Duplicate Death* brought in £400. Foyle's were now offering to buy *Cotillion* with a first printing of 140,000 copies and a 4d royalty – a potential return of more than £2,000.

Unfortunately the good news was offset by a new communiqué from Georgette's accountant, Rubens, who had written to inform her that she had drawn more money from Heron Enterprises than she should have. Consequently, the Inland Revenue had

> dug up a 1923 law not even Barclays' tax expert had ever heard of, and said these sums were undisclosed dividends. There has been a year's enquiry and argument, and we are now appealing against the decision. According to what Rubens somewhat cryptically writes, I <u>may</u> have to pay I.R. £3000 over and above all other and customary taxes, but it <u>may</u> be less, and it <u>may</u> not arise in the immediate future. He was so soothing when I last saw him that he left me with the impression that the amount I might have to disgorge would be very small, so that when I received his last letter . . . and saw this £3000 figuring on the list, I nearly had heart-failure!

It was another blow in a long series of financial setbacks which, if Georgette and Ronald had been better able to manage money, could have been avoided. It was one thing to be a successful author and quite another to make the most of the opportunities a royalty income offered. So far they had proved inept at the latter. Once she had employed Rubens Georgette tended to leave him to his own devices and become a relatively passive participant in the management of her money. It wasn't that she did not try. She certainly kept accounts (in her own idiosyncratic fashion) and would sometimes venture into Rubens' office for an explanation of the latest tax demand. This was rarely successful, however, for she would find herself defeated by his verbiage, emerging an hour or two later none the wiser.

Over the years, she and Ronald had shown themselves to be far more reactive than proactive where their finances were concerned. It was this inability to act quickly and decisively which, time and again, proved to be their financial undoing. When Georgette felt she was paying far too much tax and could not see the value in running Heron, she took no action. And when things began to go wrong and Rubens grew lax in his administration of the Heron accounts she did nothing. In the end, it would be nearly fifteen years before she and Ronald finally changed accountants and put their financial problems behind them.

30

I thought we should get <u>lots</u> of publicity if Frere invited me to lunch at the Savoy Grill, & I came with my Irish wolfhound – 33½ inches at the shoulder – & refused to be separated from her.

Georgette Heyer

By 1954 Georgette had begun to make a great deal of money. She was writing steadily, producing a novel a year, the occasional short story (*Good Housekeeping* published 'The Duel' in February), and more recently, had turned her hand to a series of short articles. In March and April *Punch* published two of her articles: 'Books about the Brontës' and 'How to be a Literary Critic'. Five other unpublished articles reflected some of Georgette's ideas about men as fathers, publishers, the state of the nation, and *Jane Eyre*'s Mr Rochester's continuing appeal:

Charlotte [Brontë] knew, perhaps instinctively, how to create a hero who would appeal to women throughout the ages; and to her must all succeeding romantic novelists acknowledge their indebtedness. For Mr Rochester was the first, and the Nonpareil, of his type. He is the rugged and dominant male, who yet can be handled by quite ordinary a female: as it might be, <u>oneself</u>! He is rude, overbearing, and often a bounder; but these blemishes, however repulsive they may be in real life, can be made in the hands of a skilled novelist extremely attractive to women. Charlotte Brontë, immensely skilled, knew just where to draw the line.

It is possible that her unpublished essays earned Georgette her first rejection slips, for after this sudden burst of non-fiction writing she wrote no more articles.

Aunt Cicely died in April. At seventy-eight Sylvia was the last of the Watkins siblings left alive. For Georgette Cicely's death was another break with the past and a reminder of her own mortality at a time when it actually seemed possible that she might yet achieve a shred of immortality through her books. They were selling in ever-increasing numbers and Heinemann were doing their utmost to promote her. Publication of *The Toll-Gate* in July coincided with 'Georgette Heyer Week' in Britain, Australia, New Zealand, South Africa and other overseas territories. It was a great success, with Georgette Heyer displays arranged in hundreds of bookshops and libraries. The jacket for *The Toll-Gate* was the work of a new artist and Georgette was delighted with Arthur Barbosa's take on her stories. Barbosa went on to design her book jackets for the next fifteen years and his elegant, distinctive style became a much-admired hallmark for her novels.

A month later Frere wrote that *The Toll-Gate* was selling a thousand copies a week and in September Pat Wallace reported that in 'the Antipodes sales of THE TOLL-GATE have already exceeded any previous work of yours in its original edition.' Heinemann was moved to issue a statement in *The Bookseller* which read: 'no less than 3½ million copies of Georgette Heyer's books have been sold.' It was a remarkable figure and it is not surprising that Foyle's chose *The Toll-Gate* as their premier book for 1955.

Immersed in a new Regency novel, Georgette paid little heed to the figures. She had promised to show Dorothy Sutherland her new novel by the end of July and a request for details had elicited a peremptory letter to Louisa Callender: 'You must fob the S.B. off for a week or two, please! Not only does it put me right off the stroke to know a part of my book is in her hands before I see my way clear to the end, but – as usual – the first chapters are in a mess, and must be altered.' She managed to send an outline of *Bath Tangle* with an assurance that 'My heroine has a lively sense of humour, and I can see some nice scenes blowing up. And – you'd <u>never</u> guess! – it all Ends Happily.' Halfway through *Bath Tangle* Georgette experienced a momentary doubt on realising that 'this is unlike my other romances in so far as it is a "Love-story" and not an "Adventure-story".' She wondered if 'The S.B. may not like that'. But Dorothy Sutherland was enthusiastic enough to write to her directly to say: 'This one's going with a wonderful swing! Alas, poor Rockingham.'

Georgette had called her 'Heyer-Hero the Marquis of Rockingham, quite forgetting that very dim Prime Minister' who had been the last Marquis of Rockingham. She felt she could not use his title for her hero and spent hours thinking of another name. It was vital to her to get it right: 'I don't choose names lightly, and once named I can't see a character under any <u>other</u> name . . . I've at last changed the gentleman's title to Rotherham. I suppose I shall get used to it in time. He looks like a stranger to me at the moment.' It was an annoying delay for she was desperate to get *Bath Tangle* finished before she and Ronald left for Scotland on 20 August. She wrote at top speed through the month, helped along by 'a certain Powerful Dope, given me once by my doctor, with instructions not to take a dose later than midday. But if one takes it at <u>dinner</u>-time one is still full of energy and inspiration at 5.0 next morning!' While there may have been side effects, the formula seemed to work for she delivered the manuscript on schedule. *Woman's Journal* paid £2,000 for *Bath Tangle* and the following year Georgette had another hit on her hands.

They went to Greywalls as usual in the summer of 1954, and Richard joined them there before returning to Cambridge for the Michaelmas term. He was enjoying university life and had met several young men and women who would become lifelong friends. Years later, a close female friend remembered him as he was in that first year at Cambridge:

He was 22 when we met and a true Heyer hero – born out of his century, slim, dark, debonair, devastatingly attractive with those piercing blue eyes and with an air of cool sophistication – but also with an ability to wither you with a cold look and a cutting phrase. I realised very early on that these sprang out of a vulnerability deeply hidden but there all his life. And how could he not be vulnerable, brought up by an adored mother totally preoccupied by her writing.

Georgette's writing inevitably affected her relationships. There is no doubt that Richard suffered from it, especially as a child. While her determination to remain out of the public eye was undoubtedly better for her family as regards their privacy, it also had the effect of keeping their world small and insular. This affected her son. She loved him, but her own repressed emotions had made it difficult for her to engage with him as a child on a childish level. To some extent Georgette lacked the kind of emotional intelligence necessary to understand him. She had no real concept of adapting her life to his so that by the time Richard became an adult he had spent twenty years learning to adapt his life to hers.

And it was not only with Richard that Georgette could be emotionally unaware. Earlier that year, Frere, Heinemann and one of their authors, Walter Baxter, had been charged with publishing an obscene libel. Baxter's second book, *The Image and the Search*, had become a *cause célèbre* when the Director of Public Prosecutions issued proceedings and the case went to the Old Bailey, the Central Criminal Court. Frere could have had the case dismissed by paying a small fine and withdrawing the book, but he did not consider *The Image and the Search* obscene. As a matter of principle he chose to fight against what he (and many others) saw as outdated censorship laws. The case dragged on through the year and Frere found it an unpleasant and, at times, distressing affair. With each court appearance he was required to spend hours as a prisoner in the cells beneath the Old Bailey before entering the dock and to suffer the indignity and humiliation of being treated like a criminal. The law did not allow the accused to call expert witnesses, testify on their own behalf or even to argue the merits of the book in question.

Many people wrote to the papers to protest against this and other trials held that year, among them Somerset Maugham, J.B. Priestley, H.E. Bates, Bertrand Russell and Graham Greene. On 18 October 1954 the case ended with a split jury and a plan for a re-trial by the prosecution. On hearing the outcome, Georgette immediately wrote Frere one of her forthright letters. She intended to be helpful but it is doubtful whether her rallying tone brought much comfort to her friend:

> I can well imagine that you are by this time, after waiting three hours for the jury to disagree, spiritually & nervously exhausted, & have probably lost all sight of the utter triviality of the whole thing – to the extent of almost seeing yourself as a Murderer. It is unpleasant, rather degrading, & altogether distasteful, but intrinsically it doesn't matter a tinker's curse. I do hope you've managed to bear this in mind, & have not allowed an excess of sensibility to get you down.

Twelve years earlier in *Penhallow* Georgette had written a description of her fictitious family: 'They were all of them imperceptive, and insensitive enough to make it impossible for them to understand why anyone should be hurt by their cheerful brutality.' It was an apt description of her letter to Frere. She meant to be kind and bracing; instead she was tactless and insensitive. Her response to her friend's anguish prompted even Ronald and Richard to tell her that she had 'a callous disposition'. For all her imaginative powers and ability to depict human foibles with such sympathetic insight in her novels, in real life there were times when Georgette could be remarkably lacking in empathy and emotional understanding.

After a second trial again returned a split verdict, a third in early December 1954 brought the Baxter case to an end. 'The whole miserable business folded up on Thursday when a fresh Judge instructed a new jury to return a verdict of "Not Guilty",' Frere reported after his eighth appearance in the dock. Tired and disillusioned he told a friend:

> The lawyers say that this may end the witch hunt for a period and that they will stop wasting public money for a while. The monstrous

thing is that any common informer can start proceedings of this sort, and put an author and a publisher into the position of having to defend themselves at enormous cost with no hope of getting costs against the Crown in any circumstances. The lawyers also say that this may be the case which will change the law. The lawyers are nearly always wrong.

But in this instance the lawyers were right, for the Baxter trial, along with several others heard that year, proved to be the catalyst for change. After representations from authors, citizens, publishers, printers, literary agents and others in the industry, the 1959 Obscene Publications Act was passed amending the laws governing such cases. In 1960, the legal suit against D.H. Lawrence's book *Lady Chatterley's Lover* would be the first to be tested under the new legislation. It would be a victory for authors and publishers. But the impetus for change had come at a high cost for Frere – and for Baxter, who never wrote another book.

Frere bore no grudge against Georgette for her bracing counsel. Genuinely liking and admiring her, he understood her better than most people. She was, furthermore, one of his top-selling authors. They lunched at Quaglino's in November and it was here that Georgette finally met Dorothy Sutherland in the flesh. A director of Amalgamated Press had come in with the editor and on seeing Georgette had 'begged permission to "present" someone who was "very anxious to meet me". And the next instant, there was the S.B., looking rather like Cassius, only hungrier, bowing from the waist, and murmuring disjointed in-audibilities.' Georgette found the encounter highly entertaining but it did not lessen her dislike of Dorothy Sutherland.

Bath Tangle came out in March 1955, but Georgette barely lifted her head from Book I, 'Richard the Redeless', of her medieval novel. By April, she had made encouraging progress and completed Book II, 'The Unquiet Time'. To her dismay she had been forced to alter its original time frame of 1399–1413 to 1399–1406, having been unable to compress Henry IV's reign into one Book. Undeterred by the manuscript's exponential growth, she had started Book III, 'Prince Excellent', and told Pat Wallace: 'I have now executed an Archbishop, and burnt a Lollard, so you will find me a bit above myself. It is a tremendous book – tremendously long, tremendously erudite, and tremendously dull.'

But she was doomed to interruptions, for Dorothy Sutherland was already asking about a new Regency for serialisation. 'It is a hellish nuisance,' Georgette told Frere, 'just as I'm getting on nicely with the Tome, but it can't be helped. If I can turn out another bleeding romance by mid-July, I can get back to *John* without – I hope to God! – losing the thread.' Louisa Callender had retired the previous December and Georgette now asked Frere about the future handling of her contracts with *Woman's Journal*: 'Is Louisa's successor going to handle the serial, or not? It is only a matter of arranging terms, of course, but I think <u>someone</u> had better do this for me, for that vulture-like creature would probably do me down if she could.' The 'someone' turned out to be Frere himself, but not before his formidable author had enjoyed an epistolary tussle with her arch-enemy.

Encouraged by their encounter at Quaglino's and by a suggestion from Kipper Landon (who had been at school with Georgette's brother Frank and had recently taken Georgette's advice on his first manuscript) that he might be able to interview Georgette, Dorothy Sutherland had written to ask if she would consent to having her photograph taken for the magazine. Unfortunately her letter was exactly the kind of missive to rouse Georgette's ire:

Dear, <u>dear</u> Georgette Heyer:

Have a heart! How could we publish an interview without a photograph? What would it look like? What would the readers think? Do please let Tom Blau come and take some with lots of background with his Leica and you shall tear them all up if you want to – but do please <u>try</u>! Please!

Georgette's reply was blunt:

I detest being photographed, and have surely reached the time of life when I can please myself. As for being photographed At Work or In My Old World Garden, that is the type of publicity which I find nauseating, and quite unnecessary. My private life concerns no one but myself and my family; and if, on the printed page, I am Miss Heyer, everywhere else I am Mrs Rougier, who makes no public appearances, and dislikes few things as much as being confronted by Fans . . . The facts of my life you can have, but not How I write My Books, or what my valueless views are on this or that question, and certainly no intimate glimpses of the author at home . . . Meanwhile, I'm trying to write a book, and, believe me it is quite fatal to badger me at such moments: it puts me in the wrong mood.

Dorothy Sutherland could mistake neither the tone nor the message and a few weeks later Georgette triumphantly told Frere that she had 'at last broken the S.B. of her repulsive habit of addressing me as "Dear Georgette Heyer." Today's post brings me the briefest note I've ever received from her – the note of one in a dudgeon: "Dear Miss Heyer: I am asking Christopher Landon to write to you to arrange a meeting. Sincerely –" That'll larn me, won't it?'

The Christopher Landon interview never did take place and Georgette refrained from pitching her 'existing manuscript (what there is of it) into the fire (which would be a good place for it)', and telling Dorothy Sutherland 'to forget my very name'. She justified her sharp response to the editor by telling Frere that she was feeling peevish after being unwell and having to look after her mother who was also ill, and being difficult. Georgette felt beset by woe. She was struggling with the new Regency and told Frere that she had 'never felt less like writing a gay romance, and am churning out heavy pastry in a slow and laborious fashion, and am quite likely to go into strong hysterics if anyone speaks a harsh word to me'. The reality was that she had been thwarted from working on her medieval novel. Having 'once again laid John of Lancaster up in lavender, I felt as I did when I saw Richard off to his prep. school for the first time', and so had taken the opportunity to vent her spleen at Dorothy Sutherland.

Although Georgette knew John of Lancaster could not possibly be finished in a matter of months like her other novels, she found it frustrating to be constantly distracted from the book. She had convinced herself that it was the one thing she wanted to be doing. Whether she truly believed in *John* as a saleable book and actually wanted to see it in print is debatable. Although she enjoyed her regular excursions into the fourteenth and fifteenth centuries and the research made her feel like a serious writer, she had already told Frere that the novel would not sell 'in huge quantities' and that admirers of 'unhistorical fiction' would 'not at all relish my book'. Her desire to succeed with her medieval tome may in part have been influenced by Carola Oman's successful transition from historical romances to more serious books. Two years previously Carola's *Sir John Moore* had won the James Tait Black Memorial Prize for biography (just as Richard Aldington's *Wellington* had in 1946). Georgette felt a direct connection to these books and their authors. Although she felt sure she would never win an award as a writer of historical fiction, there were still times when she yearned for that kind of recognition.

Meanwhile, Ronald's career was prospering nicely. He had developed a solid practice at the Parliamentary Bar and in August 1955 was elected a member of the Garrick Club (proposed by High Court judge, Sir Seymour Karminski, and seconded by Frere). Established in 1831, the Garrick's members included many of the leading lights of the theatre and literary worlds as well as lawyers, judges and journalists. The club did not admit women as members, but they could dine there in the evening as members' guests. The Garrick was home to a unique collection of paintings and theatrical memorabilia. In every room there were portraits of the theatre's most famous actors and actresses. Georgette enjoyed dining there beneath magnificent paintings by Zoffany, Samuel de Wilde and Thomas Lawrence.

Having put *John of Lancaster* away, she finally got on with her new book, *Sprig Muslin*. This would prove to be one of her most amusing, witty comedies, with an intriguing sub-plot and an older heroine whose gradual metamorphosis remains an abiding delight to Heyer readers. Soon after its publication the following spring Georgette was in the London bookstore, Truslove & Hanson, and overheard the kind of exchange guaranteed to infuriate her:

"Have you got Georgette Heyer's new book?"

"Oh yes, indeed we have! – A Sprig of Muslin, you mean: it's ever so pretty!"

Autumn brought disappointing news about her American book sales. Georgette wrote to Frere to tell him that she was thinking 'seriously about severing connections' with Putnam's, her American publisher. Since 1946 they had published nine of her novels and at best she had only ever earned a bit over the advance – itself considerably smaller than her English advances. It was frustrating for she got 'good notices, and enthusiastic fan letters; and when Doubleday handled my stuff there was never any question of not selling up to the advance.' Ted Purdy, Putnam's Managing Director, had waxed lyrical about the potential of her medieval book to sell in the States, but Georgette was convinced that 'when American publishers say that they want books about the Middle Ages they have in mind a welter of flesh, blood, sadism and general violence. Breast-sellers, in fact.' While she had no intention of giving them *John of Lancaster* she let them have *Sprig Muslin* about which one American critic wrote: 'As a plotter she has no superior.' Georgette remained unhappy with Putnam's, however, and six years later finally severed connections with the firm.

Early December found her working on a new short story for *Everybody's* magazine. For once she had not found the writing easy and had spent ten days 'churning out 8,000 words of SNOWBOUND' before deciding in the middle of the night that it would not do. Fortunately, she had 'instantly succumbed to a fit of Brilliance, during which I evolved THE NECKLACE, which is so exactly what the Fans like that I've been feeling queasy ever since'. The story never did appear in *Everybody's* and Georgette used the plot for her next Regency novel instead.

She wrote nothing over Christmas but spent the festive season peacefully at home. A few days later the cold she had caught from Ronald turned into 'flu. The two of them felt 'so bloody' that they spent the better part of an evening getting 'Stinking'. A bottle of champagne at 6.30 p.m. had gone down so well that they had progressed to Burgundy at dinner after which 'it seemed like port would be good for our throats, so we gave that a very fair trial; & ended the evening, some time later, with stout whiskeys.' Georgette enjoyed a drink.

Despite another bout of illness in the spring she began a new Regency and told Pat Wallace: 'All the time the Plucky Little Woman goes on churning out her latest novel. This one is going to touch an All Time Low. No, really, it STINKS! Frere has just rung up to ask me for the title. I told him THE NECKLACE. He took it fairly quietly, but rang up a few minutes later to say, what sort of a necklace?' Frere's reaction inspired Georgette to change the title to *April Lady* – another likely Shakespearean reference – this time from the 'men are April when they woo' speech in *As You Like It*. She planned to write two books in 1956, in the hope of freeing herself from writing romances long enough to get a clear run at *John of Lancaster*. She hoped that by having an extra novel finished and put to one side she would at last get ahead of the taxman.

Since the beginning of April, she and Ronald had paid over £7,000 to the Inland Revenue. It was a vast sum and, quite apart from having to give up so much of her hard-earned income, Georgette hated 'the thought that all this ill-gotten wealth is going to be squandered on objects I totally disapprove of, such as helping a lot of lazy sods to go out on strike for more pay and less work. If I didn't believe that the Human Race is on its way out I don't think I could <u>bear</u> it.' It was a privileged point of view. Although she had always worked hard and endured times of great strain, Georgette had never suffered actual deprivation or known what it was to go without. Her attitude was typical of someone of her upbringing, social aspirations and conservative beliefs. She would have rejected any suggestion that she was callous or unfeeling about those less fortunate than herself. As far as she was concerned, she worked hard, paid her way and was entitled to enjoy the fruits of her labours. To have the taxman take such a disproportionate share of her earnings was bad enough; to see the revenue spent on what she deemed to be pointless welfare schemes and feckless individuals was worse.

She signed the contract for *April Lady* in June 1956. 'I really can't be bothered to read the thing,' she told Frere, confident that she could disregard any clause she disliked and keen to get on with her next book. Richard had urged her to think of a new plot and with that in mind she had 'dug up a lot more Regency slang, some of it very good indeed, and the best quite unprintable'. But she would not write it until summer and the Test cricket were over. 'The English batsmen are making the Australian bowlers look like three pennorth of bad cheese,' she gleefully told Frere after listening to the Test on the radio.

She was enjoying a lazy few weeks to herself, for Ronald was away in the south of France with 'a golfing acquaintance of untold wealth', bathing, boating and playing roulette. He enjoyed gambling and often played bridge for stakes – although not always successfully. A recent evening spent partnering Richard at Crockford's had proved disastrous: 'Father never held a card, & every finesse went wrong,' Georgette confided to Frere. 'I don't know what the sum total was, but I do know that he paid Richard his share of the loss by <u>cheque</u>!' and Richard's 'balance at the club was drastically reduced!' It was not only fine food and wine, shopping trips to Fortnum's and Harrods, elegant hats, handbags, tailored suits, jewellery, first editions, and holidays at Greywalls that cost money in the Rougier household.

Richard had completed his studies earlier in 1956 and been called to the Bar by the Inner Temple. After obtaining a place in the chambers of Melford Stevenson Q.C. he had joined the South Eastern Circuit and begun working as a barrister. His suggestion that Georgette write something new had inspired her to turn 'Snowbound' into *Sylvester or The Wicked Uncle*. She told Pat Wallace that she 'hadn't enjoyed anything as much as writing this book for years'. She was also cheered by the news that after only a month on the bookstands *April Lady* was already outselling her previous novels. Serialised in *Woman's Journal* the previous October (under the annoying title 'My Lady Cardross') her fans had rushed to read the book. Georgette told Frere that she could easily 'explain April Lady's success! Almost the Top of the Popular appeal Stakes (amongst females) is the Rift in

(*Left*) Georgette and
Ronald in Paris

(*Below left*) Blackthorns
in Sussex
(*Below*) Georgette and
Misty Dawn

(*Left*) Georgette and Richard
in Cornwall

(*Below*) Richard and Johnny

(Right)
Pastel 1929

(Far right)
Barren Corn 1930

(Far left) Charles
Leslie Rougier

(Left) Sylvia Heyer

(Far left)
Jean Rougier

(Left)
'Pater' Charles
Joseph Rougier

(*Right*)
Georgette Heyer by
Howard Coster 1939

(*Above*) Georgette and Ronald at
Dmitri and Dorothy Tornow's
wedding 1944

(*Left*) Ronald, Georgette,
Boris and Richard

(*Left*) Richard,
the gillie and
Georgette in Scotland

(*Above*) Percy Hodder-Williams
(*Below*) Patricia Wallace
(*Left*) A.S. Frere
(*Below left*) C.S. Evans

Georgette's
favourite
photograph
of herself

(*Right*)
Boris Heyer

(*Far right*)
Frank Heyer

(*Above*) Richard at Cambridge

(*Above*) Aunt Ciss and Aunt Jo

(*Right*) Susie and Dominic

(*Below left*) George Ronald Rougier
(*Below right*) Richard George Rougier

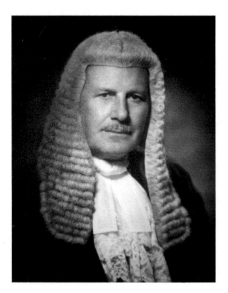

(*Above*) Georgette
by Anna Murphy 1959

(*Left*) Georgette and Ronald

(*Below*) Georgette at Greywalls

(*Left*) Max Reinhardt
and A.S. Frere by
Desmond O'Neill

(*Right*) Ronald Rougier

(*Above*) Georgette's remaining notebooks

(*Left, below left and below*) From Georgette's Regency notebooks

the Married Lute[25] – provided it All Comes Right in the End'. More good news was the sale of an option on *The Conqueror* to the British Lion Film Company for £4,000. This book had never been published in America and the film deal encouraged Georgette to think that the novel might now have a chance across the Atlantic. But even these good tidings were tempered by new tax demands.

Despite Rubens' assurances that she would pay no more than £9,000, her last tax bill had been £11,000. After handing over another £3,000 to the Inland Revenue with more still to pay, Georgette was feeling increasingly exasperated with her accountant. 'I think Jamaica would be too hot a climate for me, but what about the Channel Islands?' she asked Frere bitterly. 'If I am going to be taxed on money I never so much as touched, because I.R. got there first, I think I'll either leave the country, or go into liquidation, and not write any more books. I find it too disheartening.' Many of Britain's top-earners did leave the country during the high surtax era, but Georgette was not one of them. A complete Anglophile, once settled in England after her earlier travels she could never have returned to living overseas. Her attitude was typical of many of her generation. She once summed it up in a letter: 'I feel very much like an old man I once knew who ranked the animal creation thus: All Englishmen. Horses. Dogs. Foreigners.'

Her writing stalled in March 1957. Another bout of 'flu had been diagnosed as streptococcal throat and she could not sleep. Laboriously typing half a page a day she resolutely ignored friends' well-meant suggestions that she shelve the novel and take a holiday. Only Ronald understood that leaving a book unfinished 'would fret me into my grave'. But he had always understood her. Ronald knew better than anyone how to respond to her doubts about her writing or her struggles over a book. Georgette had once said of him during the *Penhallow* era that:

Ronald's the only one with any real tact. Having said that he thinks it a fine book, he has no more to say, & remains unmoved

---

25 A reference to the line from Tennyson's *Idylls of the King*: 'It is the little rift within the lute'.

by praise of it, shrugging his shoulders, & saying Scottishly: "Well, obviously! I told you so." When Frere liked it, Ronald "thought he would". When Percy hated it, that "confirms the opinion I've always had of that man." How to be the perfect husband!

They were great friends. Georgette and Ronald shared many common interests and she endured his irascibility and outbursts of temper while he coped with her forceful personality and determination to be right. When they did fight it was usually over a point of history (one of their more serious arguments was over the Divine Right of Kings) or a word or phrase in one of her manuscripts, rather than over more mundane things like domestic problems or money. Their deep intimacy and mutual understanding failed only in the sexual side of their relationship. If Ronald ever chose to fulfil those needs with someone else he did so with complete discretion. In the mid-1950s Georgette would sometimes joke in her letters to Richard about Father's 'Blonde' and chaff Ronald directly about his 'Floozie'. This may have been typical family humour or it may have been Georgette's way of letting her husband know that she knew and that if he *was* seeking physical comfort elsewhere she, like so many well-bred Regency wives, would always turn a blind eye.

31

It incorporates every last one of the characters which are my stock-in-trade, and ends with the sort of absurd scene which (I hope) raises my novels slightly above the Utterly Bloody Standard.

Georgette Heyer

Sylvester turned out to be one of her long books like *The Foundling* and *Friday's Child*. Worried that Dorothy Sutherland would be discouraged by the length Georgette spent a good part of April re-writing; by May she was sick of it. *Sylvester* was the first book for ages that really mattered to her. 'I <u>did</u> once think I'd got something,' she told Frere, 'it <u>was</u> better, until I got cold feet and cut out what wouldn't please the fans.' She begged him to read it and give her his views. But Frere never committed to reading her books, though he did read *Penhallow*. He thought *Sylvester* would sell, however, and in late May sent Georgette an urgent request for a synopsis: 'We go to press with the Autumn list next week. SYLVESTER is or should be one of the most important books in that list. Nobody in this office has seen a single word of it so far so, I ask you, how the hell can we describe it in the list?' She immediately sent a detailed description of the book and an assurance that it was much better than it sounded. She was going down to spend the weekend with Frere and Pat Wallace at their country house in Kent having facetiously warned them: 'you <u>do</u> know that I shall bring a MS, & Read It Aloud to you, don't you? Failing that, I shall Talk to you about My Art.'

Georgette turned fifty-five that August. She seemed increasingly susceptible to illness and a bee-sting at Greywalls had distressing repercussions. A painful attack of fibrositis was followed by internal trouble which meant 'suffering the tortures of the damned, every time I eat anything that isn't Boiled Fish or Boiled Apple'. She was stoical, however, and although she doubted she would last beyond Christmas had strength enough to express her delight at the Freres' beautiful Christmas gift: 'Darling-Frere, I shall CUT Boswell's pages, because I am going to read him.' Georgette was a voracious reader with a wide-ranging and eclectic taste – although she confessed to sometimes struggling with modern novels.

She no longer read manuscripts for Heinemann but Frere continued to send her any new title which he thought might interest her and she often requested books after reading a review or talking to a fellow Inky. Georgette could be a tough critic and had no time for what she considered verbiage. Her preference was for those skilled in the craft of writing and her favourite authors were those whose mastery of language or distinct voice set their writing apart such as Jane Austen, Charles Dickens, Ivy Compton-Burnett, Noël Coward, Angela Thirkell, Stephen Leacock, Agatha Christie, Alistair MacLean and Raymond Chandler. Georgette was even prepared to acknowledge her own ability (up to a point), though any hint of self-praise or a suggestion in a letter that what she had written was good was invariably and immediately qualified or contradicted. To have publicly admitted that she thought her writing good would mean committing the unforgivable sin of vulgarity. It was one thing to mention Ronald's or Richard's achievements, but to Georgette's mind a well-bred person never bragged about her own success.

She could not ignore her increasing sales or escalating income, however. By 1958 her annual earnings had easily passed the £10,000 mark. More money meant paying more tax and a new demand for over £4,000 on Heron prompted an angry letter to Rubens, whose soothing responses and ineffectual communication did little to placate her. Efforts to pin her accountant down to a lucid explanation brought no satisfaction: 'I never <u>can</u> make head or tail of the document he tells me to sign. Nor did it occur to me that when I employed an accountant to do my business I must watch <u>his</u> antics like a lynx.' Equally frustrating was Rubens' assurance that the company set-up was worthwhile, despite Georgette's growing doubts about the benefits of running her books through Heron:

> Whenever I say to Rubens that I can't see the advantage in being a Company, he gets annoyed – but after a flood of plausible talk from him I still don't see it. On the Company alone I pay Income Tax, Profits Tax, & Sur-Tax. On our private income, we pay Income & Sur Tax. On Richard's fees (which in actual fact are only £500) I pay P.A.Y.E. & then Sur-Tax to the tune of £600 odd – because Rubens said it would be a saving to make him the principal stake-holder. All I can say is, I've yet to see the saving – because <u>our</u> Sur-tax hasn't diminished.

After several attempts to resolve the situation she resentfully concluded: 'If this thing goes through, I shall have paid about £6000 in taxation before ever my earnings get into my private account. <u>Then</u> I shall pay private Income Tax, and Sur-tax.' To have earned over £10,000 in a year only to find herself with a balance of £2,000–£3,000 in Heron's account and an overdraft of £800 in her own was bitter indeed.

The only solution was to keep writing and within weeks Georgette had begun *Venetia*. She thought it would be short, without much plot, but with a hero who would please her readers and a heroine she even confessed to liking. But tax concerns persisted: 'I <u>cannot</u> concentrate on light & witty romances when I'm so worried.' She had no confidence in Rubens and little hope of winning her latest fight with the Inland Revenue. An offer from a German film company for a six-month option on *Arabella* would mean a £5,000 boost to her coffers if the deal went through.[26] But she was not hopeful. The BBC wanted to produce a radio play of *Sylvester* and there was an

---

26 The film was eventually made as *Die Bezaubernde Arabella*. Although it followed Georgette's story, the director gave it an early twentieth-century setting. It first screened in December 1959.

offer pending for an option on TV rights for four of her novels. But films and television serials were possibilities, not certainties. In the meantime she was having to 'contemplate a future composed of grinding out bright romances in a vain attempt to keep level with the Treasury's demands' and beginning to think that '<u>anything</u> would be preferable'.

By spring *Venetia* was half finished and Georgette was having doubts about her fans' reaction to such a simple love story – 'Except that my hero is a Rake, which always gets my silly sex.' Despite feeling that she never did her best work when worried, Georgette proceeded to produce in *Venetia* one of her finest novels. A quiet book with a great deal of subtle humour she described it as 'not quite like Me'. Although at one point in the novel she reflected on the essence of true love in a speech that may well have been a comment on her own marriage:

> "You and Damerel!" she said after a long silence. "Do you imagine he would be faithful to you?"
>
> "I don't know," said Venetia. "I think he will always love me. You see, we are such dear friends."

Almost before *Venetia* was finished, Georgette had an idea for her next book.

She spent Whitsun in Rye on the Sussex coast watching Ronald and Richard playing in the Bar Golf Tournament. Georgette had always thought Rye an ideal setting for a story. She planned to 'have a lovely week fossicking around for smugglers' haunts, & what-have-you'. The new novel would not be written for another year but she was content to keep the idea simmering in the back of her mind while she gathered her material. Much to her satisfaction, Ronald won the Bar Tournament that year (narrowly beating Richard in the semi-final round).

After nearly twenty years as a barrister, Ronald had carved out a respectable niche for himself at the Parliamentary Bar. He would never be a brilliant lawyer but he was sound, reliable and well able to argue a case. His proficiency at golf and bridge earned him the respect of his associates and he was considered a valuable member of the English Bench and Bar golf team. In March 1959 Ronald was appointed a Queen's Counsel and on 7 April he formally took silk. Georgette attended his admission ceremony and enjoyed it enormously. She was very proud of Ronald's becoming a Q.C., and for some time afterwards would refer to him teasingly as 'little Silky'.

She sometimes watched him in court but found it disconcerting to see her husband so composed and dispassionate. While she admired his court persona, she thought it a stark contrast to his personality at home. Some years later, when Ronald was Chairman of the General Optical Council, she heard him praised for his

> "Tact(!), Charm and Impartiality" when overseeing disputes and [I] expressed the fervent wish that some of this Tact might be shown in The Home; and it is with mixed feelings that I watch the Creature displaying, in Court, the calm, unemotional quiet which is at such startling variance with his Home Demeanour! In Home Arguments, I am left with the impression that he marvels that God should have cursed him with a Moron for a wife, and am frequently reminded of his mother – "Ronnie, NOT so EMPHATIC!"

Georgette sat for her portrait in 1959. Anna Murphy's painting revealed her looking every inch the *grande dame* in a magnificent black evening dress and heavy pearl necklace (Richard always said she looked as though 'someone had just trumped her ace!'). Ronald had the portrait hung above the fireplace in the sitting room in Albany where friends could admire it – although Georgette was always characteristically self-deprecating about having been 'done'.

She had finally started the novel set in Rye and decided to call it *The Unknown Ajax* after the Trojan War hero in Shakespeare's *Troilus and Cressida*. The book had another of her clever character inversions and she grew quite fond of this novel and of her large hero in particular. It helped that he was 'a new one, too, which makes an epoch!' *The Unknown Ajax* contains some of Georgette's funniest dialogue.

She finished the novel in June and sent the messy typescript to

Frere with a reassuring note and an apology: 'Sithee, love, (as my hero would say) it's noan so bad! I have just rushed through, correcting, & transcribing corrections; & I don't know, but I think it'll do. (It'll have to, anyway!) I'm sorry it's so messy.' She often apologised for her manuscripts, which were typically full of additions, deletions, interpolations, and corrections all written in a crabbed hand between the lines of typing. Frere was not concerned, however, for they were still legible and gave the typesetters no trouble. Her publisher knew her to be the consummate professional and, so far from needing to be pushed, Frere 'had to be careful not to ask too much of her'.

Her relationship with Frere and Pat Wallace gave Georgette great satisfaction: they liked and understood her and she felt completely at ease in their company. Her tendency to be brutally frank did not always make her easy to deal with, but she was a kind and generous friend with a marvellous sense of humour and she could be great fun. She and Ronald both adored Pat Wallace and Georgette once replied to an invitation to dinner by telling her friend that although she would 'love to dine . . . even more would I love to see you by yourself one day, so that I can be girlish, & let my hair down'. Living in such close proximity in Albany did not prevent her from writing regular letters to the Freres at E.1. or from revelling in their replies: 'I read your letter at the breakfast-table this morning,' she told Pat Wallace, 'and chuckled gently. Until the Creature I married (when VERY young and stupid) said, with barely restrained impatience: "Well, don't be snitchy with Wallace's letter!" So I read it to him, and now hail you (mediaevally) as a Spousebreaker, because the Nasty Old Man said wistfully: "I do love Miss Wallace!"'

Ronald's affection for Pat Wallace did not extend to her husband, however. The two men shared a mutual antipathy which each did his best to conceal. Georgette was aware that Frere thought Ronald opinionated and an 'awful ass'. But as much as she adored her publisher she would not allow him to criticise her husband. Always reticent about such things, Ronald mostly kept his feelings to himself, although his wife was aware of the spark of resentment which smouldered within him and would sometimes deliberately defer to Ronald because of it. Her relationship with the two men gave Georgette the best of both worlds: Frere was charming, clever, well-connected and successful; Ronald was understanding, supportive, intelligent and capable. They both thought the world of her.

Walter Minton of Putnam's wrote to Joyce Weiner that year to ask if he could publish four of Georgette's earlier titles in America. But Georgette had grown disillusioned with the firm's apparent inability to sell her novels properly and had already asked her agent to tell Putnam's that *The Unknown Ajax* would be her last publication with them. 'I know you are itching to do business with him,' she wrote Frere. 'Of course, I have no control over the first three titles on his list, but I will never speak to you again (except rudely) if you yield to your itch.' She had taken one of her dislikes to Minton and although she relented enough to give them one more book after *Ajax*, it was to be the last.

Georgette's mediocre sales in the United States were due in part to poor publicity. She had not yet become a household name in America as she had in Britain and, despite the sale of various film and stage rights, had never had the benefit of a successful play or movie to boost her book sales. Though sceptical of the idea, she still hoped someone might eventually make a film that did justice to her work. She was envious when she heard that Pat Wallace had sold the rights to some of her father's stories to a television production company.

They went to Greywalls as usual in September but Georgette's discovery of a lump in her breast meant surgery on her return. 'The small, sordid job was done yesterday,' she told Pat Wallace in October, '& I hope & believe that that's the end.' The tumour was benign. She recovered in a private hospital and despite feeling rather limp enjoyed several days of comfortably doing nothing with no one to make demands of her. *The Unknown Ajax* came out in November and Frere reported that sales were 'running currently much higher than VENETIA over a comparable period last year, and I can assure you that the booksellers are mighty pleased with Miss Heyer'. He also apologised for neglecting her 'with a capital N, but I cannot think of a period during our long, chequered, and to me wholly delightful association when you have not had every right to feel so'. It was not true, of course, but Georgette did not argue the point.

She spent the new year writing a short story for a new woman's magazine. Joyce Weiner had negotiated a fee of five hundred guineas for the commission – a very large sum which reflected the power of Georgette Heyer's name to sell magazines. The story was 'A Clandestine Affair' which Georgette described as 'very old rope – badly frayed . . . an unblushing crib on the works of Georgette Heyer'. She was right, for the tale had decided echoes of her 1955 novel *Bath Tangle*. It was to be her last short story.

That year, she had hopes of writing a new kind of novel but was unsure about it. She thought the book would be 'neither farcical nor adventurous, & will depend for success on whether I can make the hero as charming as I believe he was! And also, of course, if I can make a quiet story interesting.' She wanted *A Civil Contract* to be quite different from her previous books and planned to set the story in 1814–15 with 'the culminating point the financial panic in London over Waterloo. I have always had a slight yen to do that – & to see Major Percy driving in a hired hack to Carlton House, with the two Eagles sticking out of the windows.' But her writing was again destined for delay when her mother was struck down with bronchitis.

It took Sylvia a long time to recover. Having got her into a nursing home and engaged two nurses to care for her, Georgette and her brothers now tried to persuade Sylvia that she should not continue to live alone in a hotel. Frank posted up to London to try to talk his mother into moving into a nursing home on the Royal Circus in Bath. He assured her he would be nearby at Downside School and Georgette promised to visit regularly from London. It seemed the ideal solution but Sylvia refused to go. Ironically (to Georgette's mind), her main reason was that she 'did not want to be so far from me!'

Her mother then decided that what she really wanted was to live in a Home in Brighton. Consequently, Georgette and Boris (who was now in Sussex managing a country-house hotel with Evelyn) spent a 'frightful' day in Brighton looking at places – only to find on their return that Sylvia had booked herself into a room in another nursing home. It was a great relief when her mother eventually recovered and moved back into her hotel in Leicester Gardens. Georgette felt the strain of her mother's needs; it was conducive neither to tranquillity nor to writing, and 1960 was another of her rare years without a new novel.

32

My style is really a mixture of Johnson & Austen – & what I rely on is a certain gift for the farcical.

Georgette Heyer

Not wanting to disappoint her fans who had come to expect the annual Heyer novel, Georgette agreed to Joyce Weiner's suggestion that she publish an anthology of her short stories instead. She chose a selection of her published stories for the book and *Woman's Journal* chose 'Hazard' for their Christmas issue, telling readers: 'we have chosen *our* favourite, by *your* favourite author.' Some of the stories needed minor amendments or character name changes and the Coronation story 'The Pursuit of Hetty' was re-titled 'To Have the Honour'. It was a minimal amount of work for a substantial return. Georgette was so pleased with Joyce Weiner's idea that for several years afterwards she gave her ten per cent of the royalties. They called the collection *Pistols for Two*. Then Georgette returned to her neglected novel.

She did not find writing *A Civil Contract* easy. Beset by interruptions she told Pat Wallace that it remained

> much where it was – & where it <u>ought</u> to be is in an incinerator, & would be if I hadn't pledged myself to write it. To be honest with you, I do not wish to write this book. Or any other book. I have no inspiration, no energy, no enthusiasm, & no power-of-the-pen! I sit & look at the bloody thing, & wonder what can have possessed me to embark on it.

Georgette had rarely before struggled with a book and she found it disconcerting to find herself sitting at her typewriter gazing at an unfinished page. She pressed on, however, and eventually finished what some readers consider to be one of her best novels. *A Civil Contract* is about a series of unequal relationships and the different kinds of love that can make or mar them. Its prosaic romance between her plain, middle-class heroine and gentle, aristocratic hero set it apart from her other Regency novels. The book also contains one of Georgette's comic triumphs in Jonathan Chawleigh, her heroine's fabulously wealthy and vulgar father who continually 'tried to steal the whole book, & had to be firmly pushed off the stage'.

Georgette went to Paris for Christmas, spending a riotous week there with Ronald and Richard. Returning home in good spirits, a few days later she wrenched her back carrying her typewriter. Stuck at home with orders not to stoop or climb stairs she sent off the *Civil Contract* manuscript in a rather gloomy frame of mind. She also sent a message to Frere asking him to read it: 'Don't if you don't want to, but if you have, let me know what you think . . . I still feel very doubtful, and am, for once in my life anxious to see how it reads in print.' But Frere had other things on his mind. There were serious problems at Heinemann and he was facing increasing alienation and opposition to his command.

After several years of decreasing profits, the firm was near bankruptcy and there was dissension among the board members about how to address the problem. Five years earlier, Frere had attempted to get Heinemann into paperback publishing but had met with stiff resistance from the other directors. He was eventually overruled and the plan fell through. Kingswood had also become an expensive white elephant and with no significant new authors the firm was overly reliant on its long-established stars. Many of Heinemann's key writers, including Somerset Maugham, Graham Greene, John Steinbeck, J.B. Priestley, Eric Ambler and Georgette Heyer herself, were well past middle age and could not be relied on to produce bestselling novels indefinitely.

The dire financial situation had prompted Frere and Lionel Fraser, the chairman of the Thomas Tilling Group (which owned a majority share of Heinemann), to try and sell the company to McGraw-Hill, the successful American technical and academic publisher. The proposal was made in absolute secrecy, with Frere the only member of the Heinemann board to know of it. Consequently, when the deal was leaked, several of Heinemann's directors vehemently opposed it on the grounds that McGraw-Hill was too big and too American. It was a xenophobic view which conveniently ignored the fact that Heinemann had once been successfully owned by the American firm of Doubleday. The anti-McGraw-Hill lobby prevailed, however, and the deal did not go through.

Desperate to save the company in which they had invested so much, Tilling had bought up the rest of the Heinemann equity and set about re-organising the firm and its board. By April 1961 Frere's fears were realised and he was 'kicked upstairs' to occupy a new, non-managerial position as president. His long-held belief in publishing without consulting others ultimately proved his undoing.

Although Georgette was disturbed by the machinations at Heinemann, as long as Frere was still there she was content to let things continue as before. To her, at least, Frere appears to have downplayed both his anger and the true nature of the situation, for she wrote to him just as usual during that tumultuous spring and summer. By March she had already decided that it was not a good year. Her mother had had a fall and broken a rib, Frank's wife Joan was in hospital recovering from a mastectomy, Boris and Evelyn were moving north to Northumberland to run a pub, and 'a large demand from the I.R. sharks' meant calling in the *Civil Contract* advance early. When a fan wrote 'to draw your attention to a flagrant example of plagiarism' of Georgette's work it seemed the final straw.

Georgette reluctantly read *Winsome Lass* by Kathleen Lindsay and sent Frere a scathing assessment of it: 'The book is very poor stuff indeed, but not, I think, actionable. There is scarcely a character in it who wasn't suggested by me, or sometimes, two of mine, but since none of them has any life, far less charm, I hardly think I can be hurt by this utterly blatant piece of piracy. The woman hasn't a clue! . . . Utterly without wit or humour . . . You know, I can't imagine how she contrived to get some 6 books published, because she <u>can't write</u>!'[27] On Frere's advice Georgette wrote a stiff letter of protest to Kathleen Lindsay's publisher, Robert Lusty of Hurst & Blackett, which she hoped would put an end to the matter.

To her astonishment, a few weeks later she received a reply informing her that Kathleen Lindsay took 'considerable exception' to the accusations and demanded details of the alleged borrowings. Appalled by what she saw as a fellow-author's dishonesty Georgette sent Lusty a detailed summary and a two-page list of similarities. A second reply from Kathleen Lindsay demanding, 'What does it all amount to? About four incidents and two lines', shocked Georgette so profoundly that she worked up an eleven-page analysis of *Winsome Lass* cross-referenced against eight of her own novels and sent it to her solicitor. Counsel's opinion was for an injunction, but Georgette's only desire was to prevent further infringements and to put the incident behind her. Neither author was willing to give ground, however. Georgette testily told Kathleen Lindsay's publisher that 'I realize that she and I do not speak the same language, or share the same principles.' Like the Cartland case before it, this one never went to court.

Georgette's blood-pressure soared in April. Her doctor put it down to the plagiarism affair but his patient thought it was more likely the result of Richard's decision to become involved with the wife of one of his bridge-playing friends. Only a year earlier he had told his mother (much to her despair) that he had 'no intention of entering the married state' and yet now he appeared to have fallen for a married woman. Richard had known Jeremy and Susanna Flint for some time and when her marriage had foundered Susie had turned to Richard for support. The relationship had evolved from there. It was a potentially scandalous situation, however, for divorce was still seriously frowned upon in 1960s England. At first, Georgette and Ronald were horrified at the idea of Richard marrying a divorcee.

---

27 In fact, Kathleen Lindsay wrote 904 books under a series of pseudonyms and for many years held the record as the world's most prolific novelist.

It was not until Susie joined them at Greywalls in September that they were won over: 'We have had Richard's Intended with us since Tuesday, & I rather think Ronald is becoming reconciled. To Susie, if not to her circumstances – & God knows I'm not reconciled to them, & nor is Susie herself . . . But she is a charming guest, with the prettiest manner, & a gratifying way of enjoying herself.' Georgette confessed to being a little puzzled over her son's choice of bride, however: 'I should never have picked her as a suitable type for R.G. I think her intelligent, but, as far as I can discover, she is definitely not Bookish, & I do rather wonder what mutual contact there will be, since R.G. is extremely Bookish. However, he's not a boy or a fool, & I must suppose that he's weighed it all up, in his peculiarly cold-fish way.' It was a perceptive comment, for even with Susie – whom he seemed determined to marry in the face of all opposition – Richard would never be ardent or make his inner feelings known. Ronald was won over by Susie's enthusiasm and the realisation that she had endured a lot. Georgette was certain that she would be a delightful daughter-in-law.

Within a fortnight of their return to London Georgette was struck down by some kind of respiratory ailment. 'It seems strange that I was once a fairly successful novelist,' she told Pat Wallace. 'I feel today like a slow worm. It is an intolerable effort to move from one chair to another, & I wish that I were dead.' Fortunately, the feeling did not last and by Christmas she was well enough to write one of her long, chatty letters to the Freres to thank them for their gifts – including an elegant copy of *War and Peace* which Georgette thought '<u>almost</u> lovely enough to make me read it. Not quite – unless I have to go on a long sea-voyage, or into hospital for weeks & weeks – because (I say it defiantly) I am Wholly Allergic to Russian Literature, drama, & art. For one thing, they all have such Stephen Leacock names, like Ivan Ivanovitch; & for another, I loathe & despise their silly Fatalism.' Richard told his mother that she did not understand tragedy – an observation shared by Ronald who had once threatened to divorce Georgette after she had insisted that 'the sooner Anna Karenina flung herself under a train the better it would be.'

Returning from the south of France after Christmas, the Freres were greeted with news of Georgette's new book – not yet planned but in the offing: 'I cannot think whether I will write Manifold, or Gideon – but one or the other I must write, if the fantastic demands of the I.R. are to be met.' Despite her grumbles, she was more relaxed about money than she had ever been for her royalty income had grown large enough to cover even the most alarming tax bill and Joyce Weiner was negotiating the huge sum of £3,500 for the next serial in *Woman's Journal*. Meanwhile, Georgette was planning a new book *and* her son's wedding, which was to be in June. Since Susie's mother could not afford a lavish reception it was decided to hold it in Albany.

On 2 June 1962, Richard George Rougier married Susanna Whitworth Flint at the Kensington Register Office. Susie quickly found her place in the family and Georgette was delighted to discover that her new daughter-in-law 'has our own type of humour. This makes life very easy, for one doesn't have to edit one's conversation. She's quick-witted too, & dearly loves a joke.' It was a great happiness for Georgette to see her son married and to a young woman whose company she so much enjoyed. She had long thought she did not want a daughter and had clung to her maxim that 'Boys tell their mothers, and Girls tell their fathers'. But her perception was based on her own experience of having '<u>been</u> a daughter'; the advent of 'Our dear Susie' into her life soon convinced her she was wrong.

Within six months of the wedding Georgette told her old friend and former landlady, Isabella Banton, that 'I made a lot of Good Resolutions, when Richard married, about Never Intruding on them, or Making Demands, but Susie smashed the lot – so that I find myself wondering if all is well at 56 Cornwall Gardens, if I don't get a telephone call from her.' Unlike Richard, Susie talked to her mother-in-law regularly, exchanging news and gossip and keeping her up-to-date with family events. It did not take Georgette long to realise that Richard had never really told her anything. Susie's little boys also brought a new dimension to her life. She and Ronald enjoyed being step-grandparents to six-year-old Dominic and four-year-old Noel. Altogether, Georgette judged Richard's marriage a great success.

A month after the wedding she finished *The Nonesuch*. It was another of her quiet books with the action mainly centred in the fictional village of Oversett in Yorkshire. *The Nonesuch* reflected Jane Austen's famous advice that '3 or 4 families in a country village is the very thing to work on.' The book may also have been inspired by Georgette's tour of England's north earlier in the year when she had accompanied Ronald to the Northern Optical Conference where he had presided as chairman of the General Optical Council (a Privy Council appointment). During the inevitable round of factory tours, presentations, lunches and banquets Georgette had encountered several memorable characters. One local mayor had 'turned out to be a honey':

> He informed me at the outset that he was a plumber, and he had the instinctive savoir faire which characterized Bevin, and is so endearing. I may mention that he won my heart at the outset by telling me that Ee, he was glad to have me beside him, because he had wanted, at the Ball on the previous night, to coom a bit closer to me, because he couldn't hear all I said, but enough to show him that I was "a natural-born 'umorist!" so was he! We had a splendid time – and a lovely talk about cricket, with particular reference to Brian Statham.

The rest of the delegates she felt did not come 'out of quite one's own drawer, so great care had to be taken not to offend tender susceptibilities'. Georgette's particular brand of snobbery was not always clear cut. While her preference was for those individuals perceived to be from her own class or above, a person did not have to be well-born to win her over. Intelligence, strength of character and a sense of humour were the prerequisites for her friendship.

In May Frere sent through the contract for *The Nonesuch*. For the first time since sacking L.P. Moore in 1951 Georgette actually read the document. She was stunned to find that it contained an option clause giving Heinemann first refusal of her next two books. Incensed, she immediately wrote to tell Frere that she had struck out Clause 14 and that he would 'be as surprised as I was to see that it had been inserted'. She reminded him that since 1947 her contracts had been one-book deals and that their own verbal agreement (after sacking Moore) had been for the contract to be the same. It did not occur to her 'that the formula would be altered, and a clause inserted without my consent, and I regret to say that I didn't bother to read through the COTILLION contract – or any of the succeeding ones'. She now went back and read her last eleven contracts and was appalled to find that the clause appeared in every one.

As an eighteen-year-old Georgette had read her first contract with assiduous care. As the years had passed, however, she had grown less attentive to such things and more inclined to assume that her relationship with Frere was safeguard enough. It had taken forty years for her to realise 'how very unwise I had been to have taken even a Heinemann contract on trust' (and she still did not appear to notice the reduction in her royalties). After twenty-five years of regular correspondence, this was to be her last letter to Frere in his capacity as her publisher at Heinemann. While she did not blame *him*, both the tone and the contents of the letter indicated her growing dissatisfaction with the firm.

The Heinemann director appointed to manage her books in Frere's place was Derek Priestley. He did his best to win over their star author with friendly yet businesslike letters and it is possible that in time Georgette would have built a relationship with him. But Heinemann had blotted its copybook in its treatment of Frere and no one else would do. Priestley's civil communiqués were not to be compared with Frere's familiar banter and Priestley did not belong as Frere belonged. He did not yet understand her or speak her language (he fatally addressed her as Mrs Rougier). Her relationship with her publisher was a vital part of her writing life, and with Frere's time at Heinemann almost at an end Georgette felt that change was in the air.

On 16 August she celebrated her sixtieth birthday at Greywalls. A few days later she received an urgent telegram from Richard to say that her mother had suffered a stroke. She and Ronald rushed back to London and for the next three months Georgette endured the nightmare of watching her mother suffer the sorts of impairments Sylvia had most dreaded. The stroke had robbed her of her speech and left her partially paralysed and there was little anyone could do other than sit with her. Georgette made almost daily visits to the hospital and to the nursing-home where Sylvia spent her last weeks, but her mother could only speak a little and towards the end was in great distress. Georgette found some comfort in Richard's and Susie's kindness and understanding. Susie offered to share the visiting 'but quite saw that I couldn't <u>share</u> it with anyone & refrained from nagging at me'. Sylvia Heyer died on 27 November 1962 in a nursing home in Kilburn. Georgette was devastated. 'Only a monster could have wished her to linger on,' she wrote to Isabella Banton. 'Her death leaves me feeling shattered, & strangely lost. Exhausted too.'

It took Georgette some time to recover. The changes at Heinemann did not help. Ten days before *The Nonesuch* was published Derek Priestley wrote to ask about 'progress with a new novel' and then compounded this misdeed by ringing Georgette in Albany to ask again. She told him frankly that he 'should have been trained by Frere never to ask directly about plans for a book. She would let <u>us</u> know when she had a plot and a book in her head.' Priestley naïvely thought: 'No harm done, obviously by enquiring – may even have spurred her on.' Georgette *had* thought of a new book – but with the option clause now deleted from her contract, she intended that it should reach neither Priestley nor Heinemann.

By Christmas Georgette knew that Frere was resigning from Heinemann and joining the board of The Bodley Head. Although he had already cleared his desk it was not to become public knowledge until the new year. A few days after Christmas Joyce Weiner asked Georgette about rumours of change at Heinemann and offered to discuss a plan of action with her. But Georgette had no need to talk with anyone. She had already decided to follow Frere to The Bodley Head.

The rival firm was owned by his friend Max Reinhardt, who had entered publishing after the War. A tall, congenial man of cosmopolitan background and convivial manner, he lived in Albany, was a member of the Savile Club (and later the Garrick), was a talented bridge-player, knew all the right people and, as far as Georgette was concerned, was Frere's ideal replacement. A year earlier Reinhardt had been part of a proposed merger between Heinemann and The Bodley Head, but the deal had fallen through, and with it the plan to give Frere the chairmanship of the company and an active role in the management of its authors, (which would have meant a comeback for Frere). Instead, Frere accepted a position on the Board and when he left Heinemann at the end of 1962 for The Bodley Head he took Georgette, Graham Greene and Eric Ambler with him.

Shocked by her sudden departure, Derek Priestley tried to persuade Georgette to remain with Heinemann, reminding her of her forty years with the firm and their success with *The Nonesuch* (60,000 copies sold and already in its second printing). But she was adamant. She told Priestley: 'Her loyalty and her enthusiasm in writing for publication were directed to one person, Frere.' She also explained that she, Graham Greene and Eric Ambler had long since 'got together and decided there was no point in their staying now that Frere was going'. Priestley took Georgette to lunch and made one last attempt to persuade her to change her mind. It was to no avail:

> Very many thanks for your letter – & for my enjoyable lunch! The occasion was a gloomy one, but I am so glad to have met you; & I hope that my secession from the ranks won't preclude our meeting again. You were very persuasive, but my decision wasn't reached without a great deal of thought. In fact, to be asked to think any more about it almost makes me drum with my heels: Frere has been preaching Thought, Consideration, & Caution ever since I told him that I should leave the firm when he did. I don't doubt I should get on beautifully with you, but there is more to all this than the personal friendship angle. A lot of very murky water has been flowing under the Heinemann bridge, & I don't like it. It can serve no useful purpose to enlarge

upon what I said to you yesterday, so I will merely say that I am sorry, but my mind is made up.

Priestley gave up the fight and resigned himself to losing one of Heinemann's most successful authors. With rare perception he later described Georgette as 'an immensely determined woman with a good brain and a very sentimental streak which she has spent her life in covering up'.

33

Or shall I come just as Little Me – really the <u>simplest</u> of creatures, happiest when pottering about my kitchen (my books just seem to <u>come</u> to me, you know), but just <u>too</u> touched & happy for words.

Georgette Heyer

Georgette and Frere celebrated their move to The Bodley Head with a 'lovely' new year lunch. She was relieved to 'have things settled, & to be sure that my Favourite Publisher is <u>still</u> my publisher'. But Frere's position on the board gave him no direct role in the management of the firm's authors; it was to be Max Reinhardt who would fill the position Frere had held in Georgette's writing life for the past twenty-five years. She was confident that she would be in good hands, however, and was already 'toying' with her idea for her next book. 'It 'ud shake The Bodley Head a bit . . . if I favoured them with a Synopsis of my Forthcoming Work!' she told Frere before he left for an extended overseas trip.

Her first letter to Max Reinhardt was typical Georgette: 'So Frere thinks it a pleasure to deal with me, does he? He must have forgotten how broad a view I've always taken of his duties towards me.' A month later she wrote to say that her first book for the firm would be called *False Colours*. Although she assured Reinhardt that 'I <u>do</u> know what it's going to be about!', it was April before she had worked out the plot. She wrote a lengthy outline but baulked at sending it to Reinhardt for fear of causing him to 'suffer a stroke' and sent it to Frere instead.

It was another of her new plots, with identical twins who must 'rescue their entrancing but wholly irresponsible Mama from her financial difficulties' (Georgette had based her fictitious mama on Georgiana, Duchess of Devonshire). She gave Lady Denville an unlikely *cicisbeo* (gallant admirer) in Sir Bonamy Ripple, 'one of my more felicitous creations'. An enormously fat gourmand, he proved to be another of her superb comic characters. The plot was 'just the sort of nonsense which suits my particular brand of humour', she told Reinhardt. Already she had warmed to her new publisher and an early letter had begun: 'Dear Mr Reinhardt – No: on second thoughts I'll alter that to Dear Max.' Within weeks of joining The Bodley Head Georgette was writing to Reinhardt exactly as she had always written to Frere.

Determined not to put a foot wrong with his new author, Reinhardt commissioned Georgette's favourite illustrator, Arthur Barbosa, to design the jacket for *False Colours*. She loved Barbosa's subtle, elegant pictures, which she felt exactly captured the style and tone of her novels. They were a stark contrast to what she saw as the vulgar Pan paperback covers: 'I have been meaning for some time to protest against any suggestion that a book written by me will be found to contain lurid sex-scenes. I find this nauseating . . . and I have enough sense to realize that new readers, attracted by a sex-suggestive cover, will suffer nothing but disappointment if they are misled into buying the book.' She had recently signed a new agreement with Pan for a substantially increased advance and a rise in her royalty rate from three to seven per cent and was pleased when the paperback publisher informed her of their plans to improve the quality of their covers.

As promised, Georgette finished *False Colours* in June. She had written for twenty-four hours straight at the end and at 104,000 words thought the manuscript wanted cutting. 'Bits of it aren't bad,' she told Reinhardt, 'but there are moments when I look upon it with complete nausea'. She thought the fans would be happy, however, and hoped Reinhardt would read it and not be disappointed. She also asked her new publisher to tell his printers that 'I don't want my book re-punctuated, or my spelling corrected . . . when I write "realize", I do not mean "realise!"' But Reinhardt was no fool (and he had the benefit of the inside running from Frere). He wrote to her just three days after receiving the manuscript. He had read *False Colours* and was 'delighted with it . . . How clever your dialogue is and how rich all these Regency words sound . . . I enjoyed my weekend very much. Thank you.' Georgette was gratified and also pleased to learn that the printer had been instructed to follow her manuscript to the letter.

She received her advance copy of *False Colours* at the Blue Bell Hotel in Belford, Northumberland, where she and Ronald were spending September with Susie, Richard, 'the babies and the Swiss help'. She had dedicated the novel to Susie in a gesture which summed up Georgette's feelings about her daughter-in-law. 'Susie wins all hearts – including ours!' she told Isabella Banton. 'Indeed, we wonder what on earth we did <u>without</u> Our Susie. She is the daughter we never had, & thought we didn't want.' Richard's marriage was a source of happiness in Georgette's life and she enjoyed watching her son be a father to Susie's two boys. The holiday was a great success and they returned home to a letter which Georgette was to treasure for the rest of her life.

She received a lot of fan mail and, despite her protests, liked to know her books were read and enjoyed. Although she could be dismissive of her correspondents' effusive praise, she frequently took the time to write a personal reply. It would have been out of character for Georgette to openly acknowledge her readers' admiration and it had long been her 'practice to destroy all letters as soon as I have replied to them' – including those from family and friends.

The letter she kept was from a Romanian woman who, with her sister, had been held as a political prisoner there since 1949. With the help of the Leon family in America, in 1961 Nora and Annie Samuelli were ransomed and finally brought out from behind the Iron Curtain. Nora had written to Georgette from the United States to thank her 'on behalf of hundreds of women political prisoners in Rumania . . . for having helped us escape – for a few hours at least – from the weary drabness of our prison days and the evil that surrounded us'. She was referring to *Friday's Child*, which she and Annie remembered practically verbatim and which they had recited to their fellow prisoners over and over again (translating as they went) with 'all the quips and Ferdy-isms which are so much a part of it'. Thirty years later, in her memoir *Women Behind Bars in Romania*, Nora's sister Annie also recorded one of many occasions when Georgette's novel had been the saving grace in an appalling situation. Locked in a small, claustrophobic train carriage with eight other women and unsure of whether they were to live or die, she was asked:

"Do you think you could tell us a story, it would be such a help to pass the crawling hours!"

"Oh do!" exclaimed Sanda. "I would so much like to hear *Friday's Child* again! Girls it's terrific!"

I was quite willing. The exertion might stem the rising tide of panic and hysteria that engulfed me too. I was glad that Sanda had spared me the effort of thinking of a book. *Friday's Child* by Georgette Heyer was what my sister and I called my "best-seller". The pranks of Hero Wantage in the spacious mansions and cool country side of early nineteenth-century England assisted a little in whiling away the sweltering, airless afternoon. Once again, this tale like many others was the means of momentarily escaping from prison hardships without even approaching the window bars ... Never had an ancient poet had a more rapt audience.

Georgette was deeply moved by Nora Samuelli's letter; she replied to it and carefully put it away among her private papers.

On New Year's Eve Georgette contracted 'flu. She cancelled her engagements and told Reinhardt that her new novel, *Frederica*, had not progressed because 'I am not one who works well – or at all – under adversity.' It was not true. She had often worked when things were difficult, writing some of her best books when beset by worry. Her period novels, in particular, had always been an escape from adversity. Hardship in the real world heightened the pleasure of her retreat into the fictional realm.

Despite all her complaints and self-criticism, writing gave Georgette immense pleasure. Even in the sheltered world she had created for herself in Albany, she could not escape life's vagaries, uncertainties, trials or tragedies, whereas in the constructed world of the novel she could order things as she liked and ensure her (deserving) characters' happy endings. It was not all fantasy, however, for her literary worlds were linked to the real world via a wealth of carefully researched historical detail. Georgette's ability to bring the past to life and make her readers feel as though they were *there* is one of the reasons for her enduring success. The escape was not just fictional, it was historical as well, and somehow there was comfort in that.

Reinhardt was sympathetic about her illness and sent her three cheerful bits of news: Penguin had offered an unsolicited £3,000 advance for the paperback edition of *False Colours*, Longmans wanted to produce it in a school edition, and *False Colours* had sold over 50,000 copies in two months. Georgette was delighted – especially with the Penguin offer, 'for, as far as I know, they've never till now shown any interest in my deathless works' (they had published three of her detective novels in the 1940s and *Devil's Cub* in 1953. The Penguin edition of *False Colours* appeared in 1966). She was also agreeable to being read in schools and had long since given Braille a blanket permission to produce any of her books at their discretion.

She had barely begun *Frederica* when Reinhardt returned from one of his regular visits to Charlie Chaplin in Switzerland and wrote to enquire if it was all right to ask for a blurb. She sent him 'several indignant curses for DARING to ask me' and explained that 'all my faithful public wants to know is that it is the Regency mixture as before.' Possibly inspired by her recent holiday with her step-grandsons, Georgette had given her heroine two younger brothers and informed her publisher that 'I do WANT little Felix to be carried off in a balloon – waving joyously to his brothers and sisters, & followed, on the ground, by my longsuffering and very fashionable hero, driving his curricle.' The blurb which followed would eventually appear, word for word, on *Frederica*'s dustjacket. Reinhardt's response was flattering: 'With these two paragraphs of yours alone we have already booked orders for several thousand copies of *Frederica*.'

Sales of Georgette's books were booming. In 1964 she had thirty-two books in print out of a possible forty-four (six were suppressed); Pan had sold 47,000 copies of *Beauvallet* in just three months, and she was finally taking off in America. A year earlier Dutton had taken over the publication of her books from Putnam. The new firm had done well with *The Nonesuch* and *False Colours*, which was positively reviewed in *Time* magazine in February 1964. Despite some amusing inaccuracies Georgette could not help but be pleased by the *Time* review ('repulsive but eminently quotable'). Reinhardt thought it excellent and told her of his ambition to make *False Colours* her bestselling book.

In the meantime *Frederica* was progressing slowly. Having 'discovered' her heroine's younger brother's enthusiasm for steam-locomotion and coal-gas Georgette was obliged to visit the London Library several times for information. By June she had 'perpetrated some 48,000 words, & am now staring at the thing & Asking Myself (a) What the hell is this all about? [I don't know] (b) Will this work live? [NO] (c) What the hell is going to happen? [God may know: I don't] (d) Do I WANT to write the damned thing? [NO! – or anything else!]' In spite of her grumbles on reading through the manuscript she actually found it was neither 'so long or as dull as I'd thought'. After more than forty years of writing Georgette's self-deprecatory habits were established to the point of almost being an intrinsic part of her writing ritual.

Her plan to finish *Frederica* in time for the cricket Test at Lord's (she had tickets and was resolved to 'use at least <u>three</u> of them, WHATEVER') was dramatically interrupted when she was rushed to Guy's Hospital. She had been suffering stomach pains for weeks and the trouble was eventually diagnosed as kidney stones. In the 1960s this meant a major operation and a month in hospital. Friends and family visited and Max Reinhardt sent her the proofs of Charlie Chaplin's forthcoming *Autobiography* to read once she was convalescent. 'Chaplin amused me,' she told him. 'It was the only modern book which <u>did</u> amuse me: I returned to Dickens – a sure sign of old age!' She also heard from Derek Priestley of Heinemann who, not knowing of her illness, had written to ask if she would consider allowing the firm to bring out *False Colours* in their Uniform edition. Her belated reply was brief and to the point: 'As for your extraordinary proposition about *False Colours*, I imagine you must know very well what the answer is.' She did not hear from Priestley again.

Georgette left Guy's Hospital in mid-August with a scar which the hospital staff described 'as A Beautifully Neat Incision, & Ronald as A Bloody Great Gash. Ronald is right. It is some fifteen inches long, & has severed all the "torsion" muscles. Hence the pain I am still suffering.' She was lucky to be alive and her surgeon told her she could not expect a full recovery for six months. She optimistically took *Frederica* with her to Greywalls in September but after such a long break it took time to find her way back into the story. Her surgeon's promise of a Christmas recovery proved optimistic and her own doctor told her that it would be a year before she was one hundred per cent fit again.

Georgette was suffering from painful adhesions and relentless fatigue. On informing her doctor that 'a morning's shopping put paid to any real work for that day,' he 'brutally retorted that it was a <u>bloody</u> good job, since it would stop me from doing too much'. She was determined to finish *Frederica*, however, if only to get on with the next '<u>much</u> more amusing book' – ideas for which insisted on 'obtruding & have to be repressed'. Her feeling was that *Frederica* would 'sell on the reputation, the next shall be Miss Heyer's Comeback'.

The idea of spring publication for *Frederica* soon proved to be a vain hope. In mid-December Georgette remembered that she had promised it to *Woman's Journal* for serialisation which meant the book could not come out before the autumn. She felt dreadful about the delay. 'I wish I weren't failing you like this,' she told Reinhardt. 'I seethe & seethe, for Never before have I fallen down on a contract. Try to forgive me!' But her publisher could not have been as hard on her as she was on herself and Reinhardt had no intention of pressuring her. He already knew how she fretted over deadlines – even apologising if a manuscript arrived a day later than promised. He thought Georgette

'An absolute darling' and 'A marvellous pro' and told her not to worry about the delay. Greatly relieved, Georgette relaxed over the festive season and she and Ronald spent a peaceful Christmas Day at Richard and Susie's newly leased flat in Gloucester Road.

It was spring 1964 before she finished *Frederica* and Georgette told her publisher that it was too long and would need to be cut. Although she knew that her readers loved her longer books, she had never before left a Regency manuscript hanging for six months and was concerned about the effect on the final novel. When Reinhardt read it, however, he declared it first-rate and encouraged her to leave it long. He also ventured to ask if Georgette would say she liked the book so they could quote her. Her answer was explicit: 'No, I do Not like *Frederica* – and if I did, nothing would induce me to say so! For publication, too –!' She knew that those who had read the novel liked it but when she compared it 'to the three, of the same genre, which I do think good, I could weep!' But she had also thought poorly of *Sylvester*, *Venetia* and *The Unknown Ajax* at the time of their writing; only later had her opinion changed. It would eventually change for *Frederica*, too, despite the discovery of her one unwitting error.

Mistakes in a Georgette Heyer novel are rare and mostly relate to her sending her characters to places which did not exist in that form at the time when her story was set, such as the Brighton Pavilion, the Promenade Grove or the Pantheon Bazaar. In *Frederica*, however, her blunder was to send her hero to a place which did not exist at all. Setting the book in London, she had her hero take the heroine's little brother to a foundry in Soho (to see a pneumatic lift). Georgette had mistakenly taken a reference to a foundry in Soho in a book on steam-power as meaning Soho in London rather than Soho near Birmingham.[28] A fan had noticed the mistake in the *Woman's Journal* serial and written to tell her.

It was too late to correct the error and, devastated by her slip-up,

---

28 After much searching in the London Library, it appears that the book was John Sewell's, *Elementary Treatise on Steam and Locomotion* (1852) which mentions Watt and Soho on one page and on the next talks about Watt and Albion-mills, London. There is no mention of Birmingham.

Georgette wrote to Reinhardt and Frere about it: 'Far, far worse than any mere misprint is my own major error' and 'I always <u>did</u> think Soho, London, was a queer locality for a foundry!' She had meant to check it but the surgery had pushed it from her mind and the error had remained unaltered. For forty years, Georgette's idiosyncratic research methods had proven remarkably effective in enabling her to re-create a vivid sense of the past. There is no doubt, however, that there were risks in limiting her research to just the London Library and her own private reference collection.

Since first writing about the Regency in 1935, Georgette had built up a personal library of some two thousand volumes with many general reference books and dictionaries of biography, phrase, slang, dialect, place-names, Latin, French, Spanish and English. She had collected a range of history books and texts about specific subjects such as snuff-boxes, coaching inns, the military, London, etiquette and clothing. For details of life in the period and its language she favoured primary sources over secondary, and owned works by most of the late eighteenth- and early nineteenth-century diarists. Other contemporary books about Regency life included the *English Spy*, *The Hermit in London*, *Memoirs of the Court of England during the Regency*, Harriette Wilson's autobiography and Georgette's own particular favourite, Pierce Egan's *Life in London* – a treasure-trove of Regency argot and etiquette (she had her own magnificent leather-bound, two-volume edition which she lovingly polished with a special cloth). Jane Austen was a vital source and Georgette regularly sought inspiration, vocabulary and phrases from her favourite author's letters and novels.

Georgette's extensive knowledge of Regency fashion came mainly from studying contemporary magazines, including *La Belle Assemblée*, the *Ladies' Monthly Museum*, *The Gentlemen's Magazine*, *Ackermann's Repository*, the *Mirror of Fashion* and pamphlets such as *Neckclothitania*. Georgette also used books such as *Paterson's Roads*, *Advice to Young Sportsmen*, *The True Art of the Fence*, *Nimrod on Hunting*, *Household Management and Expenditure* and *Beaux of the Regency*, and would jot down useful bits in her (idiosyncratic) notebooks. These were then used as a ready reference for details on everything from costume to carriages, people, places, prices and the postal system.

She also compiled alphabetical lists of slang terms and popular expressions and gathered colloquial phrases which still made sense to the modern reader. Georgette's Regency world comes to life with the language of the period precisely because she stayed close to the sources written at the time. While her method of research was an effective (if somewhat cloistered) approach to the past, it did occasionally trip her up. To her great relief, only the one reader ever wrote to her about the Soho error in *Frederica*.

At Easter Boris and Evelyn joined them at Rye for the golf. Her brother had recently left the Lord Crewe Arms and taken a lease on an inn at Bedale in Yorkshire. Georgette thought running a pub excessively strenuous but it seemed to suit Boris. He did not see his sister all that often but they kept in touch, and Georgette and Ronald sometimes visited if they were travelling north. In May they went to Scotland again. They could afford several holidays a year now and were planning their first trip to Sweden, where Georgette's novels were being reprinted, in June.

The year 1965 marked the sesquicentenary of the Battle of Waterloo and her publishers in America, Germany and Sweden were reissuing *An Infamous Army* and were 'all very much alive to the significance of that book in this year'. Georgette also expected Heinemann to seize the opportunity to push *An Infamous Army*. She was incensed to discover that, so far from promoting it, they had actually let their stock of *An Infamous Army* run out: 'When I recall the press it had, too, it makes me rage! Why, to this day the book is recommended to Sandhurst cadets by their instructors!'[29]

It was another black mark against Heinemann and her frustration with the firm eventually culminated in what Georgette called 'a

---

29 The following year (1966) Heinemann licensed Hodder & Stoughton to bring out *An Infamous Army* as one of their 'Library of Great Historical Novels as chosen by Rosemary Sutcliff'. Rosemary Sutcliff wrote a special three-page introduction for the book which began: 'For me, the Regency Novels of Miss Georgette Heyer have always been perfect reading.'

Splendid row'. The core of the problem was Heinemann's apparent inability to keep her books on the shelves. Georgette was puzzled as to 'why, having such a Valuable Property as Me, they make no effort whatsoever to cash in on me'. It was not entirely true, but she found it maddening to receive regular letters from fans telling her they could not find one of her popular titles in the shops. It was a stark contrast to the activities of The Bodley Head who were determined to make an even bigger success of *Frederica* than they had with *False Colours*.

Frederica came out in September 1956 with Reinhardt predicting that it would be a big seller over Christmas. He was right. *Frederica* hit the top of the bestseller list on publication and remained there well into the new year. Foyle's wanted it for their book club and Pan were offering £4,500 against Penguin's £3,000 for the paperback rights. Georgette learned of the book's success by telegram. She and Ronald were in Ireland, holidaying with Richard and Susie and the children, when she received the good news: 'Congratulations subscription Frederica at least 47,000 love Max.' But it paled into insignificance against Susie's announcement that she was pregnant.

PART V

LADY OF QUALITY

1966–1974

34

I know it's useless to talk about technique in these degenerate days – but no less a technician than Noël Coward reads me because he says my technique is so good. I'm proud of that.

Georgette Heyer

The baby was due in February and Georgette and Ronald were delighted at the prospect of becoming grandparents. Georgette returned home from her holiday to further cheerful news: *Frederica* was already being reprinted and British film-maker Herbert Wilcox was planning to produce *False Colours* as a television series in America. Wilcox's wife was the famous English actress, Anna Neagle, who was a fan as well as a friend of Georgette's. It was Anna who had inspired her to create Lady Denville in *False Colours*, having once asked if Georgette 'could write a nice middle aged part for her'. Believing that Wilcox would do her work justice, this time Georgette was enthusiastic about the television proposal.

She did not count on the scheme, however, and thought that if it did come off it would not happen quickly because 'this colour TV thing is a new idea, & I've no doubt it will take time to get it started.' Nevertheless, it was an enticing proposition, and Joyce Weiner felt it would do no harm for a British producer to be promoting her books in the United States. Joyce Weiner had been working on Georgette's American publisher with the result that Dutton's had doubled her advance and were making *Frederica* their number one book for the season. Joyce's efforts looked like returning almost £14,000 – a reflection of the 'staggering interest' the Americans were now showing in Georgette's work.

Georgette was laid up again that autumn with a mosquito bite (incurred in Sweden in June) which would not heal. Her doctor was talking about specialists and skin grafts – suggestions Georgette strongly resisted, remembering the arsenic treatment specialists had subjected her to during the War. Instead she spent a good deal of time lying on the sofa (which she found a bore) and planning her next book. She had not worked out the details but in December told Reinhardt not to worry for 'somehow, or other, the New Book <u>does</u> get written!' In return he sent her the firm's latest production: a beautifully bound, limited edition (one of just 200 copies) booklet containing the balloon scene from *Frederica*: The Bodley Head's Christmas gift to their clients.

On 23 February 1966 Georgette and Ronald were delighted to learn that Susie had given birth to a boy, Nicholas Julian Rougier. It was good news at a time when Georgette was once again badly worried about the state of her finances. Her optimism over her steadily growing income had recently been dented by the discovery that her accountants had 'landed me in a real mess through their obsession with paying every penny I earn into the Company account, & paying nearly all bills out of this account . . . with the result that I now stand in the pleasing position of owing the Company something in the region of £20,000.' Susie urged them to find a new accountant and by late March, after more than a year of agonising over the decision (and a decade of dissatisfaction), Georgette and Ronald finally sacked Rubens. They now engaged the accounting firm of Black, Geoghan & Till to manage their affairs. Georgette's new accountant was Hale Crosse, a man with an international reputation for integrity and legitimately saving his authors money.

Crosse first met the Rougiers in Albany and initially found Georgette a 'very forbidding woman of few words' – an impression he later revised after they got to know one another better ('call me George' she told him). Months after that first meeting he was summoned back to Albany and asked if he could help them. It took some time to wrest the files and the company seal from Rubens, who was resisting the change. The accounts were eventually delivered to Crosse, who quickly discovered the mess their finances were in. Not only had their former accountant failed to take the necessary measures to protect Georgette when the government had closed a number of tax loopholes, but he had neglected to submit her recent tax returns and keep her accounts current. When Crosse asked Georgette about her expenses, she had no idea because she rarely claimed any.

After working his way through the tangle, Hale Crosse advised Georgette to terminate her contract with Heron in return for a lump sum payment and to ask The Bodley Head to issue all future contracts in her own name. Over the years Heron had amassed over £80,000 in its account which Georgette could not touch without paying an exorbitant amount of tax. Crosse wanted to sell the company (and its eighteen copyrights) for the sum in Heron's account, but Georgette would not entertain the concept. While she liked the idea of having a large capital sum in her account, she could not rid herself of the feeling that it was 'rather as if Susie were offered x thousand pounds for Nicholas!'

Frere thought selling her copyrights a ludicrous idea and said so. Reinhardt, too, advised caution and suggested that if she did 'want to get rid of the company I would much rather we formed a little consortium of some of your friends and bought it ourselves, with yourself or a member of your family also having an interest in it'. Georgette's other 'alternative was to run the Company down – & if I can be sure that my debt won't land me, or my heirs, in Dutch, I expect that's what I shall do'. She appreciated Reinhardt's suggestion, however. It only served to confirm her view that, like Frere, he was the perfect publisher.

By the mid-1960s, Georgette and Max Reinhardt had become great friends. She met his American wife Joan Reinhardt in 1964 and (despite Georgette's broadly anti-American sentiments) liked her very much. The Rougiers regularly invited the Reinhardts and the Freres to F.3. for dinner. Georgette and Ronald were excellent hosts and over the years the six of them enjoyed many congenial evenings in Albany (despite their mutual dislike, on the surface Ronald and Frere were always cordial to each other). They often found themselves at the same cocktail parties and dinners or arranging a table together for events like the Authors Ball.

Georgette preferred small intimate dinner parties to larger, more boisterous events where she was expected to talk to people she did not know. She enjoyed cooking and serving a sumptuous meal for a few friends, with Ronald organising the wine and changing the plates between courses. She appreciated good food, and Ronald was happy as long as there was plenty of the best fresh caviar and the 'Proper Vodka'. On social occasions Georgette would often make a point of deferring to her husband and give the impression that Ronald was in charge. Partly out of consideration for him, in her private life she was always 'Mrs Rougier', *never* 'Georgette Heyer'. She preferred not to talk about her books at dinners or parties (confining that particular discussion to her regular lunches with Max Reinhardt as she had with Frere) or to draw attention to her enormous literary success. Despite having determined the course of her own life for over forty years, Georgette still needed the presence of a strong man, and clung to the old-fashioned view of the dominant male who was master of his own house and made the decisions. Ronald could certainly be decisive (and, according to friends, stubborn) and although Georgette was herself strong and frequently the driving force in their relationship, she still relied on his approval and support.

Although Reinhardt was hoping there would be a new Heyer novel in 1966 he carefully refrained from asking Georgette about it. In April she wrote to say that 'as a reward for NOT asking me, I enclose a singularly useless description of the meretricious work.' It was entitled *Black Sheep*. The idea for it appears to have come from a story Diana Sinden had told one evening at a party in F.3. The Sindens and the Rougiers had become friends after Ronald met the great thespian Donald Sinden at the Garrick Club. The two couples occasionally dined together and also met at parties. Diana Sinden's story was about the difficult son ('a Black Sheep') of a family who had sent him out to Australia from where he had returned 'grown up and with a fortune'. As she told the story Mrs Sinden saw a 'glance pass between Georgette and Ronald; something had registered'.

Whether she had been inspired by Diana Sinden's story or not, a month later Georgette was able to tell Pat Wallace:

> My nose is sore from the grindstone, but I have made some progress with *Black Sheep*, & am feeling more hopeful about it since the appearance on the scene of the New Model Heyer-Hero. I rather wondered if I could handle him, but as he has already made my Life's Companion burst out laughing at least six times, I obviously can. But he's a bit tricky. And <u>really</u> a New Model!

Black Sheep was set in Bath with a new plot and one of her satisfyingly unromantic romances between her hero and her older, outspoken heroine. Georgette described her careless leading man as 'an amiable cynic' and admitted to having a lot of fun with him. Reinhardt immediately set things in motion for autumn publication while Joyce Weiner approached *Woman & Home* rather than *Woman's Journal* and got 4,000 guineas for the new novel, sight unseen. Dorothy Sutherland had finally retired from *Woman's Journal* but Georgette liked the new editor no better. After thirty years of successful association *Frederica* was her last publication with the magazine.

In May they learned that Ronald had been 'elected a Bencher, which affords me, & his son, great satisfaction. He is being very Scotch about it, &, when asked what it <u>means</u>, says: "Two hundred guineas!" but I think he's secretly pleased.' To be recognised as a senior member of the Inner Temple (Master of the Bench) was a feather in Ronald's cap and a timely recognition given that retirement was not far off. Three years earlier he had been named Deputy Chairman of Quarter Sessions in Essex, another appointment of which Georgette was very proud, although she would not say so directly. She went to Chelmsford to see him in action and 'found him very impressive, & (as I told him) almost <u>respected</u> him!' There was a lot of laughter in their relationship.

Georgette finished *Black Sheep* in June and Reinhardt sent a cheerful note with the contract informing her that her royalties would now start at 20% (on domestic sales). She responded in typical fashion by telling him that she hoped to start the next book 'in better time, & put some life into it!' Only Georgette could accuse her books of having no life in them. In July an interview with the famous Mersey Beat pop singer Cilla Black appeared in the teen magazine *Petticoat*. Entitled 'My Kind of Book', in it Cilla told her readers that *her* kind of book 'has to be fun and fast enough to keep you interested. F'rinstance *Arabella* by Georgette Heyer'. Several long extracts from the novel followed, interspersed with the singer's comments: '"Funny," said Cilla, "the author knows so much about the Regency period that you start to imagine yourself arriving in London, like Arabella, and taking all by storm."'

As Pan sales of Heyer books soared into the hundreds of thousands Reinhardt suggested asking for a larger advance from the paperback publisher. Georgette wrote a cautious reply: 'About Pan, I don't think I'm in favour of trying to force the price up, are you? Sooner or later they will feel it's time to call a halt, & I don't want to seem like the daughter of a horse-leech.' But when Pan's rival, the New English Library, offered a £7,500 advance for *Black Sheep*, Pan countered with their own £7,500 advance *and* a 12½% royalty. Georgette's reaction was to demand of Reinhardt if the New English Library were mad. Her response to Pan's offer was to tell him: 'Good God, yes! You haven't bullied Pan into it, have you? No, I'm sure you haven't! I don't want an unwilling publisher, or one who isn't happy to publish me, you know. The worst of bad policy!'

The lease on F.3. Albany was due to expire in November that year and was not available for renewal as the owners wished to live there themselves. Georgette had not been able to secure a ground-floor set and the steep flight of steps up to their chambers was proving too much for her. She still smoked heavily and found carrying her shopping up to the top floor left her uncomfortably breathless. After twenty-four years it would be a wrench to leave Albany but by August she was able to tell Reinhardt 'that we have practically taken a flat in Jermyn Street, & expect to get possession at the end of

September . . . It has constant hot water, & central heating, & if I had Domestic Difficulty I could run it with one hand tied behind me.' Jermyn Street was just one block south of Piccadilly and conveniently close to all of Georgette's favourite haunts.

Having decided to move, Georgette called in *Black Sheep*'s advance in order to pay for the furnishings and improvements needed for the new flat. It was exciting but also daunting. Late September found her 'engaged on the ghastly job of Turning-Out. After 25 years, the accumulation of junk is appalling. I am becoming ruthless about it!' Three weeks later her resolve quailed somewhat before 'the stacked piles, in every edition & every language of My Works! . . . What am I to do with them? I can send the foreign to a certain hospital, but what about the Duttons, Penguins, Pans, Aces, Bantams, Longmans, & God Knows how many Differently priced editions???'

In the midst of the chaos Georgette 'was rung up by a male character, who asked me if I would speak to Sir Mark M[ilbank]. As *Black Sheep* was just out, & I had been besieged by telephone calls from the worst kind of reporter, I was wary, & said, very frostily, "Who is Sir Mark?" The voice responded starchily: "I am speaking from Buckingham Palace!" Rocked off my balance, I said weakly that I would speak to Sir Mark. He turned out to be the Master of the Household, & he's quite a poppet.' He had rung to ask if Georgette would 'lunch informally with the Queen & the Duke on Nov. 3rd? ("We are all madly keen on your books here!").' Stunned, she meekly informed him that she would be honoured.

A fortnight later (the hired) Harrods' chauffeur drove her to Buckingham Palace in Ronald's Rolls Royce. Georgette was a little nervous but the chauffeur revelled in the occasion and on arrival at the Palace gate told the policeman 'haughtily, "Miss Georgette Heyer to lunch with Her Majesty!" The rozzer then bowed, & stepped back, & the chauffeur inclined his head graciously—! and swept on, visibly at bursting point!' She had been uncertain about attending but in the end found the event congenial and amusing. When Georgette eventually sat down to lunch (after drinks and conversation and the corgis jumping all over the Queen) 'a certain air of unreality came over me' and she could only think, 'like the old woman in the nursery-rhyme, "Lawks-a-mussy on me, this is none of I!"'

She enjoyed herself, though she thought 'it was the <u>oddest</u> party! There were ten or twelve guests, & I was the only Female!!! . . . I have since learnt that there is never more than <u>one</u> woman at these informal lunches she gives to People in the News.' Georgette sat on the Duke's right hand and they conversed amicably through the first two courses before he turned his back on her and spoke to his left-hand neighbour for the remainder of the meal. Having been 'brought up NEVER to slew round in my chair at a dinner-party, presenting my back to my <u>other</u> neighbour', Georgette was a little shocked and 'pleased to see that the Queen was also brought up like that!'

She had liked the Queen, whom she perceived 'had a merry twinkle, & quite a lively sense of the ridiculous' but she was amused to discover that her monarch seemed to be a little in awe of her. Carola Oman had warned her of the possibility 'because Royals are always frightened of Inkies. I didn't foresee it, but it rapidly dawned on me that she <u>was</u>! She kept on stealing sidelong looks at me, & blushing pink whenever I happened to catch her eye.' A few days after this memorable lunch Georgette visited Harrods book department, where the manager told her that the Queen had been in to buy twelve copies of *Frederica*. Her Majesty had mentioned Georgette's visit and remarked 'she's a formidable woman'. Georgette's reaction on telling Reinhardt this story was to say loudly over lunch: 'I'm not formidable! Am I formidable, Max?' But the Queen was right. It was the word friends and family most often used to describe her.

The Rougiers were due to move to Jermyn Street at the end of November. On 21 October, Georgette and Ronald held a 'house-cooling party' in Albany for about seventy guests. It was a great success and a fitting farewell to the home in which they had enjoyed so many pleasant evenings with friends. She had written twenty-two novels in F.3. Albany: many of them what Frere called her vintage works. He always said that 'Her apogee was the move to Albany.'

The shift to Jermyn Street went smoothly, although the renovations went on longer than Georgette had planned. She was still dealing with decorators at Christmas. And the new year brought bad news: Boris had suffered two strokes and was no longer capable of running an inn. Georgette wanted to help him but apart from financial support it was difficult to know how best to respond to her brother's problems. She had her own share of difficulties, although her new accountant was at last sorting out her money situation. Crosse's idea to sell Heron and its copyrights to a larger public company that would pay Georgette and Ronald a lump sum as well as annual directors' fees and bonuses was beginning to find favour. A year earlier she had declared: 'If I sold, it would only be for some astronomical sum! The Heron books, remember, include FREDERICA, which looks like being a little gold-mine.' By spring she was much less hostile to the idea of selling and even hopeful that Crosse had found the solution to their tax problems.

They went to Venice for ten days in May and stayed at the famous Cipriani's Hotel on the Island of Giudecca, having a wonderful time shopping and sight-seeing. Reinhardt had sent Georgette Ed O'Connor's novel *All in the Family* for the trip and she reported liking it

> immensely – & I'm damned if I know why! Perhaps because of his gift of creating very likeable characters in whose careers one feels great interest . . . Oddly enough – I didn't find myself compelled to skip the political part, though few things bore & disgust me more than the American political scene . . . Mind you, the book is too long, & has, I felt, too many irrelevant episodes & characters. But Americans nearly always seem to revel in verbiosity [sic].

Georgette sometimes forgot that Joan Reinhardt was an American and occasionally she would 'hold forth about Americans' before remembering her friend's nationality. She would always apologise, but Ronald was even more rigidly anti-USA and inevitably there were awkward moments.

She and Ronald were rarely averse to expressing their very decided opinions to their friends. When the Six-Day War ended in June 1967 Georgette wrote to Pat Wallace: 'I won't bore you with my valueless thoughts about the Lightning War in the Middle East. I'm not fond of Jews, but I'm delighted that they've licked the hell out of the Wogs.' She also told Reinhardt (prophetically) that 'I wish I could see a solution to the problem, but I can't. It looks like another uneasy truce in a Hundred Years' War!'

If, as she always said, her grandfather was indeed Jewish, it did not prevent Georgette from making anti-Semitic remarks, any more than her agent Joyce Weiner's Jewishness prevented them from becoming friends. In her novels Georgette usually cast her occasional Jewish characters as moneylenders and referred to them in disparaging terms. Only in *The Grand Sophy* did she ever flesh out a Jewish character beyond a walk-on part. The result, in Mr Goldhanger, was a literary caricature of an avaricious moneylender whose antecedents were undoubtedly Dickens' Fagin and Shakespeare's Shylock. She did not repeat the experiment. Frere once described Georgette as 'a strict old fashioned High Tory like Dr. Johnson' and Ronald as 'even more conservative'. Certainly those who knew the Rougiers well tended to avoid discussing politics or foreign affairs with them on social occasions.

In June Ronald was named in the Queen's Birthday Honours List for his services to the General Optical Council. They returned home from Venice in time for him to receive his CBE. Soon afterwards Georgette sent Reinhardt an outline of her next novel with a warning not to 'ask me a whole lot of questions about this epic! I know what it's ABOUT, but I also know (knowing myself) that it will probably undergo many changes as my Fluid Pen progresses. No doubt some utterly unforeseen person will push himself into the plot, and do his best to disrupt it.'

Cousin Kate was to be a departure from her usual style of book. As Georgette's own version of the Gothic novel, its characters included a sinister matriarch in Lady Minerva Brede (Broome in the final book), a mentally unstable pseudo-hero with homicidal and suicidal tendencies, a charming heroine and a hero designed to look like the villain. Reinhardt was delighted with the synopsis and keen to achieve 'a bumper subscription of 60,000 odd before you have even started writing a single word'. He was certain that *Cousin Kate* would be another bestseller. Frere was also convinced and a few months earlier had made a point of highlighting Georgette's enormous success with *Black Sheep* in a letter to *The Times*:

> Sir, – Ten thousand was a best-selling figure in the pre-paperback days when Galsworthy, Bennett and Wells were writing. Miss Georgette Heyer's latest novel, published in hard-back and not yet in paperback, has to date sold 62,000. This seems to make a nonsense of Mr Temple Smith's 'fact that fewer people now buy hard-cover books'. Within my knowledge, inaccurately informed writers have been burying publishers for the past 40 years. In spite of that, some of them seem to be doing pretty well. Yours faithfully, A.S. Frere H5 & 6 Albany

A few months later Hale Crosse conveyed to Georgette an offer from Booker Bros. to buy Heron Enterprises. A large food wholesaler, this company had recently set about diversifying its interests. One of Jock Campbell's (the chairman) most unusual investments was in literary copyrights. The company had discovered a loophole in the British tax system which enabled them to buy an author's copyrights, and pay her fees or bonuses (partly at the taxpayer's expense) while the company collected the royalties. Booker Bros. had already purchased the Ian Fleming estate and 51% of Agatha Christie Ltd. Now they wanted Heron and its eighteen copyrights.

Crosse thought it the ideal solution but Max Reinhardt was also interested in buying Heron Enterprises and sought a meeting. However, the idea came to nothing after it was discovered that The Bodley Head and Heron were both 'closed' companies (a closed company could not buy another closed company). Disappointed, Reinhardt suggested to Georgette she accept the Booker deal. Ronald was keenly in favour of the proposal but Frere baulked at the sale of her copyrights. Georgette found his attitude distressing – especially as it was so at odds with Ronald's view. Since leaving Albany they had not seen nearly as much of the Freres who now spent several months each year in Barbados.

It took twelve months to finalise the Booker scheme but it ended satisfactorily. In buying Heron, Booker Bros. would effectively pay Georgette what was in the company and she would finally get her money without having to pay an enormous amount of tax: 'The thing I like 'enormously about the new scheme is that I should be handing over to Bloody Wilson 7/- in the pound, instead of 17/9!!' (Harold Wilson was then Prime Minister.) On 18 November 1968, Georgette and Richard (Ronald was ill) attended a grand lunch at Bucklersbury House for the contract signing. The Booker directors handed 'three Enormous cheques' to Georgette and the deal was done.[30]

She, Ronald and Richard had sold their shares in Heron Enterprises for £80,000, with a gentleman's agreement that she could buy back the copyrights at any time. Georgette remained as managing director of Heron with Ronald and Richard as directors, each to receive a salary and regular bonuses. Hale Crosse had managed to reduce her capital gains liability from £24,000 to £100 so all she had to do was bank her cheque. For the first time since her father's death Georgette felt the financial burden slip from her shoulders.

---

30 In 1968 Booker Bros. became Booker McConnell. The following year, after a suggestion from Ian Fleming's publisher Tom Maschler, Jock Campbell announced the first 'Booker Prize for Fiction'. Ironically, none of the writers (Fleming, Christie and Heyer) whose royalties had made the prize possible wrote the sort of fiction likely to be considered for the Booker.

35

To be, in one's small way, a creative artist, wholly unable
to create, is a malady known only to a few.

Georgette Heyer

It was with a new sense of financial freedom that Georgette and
Ronald went up to Gloucestershire to spend Christmas with Richard
and Susie at their new country house at Murrell's End. Before they
left London Georgette invited Hale Crosse to Albany and presented
him with a gold Rolex watch inscribed with his initials and the
year of the Booker deal. It was a graceful gesture and he was
delighted. By now, he and Georgette were on excellent terms and
Crosse had discovered that 'once you got past the crust (which she
made sure was fairly thick) she was fine.' Although 1968 had ended
on a high note with the magnificent Booker lunch and a lovely
Christmas at Murrell's End, it had not been an easy year for
Georgette.

From January to August she had been stricken with an oedema
which had caused dreadful swelling in her feet and ankles. An
extended course of diuretics had affected her badly: 'I felt sick from
morning till night, and became afflicted with what I believe is called
aphasia' (a condition of the brain affecting speech). Although she
eventually recovered, she felt that *Cousin Kate* had suffered as a result.
She thought it one of her worst novels. Her fans disagreed. When
the book came out in September it went straight to the top of the
bestseller list. But neither 'Rave letters' from her readers about it nor

'the fervent assurances of my son and my brothers (my most severe critics) that they thought her (a) Very good! (b) Different, but MOST interesting; and (c) Compulsive!' convinced her of the book's worth. She did not 'believe a word of their kindly encomiums, and they don't change my opinion of *Kate!*'

Given her poor health Georgette made no plans for a new book in 1969. She and Ronald went to Iceland in July and the bracing Icelandic air proved to be exactly what she needed. She was letting herself relax at last: 'I <u>am</u> enjoying my idle year!' she told Reinhardt. Her plan to spend August at Greywalls was thwarted, however, after it was damaged by fire. She and Ronald had booked into the famous Gleneagles Hotel instead but it was not a success. They found the hotel so large (guests were given a map) and so full of loud American tourists that they left after a week.

Georgette and Ronald spent the remainder of their holiday at the Marine Hotel in North Berwick. Even in those peaceful surrounds it was not her usual restful month, however, for issues with her American publishers meant writing long letters to Joyce Weiner to resolve them. Reinhardt also wrote, enclosing the contract for her next book and an article from the August edition of *Nova* magazine written by the well-known author A.S. Byatt. Entitled 'Georgette Heyer is a Better Writer Than You Think', it was the first article to offer a serious appraisal of Georgette's novels and to ask: 'Why *is* she so good?' For Byatt, the answer lay

> in the *precise* balance she achieves between romance and reality, fantastic plot and real detail. Her good taste, her knowledge, and the literary and social conventions of the time she is writing about all contribute to a romanticised anti-romanticism: an impossibly desirable world of prettiness, silliness and ultimate good sense where men and women *really* talk to each other, know what is going on between them, and plan to spend the rest of their lives together developing the relationship.

It was a perceptive assessment, for Byatt described precisely Georgette's own view of the ideal relationship between a man and a woman

– one with a deep mutual understanding and a lasting connection that was much more than purely physical or emotional – exactly what Georgette shared with Ronald.

Towards the end of the year she began writing again and penned a note to Reinhardt to tell him the good news. She asked him to keep the new book's title, *Charity Girl*, secret and to tell no one about the novel until she had it well in hand. 'I hope (and even dare to believe!) that this will be a better, and certainly more lighthearted a book than *Cousin Kate*. The fact that that lamentable effort has earned, to date, £12,728 [over £200,000 at today's values] in no way changes my opinion of it!' She wrote steadily until a fortnight before Christmas when she was suddenly beset with what she called 'One of My Queer Turns'. For the past five or six years she had ascribed these to indigestion but after suffering four attacks in forty-eight hours had called her doctor. He diagnosed the problem as 'a temporary failure of the main artery which runs up the back of one's neck to feed the brain'. Years of smoking were taking their toll on Georgette's cardiovascular system and any compression of the carotid artery had an unpleasant effect. She nobly went to Murrell's End for Christmas – although if she could have convinced Ronald to go without her she would have gladly stayed in bed.

She pressed on with her novel, however, and contrary to her expectations completed it in mid-February 1970, writing to tell Reinhardt, who sent his congratulations from Barbados where he had seen the Freres. Georgette still occasionally lunched with Frere and saw him and Pat Wallace at parties, but the literary link which had brought them together was gone. Georgette had been writing for nearly fifty years and in many ways her books were her life. As her publisher Frere had been a central figure in that life; as her friend – although he was still valued – he was much more on the periphery. After leaving Albany their paths had diverged and Georgette's involvement in the Freres' lives, her intimate association with Pat Wallace and her affectionate, regular communication with them, had gradually diminished until she was more likely to speak *of* them than to them: 'I saw the Freres last night, at L'Aperitif, where they were dining with Harry, and we were dining with Richard. They both seemed to be in excellent form.' Though they were still friends, the relationship had shifted and by the year's end, inexplicably for everyone but Georgette, it would be over.

With *Charity Girl* complete, Joyce Weiner urged Georgette to take life easy for a while. She disagreed: 'Now that my hand is "in" I rather think I'll write another book, and have already begun to plan it.' Demand for her novels was enormous and in America her sales had improved dramatically. On receiving *Charity Girl* Jack Macrae of Dutton had written to say that they 'loved it and feel our distinguished author is on top of her form'. She was glad she had finally taken off in America but, try as she would, she could not warm to the new generation of American publishers. She had liked Elliot Macrae at Dutton, but his son Jack was too energetic, his manners far too relaxed to please Georgette. Nor did his proposal for promoting *Charity Girl* find favour with her. While she did not wish to offend him by telling him what she thought of his 'horrid' idea of having her meet a fan for a drink at the Ritz, she considered the notion 'quite fatuous'.

Georgette was now an established household name, her birthday listed annually in *The Times*. Every week brought more letters from around the world praising her books and asking for sequels and autographs and information about the suppressed novels. She answered some and discarded others. A letter from a Chicago reader infuriated her so much that she told Reinhardt: 'she wrote that my books had induced her to overcome her dislike of "the classics," and that she had just succeeded in "wading thru' *Pride and Prejudice*." Her rating of this masterpiece was that it was a Heyer book "with a lot of unnecessary padding." I don't know what else she had to say, for at that point I tore the letter up.' Max Reinhardt thought this hilarious but Georgette was not amused. Her huge popularity also brought a steady stream of requests for interviews, guest appearances and invitations to literary functions. She refused them all.

In spite of the effusions, massive sales, good reviews and the affirmation of her publishers, Georgette still found it hard to accept her success. She knew she was a bestseller but felt it had less to do with her ability or style (she never could allow herself to share the same sphere with other, more 'serious', writers) and more to do with the fact that 'since I write historical romances, my books don't date, so that the very first I wrote, over 50 years ago, is still one of my most consistent money-makers.' This was true but it did not explain why so many bestselling historical novelists had faded from view while Georgette Heyer novels had continued selling for five decades.

Frere tried to explain it to her over lunch one day but his assertion 'that there is No Other Novelist today who can rival my World-Wide sales' only caused Georgette to 'cock a disbelieving eyebrow at him'. But Frere was adamant and

> said acidly that I had always had an apparently ineradicable belief in the huge sales enjoyed by authors who don't come within touching reach of <u>my</u> sales, but that I would PERHAPS allow him to know rather more than I did about such matters. He added, still more acidly, when I murmured "That'll be the day!", that there are many problems confronting publishers, but there is only one confronting the publisher of Miss Georgette Heyer's new books: whether to publish a first edition of 40, 50, or 60 thousand copies! I still don't entirely believe him.

Her former publisher had, in fact, underestimated the dilemma for she was now selling in excess of 60,000 copies in the first months of a book's release. Joyce Weiner summed it up: 'This, madam, is a PHENOMENON – indubitably.'

In August the Rougiers returned to Scandinavia, this time touring Norway for a fortnight before going to Greywalls. While in Scotland, Georgette received a letter from the Literary Editor of *The Times* asking her to sit for a photograph. The portrait was needed to accompany an article about Georgette and *Charity Girl* which Marghanita Laski, 'a great admirer of your work', was writing. Georgette's initial reaction was to 'tell him I'm just off to the South Pole', but Ronald intervened and persuaded her to agree. In October 1970 the article appeared (with picture) under the somewhat misleading title 'The Appeal of Georgette Heyer'. The heading was not a statement but a question as to why her books (whose 'appeal to simple females of all ages is readily comprehensible') had 'become something of a cult for many well-educated middle-aged women who read serious novels too?' Marghanita Laski had apparently forgotten her earlier comment that 'Georgette Heyer is a genius and defies description', and chose instead to use the column to belittle the author, her novels and her admirers.

The article prompted a storm of protest from her readers, many of whom wrote outraged letters to *The Times* – including one which explained Georgette's appeal in a single sentence: 'What Miss Heyer provides is a beautifully written novel with a neat plot, witty dialogue and good characterisation.' The correspondence to the newspaper was so heavy that a few days later the editor was forced to declare the matter closed. A great many readers wrote directly to Georgette and she told her agent that 'to judge from the furious letters I've received from Indignant Fans, [the editor] must have been snowed under by the letters they've written him!' She also had a charming letter from Lucy Boston, the well-known children's author, which pleased her 'more than somewhat!' It was all immensely gratifying and although she could not help but be a little stung by the piece, she told Frere: 'What a remarkably silly "review" of *Charity Girl* it was! I thought, as I read it, that I could have torn ME to bits far better than she did. Not that it has done me the slightest harm, so it has left my withers wholly unwrung.'

That month the BBC wrote to ask if Georgette would allow them to record her voice for future generations but she thought the suggestion laughable: 'Record my voice for posterity indeed! Few things are more unlikely than that posterity will have the smallest interest in either me or my works.' She could not deny that she was in demand, however, and an offer of £5,000 for a film option on *These Old Shades* came to fruition in the autumn. It had taken more than a year to finalise the deal and, perusing her old contracts,

Georgette was reminded of the sale of her copyrights three decades earlier:

> Doesn't it seem fantastic thirty years later, that £750 should have been considered by the valuers on both sides to have been a pretty generous price? It led me to rout out my old account book, and I see that it <u>was</u> generous! In those days my gross income very rarely got into four figures. It is now in five figures – and the wry thought in my mind is that I was better off then than I am now! And it is still more fantastic to think that Heinemann's weren't at all keen to buy my copyrights! I heard, years later, that Frere had the devil of a job persuading the Board to do it! Well, they got a very good bargain, but I don't begrudge it them, remembering, as I do, to what straits we were reduced at the time.

She did not comment on the fact that the terms of that thirty-year-old agreement meant she received only half of the £5,000 paid for the film rights to *These Old Shades*. The realisation must have been an unpleasant one and it may have been a factor in her eventual estrangement from Frere.

With her income now in the region of £50,000 a year, the old pressure to write for money was gone and it was partly the need to fulfil her fans' and her publishers' eager expectation of an annual Heyer novel that kept Georgette writing. Her lifelong compulsion to write was still a force but now considerably less intense. Her determination to start a new book 'with plenty of time on hand' had waned as the year progressed. By year's end she still had not put pen to paper. She suffered another spate of ill-health in December, with her left foot so swollen it would not go into a shoe and a streptococcal infection which made it difficult to breathe. She wrote to Pat Wallace with a touch of her old humour: 'Yes dear: Foot-and-Mouth disease!' It was to be her last letter to her old friend: a brief chatty missive, not quite in the old manner, but still addressed to 'My dear Wallace' and ending 'My love to Frere, and also to yourself.' It is not known why Georgette's relationship with Frere and Pat Wallace came to an end but her lunch with them in October 1970 at L'Aperitif was to be her last.

Twelve months later, Georgette told Max Reinhardt sadly:

It is now more than a year since I had any direct contact with either of the Freres. Ronald meets Frere at the Garrick, and says he is always very friendly and chatty, so I must assume that in some way, unknown to me, I have offended him, and Pat. But, if the truth was told, the boot is on the other leg – though remembering our long friendship, and how much I owed to Frere, I did NOT slap him down, when perhaps I ought to have done so.

The hurt went deep on both sides and neither Frere nor Pat Wallace ever understood the cause of the estrangement. Whatever the reasons behind the breach, Georgette did not know how to resolve it. She could only end by telling Reinhardt, 'Oh, well! It's all water under the bridge now, I suppose, but it has left a scar of sadness'.

The cause of the rift never would be explained. Ronald, Frere and Richard would eventually write to each other after Georgette's death: Ronald to tell Frere that Georgette 'would never tell me the cause' and Richard to suggest that the continuing enmity between Ronald and Frere had played on his mother's strong sense of loyalty until finally she had chosen her husband over her friend. Frere's letter would express all their feelings best:

So far as we are concerned it must now be something which never will be solved and a sadness we must always live with. Of course we must try to forget it and remember instead the long years of happiness we found in our intimate friendship with her; full of light, laughter and the joy of living.

36

*Most of my works would die with me, I fear; but one or
two might continue selling for a while.*

Georgette Heyer

Christmas was at Murrell's End again that year. Georgette always
found the season more enjoyable when there were children present
and she and Ronald took great delight in buying their three grandsons
gifts and acting as 'perennial Santa Clauses'. Richard was increasingly
busy at the Bar and planning to take silk in another year or two, but
he took a break over the festive season and enlivened the household
by giving Noel a baby chinchilla. Ronald had retired from the Bar,
though he continued as a Bencher for another year, presiding over
cases in Cambridge and Wisbech, and he was still chairman of the
General Optical Council.

Georgette's agent, Joyce Weiner, was also thinking about retirement.
She had suffered intermittent bouts of illness throughout the year but
by January 1971 was well enough to invite Georgette to lunch to mark
her agency's Silver Jubilee. It was a short-lived celebration. By March
they were both unwell: Georgette's foot was still swollen and she had
developed a persistent cough, while her agent's condition resisted all
attempts at a cure. That spring Joyce Weiner finally gave in and
announced her retirement. She did her best to mitigate the disappointment to her most important author by suggesting to Georgette that
Deborah Owen, an American married to British MP David Owen,
might do very well as her replacement. The news still came as a blow.

Georgette had learned to rely on Joyce Weiner's management of her foreign and serial rights. When her agent talked 'of "the kindness, tolerance, loyalty and understanding"' Georgette had shown her, Georgette demanded she 'put a sock in it!' A few weeks later, she met Deborah Owen and agreed that she should take over.

By May Georgette was feeling better so Ronald took her on an Aegean cruise 'by way of setting me completely on my feet once more'. They had a marvellous time; Georgette thought Rhodes and Knossos wonderful. They ended their holiday in Venice. But on their last day there Georgette gashed her right shin badly while getting into a water-taxi outside Cipriani's. Weeks later it still had not healed. The injury left her rather lame, making it difficult to walk more than a few hundred yards at a time, but she remained stubbornly optimistic that she would be completely healed when they returned from Greywalls, midway through September.

The year 1971 was another without a new novel. Reinhardt sent a gentle hint via a fan-letter from Argentina (pointing to the reader's query about 'new works'), but Georgette did not rise to the bait. That autumn, any plans she might have had for a new novel were put on hold as she and Ronald prepared to move house once more.

After four years they had decided that the Jermyn Street flat was too noisy and had finally found a charming apartment at 28 Parkside, Knightsbridge. The move meant another major disruption but the new place had the benefit of being 'beautifully spacious and blessedly quiet'. It also had views directly on to Hyde Park from their bedroom, the sitting room and Georgette's study, and a staff of day and night porters to manage things. Ronald had now fully retired from legal practice but was continuing his role with the General Optical Council for one more year. Georgette hoped that a gradual transition would 'let him down lightly'; she had concerns for him in retirement – Ronald being the sort of person 'who can't thrive unless his brain is fully occupied'.

They had plenty to occupy them that Christmas, however, for Frank's wife Joan died on 16 December after a long battle with cancer and Boris's wife, Evelyn, was also unwell. Georgette did not expect it to be a particularly merry Christmas but she had invited her brothers and sister-in-law to spend the day with them and hoped to make the occasion a pleasant one. Entertaining her family was an effort, especially when she was 'longing . . . to remember that I am not only a Sister, and a Housewife, but a NOVELIST!' She was tired but she wanted to return to her writing and assured her publisher that 'suddenly an Idea will burst upon me – after which I shall forget that I'm a Sister and a Housewife, and shall plunge deep into the early XIXth Century, and be lost to Society until I have written THE END!'

Early in January 1972 Georgette received the second of the two fan letters which she would keep. It came from Roy Pfautch, President of Civic Service Incorporated in St Louis, Missouri, and began:

> I am not given to the writing of letters of praise to famous individuals. In this instance, I am literally compelled to do so by a feeling of gratitude so strong that the peace of my nerves demands an assuaging through the process of thanking you for the grace, the marvels and the sheer magic of your writing.

He assured her that her Regency novels were 'read and re-read' and told Georgette he could 'only hope . . . only anticipate . . . and only wait' for her next novel. It was a delightful letter to receive and she wrote a pleased reply in which she assured the American businessman that 'I'm not really as good as you think I am, but it is very nice to be told I am!' Perhaps inspired by this unlooked-for praise, a week later she told Reinhardt that she was starting a new book.

The Rougiers moved to Parkside in January, celebrating with a cocktail party for sixty friends. It was a great success but a few days later Georgette fractured her fibula and once again became housebound. Her leg was very painful and not at all conducive to positive thought. As well as feeling that she had 'become Accident Prone, in my old age', she was finding the new book unexpectedly difficult. 'There are moments when I feel I have written myself out,' she told Joyce Weiner. She was pushing herself again, trying to meet her self-imposed deadline in order to give Reinhardt the book in time for autumn publication. Family and friends tried to soothe her concerns but she refused to listen. While she recognised that she had not been in good health for some while, Georgette was also convinced 'that ten years ago it wouldn't have affected my brain as today it has'.

A month later, despite her struggles with the book, Georgette told Reinhardt the title was *Lady of Quality* and that 'Ronald says the operative words are "the rudest man in London."' The new book had several things in common with *Black Sheep*, although *Lady of Quality* was a quieter, more thoughtful book than its predecessor. It was also the first of Georgette's novels in which the older heroine openly struggles with 'the question of being obliged to give up her freedom, to turn her life upside down' by choosing to marry. Georgette had been thinking deeply about love and marriage and the novel offers a rare insight into the bond between a happily married couple (the heroine's brother, Sir Geoffrey, and his wife Amabel). Their marriage is depicted not as a fairytale romance but as a practical, loving relationship. Georgette imbued the book with her usual humour, created another of her memorable characters in the dreadful Maria Farlow (an 'infernal gabster' who would be magnificently dispatched by the hero) and ended the novel on a note of domestic felicity between Sir Geoffrey and Amabel which in some ways reflected her own happy *ménage*.

It was a race to get the book finished. She worked at breakneck speed through the spring, stopping only to celebrate Richard's appointment as a Queen's Counsel in April (he would be made a Bencher in 1979 and knighted in 1986 after being appointed to the High Court. He and Susie would divorce in 1996 and Richard would remarry that year), and to attend a 'Grand Day' at Lincoln's Inn at which she (along with the Duke of Kent) was a guest of honour. The rest of the time she worked in 'strict retirement', eschewing lunches and social engagements and only going away for a short break to Greywalls over Whitsun. She worried over her writing and was relieved when, after reading the bulk of the manuscript to Ronald, he assured her that it was not dull.

She finished the book on 17 June. It meant a tight schedule if Reinhardt was to achieve October publication, but he collected the last 30,000 words himself, had everyone on standby and, when Barbosa unexpectedly fell ill, 'managed to get hold of another artist, who agreed (for a sum!) to do the job instanter [sic], AND to copy Barbosa's style!' Georgette eventually pronounced the dustjacket as one of her best. She was less convinced about the book, thinking *Lady of Quality* well below the standard of her 'Vintage works'. But booksellers found nothing wanting. Even before she had finished writing it, her new novel had sold 25,000 copies on the strength of her name and the title alone.

Reinhardt sent the new contract in May and told Georgette he had doubled her advance. In June she called it in: 'When I grandly said that I didn't want £10,000 I was reckoning without the Treasury Sharks.' Since the beginning of the financial year she had paid £28,000 in tax and had just received a bill for another £6,000. Her sentiments about taxation and the 'National Drain' had not altered over the years, although a new purchase tax a few years earlier had made her more sympathetic to 'the countless millions who subsist by the skin of their teeth on low incomes'. She knew she was fortunate and, although she worked hard for it, she was never tempted to take her income for granted – even telling Max Reinhardt: 'Mind, now! I don't want you to pay me this ridiculous sum without having read the book! You may well feel it isn't worth it.' But Reinhardt did not need convincing. Georgette's lament that she would 'have to revert to the One-Book-A-Year routine' in order to satisfy the Inland Revenue was deemed by her publisher to be wonderful news.

Lady of Quality left Georgette exhausted. She wrote to thank Reinhardt for all his efforts with the novel as well as for his 'quite Divine Patience with your most tiresome author!' She was no such thing, of course, and Reinhardt knew it. Though she could be demanding, she was not difficult, and after more than fifty years of writing was still the consummate professional. With the book done, she enjoyed a leisurely July watching the cricket on the television and preferring to stay in to see the fourth test to going out to lunch or shopping. She had slowed down considerably since suffering the injuries to her legs and would not cross Knightsbridge without Ronald beside her for fear of being run over by the 'cars and busses which come hurtling round the corner the entire time'.

They were at Greywalls for Georgette's seventieth birthday in

August, and celebrated with a bottle of champagne. Ronald's gift was the promise of a long silver chain – once she had found one she liked. Joyce Weiner sent an 'enchanting little pill-box' and Reinhardt wrote to congratulate her, convey 'the good news that *Lady of Quality* is selling like hot cakes' and to tell her that Pan had offered £15,000 for the paperback rights. Georgette was pleased, especially about Pan, though she could not refrain from asking Reinhardt: 'Did you have to wring it out of them, or did they actually <u>offer</u> it?'

Georgette returned from Greywalls feeling restored to health and ready to start work on a new book 'if I can think of one!' A few weeks later she had a fall in her dining room, cut her scalp open and bruised her spine and ribs. It was several weeks before she could cough without pain or lie down comfortably and the accident put paid to any thought of a new novel. Instead, she got out her long-neglected medieval manuscript and spent the dreary days of recovery reading it through and 'toying with the idea of bringing it to an end, with the death of Henry IV'.

It was years since she had looked at the book and a relief to discover it was 'definitely GOOD' and 'absorbingly interesting' – though not at all in her usual style. She did not know if it should be published and hoped Reinhardt would read it and advise her. The third part was still unfinished and would need a lot of work to complete but with *Lady of Quality* already heading the bestseller lists and her income secure the task now seemed feasible. Whether *John of Lancaster* was published or not, Georgette was certain she wanted to finish it. If Reinhardt thought it would be 'disastrous to publish it' then she would 'put it away to be published after my death!'

She never did finish the book that became *My Lord John*. Perhaps she recognised the novel's shortcomings and her own inability to grasp the medieval era. When it was eventually published the year after her death her reviewers praised her research, her knowledge and her skill as an outstanding storyteller, but the majority view was that *My Lord John* did not match the standard set by her Regency novels. Most readers found her posthumous novel a dull book crammed with too much historical detail, contrived dialogue and a confusing cast of characters. Georgette's inability to understand the importance of religion in medieval times was a major flaw and she was unable to bring the era to life as she had the Regency. In this book at least Georgette failed to wear her learning lightly – and in her heart of hearts she must have known it. If she had really wanted to finish the manuscript she would not have put it away for eighteen years. By keeping it 'in lavender', however, Georgette avoided the sort of disappointment she had experienced with *Penhallow* and her medieval dream remained inviolate until the end.

Death seemed a little nearer that Christmas. In a card to Joyce Weiner, Georgette told her former agent that she had 'been through a pretty grim period . . . and begin to wonder whether I ever shall be fit again'. The accident in her apartment was her fourth unlucky incident in less than two years. It had knocked her confidence and made her feel her age. By January 1973, though her spine was still sore, she was feeling a little better and able to write Reinhardt a pithy letter criticising W.H. Smith's latest advertising gambit. Her publisher was hoping for news of her next book but a few weeks later Georgette wrote to say she had been 'laid up with bronchitis, & am only just – precariously – on my feet again'.

She had a new doctor whom she and Ronald thought excellent and hoped would see them to their last. His response to her worries about her writing was to assure her that 'if I take things very easily for some weeks, don't over exert myself, don't let anything worry me, & don't have Any More Accidents, I shall in all probability regain all my lost vitality, & perpetrate a Masterpiece!' She was not convinced. She thought it unlikely she would produce a book that year and apologised to Reinhardt for letting him down.

By late March Georgette was, if not quite well again, on her feet and able to walk through Green Park with Ronald. She found herself easily tired and overwhelmed by noise, traffic or anything else frenetic or fast. She loved her view across Hyde Park and would often spend time in the gardens, finding it 'a blessed relief to be surrounded by grass, and trees, and flowers, instead of houses!' She missed Albany's peaceful environs and the sense of being tucked away in a haven in the heart of busy London. Parkside was an improvement on Jermyn Street but as her health continued poor, Georgette found it increasingly exhausting to be out in the world. She managed a trip to Provence with Ronald and Frank in the spring but confessed to Reinhardt afterwards that she felt 'about Provence much as I felt about Iceland: it was extremely interesting, I wouldn't have missed it, but I don't want to go there again. It isn't my kind of country.'

But the holiday did her good and by July she was more or less restored to health and catching up on her 'Social Arrears'. This meant occasional lunches with friends, for she found that more than one engagement on the same day left her exhausted. A few weeks later her plan to meet Joyce Weiner for lunch had to be postponed after Georgette suffered a slight stroke. Desperate to see her well again Ronald took her north to the Summer Isles Hotel in Scotland. He hoped the magnificent views and wonderful air would be a tonic to her exhausted nerves and afflicted body. They had three glorious, untroubled weeks before Georgette became ill again and had to be transferred to a nursing home in Edinburgh, where she stayed for the remainder of their holiday. Ronald was a tower of strength, organising everything and eventually bringing her home on the day train.

By late September she was over the worst of it and able to meet Max Reinhardt for lunch, but his pleasure in her recovery and belief that she was well again proved premature. The stroke had left her with a semi-paralysed right hand, she was now losing weight and had developed a little, dry cough. She wrote to Joyce Weiner in October to apologise for their delayed lunch but explained that 'At the moment I am keeping my social engagements to the barest minimum, which is very boring, but also very necessary, if I am ever to think of writing another book.'

Georgette was fighting against the odds but refusing to give in. In November she told her old friend Dorothy Tornow that she was 'at last making progress, & no longer feel better one day and worse the next. I can't do very much yet, but I no longer feel a longing for death!' Ronald was doing all he could to aid her recovery and Georgette admitted that 'the ministrations of my peerless husband' were the only thing that helped. Now fully retired, he was always there and ready to do the shopping or any other errand no longer within her power, while their housekeeper's sister did the cooking.

On 10 November 1973 Georgette learned that her brother Boris had died after a long illness in the Radcliffe Infirmary. She had longed to visit him during the last months of his life but her doctor would not allow it. It was small comfort to know that even if she had made the journey her brother was beyond recognising anyone. She had made up *The Black Moth* for Boris and he had always been one of her most enthusiastic readers. Now he was gone, and she had to 'try not to let it get me down'.

Georgette and Ronald had a quiet Christmas. She sent her usual Fortnum & Mason hampers to family and friends but was incapable of travelling to Murrell's End. Richard and Susie held the festivities at their Gloucester Road flat and Georgette spent a 'very happy, lazy day with them' and her grandsons, who were as engaging as ever. She was proud of Richard's family and told Isabella Banton that her son 'was born lucky'.

In January 1974 the international oil crisis found them enduring all sorts of inconveniences in order to save fuel. The crisis deepened through the new year until Georgette felt they could stand no more. 'We are neither of us of an age, or in the right state of health, either to cope with life in a flat which has no light or heat other than that provided by electricity – let alone the lift!' she told Reinhardt. Her pronouncement to friends that her health was better had been short-lived. Her doctor told her she would not be well before June. This was frustrating because she was 'trying to think of a Plot for a book, & finding it almost impossible'. Her doctor had urged her to start writing as a form of "excellent mental therapy", but Georgette found the idea of writing a book as therapy unappealing. She had thought of several possible characters, however, and hoped that if she began writing, inspiration might come. Reinhardt assured her that he did not want her to feel pressured – only that if she was writing a new novel they would 'all be thrilled'.

A month later, finding that she was constantly tired and with her energy sapped by midday, Georgette decided to escape the misery of ill-health, fuel shortages and blackouts and fly to Gibraltar for a fortnight's respite. It was with real anticipation that she and Ronald flew out of England on a holiday which Georgette hoped would restore some of her vigour. Those hopes were dashed on the first day when she slipped on a marble floor and wrenched the ligaments in her bad leg. It was a disastrous start to their trip and the discovery that 'every hotel is built on the side of a steep hill' made Gibraltar less than ideal for the sort of convalescence she had envisaged. Despite the difficulties, a fortnight later she arrived home in such good spirits that she decided she 'must indeed be much better'.

By May, however, the pain in her back and legs was so severe that Georgette was unable to write. She had been enduring more and more pain and although he knew she was stoical by nature, Ronald found it increasingly difficult to cope with watching her in such agony. A few days later, having done his best to alleviate the pain and keep her at home, her doctor had no choice but to admit her to Guy's Hospital. Georgette was seriously ill. She knew, without being told, that there was not much time left. After weeks of tests and examinations Ronald hoped to be able to bring her home with a day and a night nurse to look after her, but it proved to be impossible.

A few months earlier, Georgette had told Joyce Weiner that 'I never wanted to live (as too many of my forebears have) to a very unripe old age, & my hope now is that I may go quickly, & NOT by inches.' A moment later she had looked from her window and added, 'The sun has now pierced through the lowering cloud, & I instantly feel a bit better.' She wanted to be well again and to get on with the writing she had loved for so long. But age and imminent death would not permit it. By the time lung cancer was diagnosed she was in the last weeks of her life and Ronald told friends that she was passing 'most of the time in a rather comatose state due, no doubt, to the drugs she is given'. Every afternoon and evening her husband sat at her bedside, waiting for the lucid moments when his companion of nearly fifty years would look into his eyes and recognise him. Ronald was there when, on 4 July 1974, Georgette Heyer died.

AFTERWORD

Two days after Georgette's death the first obituaries appeared. The world learned that 'the Queen of Regency Romance' was dead at the age of seventy-one, and her fans finally discovered that Georgette Heyer was also Mrs Ronald Rougier. Major newspapers around the world offered tributes with the *Daily Telegraph* calling her the '20th Century Jane Austen'. A week later Georgette's funeral was held at St Paul's Knightsbridge. It was a simple service with only her closest friends and family in attendance. In keeping with her wishes, Georgette was cremated and her ashes scattered.

A month after the funeral Ronald went north for an extended holiday. Georgette's death had affected him deeply and he hoped that time away would help him to recover from his loss. On his return he contacted the well-known writer A.S. Byatt and invited her to lunch to discuss a possible article about Georgette's life and writing. Ronald had admired Byatt's 1969 *Nova* article and the radio interview she had given on the BBC's *Kaleidoscope* programme the day after Georgette's death. He told Byatt she could have access to his wife's notebooks and family photographs and also promised introductions to those who had known Georgette best. It was suggested that the piece coincide with the publication of *My Lord John.*

Rumours that Georgette had left a number of unpublished manuscripts had prompted an influx of letters to The Bodley Head from fans urging the firm to publish anything they had by Georgette Heyer. But the only uncompleted manuscript was *My Lord John* and Max Reinhardt had already asked one of his editors, Jill Black, to help Ronald prepare it for publication. Although Georgette had completed the first 80,000 words of the novel there were still another 25,000 words in rough draft, with a great many pencilled notes and corrections to be deciphered and incorporated. Ronald took on the job of compiling the book's glossary and also wrote the historical note needed to end the book, given that Georgette's manuscript stopped in mid-sentence. He and Jill Black worked on My Lord John through the winter and finalised the proofs late in March 1975. Max Reinhardt scheduled the novel for October publication with hopes of a great success.

A.S. Byatt's piece appeared in The Sunday Times three days after publication of My Lord John. The first independent biographical account of Georgette Heyer ever published, the eight-page article also included many never-before-seen photographs of Georgette from the Heyer family albums. Entitled 'The Ferocious Reticence of Georgette Heyer', Byatt had written a magnificent tribute to Georgette, full of new insightful commentary and humorous anecdotes. Ronald was delighted with the piece and told a friend: 'Seeing Antonia Byatt had never actually met Georgette I thought it extremely perceptive.'

On 26 August 1976, almost a year after the publication of My Lord John and two years after his wife's death, Ronald took his own life. He had cancer of the jaw and was lonely without Georgette. In his precise, careful way, he had decided to end things while he was still in control of his mind and body. There was no fuss or scandal, just a brief report in The Times and an obituary written by his son. Richard mourned his father deeply and found the manner of his death very difficult. Ronald had arranged his suicide in the same methodical way that he had once devised the plots for Georgette's detective novels. His intention was to spare his son and his family pain, but in the end it was unavoidable.

Richard inherited the bulk of his parents' estate including those of Georgette's copyrights not owned by Booker (he eventually bought these back). His mother's death had not diminished her sales. By 1977 Pan were selling more than a million copies of her novels a year in Britain alone. A year later The Bodley Head announced The

Historical Novel Prize in memory of Georgette Heyer, with an award of £1,500 and a publishing contract for the winner. Sponsored jointly by The Bodley Head and the Heyer Estate, over the next decade the prize became an important part of the literary calendar, attracting between 200 and 300 manuscripts annually and launching the careers of some fine writers. In 1992 it was felt that the administration of the prize (and finding manuscript readers) had become too difficult and The Bodley Head reluctantly decided to bring it to a close.

Despite her intensely private personal life, Georgette Heyer remains a very public writer. Her novels have been continuously in print since their first publication in 1921 and she is still selling. Interest in her life and writing also continues. In 1983, the year before he died, Frere told Jane Aiken Hodge that he thought the intelligentsia would eventually recognise Georgette's achievement and that she would become a respectable subject for study and debate. Rosemary Sutcliff and A.S. Byatt were the first to give her serious recognition and in 1970 Germaine Greer included a lengthy commentary on *Regency Buck* in *The Female Eunuch*. Since then a growing number of scholars and commentators have written about Georgette Heyer and her novels in articles, essays, papers, chapters, theses and books.

Georgette Heyer has been included in more than twenty literary companions and dictionaries, including the *Dictionary of National Biography* and the *Oxford Companion to English Literature*. She is cited eighty times in the complete *Oxford English Dictionary*. In 2008 the Public Lending Right Registry listed her fourth in the top twenty of the 'classic writers' most frequently borrowed from UK libraries, along with Enid Blyton, Roald Dahl, Agatha Christie, Beatrix Potter, Jane Austen, Charles Dickens, Daphne du Maurier, C.S. Lewis, J.R.R. Tolkien and Shakespeare among others. The writer George MacDonald Fraser described her as 'a splendid historical novelist, certainly one of the best of the last century'. Carmen Callil and Colm Tóibín included *The Grand Sophy* in *The 200 Best Novels in English since 1950* and in 1964 a Professor of Military Studies at the Belgium Military Academy declared the battle scenes in *An Infamous Army* 'the nearest to reality that one will ever come without having been there'. Today, Georgette Heyer continues to be one of the great bestsellers.

In her fifty-year career Georgette wrote fifty-five novels and never had a failure. With the exception of the five books that remain suppressed, all of her titles are still in print. She wrote across several different genres and historical periods but it is with the English Regency that her name has become synonymous. Today Georgette Heyer is universally recognised as the creator of the Regency genre of historical fiction.

Although the Regency world she created was faithful in its historical detail, it was also a carefully constructed entity which reflected the Edwardian values, ideas and social mores with which she had grown up. Georgette felt at home in the Regency because it was an era which reached forward into her childhood and writing about it enabled her to escape to a time which felt safe, comfortable and familiar. In the twenty-first century it is her version of the Regency which has set the standard for research, writing and the re-creation of the period. Since her death her books have continued to inspire readers and writers across the globe. Georgette Heyer's literary legacy endures.

References to Published Sources

Page 14   **'most amusing'** Winifred Whitehead, *Wimbledon 1885–1965*, W. Whitehead, Wimbledon, 1979, p.12.

Page 15   **'As she grew older'** Darley Dale, *The Shepherd's Fairy*, The Religious Tract Society, London, 1888, pp. 163–4.

Page 16   **'We are never unkind'** J.W. Fortescue, *The Story of a Red Deer*, Pan Books, London, 1976 [First published in 1897], p.6.

Page 20   **'The most popular master'** G.S. Szlumper quoted in Frank Miles and Graeme Cranch, *Kings College School*, Kings College School, 1979, p.210.

Page 27   **'I don't want Helen'** Georgette Heyer, *Helen*, Part I: chapter VI.

Page 28   **'Himself had taught Helen'** *Helen*, Part I: chapter VI.

Page 32   **'Never were more inveterate'** *Helen*, Part II: chapter I.
           'the afternoons were free' *Helen*, Part II: chapter I.

Page 34   **'We thought the War'** *Helen*, Part II: chapter IV.

Page 34   **'She was not cold'** *Helen*, Part II: chapter IV.

Page 38   **'the persuasive English officer'** John Hales, Obituary Notice, *The Times*, 22.6.1925, p.16, col. b.

Page 41   **'Mamma always admitted'** Josephine, Diana and Christine Pullein-Thompson, *Fair Girls and Grey Horses*, Allison & Busby, London, 1997, p.10.

Page 42   **'Carola was five'** Carola Oman, *An Oxford Childhood*, Hodder & Stoughton, London, 1976, p.76.

Page 48   **'Smilingly, she called herself'** Jane Mander, 'Two Clever Writers: the Work of Georgette Heyer and Carola Oman', *The Sun*, New Zealand [n.d. but early 1929 from textual evidence within the article].

Page 49 *'young men abandoned'* Jane Aiken Hodge, *The Private World of Georgette Heyer*, chapter 1.

Page 56 *'a young girl's wildly romantic'* Jane Aiken Hodge, *The Private World of Georgette Heyer*, chapter 1.

Page 59 *'There's no peace for me in England'* Georgette Heyer, *The Great Roxhythe*, Book IV, chapter VI.

Page 68 *'the best historical novels'* George Heyer, 'History in Fiction', 1923, from the minutes of the Wimbledon Literary and Scientific Society, transcribed for me by Mrs Pauline Prest in 2002.

Page 70 *'There's a deal of give and take'* Heyer, *Instead of the Thorn*, chapter 26.

Page 72 *'considered too frank'* Ainslie Ellis, 'Hoppé at Ninety' in the *British Journal of Photography*, 19 April 1968, p.326.

Page 80 *'Historical novels are of two kinds'* Isabelle Wentworth Lawrence, *Boston Evening Transcript*, 23 May 1925 in Mary Fahnestock-Thomas, *Georgette Heyer: A Critical Retrospective*, Prinny World Press, Alabama, 2001, p.69.

Page 83 *'What is it, then'* Austin Dobson, *Epilogue to Eighteenth Century Vignettes (second series)*, 1894 in *The Complete Poetical Works of Austin Dobson*, Oxford University Press, 1923.

Page 84 *'at the close of literally dozens'* Marjorie Garber, *Vested Interests: Cross-Dressing and Cultural Anxiety*, Penguin, London, 1992.

Page 85 *'Suddenly, as though something had snapped'* Helen, Part III: chapter VII.

Page 86 *'misplaced attempt'* Helen, Part III: chapter VII.

Page 88 *'She unearthed the manuscript'* Helen, Part III: chapter VII.
        'writing with an easy pen' Hodge, *Private World*, chapter 1.

Page 92 *'unspeakably slimy and slippery'* Elsie M. Kimball, letter dated 12 February 1926, The Elsie M. Kimball Papers, Mount Holyoke College, Archives and Special Collections.

Page 98 *'cheap and easy device'* 'Latest Works of Fiction', *The New York Times Book Review*, 27.5.28, p.17.

Page 99 *'He was not Romance'* Heyer, *Pastel*, chapter XXVII.

Page 100 *'you all fall into the error'* *Pastel*, chapter XXIII.
        'Life was bound up with Norman' *Pastel*, chapter XXIII.

Page 101 *'much faith in the lasting qualities'* *Pastel*, chapter VI.
        'I used to think' *Pastel*, chapter XX.

Page 101   *'my own authors'* Jane Mander, 'Women Writers I Have Known', *The Sun*, New Zealand, 1933.

Page 102   *'very shy and brusque'* Helen, Part I: chapter VI.

Page 104   *'Lorna Coote was thirty-three'* David Footman, *Halfway East*, Heinemann, 1935, pp.52–3.

Page 105   *'forget the accident of her birth'* Heyer, *Barren Corn*, chapter III.

Page 110   *'In the first version, he wins her'* Hodge, *Private World*, chapter 1.

Page 113   *'Cynthia Bechler was a historical novelist'* Joanna Cannan, *No Walls of Jasper*, Ernest Benn, 1930, p.34.
         'I've been trying to imagine' Cannan, *No Walls of Jasper*, p.158.

Page 114   *'spent over a year'* Mander, 'Two Clever Writers', *The Sun*, New Zealand.

Page 122   *'"And now," said Vidal silkily'* *Devil's Cub*, chapter VI.

Page 127   *'At the time, Mother was writing'* Richard Rougier in 'She Wasn't Like Other Mothers', *Woman's Own*, 2 September 1978, p.25.
         'at this time' Hodge, *Private World*, chapter 2.

Page 129   *'Somebody in the* **Westminster Record'** John Byers, *The Record and West London News*, 20 May 1933, p.6.

Page 137   *'I said last week'* Dorothy Sayers, *The Sunday Times*, 1 April 1934.

Page 139   *'There was not a bookshop'* John Attenborough, *In Living Memory: Hodder & Stoughton Publishers 1868–1975*, Hodder & Stoughton, London, 1975, p.98.

Page 140   *'the last of the puritans'* Attenborough, *In Living Memory*, p.122.
         'nothing in them' Attenborough, *In Living Memory*, p.103.
         'it was too much of an affront' Attenborough, *In Living Memory*, p.233.

Page 159   *'You think that if a man'* Heyer, *They Found Him Dead*, chapter 13.
         'You see, I know myself' *They Found Him Dead*, chapter 1.

Page 163   *'One of Heinemann's stars'* John St John, *William Heinemann: A Century of Publishing 1890–1990*, Heinemann, 1990, p.210.

Page 168   *'understood and liked authors'* St John, *William Heinemann*, p.204.

Page 178   **'Jim tells me'** *They Found Him Dead*, chapter 9.

Page 180   **'Here is a romance'** *The Times Literary Supplement*, 13 November 1937, p.869.

            'One of the clearest' the *Daily Mail*, November 1937.

Page 192   **'tackling a crossword puzzle'** Letter from Richard Rougier to James P. Devlin and quoted in Devlin's article 'The Mysteries of Georgette Heyer: A Janeite's Life of Crime' in *The Armchair Detective* no.17, Vol. 3, summer 1984, p.301.

Page 201   **'Once more unto the breach'** Shakespeare, *Henry V*, Act 3, scene 1.

            'We band of brothers' Shakespeare, Henry V, Act 4, scene 3.

Page 203   **'Evans, Hall and Oliver'** St John, *William Heinemann*, p.301.

Page 209   **'I see now that there is a great deal'** Heyer, *The Corinthian*, chapter 7.

Page 215   **'one of Miss Georgette Heyer's admirers'** Frank Swinnerton, the *Observer*, 20 October 1940, p.5.

Page 242   **'In December 1942 the Irish Censorship'** Minutes of The Censorship of Publications Board meeting 11 December 1942 at which it was decided that 'this book in all its editions be prohibited.' The recommendation was made to the Minister of Justice and *Penhallow* was prohibited from 18 December 1942. Office of Censorship Publications, Dublin 2, Republic of Ireland.

Page 253   **'In our opinion'** Assistant Secretary to Georgette Heyer, Correspondence with the Society of Authors 1921–1948, Add.63262 ff.185–200, British Library MS collection, 3 April 1944.

Page 256   **'one of the most influential'** J.B. Priestley, 'Mr C.S. Evans' in *The Times*, 2 December 1944, p.7.

Page 266   **The Chairman: Perhaps I might say to you'** House of Commons: Minutes of Evidence taken before the Committee on Group B of Private Bills on the South Bucks & Oxfordshire Water Bill, Bucks. Water Bill, Readings Berkshire Gate Bill, Mid-Wessex Water Bill, Wednesday 4th February 1959.

Page 269   **'To write romantic comedy'** Hodge, *Private World*, chapter 3.

Page 273   **'I daresay she doesn't live at Hitchin'** Heyer, *The Foundling*, chapter XIII.

Page 275   **'the greatest writer'** *Australian Women's Weekly*, 10 July 1937, p.8.

Page 287   **'Once again Georgette Heyer has demonstrated'** Kelsy Guilfoil, 'Entertaining 18th Century English Life', *Chicago Sunday Tribune*, 22 October 1950, part 4, p.4 in Fahnestock-Thomas, *Critical Retrospective*, pp.156–157.

Page 301   **'one of the most widely read'** 'Georgette Heyer – The Shy Best-Seller', Coral Craig at our London Office, *Australian Woman's Day*, 27 October 1952, p.26.

Page 319   **'men are April'** Shakespeare, *As You Like It*, Act 4, scene 1.

Page 326   **'You and Damerel!'** Heyer, *Venetia*, chapter 19.

Page 339   **'3 or 4 families in a country village'** Jane Austen, Letter to Anna Austen, 9 September 1814, in R.W. Chapman (ed.), *Jane Austen's Letters*, Oxford University Press, 1932.

Page 348   **'Do you think you could tell us'** Annie Samuelli, *Women Behind Bars in Romania*, Frank Cass & Co., London, 1997, pp.143–44.

Page 364   **'has to be fun and fast enough'** Cilla Black in 'My Kind of Book', *Petticoat*, 16 July 1966, pp. 8–11 & 42–43.

Page 369   **'Sir, – Ten thousand was a best-selling figure'** A.S. Frere, *The Times*, Tuesday 16 May, 1967; p. 11; Issue 56942; col G.

Page 372   **'in the precise balance she achieves'** A.S. Byatt, 'Georgette Heyer is a Better Writer than You Think', *Nova*, August 1969, p.22.

Page 376   **'The Appeal of Georgette Heyer'** Marghanita Laski, *The Times*, Thursday, 1 Oct, 1970; p. 16; Issue 57985; col A.
            'What Miss Heyer provides' Susan Horsley, *The Times*, Wednesday, 7 Oct, 1970; p. 9; Issue 57990; col G.

Page 393   **'a splendid historical novelist'** George MacDonald Fraser, letter to the Author, 25 March 2002, extract reproduced with the permission of Curtis Brown Group Ltd, London on behalf of the Estate of George MacDonald Fraser.

Georgette Heyer's Novels
(UK First Editions)

1.	*The Black Moth*	1921 Sept	Constable	18thC
2.	*The Great Roxhythe*	1922 Nov	Hutchinson	17thC
3.	*The Transformation of Philip Jettan*	1923 April	Mills & Boon	18thC
4.	*Instead of the Thorn*	1923 Nov	Hutchinson	Modern
*	* *	1924 *	* * *	*
5.	*Simon the Coldheart*	1925 Oct	Heinemann	Medieval
6.	*These Old Shades*	1926 Oct	Heinemann	18thC
*	* *	1927 *	* * *	*
7.	*Helen*	1928 April	Longmans	Modern
8.	*The Masqueraders*	1928 Sept	Heinemann	18thC
**	*The Black Moth* (reprint)	1929 Jan	Heinemann	18thC
**	*The Great Roxhythe* (reprint)	1929 Jan	Heinemann	17thC
9.	*Pastel*	1929 April	Longmans	Modern
**	*Instead of the Thorn* (reprint)	1929 April	Longmans	Modern
10.	*Beauvallet*	1929 Sept	Heinemann	16thC
**	*Powder and Patch* (reprint)	1930 March	Heinemann	18thC
11.	*Barren Corn*	1930 April	Longmans	Modern
12.	*The Conqueror*	1931 March	Heinemann	11thC
13.	*Footsteps in the Dark*	1932 Feb	Longmans	Crime
14.	*Devil's Cub*	1932 Nov	Heinemann	18thC
15.	*Why Shoot a Butler?*	1933 Feb	Longmans	Crime
16.	*The Convenient Marriage*	1934 Feb	Heinemann	18thC
17.	*The Unfinished Clue*	1934 March	Longmans	Crime
18.	*Death in the Stocks*	1935 April	Longmans	Crime
19.	*Regency Buck*	1935 Sept	Heinemann	Regency

20. *Behold, Here's Poison*	1936 May	Hodder.	Crime
21. *The Talisman Ring*	1936 Oct	Heinemann	18thC
22. *They Found Him Dead*	1937 May	Hodder.	Crime
23. *An Infamous Army*	1937 Nov	Heinemann	Regency
24. *A Blunt Instrument*	1938 May	Hodder.	Crime
25. *Royal Escape*	1938 Sept	Heinemann	17thC
26. *No Wind of Blame*	1939 June	Hodder.	Crime
27. *The Spanish Bride*	1940 April	Heinemann	Regency
28. *The Corinthian*	1940 Oct	Heinemann	Regency
29. *Envious Casca*	1941 Oct	Hodder.	Crime
30. *Faro's Daughter*	1941 Oct	Heinemann	18thC
31. *Penhallow*	1942 Oct	Heinemann	Crime
* * *	1943 *	* *	*
32. *Friday's Child*	1944 July	Heinemann	Regency
* * *	1945 *	* *	*
33. *The Reluctant Widow*	1946 July	Heinemann	Regency
* * *	1947 *	* *	*
34. *The Foundling*	1948 April	Heinemann	Regency
35. *Arabella*	1949 July	Heinemann	Regency
36. *The Grand Sophy*	1950 Sept	Heinemann	Regency
37. *Duplicate Death*	1951 July	Heinemann	Crime
38. *The Quiet Gentleman*	1951 Oct	Heinemann	Regency
* * *	1952 *	* *	*
39. *Cotillion*	1953 Jan	Heinemann	Regency
40. *Detection Unlimited*	1953 Dec	Heinemann	Crime
41. *The Toll-Gate*	1954 July	Heinemann	Regency
42. *Bath Tangle*	1955 March	Heinemann	Regency
43. *Sprig Muslin*	1956 March	Heinemann	Regency
44. *April Lady*	1957 Jan	Heinemann	Regency
45. *Sylvester*	1957 Nov	Heinemann	Regency
46. *Venetia*	1958 Nov	Heinemann	Regency
47. *The Unknown Ajax*	1959 Nov	Heinemann	Regency
Pistols for Two[1]	1960 Nov	Heinemann	Regency
48. *A Civil Contract*	1961 Oct	Heinemann	Regency
49. *The Nonesuch*	1962 Oct	Heinemann	Regency
50. *False Colours*	1963 Oct	Bodley Head	Regency
* * *	1964 *	* *	*

51. *Frederica*	1965 Sept	Bodley Head	Regency
52. *Black Sheep*	1966 Oct	Bodley Head	Regency
* * *	1967 *	* * *	
53. *Cousin Kate*	1968 Sept	Bodley Head	Regency
* * *	1969 *	* * *	
54. *Charity Girl*	1970 Oct	Bodley Head	Regency
* * *	1971 *	* * *	
55. *Lady of Quality* \	1972 Oct	Bodley Head	Regency
* * *	1973 *	* * *	
* * *	1974 *	[GH dies 4 July]*	*
56. *My Lord John*	1975 Oct	Bodley Head	Medieval
** *Simon the Coldheart* (reprint)	1978 Sept	Bodley Head	Medieval

* A year without a book
** A reissue of an earlier title
¹ An anthology of short stories

Georgette Heyer's Novels
(USA First Editions)

1. *The Black Moth*	1921 Nov	Houghton Mifflin	18thC
* * *	1922 *	* *	*
2. *The Great Roxhythe*	1923 June	Small Maynard	17thC
3. *Instead of the Thorn*	1924 Apr	Small Maynard	Modern
4. *Simon the Coldheart*	1925 May	Small Maynard	Medieval
5. *These Old Shades*	1926	Small Maynard	18thC
* * *	1927 *	* *	*
6. *Helen*	1928 May	Longmans	Modern
7. *Pastel*	1929 May	Longmans	Modern
8. *The Masqueraders*	1929 Jul	Longmans	18thC
9. *Beauvallet*	1930 Feb	Longmans	16thC
10. *Barren Corn*	1930 Sep	Longmans	Modern
* * *	1931 *	* *	*
* * *	1932 *	* *	*
* * *	1933 *	* *	*
* * *	1934 *	* *	*
11. *Merely Murder*[1]	1935 Sep	Doubleday	Crime
12. *Why Shoot a Butler?*	1936 Feb	Doubleday	Crime
13. *Behold, Here's Poison*	1936 April	Doubleday	Crime
14. *The Unfinished Clue*	1937 Feb	Doubleday	Crime
15. *The Talisman Ring*	1937 Jun	Doubleday	18thC

16. *They Found Him Dead*	1937 Aug	Doubleday	Crime
17. *An Infamous Army*	1938 Apr	Doubleday	Regency
18. *A Blunt Instrument*	1938 Oct	Doubleday	Crime
19. *Royal Escape*	1939 Feb	Doubleday	17thC
20. *No Wind of Blame*	1939 Nov	Doubleday	Crime
21. *The Spanish Bride*	1940 Oct	Doubleday	Regency
22. *Beau Wyndham*[2]	1941 Apr	Doubleday	Regency
23. *Envious Casca*	1941 Dec	Doubleday	Crime
24. *Faro's Daughter*	1942 May	Doubleday	18thC
25. *Penhallow*	1943 Aug	Doubleday	Crime
* * *	1944 *	* * *	*
* * *	1945 *	* * *	*
26. *Friday's Child*	1946 Feb	Putnam	Regency
27. *The Reluctant Widow*	1947 Feb	Putnam	Regency
28. *The Foundling*	1948 Mar	Putnam	Regency
29. *Arabella*	1949 May	Putnam	Regency
30. *The Grand Sophy*	1950 Oct	Putnam	Regency
* * *	1951 *	* * *	*
31. *The Quiet Gentleman*	1952 Mar	Putnam	Regency
32. *Cotillion*	1953 Feb	Putnam	Regency
33. *The Toll-Gate*	1954 Aug	Putnam	Regency
34. *Bath Tangle*	1955 Aug	Putnam	Regency
35. *Sprig Muslin*	1956 Aug	Putnam	Regency
36. *April Lady*	1957 Aug	Putnam	Regency
37. *Sylvester*	1958 Mar	Putnam	Regency
38. *Venetia*	1959 Feb	Putnam	Regency
39. *The Unknown Ajax*	1960 Apr	Putnam	Regency
* * *	1961 *	* * *	*
40. *A Civil Contract*	1962 Jan	Putnam	Regency
41. *The Nonesuch*	1963 Mar	Dutton	Regency
42. *False Colours*	1964 Feb	Dutton	Regency
Pistols for Two[3]	1964 Aug	Dutton	Regency
** *An Infamous Army*	1965 Mar	Dutton	Regency
** *The Spanish Bride*	1965 Mar	Dutton	Regency
43. *Frederica*	1965 Oct	Dutton	Regency
** *Beau Wyndham*	1966 Jan	Dutton	Regency
** *These Old Shades*	1966 Aug	Dutton	18thC
44. *Devil's Cub*	1966 Aug	Dutton	18thC

45. The Conqueror	1966 Oct	Dutton	Medieval
46. The Convenient Marriage	1966	Dutton	18thC
47. Regency Buck	1966	Dutton	Regency
48. Black Sheep	1967 Mar	Dutton	Regency
** The Talisman Ring	1967 Aug	Dutton	18thC
** Faro's Daughter	1967 Aug	Dutton	18thC
** Royal Escape	1967 Nov	Dutton	17thC
** The Masqueraders	1967 Nov	Dutton	18thC
** The Black Moth	1968 Mar	Dutton	18thC
** Beauvallet	1968 Mar	Dutton	16thC
49. Powder and Patch	1968 Jun	Dutton	18thC
50. Cousin Kate	1968 Nov	Dutton	Regency
51. Duplicate Death	1969 Jun	Dutton	Crime
52. Detection Unlimited	1969 Aug	Dutton	Crime
** Envious Casca	1969	Dutton	Crime
** The Unfinished Clue	1970 Feb	Dutton	Crime
** Merely Murder[1]	1970 Mar	Dutton	Crime
** A Blunt Instrument	1970 Aug	Dutton	Crime
53. Charity Girl	1970 Oct	Dutton	Regency
** No Wind of Blame	1970 Nov	Dutton	Crime
** Behold, Here's Poison	1971 Jun	Dutton	Crime
54. Lady of Quality	1972 Oct	Dutton	Regency
** They Found Him Dead	1973	Dutton	Crime
** Why Shoot a Butler?	1973 May	Dutton	Crime
* * *	1974 *	* *	*
55. My Lord John	1975 Nov	Dutton	Medieval
** Simon the Coldheart	1979 Nov	Dutton	Medieval
56. Footsteps in the Dark	1987	Berkeley	Crime

* A year without a book
** A reissue of an earlier title
[1] English title *Death in the Stocks*
[2] English title *The Corinthian*
[3] An anthology of short stories

Georgette Heyer's (Known) Short Stories

1.	A Proposal for Cicely	1922 Sept	*The Happy Mag*
2.	The Little Lady	1922 Dec	*The Red Magazine*
3.	Bulldog and the Beast	1923 March	*The Happy Mag*
4.	Linckes' Great Case	1923 March	*The Detective Magazine*
5.	Acting on Impulse	1923 June	*The Red Magazine*
6.	Whose Fault Was It?	1923 August	*The Happy Mag*
7.	Love	1923 Nov	*Sovereign Magazine*
8.	Chinese Shawl	1924 Feb	*Tvidenskronder*
9	The Old Maid	1925 August	*Woman's Pictorial*
10.	On Such a Night	1935	Unknown
11.	Runaway Match	1936 April	*Woman's Journal*
12.	Incident on the Bath Road	1936 May	*Woman's Journal*
13.	*Hazard	1936 June	*Woman's Journal*
14.	Lady, Your Pardon	1936	*Australian Women's Weekly*
15.	Pursuit	1939 Nov	*Queen's Book of the Red Cross*
16.	*Snowdrift	1948 Nov	*The Illustrated London News*
17.	*Full Moon	1948 Nov	*Woman's Journal*
18.	*Pistols at Dawn	1949 Dec	*Woman's Journal*
19.	*Night at the Inn	1950 March	*John Bull*
20.	*A Husband for Fanny	1951 Nov	*The Illustrated London News*
21.	*Bath Miss	1952 Sept	*Good Housekeeping*
22.	*The Pursuit of Hetty	1953 June	*Good Housekeeping*

23.	*The Duel	1953 Feb	*Good Housekeeping*
24.	The Quarrel	1953 Dec	*Everywoman*
25.	*Pink Domino	1953 Dec	*Woman's Journal*
26.	*A Clandestine Affair	1960	Magazine title unknown

*Indicates those stories included in the Georgette Heyer anthology *Pistols for Two* (1960) in which the 1953 short story 'The Pursuit of Hetty' was renamed 'To Have the Honour'

Heyer-related Archives

1890s–1970s	Heyer and Rougier family photo albums, Heyer Estate
1902–1908	Georgette Heyer's Baby Book written by her mother, Sylvia Heyer, Heyer Estate
1920s–1974	Georgette Heyer's Notebooks & Private Papers, Heyer Estate
1921–1944	Correspondence with the Society of Authors Archive (11 letters), The British Library
1923–1945	The Georgette Rougier (Heyer) Correspondence, McFarlin Collection, The University of Tulsa (251 letters), Oklahoma, USA
1935	The John Hayward letter, King's College Library Archive (1 letter), Cambridge, UK
1937	Lady Juliet Townsend letter (1 letter), privately held
1937–1970	The Frere Family Archive (93 letters), privately held
1941–1942	Alice Heyer Bowden, *My Memoir*, privately held
1942–1974	The Dorothy and Dmitri Tornow letters (12 letters), privately held
1943–1963	The Heinemann Correspondence, Random House Archive (326 letters)*, Northamptonshire, UK
1946–1951	The Rosemary Marriott Archive (6 letters), privately held
1948–1951	The William Heinemann Ltd correspondence in the Meanjin Archive, The University of Melbourne Special Collections, Baillieu Library, Victoria, Australia
1952	Arnold Gyde's diary extract, privately held
1950–1952	Duke University, William R. Perkins Library Archive (28 letters), North Carolina, USA
1952–1959	Incidental Hodder & Stoughton correspondence (8 letters), Reading University, Reading, UK
1957–1974	The Isabella Banton letters (14 letters), privately held

pre-1960	The Random House Archive (4 additional letters)
1962–1974	Correspondence between Georgette Heyer and Joyce Weiner (163 letters)*, privately held
1963	Derek Priestley, notes on conversations with Georgette Heyer, in the Heinemann Correspondence, Random House Archive
1963–1974	The Max Reinhardt Archive (414 letters)*, Reading University, Reading, UK
1963–1984	The Jane Aiken Hodge Archive, privately held
post-1963	The Bodley Head Archive at Reading University (miscellaneous)
1966 & 1973	Enid Chasemore letters (2 letters), privately held
1970	The Roy Pfautch letter (1 letter), privately held
1972	The Mrs Matthews letter (1 letter), privately held

* Indicates two-way correspondence. Within these collections there are 164 Heyer letters in the Heinemann Correspondence, 64 letters to Joyce Weiner and 153 Heyer letters in the Max Reinhardt Archive. To date there are over 800 Georgette Heyer letters extant.

Additional material was drawn from:
- The Aldington Archive, Random House Archive, Northamptonshire
- The King's College Hospital Archive, London
- The King's College School Archive, Wimbledon
- The Lancing College Archive, Sussex
- The Marlborough College Archive, Wiltshire
- The William Heinemann Ltd correspondence (1948–1951) in the Meanjin Archive, the University of Melbourne Archives
- The Frank Heyer papers, privately held
- The Sidney Sussex College Archive, Cambridge
- The Victoria & Albert Museum Archive, London
- The Wimbledon Literary and Scientific Society Archive
- Elsie Kimball Archive held by Mt Holyoke College, Massachusetts
- Arnold Gyde Diary Extracts
- George MacDonald Fraser letters to the author
- Jane Mander letters held by the Auckland Central City Library, New Zealand
- The Fiction Mags Index internet database

Permissions

I am grateful to all those who gave their permission for the use of quotations and photographs. All Georgette Heyer letters, novels and short stories are used with the permission of Sir Richard Rougier and the Heyer Estate. *Correspondence with the Society of Authors 1921–1948*, Add.63262 ff.185–200, British Library MS collection, London, used with the permission of the Society of Authors. The Georgette Rougier (Heyer) Correspondence used with the permission of the McFarlin Library, University of Tulsa. John Hayward Papers, the JDH/26/45 from the Archives Centre, King's College, Cambridge, used with the permission of King's College Cambridge. The Juliet Townsend letter used with the permission of Lady Townsend. The Georgette Heyer letters in the Frere Family Archive used with the permission of the Frere family. The Dorothy & Dmitri Tornow letters used with the permission of Sally and Stephen Tornow. The Heinemann Correspondence used with the permission of Random House. Letters to Clem Christensen at Heinemann Australia from the Meanjin Archive used with the permission of University of Melbourne, Baillieu Library, Special Collections. The Rosemary Marriott Archive used with the permission of Ro Marriott. Barbara Cartland plagiarism letters from the William R. Perkins Archive, Rare Book, Manuscript and Special Collections Library, Duke University Libraries, used with the permission of Duke University. Isabella Banton letters used with the permission of Pam Stevenson, Tim Brearley, and Marianne Sunier. The Max Reinhardt Archive used with the permission of Mrs Joan Reinhardt. Material from the Jane Aiken Hodge Archive and quotations from *The Private World*

of Georgette Heyer used with the permission of Mrs Jane Aiken Hodge.
The Roy Pfautch letters used with the permission of Mr Roy Pfautch.
Excerpts from the Elsie Kimball papers, 1919–ca.1950: MS 0562,
used with the permission of Mt Holyoke College Archives and Special
Collections, Massachusetts. George MacDonald Fraser letter extract
reproduced with the permission of Curtis Brown Group Ltd, London
on behalf of the Estate of George MacDonald Fraser. Extracts from
Arnold Gyde's diary used with the permission of Dr Humphrey Gyde.
Dr Jonathan Ray's thesis on Albany used with his permission.
Elizabeth-Ann Malden's tribute to Sir Richard Rougier used with her
permission. Quotations from John St John's *William Heinemann: A
Century of Publishing, 1890–1990* used with the permission of Random
House. The excerpt from *Women Behind Bars in Romania* by Annie
Samuelli used with the permission of Taylor & Francis publishers
(for Frank Cass & Co.). The excerpts from the *Petticoat* interview
with Cilla Black used with the permission of IPC Media. The excerpts
from *Australian Woman's Day* and *Australian Women's Weekly* used
with permission of Australian Consolidated Press. The Joanna Cannan
photograph and excerpts from her book, *No Walls of Jasper,* and the
extract from *Fair Girls and Grey Horses* used with the permission of
Mrs Josephine Pullein-Thompson. Access to the Richard Aldington
Archive at the Random House Archive UK (© The Estate of Richard
Aldington) granted with the kind permission of the Estate of Richard
Aldington c/o Rosica Collins, London. Photograph of Georgette
Heyer by E.O. Hoppé reproduced and supplied with the kind permis-
sion of The E.O. Hoppé Estate Collection. Photograph of Georgette
Heyer by Howard Coster reproduced with the kind permission of the
National Portrait Gallery, London. Photograph of A.S. Frere and
Max Reinhardt by Desmond O'Neill reproduced with the kind permis-
sion of Dominic O'Neill.

Acknowledgements

A great many people have assisted me during the last ten years of research and writing and without them this biography would not exist. All have given unstintingly of their time, knowledge, and expertise and many have gone above and beyond the call to provide me with information or point me in the right direction. I have enjoyed extraordinary kindness and wonderful hospitality – and many who were strangers have now become friends. I have been inspired, encouraged and supported and I have learned far more about Georgette Heyer than I ever expected to know. I am enormously grateful to all who have helped me but especially to Sir Richard and Judy, Lady Rougier. Their kindness, generosity, hospitality and friendship enriched my experience and made the vision a possibility; their permission to quote from Georgette Heyer's letters, novels and short stories made it a reality. Sir Richard's continuing faith in me opened many doors and ensured that I would finish the book no matter what. Jane Aiken Hodge led the way with the first biography and continued to inspire me with her keen intellect, stimulating conversation and perceptive reading of my work, as well as the extraordinary gift of her entire research archive. Susanna, Lady Rougier has been a constant support and a kind and generous friend, sharing with me a wealth of information, insight and memories of Georgette Heyer. She also introduced me to others who knew her mother-in-law with plenty of laughter and memorable conversations along the way. Jean and Harry Frere made me welcome and allowed me exclusive access to the Georgette Heyer letters in the Frere Family Archive. Their unfailing kindness, generosity and friendship will always be treasured.

Special thanks to Jean Frere for reading the drafts, meticulous editing, wise counsel, invaluable suggestions and for responding to my emails and phone calls with such magnificent insight and patience. Dr Paul Nicholls brought a wealth of wisdom to the work with superb editing and rigorous reading and shared his delight of Georgette Heyer and her novels with me at regular intervals. J. Roy Hay, mentor and friend, set me on this path and has never stopped encouraging and supporting me; Frances Hay was always interested and happy to answer questions about punctuation. Jeremy and Judith Rougier shared their family history with me and were unfailingly kind and hospitable. Joan Reinhardt generously allowed me to borrow and copy the entire Max Reinhardt Archive and she and Belinda McGill told me many stories about Georgette Heyer and The Bodley Head. Jean Rose at the Random House Archives helped me to fill in several pieces of the puzzle and her generous replies to my emails, her kindness during my visits to Rushden and her extensive knowledge of the Archives greatly enhanced this book. Hale Crosse provided the inside story on the Booker deal and other useful Heyer information, and he and Eunice Crosse gave me the pleasure of their company. Jay Dixon has been a great support and I will always be immeasurably grateful to her for an unforgettable day spent touring Sussex in pursuit of Georgette Heyer. Dr Peter Sherlock gave unstintingly of his time, wisdom and expertise, which enabled me to fill in many missing details in Georgette Heyer's family tree. Ro Marriott generously shared her wonderful Georgette Heyer letters and her memories of their correspondence with me. Dr Dolly MacKinnon remains a wise counsellor and wonderful friend and her keen perception helped me to overcome many challenges. Dianne Tobias and Fiona Skinner have listened to me for ten years and have always responded with patience and insight and their friendship is priceless. Mary Fahnestock-Thomas generously gave me the benefit of her years of research, and her remarkable research archive was a timely addition to this book, and thanks to Alan Homes who kindly shared his years of Watkins family research with me. Special thanks to Jenny Walshe, Dianne Tobias and John Nolan for reading the manuscript and to Dr Helen MacDonald for her generosity, wisdom and insight.

Many other people have helped to make this book possible by enabling me to follow up the myriad of research lines, sharing memories, photographs, letters, ideas and insight and offering practical assistance, encouragement, information, hospitality or permission. Thank you: May and Neil Aaldwark-Clegg, Dilip Abraham at the Port of Geelong, Catherine Aldington, Ginny Andrews, Verity Andrews and Michael Bott at the University of Reading Archives, Esther Sherman Arlan, Marigold Atkey, the Australia Council for the Arts, Dr Jack Ayerbe, Paul Baker, Jeremy Barron, Diana Baty, Donica Bettanin, Jill Black, Charles and Joy Boldero and the Old Weymouthians Club, Martin Boswell, Rex Bowley, Peter and Rosemarie Buckman, Milissa Burkart, Dame Antonia Byatt, Leslie Caelli, Euan Cameron, Luke Carruthers, Lori Curtis and Marc Carlson at the McFarlin Library Special Collection University of Tulsa, Loreen Chambers, Mercia Chapman, Margot Charlton at the *Oxford English Dictionary*, Teresa Chris, Simon Clews, William G. Contento, Damien Connelly, Glenda Cooper, Matt and Maryanne Cotter, John Coulter at the Lewisham Local History and Archive Centre, Nick Cross, Jenny Darling, Emma Darwin, Professor Martin Daunton, Simon & Annie Davies, Jane Davis, Christopher Dean, Donald Derrick & Patricia (Lamburn) Derrick CBE, Ian Dinwiddy at Hodder & Stoughton, Ralitsa Donkova at the Mount Holyoke College Archives and Special Collections, Professor David Dorward, Peter and Anne Downie at Barwon Books, Darren Drake, Nell Duffie, Richard Edgar, Alan and Pat Elliot, Kirsten Elliot, The English-Speaking Union (Melb.), John and Penny Fabb, Leigh Finch, Dr Juliet Flesch, Dr Lisa Fletcher, Dominic Flint, Noel Flint, Elizabeth Frere Jones, Susannah Fullerton, Peggy Garvey at the Office of Censorship of Publications Ireland, Pat Gaskin, David Gibb, Chris Wright and the staff at Goodenough College, Kay Gooding, Juliet and Victor Gordon, Gordon Grant, John Gray, Terry and Myrna Green, Deirdrie Gregory, Dr Humphrey Gyde, Karl Hahn, Lawrie Hall, Towse Harrison, Dr Jane Harrold, Jane Hawtin, Tim Heald and Alexander Heald for information about the Mills & Boon archive, The Heyer Estate, The Heyer List (now Almacks), Tessa and Rupert Hinds, The Historical

Novel Society, Roy & Hilary Hoevenaars, Dr Sally Houghton, Graham Howe and Pam Moffat at the E.O. Hoppé Collection, Valerie Howe, Bruce Hunter, Professor John Iliffe, The Institute of Materials, Minerals & Mining UK, The Jane Austen Society of Australia (Melbourne and Sydney), Peter Janson-Smith, Bill Jay, Debbie Jay, Marjorie Johnston, Dr Susan Johnston, Dr Peter Johnston, Adrien Joly the Interpretation Officer at the Brighton Pavilion, Anna Karpinski, Sir John Keegan, Tamara Kichakov, Jeremy Knight and the staff at Horsham Museum, Mary Kosiak at Adelaide Booksellers, Kwik Kopy Geelong, Savannah Lambis, George Lawrie, Miss Deirdre Le Faye, John Letts, Pamela Lindsay, Dr Joseph McAleer, Bruce McBrien OAM, George MacDonald Fraser, Belinda McGill, Rae McGregor, Victoria McNair, Hilary McPhee, Elizabeth-Ann Malden, The Melbourne University Writers' Centre, Rosalind Moad at King's College Library Archives, Cambridge, Dr Sandor Monostori, Gabrielle Murphy, Ian Murray, Jennifer Nason and Alex Lipe, The National Portrait Gallery in London, The New York Public Library for the Performing Arts, Miss Elizabeth Oliver and the Albany Trustees, John Olsson at the Forensic Language Institute, Alice O'Neill, Christine Owen, Deborah Owen, Richard Page, Bridget Palmer at The Royal Academy of Music, Dr Pauline Parker, Anna Paterson, Vija Pattison, Sue Payne, Lynn Penfold, Roy Pfautch, Professor David Philips, Christopher Phipps, Joanne Playfoot at IPC Media, Virgil Pomfret, Pauline Prest and the Wimbledon Literary and Scientific Society, Diane and Antony Price, Josephine Pullein-Thompson, Dr Jonathan Ray, Phil and Mary Rebakis, Dr Clare Rider at the Inner Temple Archives, Professor Ronald T. Ridley, J.S. Ringrose at the Pembroke College Archives, Marcus Risdell at The Garrick Club, Nicholas Rogers at the Sidney Sussex College Archives, Terry Rogers at the Marlborough College Archives, Romance Writers of Australia, Emma Rose, Nicholas Rougier, The Royal School of Mines, Mrs Jane de Salis, Oliver Saxby, Diana Schaffer, Adele Schaverien, the School of Historical Studies at the University of Melbourne, Nikola Scott, Teresa J. Sergot at the Royal School of Mines, David Shannon, Iain Sharp at the Auckland Central City Library, Mike Sims at A Book

For All Reasons, Sir Donald Sinden, David Smith at the New York Public Library, Kentley and Angela Smith at Smith's Bookbinders, The Society of Authors (UK), Sotheby's London, Henry Speagle, Ann-Marie & Peter Spolton-Dean, the staff at the National Army Museum Chelsea, the staff at the Baillieu Library University of Melbourne, the staff at Barwon Books, the staff at the Billy Rose Theatre Collection in New York, the staff at the Brighton Pavilion, the staff at the Britannia Royal Naval College, the staff at the Rare Books and Music Reading Room at the British Library, the staff at the Family Resource Centre London, the staff at *The Illustrated London News*, the staff at the Imperial War Museum, the staff at the London Library, the staff at the London Probate Office, the staff at the Newspaper Library at Colindale, the staff at the Public Record Office Kew, the staff at the State Library of Victoria, the staff at the Westminster City Archives, Mrs Margaret Stankiewicz at the Lancing College Archives, Mr William Staples the Head Porter in Albany, Pam Stevenson at Boris Books, Bryan Stokes at the King's College School Archives, Jean Strathdee-Cook, Pat Stubbings, Francis Sultana, Mike Swales, Satu Tähtinen, Pia Tapper Fenton, Dr Valerie Tarrant, Robyn Tooth, Sally Tornow, Stephen Tornow, Lady Juliet Townsend, James Travers, Julia Trevelyan Oman (Lady Strong), John Trier, Professor Stephanie Trigg, Elizabeth (Lizzie) Tucker, Dr Clara Tuite, Bruce and Jenny Walshe, Steven Walshe, Giles Weaver at Greywalls, Cdr Ian Wellesley-Harding RN, Vicki West, Professor Stephen Wheatcroft, Anne White, Eva White and the staff at the Victoria & Albert Museum Archives, Lydia Whitehand, John Whitehouse, Professor Martin Wiener, Damien Williams, The Wimbledon Local History Museum, Mark Wolfson OBE, Dr J.G.M. Woodrow, Ruth and Andrew Woolaston and Gavan and Anna Wright. Thanks also to my wonderful editors Jay Dixon and Georgina Hawtrey-Woore.

For a lifetime of love and support, special thanks to
Elanor, Christopher and Benjamin.
And to Barry for everything.

Index